Game Theory with Applications to Economics

Game Theory with Applications to Economics

JAMES W. FRIEDMAN
University of North Carolina

New York   Oxford
OXFORD UNIVERSITY PRESS
1986

Oxford University Press

Oxford New York Toronto
Delhi Bombay Calcutta Madras Karachi
Petaling Jaya Singapore Hong Kong Tokyo
Nairobi Dar es Salaam Cape Town
Melbourne Auckland

and associated companies in
Beirut Berlin Ibadan Nicosia

Published by Oxford University Press, Inc.,
200 Madison Avenue, New York, NY 10016

Oxford is a registered trademark of Oxford University Press.

Library of Congress Cataloging in Publication Data

Friedman, James W.
  Game theory with applications to economics.

  Bibliography: p.
  Includes index.
  1. Game theory.   2. Economics, Mathematical.
I. Title.
HB144.F75   1986   330'.01'193   85–5036
ISBN 0-19-503660-3

Printing (last digit): 9 8 7 6 5 4 3 2

Printed in the United States of America

To Stewart

Preface

In writing this book, I have tried to reach an honors undergraduate or first-year graduate school audience in economics, having a moderate background in mathematics. The book discusses game theory, with examples from economics and sometimes from politics. It is, to quote a source I cannot now recall, "introductory but not elementary." It presumes no prior knowledge of game theory, but many topics are handled in considerable depth. There are two major respects in which the book is aimed at an economics audience. First, the selection of topics is influenced by my views of what is particularly fruitful for economics and, second, the examples are drawn mainly from economics in a way intended to illustrate the breadth and depth of game theoretic influence on that discipline. In addition to serving as a text for courses in game theory, I hope that this book will prove helpful to economists who have not specialized in game theory, and who wish to gain a knowledge of useful developments in the field.

The book can be read on any of several levels, depending on the mathematical background of the reader and on her or his willingness to work hard. A reader with only a working problem-solving knowledge of calculus, and with the ability to accept prose occasionally littered with mathematical symbols, should be able to understand all the examples and to follow everything except the proofs of theorems and lemmas. The proofs themselves vary greatly in their length and difficulty. Undoubtedly, many readers will find some proofs easy and others impenetrable. Although I intended to keep the mathematical depth uniformly modest, I soon found that doing so would force certain topics to be either omitted entirely or treated with insufficient completeness. Consequently, I compromised by including topics of varied technical difficulty. The most mathematically difficult portions are explained in words that give the reader an intuitive grasp.

The coverage of the book is conventional in some respects and particularly up to date in others. Chapters 1, 2, 5, and 6 provide most of the conventional material. Chapter 1 is introductory, Chapter 2 deals with two-person, zero-sum games and with (Nash) noncooperative equilibrium for n-person noncooperative games, touching on both uniqueness of equilibrium and on games of incomplete information as well. Chapter 5 is devoted to two-person cooperative games, and Chapter 6 covers solution concepts for cooperative games having transferable utility. The most recent material occurs in Chapters 3 and 4, which are on noncooperative supergames and include trigger strategy equilibria, cooperation supported by self-enforcing agreements, and refinements of the Nash noncooperative equilibrium such as perfect equilibrium and sequential equilibrium. Chapter 7 is primarily concerned with the generalizations of the core and the Shapley value to nontransferable utility games.

Many writers have commented on their great intellectual debt to others, and my debt must be as large as most. In addition to the influence over the years of many teachers, colleagues, and students, there are two people whom I particularly want to single out: the late William Fellner and Martin Shubik. Willy taught the first-year graduate theory course at Yale when I entered the graduate program there. He was a man of great thoughtfulness and subtlety: in that course came my first introduction to a game-theoretic topic when we studied oligopoly. That provided a glimpse into an interesting area that shortly became a fascination. The following year, Martin Shubik was a visiting professor who taught a game theory/oligopoly course in which his knowledge, point of view, insight, and enthusiasm influenced my main lines of interest in economics.

Several people have read parts of an earlier draft of this book and have given me helpful comments, including Catherine Eckel, Nicholas Economides, Val Lambson, Douglas McManus, John McMillan, David Salant, Patricia Smith, Richard Steinberg, Manolis Tsiritakis, Chang-Chen Yang, and Allan Young. They eliminated typographical errors, improved the clarity of exposition, and corrected my errors. Robert Rosenthal read most of the previous draft and provided comments that helped me eliminate much nonsense and much murky prose. At many points in the text he has saved me from serious error. Some typing was done by Barbara Barker, Irene Dowdy, and Wadine Williams. I am grateful to them for pitching in when there was some time pressure. Most of the typing was done, with great skill, speed, and good humor, by Vickie Carroll and Jay Willard. Much of what is good in the following pages results from the help of all these people. Any blame, of course, for any remaining mistakes and inaccuracies rests with me.

Chapel Hill, North Carolina   J. W. F.
June 1985

A note on other books in game theory

There are many other books from which a reader might gain greatly, a few of which are Luce and Raiffa (1957), Owen (1982), Shubik (1982, 1984), Roth (1979), and van Damme (1983). Luce and Raiffa have written the sort of classic book to which many of us must aspire. Despite being much out of date, due to the developments of nearly 30 active years, it is a superb source for much of the central material of the field. The writing is extremely lucid, the intuition supporting various models and the criticisms of them is insightful and illuminating, and the technical demands are never more than the necessary minimum for the subject. Owen has a fine modern text that is particularly strong on cooperative game theory. Shubik's two volumes, totaling over 1200 pages between them, cover immense ground in game theory proper and on applications of game theory to social science disciplines. Shubik surely provides the most comprehensive coverage of game theory and applications by a single hand and will be an invaluable source to serious students of the subject. Roth and van Damme's books are specialized in scope, each treating in a unified way a topic of great importance that has developed in the recent past. Roth's monograph is on axiomatic bargaining models; van Damme's is on refinements of the noncooperative equilibrium.

Contents

7. *n*-Person Cooperative Games without Transferable Utility   218

List of Figures

List of Tables

Game Theory with Applications to Economics

1

Introduction to games

In Samuel Johnson's (1755) dictionary, the first definition of the noun *game* is "sport of any kind," and our modern notion typically would add that games usually have some particular rules associated with them. Examples include athletic games such as soccer, golf, basketball, and tennis; card games such as bridge, poker, and cribbage; and board games such as chess, backgammon, and Go. Most of these games share an interactive and competitive element. That is, a player strives to outdo the other players in the game, and her success and effectiveness depend on the actions of the remaining players, as well as her own actions. For instance, in playing tennis, one does not merely try to hit the ball back to the other player, one tries to hit it back so that the other player cannot return it, so where the ball is aimed will depend on where the other player is placed. An exception to the interactive and competitive element in the preceding list of games is golf, where each player struggles against an absolute standard, and the actual performance of a player does not depend on the actions chosen by other players.

There are several features that are typical of most games. First, games have rules that govern the order in which actions are taken, describe the array of allowed actions, and define how the outcome of the game is related to the actions taken. Second, there are two or more players, each of whom is struggling consciously to do the best he can for himself. Third, the outcome to a player depends on the actions of the other players. The player knows this, and knows that choosing the best action requires making an intelligent assessment of the actions likely to be taken by the other players.

These general characteristics of games typify many situations in life that are not *games* in the sense of being *sport*. For example, when the management of a company and the leadership of a union face each other over the bargaining table to work out a new contract, they are in a gamelike situation. The rules are not as formal and detailed as for chess, but there are rules. Offers and counteroffers are made with a view on each side to making the final settlement as favorable as possible, and what offer one side should make to best further its interest depends on just how that

1

offer will be received and responded to by the other side. In 1979, the new head of the International Harvester Company bargained so hard with the United Auto Workers Union that he went far beyond the bounds of what the union found reasonable. Union members had the impression that he wished to kill their organization. After a long and bitter strike, there was a settlement; however, the union became so intransigent at the subsequent contract negotiations three years later that they did not settle with the company until (coincidentally) that same head resigned from his job.

Many people face bargaining situations at one time or another, for example, when buying or selling a house or an automobile. These are games in quite the same sense that the labor-management situation is a game.

The first important theorem in game theory, the *saddle point theorem* for two-person, zero-sum games, was published by von Neumann (1928). This was followed by the rich collaboration culminating in von Neumann and Morgenstern (1944), which contains approaches to the treatment of many kinds of games along with much discussion of the potential applications of game theory. The early history of game theory, going back to von Neumann's precursors, is discussed in Rives (1975).

1   Examples of games

Several illustrative games are described below. The first is an oligopolistic market with three firms, and the two following are political science models of the election process. All of these are *noncooperative games*, which means that the players are unable to make contractual agreements with one another. The final example is a labor-management dispute whose outcome should be a contract signed by the two players.

1.1   A three-firm computer market

Suppose a market in which the number of active firms is not very large, but is more than one. Imagine firms in the rapidly changing computer industry. Each firm must decide how to direct its efforts in developing and marketing new equipment, and the best plan for one to follow is dependent on the plans adopted by all of the others. A small- to middle-sized firm might be able to seriously tackle the market for just one size of computer, and, to survive, it must select a size that will not have many competing firms. Meanwhile, problems of product development require that it commit itself to a course of action years in advance and before it can possibly have a clear idea of what the others have chosen. As a simple numerical illustration, imagine that there are three firms, each of which can choose to make large (L) or small (S) computers. The choice of firm 1 is denoted S_1 or L_1, and, similarly, the choices of firms 2 and 3 are denoted S_i or L_i where $i = 2$ or 3 indicates the firm. Table 1.1 shows the profit each firm would receive according to the choices which the three firms could make. For

TABLE 1.1   Profits to three computer firms, according to the size of computer which each produces

	S_2S_3	S_2L_3	L_2S_3	L_2L_3
S_1	−10 −15 −20	0 −10 60	0 10 10	20 5 15
L_1	5 −5 0	−5 35 15	−5 0 15	−20 10 10

example, the second entry in the first row is $(0, -10, 60)$ indicating profit of 0 for firm 1, -10 for firm 2, and 60 for firm 3. This results from the choices $(S_1S_2L_3)$. Firms 1 and 2 choose to produce small computers, while firm 3 produces large ones. Note that this is the most profitable possible outcome for firm 3; however, if firm 2 had foreseen the choices of firms 1 and 3, then it would have done better by choosing L_2.

Suppose that each of the firms has the information in Table 1.1. We can easily analyze the situation from the vantage point of a single firm, say firm 1. It is better off choosing S_1 if either or both of the others choose L, but it is best off with L_1 if both of the others decide on S. Thus it is impossible to ignore the probable choices of firms 2 and 3. Whether to make large or small computers depends on its assessment of what the other two firms select. With each of the other two firms, large is the better choice as long as at least one firm selects small. This immediately suggests choices that may be a plausible equilibrium outcome: S_1, L_2, and L_3. From Table 1.1, it is clear that this combination causes no ex post regret. That is, given the choices of the other two, no one firm could have done better by choosing something else. The same cannot be said for any other selection open to the firms. For any other outcome, at least one firm could have done better by making the other choice, given the choices of the rival firms. The outcome (S_1, L_2, L_3) is a *noncooperative equilibrium* for the game. Such equilibria are studied extensively in Chapters 2 to 4 in a variety of models. The defining feature of this equilibrium is that no single player would have obtained a larger payoff had she used an alternative strategy, given the strategies of the other players. In the present instance, a player's strategy is either S or L.

1.2   Two political election games

Politics provides ready examples of game theoretic situations. Picture several candidates who are running for office, say for mayor of a city. Prior to the start of the electoral campaign, each candidate must select a position, which means that a particular stand must be taken on each of several issues. In one version of the example, the original position is immutable, and, supposing each candidate merely seeks election and is equally willing to be elected on the basis of any position, the best position

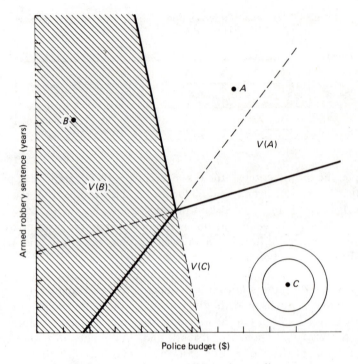

FIGURE 1.1   Voters and candidates in a policy space.

for a candidate depends on the positions chosen by the others. Figure 1.1 illustrates this for two issues, with the issue on the horizontal axis being the annual budget for the police force, and, on the vertical axis, the jail sentence to be imposed for armed robbery.

Each voter has preferences regarding positions in this two-dimensional issue space. For simplicity, suppose each voter has a favorite position, that the farther a point is from this best point, the worse it is, and that all positions equidistant from this best point are equally good. A voter's favorite position can be thought of as her *location* in the issue space, and a voter located at *c* in Figure 1.1 has indifference contours that are concentric circles around *c*. Suppose that a voter will vote for that candidate whose position stands highest on the voter's utility scale. Then, for this example, the candidate nearest to the voter receives her vote. With three candidates located at *A*, *B*, and *C*, respectively, those voters located in the region $V(A)$ will vote for *A*, and similarly for $V(B)$ and $V(C)$. Letting v_A, v_B, and v_C denote the number of voters in the three regions, the winner is the candidate having the largest number of votes. In this game, the players are the three candidates, while the voters behave according to clearcut rules that imply they make no judgments. For each candidate, a location is a strategy; hence, choosing a strategy means choosing a location. A complete specification of this game would include a utility, or payoff, function for each candidate, based, ultimately, on the distribution of votes and on whether the candidate won or lost.

The preceding example can be modified by supposing the voters are also players. As before, the candidates are players who choose positions. Each voter chooses a candidate to vote for; however, a voter's utility depends on whether she has voted for one of the two top vote getters. The rationale for this is the view that voting for a third place candidate is to throw one's vote away. Thus a voter maximizes her payoff by voting for the candidate (i.e., position) she prefers among the two top vote getters. In three candidate presidential elections in the United States, it is nearly always clear during the campaign which candidate has the smallest following (i.e., which candidate would get fewest votes if each voter voted for the nearest candidate). If, for example, $v_A > v_B > v_C$, then those voters favoring C would not vote for him on the supposition that he would run behind the other two. The actual vote would split between A and B with the winner being determined by the voting preferences of the voters in region $V(C)$.

The two voting models embody different views concerning the purpose of voting. The first method is consistent with the view that, by voting, a person intends to go on record saying who he believes to be best among all candidates. The second method applies to voters who wish to use their votes to bring about as good an outcome as they can. If your favorite is doomed to be a distant third, you will do more to bring about an outcome favorable to yourself by casting your vote for your second choice, thereby reducing the chance that your third choice will win. Abandoning your first choice in this case does not hurt you because he cannot win anyway.

Whichever rule is used to determine who votes for whom, it is clear that the position chosen by a candidate will depend on more than the way voters are distributed; it will also depend on how the candidate presumes the other candidates will position themselves.

1.3 Labor-management: A cooperative game example

The political examples and the computer firm example are all instances of what is called *noncooperative games*. The essential feature setting these games apart is that the decision makers (players) are unable to make legally binding contracts with one another. The computer firms cannot collude, nor can the voters or the candidates for mayor. This inability to collude is part of the *rules of the game*; hence, is assumed beyond the players' control. This may be contrasted with a labor-management situation in which the outcome of the game is a contract if the two sides (players) agree or a threat outcome if they do not. The threat outcome may be something even more severe than a strike; it could be such a complete breakdown between the two that they go their separate ways and have no more to do with each other. In this case, the workers seek jobs elsewhere, refusing to go back to the company, and the company must set about acquiring and training a whole new workforce. This is represented in Figure 1.2, where the horizontal axis is the total income of the workers in the union and the vertical is the profit of the company. Point T shows the threat payoffs that

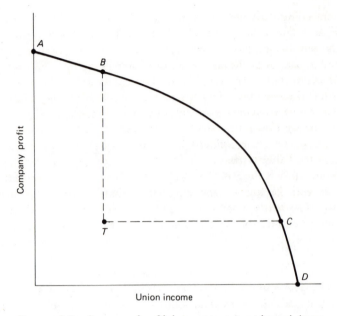

FIGURE 1.2   An example of labor-management bargaining.

they will obtain if they cannot agree, and the points on and beneath the curve *ABCD* show the payoffs that are achievable through agreement.

Because the game is cooperative, that is, admitting of binding agreements, it is natural to focus attention on what the players ought, in some sense, to agree on. Two natural restrictions on their agreements are, first, that they would agree to an outcome giving each player at least what he would get at *T*. For someone to accept less would be irrational. The reasoning behind this is that a player can guarantee that much without the help of the other player. Second, players should agree on something that they cannot jointly improve on. The first restriction, called *individual rationality*, limits attention to outcomes that lie above and to the right of *T*, while the second, called *group rationality*, restricts outcomes to the payoff possibility frontier *ABCD*. Between the two restrictions, the outcomes must lie on the part of the frontier going from *B* to *C*.

2   Forms in which games are represented

You may have noticed that the noncooperative game examples and the cooperative example have been organized and discussed in very different forms. In the noncooperative example, attention is focused on the actions that each player is able to take, and on how these actions jointly determine each player's payoff. In the labor–management example, the actions of the players are largely suppressed. What matters is what the players are able to obtain, separately and together. How they obtain an outcome is not of central importance. That is, if they fail to agree, they are at *T*. It does not really matter what they do to achieve T. Similarly, if they agree, they are capable of attaining any point on or below the payoff frontier. Again, it is not important to know how they behave to achieve a particular outcome. It only matters that a particular set of outcomes is freely available to them if they choose to cooperate.

Noncooperative games are often expressed in a fashion that exposes each individual move a player can make; this is called the *extensive form*. Or they are expressed in a way that suppresses individual moves but highlights the overall plans, or *strategies*, which are available to players. This form, illustrated by Table 1.1 has been called the *normal form*, but recently it has been more aptly called the *strategic form*. Cooperative games are often shown, as with Figure 1.2, in a fashion underlining achievable outcomes; called the *characteristic function form*, or the *coalitional form*. More is said on these matters in later chapters.

2.1   The extensive form and some basic concepts applying to all games

In this section, games are informally described in extensive, strategic, and coalitional forms. Although there are some elements common to each form, there are also substantial differences. The extensive form, represented by a *game tree*, is discussed first and is used as a vehicle to introduce concepts of wider interest. *Every game has a set of rational decision makers, called* **players**, *whose decisions are central to the study of games. The* **set of players** *is denoted N where $N = \{1, 2, \ldots, n\}$.* Throughout the book, n is generally finite, and each player knows how many players are in the game. Putting random actions aside for a moment, a game in extensive form starts with a particular player making a move. After the first player moves, some other player has a turn to move, and so on until the game terminates. When it ends, the players receive their payoffs. Randomness can be added by having certain decision points at which *player* 0 moves. Player 0 is called *nature* or *chance*, and chooses its move by drawing from a probability distribution which is known to all the other players (i.e., the players in N).

Simultaneous moves by two or more players are modeled using *information sets*. When it is the turn of a player to make a move, she is always located at a specific decision point, called a *node*. If she knows precisely which node she is at, then that node, by itself, constitutes an information set. Suppose two players move simultaneously, that player 1 is treated by the extensive form representation as moving first, and that both players know which specific node he is moving from. If he has m possible moves, then each move leads to a different node. Player 2 will not know at which of these m nodes she is actually located, and, thus, these m nodes will constitute an information set.

2.1.1   A game in extensive form

As an example of a game in extensive form, imagine two people who are going to match pennies twice in succession for stakes of $5.00. The

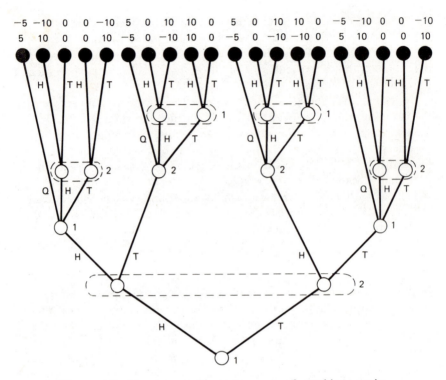

FIGURE 1.3   Game tree to illustrate a game of matching pennies.

procedure is that each will choose heads (H) or tails (T) without knowing what the other has chosen. They then reveal their choices to one another. If the two coins do not match (i.e., if there is one H and one T), then player 1 wins $5 from player 2. If the coins match, player 2 wins $5 from player 1. At the second stage, the player who lost at stage 1 has the right to decide whether they proceed to another matching or simply quit. Thus the loser can now select quit (Q) or H or T. If he chooses H or T, then, simultaneously with that choice, the winner chooses H or T. This is illustrated in the game tree shown in Figure 1.3. To simplify the illustration, it is assumed that utility is measured by money. In the figure, an open circle denotes a point at which a player makes a decision, and this point is called a *decision node*. A filled circle, called a *terminal node*, is an endpoint of the game. Payoffs are written at each terminal node. The left-most node is reached by player 1 first choosing H, followed by player 2 choosing H, followed by player 1 electing to end the game (choosing Q). The first (top) payoff is that of player 1 (−5). A game tree represents the action of a game as if moves are always sequential. In the figure, player 1 is shown to move, after which player 2 moves. This sequential action is made equivalent to the simultaneous action described above by the *information sets*. The broken figures in Figure 1.3 that enclose two decision nodes are information sets. Next to each information set is the name of the player who moves. If a node is not enclosed by a broken figure, then that node, by itself, is an information set. This means that the player who is to move at those nodes does not know which node he is actually at. He only knows which information set he is in. It is as if player 1 actually does choose first and then reveals his choice to an umpire, followed by player 2 making and revealing her choice in the same way. Then the umpire discloses the choices to them and they proceed to the next stage. In general, an information set can contain any number of nodes; however, each node of an information set must have the same number of branches leading on from it. This is because the number of branches is the number of choices a player has at that point, and, if she does not have exactly the same number of choices at each node, she has a means of telling the nodes apart. Also if one node follows another in the game tree, by one or more moves, the two nodes cannot be in the same information set.

2.1.2 *Complete information, perfect information, and perfect recall*

It is obviously important to be clear concerning the information which a player possesses in a game, and several kinds of information must be distinguished. First, **complete information** *versus* **incomplete information** *refers to whether or not each player knows (a) who the set of players is, (b) all actions available to all players, and (c) all potential outcomes to all players. Essentially,* **complete information** *obtains when each player knows (a), (b), and (c).* This is like saying each player knows the whole game tree, including the payoffs listed at each terminal node. In the game of Figure 1.3, complete information requires that each player have a copy of Figure 1.3 itself (or equivalent information). Suppose, by contrast, that player 1 only knew the payoffs in the top row (his own payoffs), while player 2 knew only the payoffs in the second row. This would be a case of *incomplete information*. If one or more players lack knowledge of (a), (b), and/or (c) above, then the game is one of incomplete information. Most of the models in this book assume complete information, and that assumption should be understood to hold unless incomplete information is explicitly stated.

A second sort of information relates to the information sets. If each information set in the game consists of just one node, then the game is one of **perfect information**, *while, if that is not the case, the game is one of* **imperfect information**. Figure 1.3 depicts a game of complete and imperfect information. The last aspect of information concerns a relationship between the information sets and the moves of the players. *If the information sets are always consistent with a player remembering all past moves she has selected, then the game is one of* **perfect recall**. *If this does not hold, the game is one of* **imperfect recall**. The game in Figure 1.3 is one of perfect recall, but the variant of it shown in Figure 1.4 is one of imperfect recall. Note that player 1 has an information set that contains four nodes. It can only be possible for player 1 to have this information set

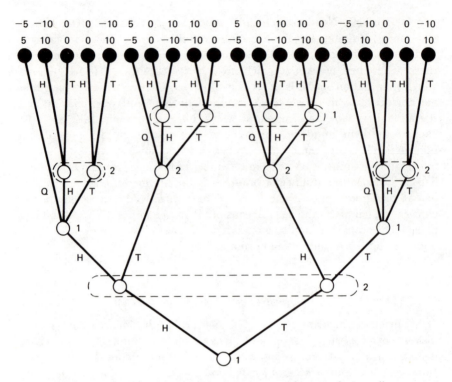

FIGURE 1.4   Matching pennies in a game without perfect recall.

if she has forgotten whether she chose H or T at her first move. If she remembered, then the right two nodes and the left two nodes would be in different information sets, as in Figure 1.3.

Most of the games studied in later chapters assume imperfect information and perfect recall. This is because the selection of game theory models is biased towards models with applicability in the social sciences. Simultaneous move games are commonly encountered in applications, and such games embody imperfect information. Perfect recall is also a natural choice for applications because players are generally either individuals or firms. If they are firms, then they are assumed to have centralized information and decision making. To see where imperfect recall might arise, consider the bidding process in a game of bridge. It is natural to regard bridge as a two-player game, with each player being a two person team. Suppose Alice and Ben are partners. The early moves of the game involve each person picking up her or his cards and examining them. Alice will not recall what Ben saw, and vice versa. When it is Alice's turn to move (i.e., to bid), she does not know Ben's hand, but she knows her own. When that player (i.e., Alice and Ben) has its next move, it is Ben who bids, and he does not know the contents of Alice's hand.

2.1.3　*The rules of the game, common knowledge, binding agreements, and commitments*

The extensive form of the game shows the complete move, information set, and payoff structure. It does not quite give a total definition of the game. The missing elements, covered under the rubric *rules of the game*, include (a) whether information is complete or incomplete, (b) common knowledge and (c) whether it is possible for the players to make binding agreements or commitments. Other aspects of information previously mentioned (perfect or imperfect information, perfect or imperfect recall) are captured by the extensive form. It would even be possible to represent incomplete information in the extensive form if a separate game tree were drawn up for each player showing, for each, the information she was to have. *Common knowledge* refers to those things that are known by all players, and known by each to be known to all of them, and so forth. See Aumann (1976) and Milgrom (1981). Usually, and always throughout this book, games of complete information are characterized by each player knowing the entire structure and payoffs of the game, by each player knowing that all players possess this information, and by all players knowing that all players have this information. There is, for example, an important conceptual distinction to be made between (a) a complete information game in which complete information is common knowledge and (b) a complete information game in which each player does not actually know whether the other players also have complete information. In general, there is no reason to suppose that intelligent behavior and equilibrium will be the same in both cases. To repeat, in this book, complete information games are restricted to games in which complete information is common knowledge.

To illustrate these informational considerations, look at the game in Figure 1.3. It is a game of complete information if all the information in the figure is known to both players. It is a game of incomplete information if everything in the figure, except some of the payoffs at some of the terminal nodes, is known to each player. The gaps of knowledge need not be the same for each player. The information situation is common knowledge if each player is correctly informed about what the other knows (and each knows that the other knows that he knows this, and so forth).

Concerning binding agreements, it is common knowledge among the players whether they may be made. In motivating the notion of a binding agreement, it is usual to note that the game requires an outside authority that enforces any such agreements. The situation is as if the parties to a binding agreement write and sign a contract that they register with this authority. The authority can monitor the agreement at no cost, can tell with certainty whether its terms are being carried out, and can, like an avenging angel, impose on violators sanctions so severe that cheating is absolutely out of the question. Related to binding agreement is commitment. *A* **commitment** *is an action taken by a single player that is binding on* *him* and that, to be of any use, must be known to the other players. The point of a commitment is to persuade others to take actions more favorable to oneself with the threat of taking a particular (costly to oneself) action if they do not do so. A rather fanciful example is that of the perfectly sane and rational person who demands a payment from each of several others, saying that he will kill himself if the payments are not made. The others would rather make the payments than see the person die, but they are unlikely to believe he would carry out such a threat. The threat can be made credible if the person can make a contract with some outside agent to kill him should the payments fail to be made. **Binding agreements** *and* **commitments** *are both instances of voluntary restrictions on the actions available, where those restrictions are enforced. With* **binding agreements**, *two ore more players make jointly agreed upon restrictions, while* **commitments** *are unilateral restrictions.*

Another point, probably obvious to the reader, should be noted about game trees: They are cumbersome and unwieldy for all but very simple games. Anyone doubting this is invited to make a complete game tree for the game of tic-tac-toe. At the first move, player 1 has nine choices. At the second move, player 2 has eight choices, but he can be at any one of nine nodes. Thus, at the third move, player 1 can be at any one of 72 nodes. The game must go to at least five moves, and, at the fifth (the third move of player 1), player 1 could be at any one of $9 \cdot 8 \cdot 7 \cdot 6 = 3024$ nodes. Game trees are handy for illustrating basic game theoretic concepts and for analyzing particularly simple games, but other forms are required to deal with large classes of games. Many games in later chapters have uncountably infinite strategy spaces. For these games, it is not clear that an extensive form could be fruitfully specified.

2.2   The strategic form

Imagine a game in extensive form such as the one in Figure 1.3. Suppose a player were committed to play this game, but were unable to show up for the execution of it. He could find a person to stand in for him, but it would be necessary to give the stand-in a complete set of instructions on what choices to make. This amounts to telling the stand-in a decision rule for each information set in the game belonging to the player. Two information sets can have different decision rules associated with them. Suppose the player to be player 1. An example of his instructions is: Choose H on the first move; then, if player 2 has chosen H on her first move, choose Q; but if player 2 has chosen T on her first move, choose H on the second move. A set of instructions like this is called a **strategy**. *What characterizes a strategy is that, at every point of decision for a player, the strategy dictates precisely what the player does.* In general, games are played by a sequence of moves, but individual moves have interest insofar as they contribute to an overall plan of action—a strategy. Strategies can allow for players to randomize in choosing moves. For example, a valid strategy for player 1 is to choose H on his first move; then, if player 2 has chosen H, to choose Q with probability .4, H with probability .5 and T with probability .1; and if player 2 has chosen T, player 1 chooses T. For a particular strategy for player 1 and a particular strategy for player 2, it is possible to calculate an expected payoff for each player. Given a pair of strategies, the probability of reaching any specific terminal node is determined. If a strategy has no randomly determined choices, it is called a *pure strategy*; otherwise it is called a *mixed strategy*.

Table 1.2 contains a complete enumeration of all of the pure (i.e., nonrandomized) strategies of players 1 and 2 for the game in Figure 1.3, and Table 1.3 is a double-entry payoff matrix giving the payoffs associated with any pair of pure strategies that the players might choose for this game. In Table 1.3, the strategies of player 1 are the row headings, while those of player 2 are the column headings. The numbers, 1, ..., 12, correspond to the strategies as they are defined in Table 1.2. For any particular *strategy combination* (i.e., a pair of strategies, one for player 1 and one for player 2) the two corresponding numbers in the table are the payoffs of the two players; the figure that is higher and to the left is the payoff of player 1. For

TABLE 1.2 Strategies of players 1 and 2 for the strategic form of the game shown in Figure 1.3

	Strategies of player 1			Strategies of player 2		
	First move	Second move if the first move of player 2 is		First move	Second move if the first move of player 1 is	
		H	T		H	T
1	H	Q	H	H	H	Q
2	H	Q	T	H	T	Q
3	H	H	H	H	H	H
4	H	H	T	H	T	H
5	H	T	H	H	H	T
6	H	T	T	H	T	T
7	T	H	Q	T	Q	H
8	T	T	Q	T	Q	T
9	T	H	H	T	H	H
10	T	T	H	T	H	T
11	T	H	T	T	T	H
12	T	T	T	T	T	T

TABLE 1.3   Payoff matrix showing the strategic form of the game in Figure 1.3

Strategies of player 2

		1	2	3	4	5	6	7	8	9	10	11	12
Strategies of player 1	1	-5 / 5	-5 / 5	-5 / 5	-5 / 5	-5 / 5	-5 / 5	5 / -5	5 / -5	0 / 0	0 / 0	10 / -10	10 / -10
	2	-5 / 5	-5 / 5	-5 / 5	-5 / 5	-5 / 5	-5 / 5	5 / -5	5 / -5	10 / -10	10 / -10	0 / 0	0 / 0
	3	-10 / 10	0 / 0	-10 / 10	0 / 0	-10 / 10	0 / 0	5 / -5	5 / -5	0 / 0	0 / 0	10 / -10	10 / -10
	4	-10 / 10	0 / 0	-10 / 10	0 / 0	-10 / 10	0 / 0	5 / -5	5 / -5	10 / -10	10 / -10	0 / 0	0 / 0
	5	0 / 0	-10 / 10	0 / 0	-10 / 10	0 / 0	-10 / 10	5 / -5	5 / -5	0 / 0	0 / 0	10 / -10	10 / -10
	6	0 / 0	-10 / 10	0 / 0	-10 / 10	0 / 0	-10 / 10	5 / -5	5 / -5	10 / -10	10 / -10	0 / 0	0 / 0
	7	5 / -5	5 / -5	0 / 0	0 / 0	10 / -10	10 / -10	-5 / 5	-5 / 5	-5 / 5	-5 / 5	-5 / 5	-5 / 5
	8	5 / -5	5 / -5	10 / -10	10 / -10	0 / 0	0 / 0	-5 / 5	-5 / 5	-5 / 5	-5 / 5	-5 / 5	-5 / 5
	9	5 / -5	5 / -5	0 / 0	0 / 0	10 / -10	10 / -10	-10 / 10	0 / 0	-10 / 10	0 / 0	-10 / 10	0 / 0
	10	5 / -5	5 / -5	10 / -10	10 / -10	0 / 0	0 / 0	-10 / 10	0 / 0	-10 / 10	0 / 0	-10 / 10	0 / 0
	11	5 / -5	5 / -5	0 / 0	0 / 0	10 / -10	10 / -10	0 / 0	-10 / 10	0 / 0	-10 / 10	0 / 0	-10 / 10
	12	5 / -5	5 / -5	10 / -10	10 / -10	0 / 0	0 / 0	0 / 0	-10 / 10	0 / 0	-10 / 10	0 / 0	-10 / 10

example, suppose player 1 chooses 8 and player 2 chooses 3. Then the payoff to player 1 is 10, and the payoff to player 2 is −10. Notice that the *strategic form* represented in Table 1.3 completely hides the underlying move structure of the game. In general, the strategic form of a game, although very handy to work with, suppresses information about the underlying move structure of the game that may be of interest. The treatment of noncooperative games and of equilibrium points for them, in Chapters 2 to 4, brings this out.

2.3 The coalitional, or characteristic function, form

The hallmark of cooperative games is that the players or any subgroup of them have the right to make contractual agreements that are 100% binding. A subset of players that has the right to make an agreement is called a *coalition*, and, usually it is assumed that any subset of the players can form a coalition. In such a cooperative setting, the strategies are of less direct interest to someone wanting to analyze a game, and, instead, the payoff opportunities open to each player and to each coalition are of central concern. Indeed, some games are most naturally described in ways that make it unclear just how strategies ought to be described. Other games in which strategies are clearly present and easily described must have another description that easily captures the power and opportunities of the coalitions. Some examples should clarify these comments.

First take a common example in which strategies make no explicit appearance. Suppose there are three persons who are told that they can divide (up to) $100 in any way they wish. The rules are that a division of the money, denoted $x = (x_1, x_2, x_3)$, (a) must satisfy the condition $x \geq 0$, (b) must allocate not more than $100 (i.e., $x_1 + x_2 + x_3 \leq 100$), and (c) at least two of the three players must agree to an allocation. Suppose that utility is measured by money for each player. Then the payoff possibilities open to each coalition can be described by means of a *characteristic function*, denoted $v(K)$, that associates with each coalition K the total utility that the members of that coalition can achieve when they act in concert. Thus, for the game of dividing $100, the characteristic function is (a) $v(\{i\}) = 0$ for $i = 1, 2, 3$, (b) $v(\{i, j\}) = 100$ for any two (distinct) players i and j, and (c) $v(\{1, 2, 3\}) = 100$. It is hard to see how any helpful additional information would be added by knowing what strategies the players used to achieve these various enforceable outcomes.

One cooperative game solution concept, the *core*, is a generalization of Edgeworth's (1881) *contract curve*, and is based on the notion that an outcome agreeable to all players must give as much to each single player and to each coalition as it (the player or coalition) can achieve for itself. The reasoning behind this solution is that such requirements are needed to obtain the agreement of all players and coalitions. If, for example, a proposed solution gives to a player less than the player can guarantee himself on his own, then the player will not agree to the joint outcome. Similarly, if a coalition can, on its own, achieve an outcome that gives more to each player than each received under a proposed outcome, then the coalition will not agree to the proposal.

In the present game, this requires that each individual receive at least 0 and each pair of individuals receive at least $100 between them. For the three-person game of splitting $100, the core is empty. It is impossible to divide $100 so that players 1 and 2 receive $100, players 1 and 3 receive $100, and players 2 and 3 receive $100. These conditions could be met in a game where any two players can obtain $100, but a coalition of three players can obtain $150 (or more). Then an outcome in which each player receives at least $50 satisfies all the required conditions.

The situation is substantially the same if utility is not measured by money. Suppose that the utility of money for each player were $u_1(x_1) = x_1^{.5}$ for player 1, $u_2(x_2) = x_2$ for player 2, and $u_3(x_3) = \ln(1 + x_3)$ for player 3. It is no longer possible to describe with a single number the possibilities open to a coalition of two or more players. Instead, a set is used to describe them. Take, for example, the coalition $K = \{1, 2\}$, consisting of players 1 and 2. Each player alone can guarantee a payoff of zero; therefore, the only coalitional outcomes that are of interest are the ones giving each player at least these minima. What this coalition can achieve is pictured in Figure 1.5, where the upper right frontier gives all the outcomes to players 1 and 2 corresponding to the division of the $100 between the two of them. On and below this frontier, bounded underneath and at the left by the two axes, are all two-person payoffs achievable by the two of them.

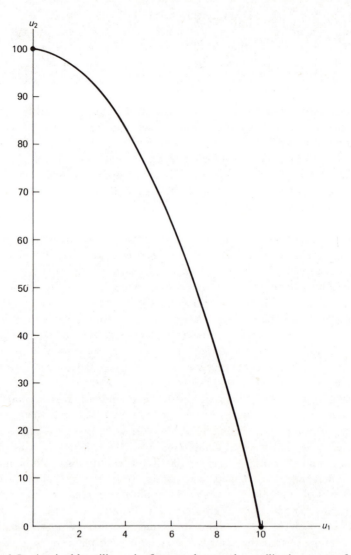

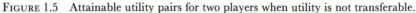

FIGURE 1.5   Attainable utility pairs for two players when utility is not transferable.

Oligopoly provides an example in which the players naturally have strategy sets. Let there be a duopoly in which the two players can collude and form a cartel with a binding agreement. Assume an inverse market demand function of $p = 100 - q_1 - q_2$. The two firms' total cost functions are $C_1(q_1) = 5q_1$ and $C_2(q_2) = 10q_2 + .5q_2^2$, respectively. Letting $\pi_i = pq_i - C_i(q_i)$ denote the profit of firm i, the payoff possibility frontier for the two firms is calculated by maximizing $\lambda\pi_1 + (1 - \lambda)\pi_2$ with respect to q_1 and q_2 for all values of λ between 0 and 1 (subject to $q_1 \geqslant 0$ and $q_2 \geqslant 0$). This frontier is calculated assuming the firms cannot make direct money transfers among themselves. In game theoretic terms, *side payments* are ruled out. The strategy sets for each player can be taken as the output levels in the interval $[0, 100]$, but the strategies themselves are not of any real interest. Clearly, either player can guarantee herself a payoff of at least zero by producing nothing; therefore, the set of payoffs attainable by the coalition consists of the payoffs on and below the payoff possibility frontier that also give at least zero to each player. For the present example, these are shown in Figure 1.6. In this two player game, any outcome on the

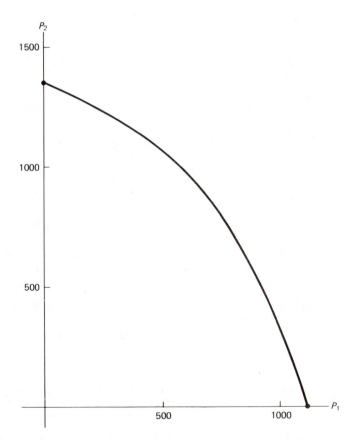

FIGURE 1.6 The payoff possibility frontier for a duopoly.

profit possibility frontier that gives at least zero to each player is in the core.

3   Outline of the book

Six chapters follow the present chapter; the next three are devoted to noncooperative games and the last three to cooperative games. Many of these chapters contain a section that illustrates the models by applications to economics and, sometimes, politics.

3.1   *Chapters on noncooperative games*

Chapter 2 takes up noncooperative games in strategic form. Games are directly described in the strategic form instead of being formulated in the extensive form with the strategic form being derived from it. After some basics about such games, two-person, zero-sum games are discussed, along with von Neumann's (1928) saddle point (minimax) theorem, and two-person, strictly competitive games. The latter are two-person games in which all outcomes are Pareto optimal, and they form a generalization of two-person, zero-sum games that preserves the essential strategic feature of these games: in both two-person, zero-sum games and two-person, strictly competitive games there is no room whatever for any cooperation between any players. In a two-person game that is not strictly competitive or in a three- or more-person, zero-sum game, there is room for some cooperation between at least one pair of players. The remainder of the chapter deals with general n-person noncooperative games in strategic form, centering about Nash's (1951) theorem on existence of equilibrium points for noncooperative games. The Nash theorem was stated in his article for finite games, that is, for games in which each player has only a finite number of pure strategies; however, generalizations are considered in Chapter 2 that go beyond Nash and that are particularly useful in economic and political applications.

Chapters 3 and 4 deal with games that can be thought of in either of two ways: as dynamic games or as games in a form similar to the extensive form. For illustration, picture the foregoing duopoly as a noncooperative game in which each player will *once and only once* select an output level, with the two players choosing their output levels simultaneously. Such a game is more naturally described in strategic form than in extensive form. Now suppose that the two players will repeat this very same game in a countable sequence of time periods, $t = 1, 2, 3, \ldots$. This *repeated game* or *supergame* is dynamic in the sense that time explicitly enters. The game could be reduced to a strategic form, thus becoming subsumed in the material of Chapter 2, but this reduction would obscure elements of the game that may be of interest. In the duopoly example, one wants to know more than whether the game has an equilibrium. One wants to know things about the nature and characterization of the equilibrium and about the nature of the specific single-period choices that are part of an equilibrium strategy.

Clearly in the duopoly game, one choice of an output level by a firm constitutes a single move of that player. In the one iteration version of the game, move and strategy coincide; however, in the repeated version, a strategy consists of an initial move and the rules by which each later move will be chosen as a function of the information that will come into the hands of the player. In this application, it would be very desirable to keep track of individual moves, rather than to have them buried in a strategic form. The extensive form is a little cumbersome because the players actually move simultaneously, while the extensive form requires that moves of players be treated formally as if they were sequential. The formulations in Chapters 3 and 4 are a compromise between the two forms in which the individual moves of the players remain visible.

The difference in material between the two chapters is based on *structural time dependence*. In Chapter 3, all models are either games in which each period repeats an identical structure to the preceding period, and, like the duopoly example, each period's activity could be thought of as an individual game, or, in each period a different situation may be encountered, but each period's situation is independent of all other periods. This independence is *structural* in the sense that the payoffs in a single time period depend only on the moves of that very same period. The behavior of the players may depend on observations of past choices made by rival players. In other words, structural time dependence may be absent while behavioral time dependence is present. The models of Chapter 4 allow for structural time dependence by permitting the payoffs associated with each period t to depend on the moves of both periods t and $t - 1$.

3.2 Chapters on cooperative games

Chapters 5, 6, and 7 are concerned with cooperative games. There is no single solution concept for cooperative games that has had the central role occupied by the Nash equilibrium in noncooperative games, and, as a consequence, these chapters do not have such a strong unifying theme as do Chapters 2 to 4. Because of the complications added by possible agreements among individual coalitions, there is a big difference between the analysis of two-person and $n > 2$-person cooperative games. Therefore, Chapter 5 is devoted exclusively to two-person cooperative games, focusing mainly on the Nash (1950, 1953) models and related approaches.

Another difference between cooperative and noncooperative games is the transferable/nontransferable utility division. Transferable utility is a simplifying assumption that is undesirable in many applications but that is a great analytical convenience in many cooperative game models. Chapter 6 takes up transferable utility models, introducing the *core*, the *von Neumann–Morgenstern solution*, the *bargaining set*, and the *Shapley* (1953b) *value*. The value approach to cooperative games provides a strong contrast with the core concerning multiplicity of solutions. The core is often empty, as in the game of splitting $100; it is often very large, as in the game where two players can achieve $100, but all three players can achieve $200. The Shapley value, in contrast, exists for a large class of games and is always unique when it exists. Chapter 7 is devoted to nontransferable utility models, taking up the core and a generalization of both the Nash bargaining model and the Shapley value.

There is a cross link between the cooperative game chapters and some of the material on noncooperative games, because a central aspect of the *repeated games* literature (see Chapter 3) is that a repeated game allows a *cooperative outcome* to be supported by (i.e., be the result of) a *noncooperative equilibrium*. In a way, this causes a blurring of the distinction between cooperative and noncooperative games; however, this blurring need not be confusing if a distinction is kept in mind between cooperative versus noncooperative games (i.e., the structures) on the one hand, and cooperative versus noncooperative outcomes on the other. The presence or absence of binding agreements is the definitive element for cooperative versus noncooperative games. If binding agreements are possible, then the game (structure) is cooperative, otherwise it is noncooperative. A cooperative outcome can be defined as an outcome that is Pareto optimal in a game where not all outcomes are Pareto optimal. A noncooperative outcome is merely an outcome supported by a noncooperative equilibrium. Thus the *cooperative* outcome of repeated games are *both cooperative and noncooperative outcomes*. Such outcomes are noncooperative because they are supported by noncooperative equilibrium strategies and they are the former because they are Pareto optimal. By contrast, a structure is either cooperative or noncooperative but not both. With respect to structure, these properties are mutually exclusive and exhaustive, but with regard to outcomes they are neither.

3.3 Application to economics and political science

Most, although not all, chapters conclude with a few pages devoted to applications in the social sciences. Most applications are to economics, and a few are to political science. These examples are not intended to substitute for textbook presentations of the subjects they deal with; however, they are serious applications in the sense that they are usually well-accepted models of the processes they describe. An attempt is made to keep these models relatively simple without making them so unreasonably simple minded that people teaching the subjects they cover would never use them.

The collection of applications is somewhat idiosyncratic, reflecting the things I happen to know about, and is not put forth as a perfectly representative sample of the ways that game theory has been used in economics and politics. Still, for economics especially, I think the examples are good individual representatives even if the collection may leave out some important topics. Above all, these applications are intended to show the reader what some interesting uses of game theory look like and, in each instance, to link clearly a game theoretic model with an economic or political model.

4 A note on the exposition

If the "ideas" of game theory are presented in a largely nontechnical way, the reader can only glean a pale shadow of their meaning and power; therefore, a moderate level of technical sophistication must be assumed in order to present models with enough precision and generality. Following this course need not mean that the text be continually extremely difficult. For readers having a moderate ability to follow logical argument and having enough familiarity with mathematics that they are comfortable with models formulated using symbols, the bulk of the book should be within their grasp. The mathematical appendix at the end of the book contains some notation and definitions that are used at various places in the book. The appendix is no substitute for a mathematics text, but it may serve as a handy source for refreshing one's memory.

In addition to the sections containing applications, there are many examples included in the purely game theoretic sections of the book. I hope that between these examples and considerable verbal explanation, the material presented in the remaining chapters is readable with only a sound grasp of basic calculus. There does remain one source of potential difficulties: Some of the proofs will not be easy; however, for the reader who sometimes encounters a proof too difficult to work through, the presentation and discussion of the model and results should still be accessible and useful.

2

Noncooperative games in strategic form

This chapter is the first of three chapters covering noncooperative games. The games studied in this chapter are often characterized as *one-shot* or *single-period* games. The real significance of this characterization is that the temporal structure of the game—that is, the extensive form—is considered to be uninteresting. Consequently, the usual practice, followed in the present chapter, is to ignore the extensive form and define games in strategic form from the outset. As an example of why the extensive form might lack interest, imagine an *n*-person game in which each player has only one move and all players must move simultaneously. The extensive form of this game would impose on it a temporal structure that was artificial, because the players would have to be treated as if they moved sequentially. The games covered in Chapters 3 and 4 are explicitly intertemporal, with a set of players in a *supergame* in which a sequence of ordinary games, each like a game from the present chapter, is played. In these supergames, the nature of individual moves is interesting; therefore, they are studied in a *semiextensive form* that lies between the strategic form and a true extensive form; however, the semiextensive form retains all the essential parts of the move structure.

In most complete-information, noncooperative games examined in Chapters 2 to 4, there is only one concept of equilibrium studied: the noncooperative equilibrium due to Nash (1951), which is referred to variously as *equilibrium point*, *noncooperative equilibrium*, *Nash–Cournot equilibrium*, and where the context assures there will be no confusion with Nash's (1950, 1953) cooperative solution, the *Nash equilibrium*. He is the great pioneer in noncooperative game theory, although the Cournot (1838) equilibrium is a precursor of the Nash (noncooperative) equilibrium. The fundamental idea behind the equilibrium point is that each player in a complete information game has chosen a strategy that maximizes his own payoff given the strategies of the other players. Of course, it is commonplace in economic theory to postulate that each decision maker chooses, in equilibrium, behavior that maximizes her objective function; however, it is also usual in much of economic theory that the behavior of a single decision maker has no effect on the circumstances facing any other decision maker. In game theory, this latter simplification is abandoned; the behavior of any one player may well affect the payoff functions of all others. It will be seen in Chapters 3 and 4 that some noncooperative equilibria are clearly unsatisfactory. This observation leads to a subclass of noncooperative equilibria, called *subgame perfect equilibrium points*, which are introduced in Chapter 3 and are important to models in semiextensive form.

The games studied in this chapter reveal many of the basic insights to be gained from the study of noncooperative games. They have many valuable direct applications and, additionally, provide a basis for and introduction to the models in Chapters 3 and 4. Indeed, as the chapters on cooperative games reveal, noncooperative game theory can aid in the analysis of cooperative games.

Section 1 of this chapter contains basic definitions, assumptions, and rules used throughout the chapter, as well as in Chapters 3 and 4. Section 2 is devoted to *finite two-person, zero-sum games*. von Neumann (1928) proved that all such games have an *equilibrium point*, thus providing game theory with its first major theorem. A remarkably short and elementary proof of von Neumann's theorem, due to Owen (1967), is presented. In Section 3, *strictly competitive two-person games* are examined. These are games in which the interests of the two players are strictly opposed in the sense that anything that benefits one player is necessarily hurtful to the other. The *saddle point equilibrium* for two-person, zero-sum games has some special properties that carry over to strictly competitive games but that do not carry over to two- or more-person noncooperative games in general. In Section 4, a general n-person noncooperative game is formulated and it is shown that such games have equilibrium points. In general, equilibrium is not unique; however, conditions ensuring uniqueness are given in Section 5. Section 6 deals with noncooperative games under incomplete information; that is, games in which a player does not know the payoff functions of the other players. Harsanyi's (1967, 1968a, 1968b) work in this very difficult area is followed. Then, in Section 7, several examples applying noncooperative games are examined. The final section contains concluding comments.

1 Basic concepts for noncooperative games

This section contains definitions of the basic concepts needed for the chapter. In addition to defining notation and various terms, assumptions usually made in noncooperative game theory are also stated. The material of this section provides a basic framework from which all other sections draw heavily. Certain concepts and notation that recur throughout this chapter are:

$N = \{1, \ldots, n\}$ is the **set of players**.

S_i is the **strategy space of player** i and, for this chapter, is a subset of the Euclidean space R^m.

$S = S_1 \times \cdots \times S_n$ *is the Cartesian product of the individual strategy spaces and is the* **strategy space of the game**.

$s_i \in S_i$ *denotes a* **strategy of player** i, *and is therefore an element of* S_i.

$s = (s_1, \ldots, s_n) \in S$ *is called a* **combination**, *or more formally, a* **strategy combination**, *and it consists of n strategies, one for each player.*

$P_i(s) \in R$ *is the* **payoff function of player** i *and is scalar valued.*

$P(s) = (P_1(s), \ldots, P_n(s)) \in R^n$ *is the* **payoff vector.**

It is also convenient to have a notation for strategy combinations that allows for the strategy of one player to be varied while the strategies of the remaining players are fixed. This is done in the following way: let $s \in S$ and $t_i \in S_i$. Then $s\backslash t_i$ denotes $(s_1, \ldots, s_{i-1}, t_i, s_{i+1}, \ldots, s_n)$. Thus $s\backslash t_i$ is the combination s with t_i substituted in place of s_i.

An **equilibrium point** is a combination, s^*, which is feasible (i.e., is contained in S) and for which each player maximizes his own payoff with respect to his own strategy choice, given the strategy choices of the other players. More formally:

DEFINITION 2.1   *An* **equilibrium point** *is a combination* $s^* \in S$ *that satisfies* $P_i(s^*) \geq P_i(s^*\backslash s_i)$ *for all* $s_i \in S_i$ *and for all* $i \in N$.

The equilibrium point was introduced by Nash (1951); however, the saddle point equilibrium of von Neumann (1928) is a special instance of it, as is the Cournot (1838) equilibrium in oligopoly theory.

There is a set of common assumptions that many models considered in the next three sections obey; these are that the strategy sets are both compact and convex, that the payoff functions are defined, continuous and bounded on S, and that each payoff function, P_i, is concave with respect to s_i. Concave functions of one variable are illustrated in Figure 2.1.

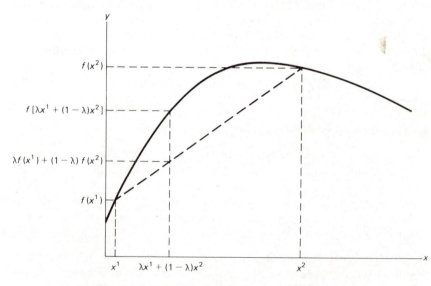

FIGURE 2.1   Illustration of a concave function.

A function $y = f(x)$ *is* **concave** *if, for any* x^1 *and* x^2 *in the domain of the function, and any scalar* $\lambda \in [0, 1]$

$$f[\lambda x^1 + (1 - \lambda)x^2] \geq \lambda f(x^1) + (1 - \lambda)f(x^2) \tag{2.1}$$

A **compact set** *in* R^n *is a set that is both* **closed** *(i.e., contains its own boundary) and* **bounded** *(i.e., can be contained within a ball of finite radius). A* **convex set** *has the property that the straight line segment connecting any two points in the set is also in the set.*

The common assumptions, again, are:

ASSUMPTION 2.1 $S_i \subset R^m$ *is compact and convex for each* $i \in N$.

ASSUMPTION 2.2 $P_i(s) \in R$ *is defined, continuous, and bounded for all* $s \in S$ *and all* $i \in N$.

ASSUMPTION 2.3 $P_i(s \backslash t_i)$ *is concave with respect to* $t_i \in S_i$ *for all* $s \in S$ *and all* $i \in N$.

Assumptions 2.1 to 2.3 pertain to the structure of the game. There are additional conditions relating to the rules of the game and to the information conditions.

RULE 2.1   *The players are not able to make binding agreements.* ~non-Cooperative~

RULE 2.2   *The strategy choice made by each player is made prior to the beginning of the play of the game, and without prior knowledge of the strategy choices made by other players.* ~complete info~

DEFINITION 2.2   *A* **game of complete information** *is a game in which each player i knows all the strategy sets* $S_j, j \in N$, *each knows all payoff functions* $P_j(s), j \in N$, *all players know that this information is in the possession of each of them, and all players know that everyone in the game knows all of these things.*

Rule 2.1 defines a noncooperative game. Rule 2.2 states that players may be thought of as choosing their strategies simultaneously; however, this places no restriction on the structure of the game. All it does is underscore the definition of *strategy*. For example, it does not mean that a particular move of a player takes no account of the known past moves of other players. Quite the contrary, even at the start of a game, a player can anticipate the whole array of situations in which he might find himself at, say, his fifth move, and his choice of a fifth move can be different according to which of these situations actually takes place. All of this is easily spelled out prior to the start of play. The games examined in Sections 2 to 4 are all games of complete information that satisfy Assumptions 2.1 to 2.3 and Rules 2.1 and 2.2. All such games have equilibrium points.

In a game satisfying Assumptions 2.1 to 2.3, the *set of attainable payoffs*, $H = \{P(s) \mid s \in S\}$ is necessarily compact. Related to this set is its upper frontier, the *Pareto optimal set*, also called the *payoff possibility frontier*. Formally, it is defined by $H^* = \{y \in H \mid z \in H$ implies $y_i \geq z_i$ for at least one

$i \in N$}. That is, the payoff vector y is Pareto optimal if there is no other attainable payoff vector that gives a higher payoff to each player.

2 Finite two-person, zero-sum games

The class of games described by Assumptions 2.1 to 2.3 is easily restricted to being two person by letting $N = \{1, 2\}$ and is further restricted to being zero sum by defining $P_2(s)$ as the negative of $P_1(s)$. Finite two-person, zero-sum games are a special category of two-person, zero-sum games, and it is easiest to describe them without referring to the material of the preceding section. After the description is complete, it is a simple matter to relate them to the foregoing games. This is done below, after which a simple proof is given that all such games have a noncooperative equilibrium.

2.1 A finite matrix game

Suppose that player 1 has a finite set of m strategies, called pure strategies, from which to choose, and that player 2 has n pure strategies. Then the payoff functions of the game can be completely described by a matrix A having m rows and n columns. The entry a_{ij} is the payoff to player 1 when he chooses strategy i and player 2 chooses her strategy j. The payoff to player 2 under these circumstances is $-a_{ij}$. In general, this game need not have an equilibrium point; however, the game does not satisfy Assumption 2.1, because the strategy sets are not convex. The absence of convexity can be seen by noting that convex combinations of, say, strategy 1 and strategy 2 are not available. For example, a strategy defined as being one-third of strategy 1 and two-thirds of strategy 2 is not in the (finite) strategy space. This deficiency is remedied below by the device of *mixed strategies*. Tables 2.1 and 2.2 each contain two-person, zero-sum games. The game in Table 2.1 has an equilibrium point and the game in Table 2.2 does not—as long as the strategy sets are taken to be the pure strategy sets $\{1, \ldots, m\}$ and $\{1, \ldots, n\}$. The equilibrium point in the first game is $(3, 3)$ where the

TABLE 2.1 A two-person, zero-sum game with a pure strategy equilibrium point

		Strategies of player 2			
		1	2	3	4
Strategies of player 1	1	5	10	5	4
	2	6	3	0	15
	3	15	20	8	10
	4	6	15	7	2

TABLE 2.2 A two person, zero-sum game
with no pure strategy equilibrium point

		\multicolumn{4}{c}{Strategies of player 2}			
		1	2	3	4
Strategies of player 1	1	5	10	5	4
	2	6	3	10	15
	3	15	20	8	10
	4	6	15	7	2

payoff to player 1 is 8. Note that for player 1 to use a different strategy, given the strategy of player 2, means moving to a different row but staying in the same column. Any such move will lower the payoff to player 1. Similarly, changing the strategy of player 2, given the strategy of player 1, means moving to a different column while staying in the same row, and such a change cannot be done to the benefit of player 2. By contrast, choose any entry in the payoff matrix shown in Table 2.2 and note that there is at least one player who could have a higher payoff at another strategy while keeping fixed the strategy of the other player.

2.2 Mixed strategies

There is a natural extension of the strategy sets, and of the payoff functions, that makes them conform to Assumption 2.1. Suppose that player 1 can use a random mechanism to select from among her original strategies. *The original strategies are called* **pure strategies** *and a strategy consisting of a probability distribution over the pure strategies is called a* **mixed strategy.** The set of mixed strategies for player 1 is $S_1 = \{s_1 \in R^m_+ \mid \sum_{k=1}^m s_{1k} = 1\}$ and for player 2 is $S_2 = \{s_2 \in R^n_+ \mid \sum_{k=1}^n s_{2k} = 1\}$. S_1 is the *unit simplex* in R^m and S_2 is the unit simplex in R^n. The payoff function of player 1 is

$$P_1(s) = s_1^T A s_2 = \sum_{i=1}^m \sum_{j=1}^n s_{1i} a_{ij} s_{2j} \tag{2.2}$$

and the payoff function of player 2 is $P_2(s) = -P_1(s)$. The justification for defining a player's payoff as an expected value lies in von Neumann–Morgenstern utility theory.[1] Note that the strategy space of a player, S_i, which contains all of player i's mixed strategies, also contains all of her pure strategies. These appear in the form of the (degenerate) probability distributions, such as $s_1 = (1, 0, \dots, 0)$, which have zeros in all but one component, and the value of that component is 1. Each of these points of the simplex is called a *vertex*. There are m of them for player 1, corresponding to each of her pure strategies, and n of them for player 2. The strategy sets S_i are compact and convex and the game based on them obeys Assumptions 2.1 to 2.3.

DEFINITION 2.3   *A* **finite two-person, zero-sum game** *is a two-person, zero-sum game of complete information that satisfies Assumptions 2.1 to 2.3 and Rules 2.1 and 2.2, in which the strategy sets,* S_i, *are unit simplexes, and in which* $P_1(s) = \sum_{i=1}^{m} \sum_{j=1}^{n} s_{1i} a_{ij} s_{2j}$ *where* a_{ij} *is the payoff to player 1 when his strategy is the ith vertex of his strategy simplex and the strategy of player 2 is the jth vertex of her strategy simplex.*

2.3   *Existence of equilibrium points*

With the understanding that Rules 2.1 and 2.2 hold, complete information is assumed, and mixed strategies are allowed, a matrix A with m rows and n columns fully describes a finite two-person, zero-sum game. The proof that such a game has an equilibrium point in mixed strategies is carried out in several steps. First, the concept of security level of the player is defined. Next, a lemma is proved showing that a game has an equilibrium point if and only if the two players have identical security levels. Third, it is proved in a lemma that if any game obtained by deleting some rows or columns from a matrix A has an equilibrium point, then the game based on A has an equilibrium point. Finally, in Theorem 2.1, it is proved by induction that any finite two-person, zero-sum game has an equilibrium point.

Let $V_1(s_1) = \min_{s_2 \in S_2} s_1^T A s_2$ and $V_2(s_2) = \max_{s_1 \in S_1} s_1^T A s_2$. Then $V_1(s_1)$ is the lowest payoff that player 1 could possibly obtain if he used strategy s_1. Similarly, $V_2(s_2)$ is the largest loss that player 2 could possibly sustain if she used s_2.

DEFINITION 2.4   *A* **security level** *for a player in a two-person, zero-sum game is the best payoff which that player can guarantee to himself, irrespective of the actions of other players. The security level of player 1 is* $v_1 = \max_{s_1 \in S_1} V_1(s_1)$, *and that of player 2 is* $v_2 = \min_{s_2 \in S_2} V_2(s_2)$.

The security levels v_1 and v_2 are clearly both attainable, which imples that $v_1 \leqslant v_2$. That is, if player 1 can surely obtain at least v_1 and player 2 can keep player 1 from obtaining more than v_2, then v_1 cannot be larger than v_2. If $v_1 = v_2 = v$, then v is called the *value* of the game.

LEMMA 2.1   (t_1, t_2) *is an equilibrium point for a two-person, zero-sum game if and only if (a)* $v_1 = V_1(t_1)$, *(b)* $v_2 = V_2(t_2)$, *and (c)* $v_1 = v_2$.

Proof   It is first shown that, if (a), (b), and (c) hold, then (t_1, t_2) is an equilibrium point; then the converse is proved.

Suppose (a), (b), and (c) are true. Then $t_1^T A t_2 \geqslant s_1^T A t_2$ for all $s_1 \in S_1$ and $t_1^T A t_2 \leqslant t_1^T A s_2$ for all $s_2 \in S_2$, which is the definition of an equilibrium point in this context.

Suppose that (t_1, t_2) is an equilibrium point. If $v_1 > V_1(t_1)$, then t_1 is not optimal for player 1. There is some $s_1 \in S_1$ such that $s_1^T A t_2 = v_1$. On the other hand, $v_1 < V_1(t_1)$ is impossible. Thus, if (t_1, t_2) is an equilibrium point, then $v_1 = V_1(t_1)$. A parallel argument establishes $v_2 = V_2(t_2)$.

It remains to show that $v_1 < v_2$ is incompatible with the existence of equilibrium. Suppose that $v_1 < v_2$. Then, for any combination (t_1, t_2), at least one of the following must hold: (a) $v_1 < t_1^T A t_2$ or (b) $t_1^T A t_2 < v_2$. If (a) holds and (u_1, u_2) satisfies $u_1^T A u_2 = \max_{s_1 \in S_1} \min_{s_2 \in S_2} s_1^T A s_2$, then player 2, by choosing u_2, can hold her loss to $t_1^T A u_2 \le v_1 < t_1^T A t_2$. For (b), a parallel argument can be made for player 1. Therefore, if (t_1, t_2) is an equilibrium point, $v_1 = v_2 = V_1(t_1) = V_2(t_2)$.   QED

DEFINITION 2.5   *Let A be an $m \times n$ matrix. B is a **submatrix** of A if it can be derived from A by the deletion of one or more rows, one or more columns, or both.*

LEMMA 2.2   *Let A be an $m \times n$ matrix representing a two-person, zero-sum game. If all games represented by submatrices of A have equilibrium points, then A has an equilibrium point.*

Proof   Let v_1 and v_2 be the security levels for the game A, and let $t = (t_1, t_2)$ be the strategies that achieve the security levels. That is, $v_i = V_i(t_i)$ for $i = 1, 2$. By Lemma 2.1, if $v_1 = v_2$, then t is an equilibrium point. Therefore, suppose that $v_1 < v_2$. Then, either (a) $v_1 < t_1^T A t_2$ or (b) $t_1^T A t_2 < v_2$. If (b) holds, then for some k and some $\varepsilon > 0$, $A_{k.} t_2 = v_2 - \varepsilon$, where $A_{k.}$ denotes the kth row of A. Let the game B be obtained from A by deleting the kth row of A. By hypothesis, B has a value, denoted v_B, and an equilibrium pair of mixed strategies. Note that the strategy space of player 2 is the same in the game B as in A; however, this is not the case for player 1. The game B strategy space of player 1 can be represented as a subset of his space for game A; it is $S_1' = \{s_1 \in S_1 \mid s_{ik} = 0\}$. It is convenient to view the strategy space of player 1 in this way. Let $u = (u_1, u_2) \in S_1' \times S_2$ be an equilibrium point of game B. Then, letting $A_{.j}$ denote the jth column of A, $\min_j u_1^T A_{.j} = \max_{i \ne k} A_{i.} u_2 = v_B$. Letting a denote the absolute value of the largest element of A, clearly $v_B \le a$.

Now, for the original game, define the strategies w_1 and w_2 by $w_i = (1 - r) t_i + r u_i$ where r is chosen so that $0 < r < \varepsilon / (a - v_B + \varepsilon)$, and $\varepsilon > 0$. Since $\varepsilon / (a - v_B + \varepsilon) < 1$, w_1 and w_2 are contained in S_m and S_n, respectively. Note that $V_1(w_1) = \min_j w_1^T A_{.j} \ge (1 - r) v_1 + r v_B$ and $V_2(w_2) = \max_i A_{i.} w_2 \le (1 - r) v_2 + r v_B$. Thus, $V_2(w_2) - V_1(w_1) \le (1 - r)(v_2 - v_1) < v_2 - v_1$, which implies that $V_2(w_2) < v_2$ or $V_1(w_1) > v_1$. Either is a contradiction, because the latter implies that player 1 has a security level higher than v_1 and the former implies that player 2 has a security level below v_2. A parallel argument follows starting from condition (a); therefore $v_1 = v_2$ and the game has an equilibrium point.   QED

THEOREM 2.1   *Any finite two-person, zero-sum game A has an equilibrium point.*

Proof   Suppose that A is $m \times n$. The argument proceeds constructively by induction from small to large games. Suppose that B is any game with 1 row and n columns. Such a game has an equilibrium point; for, a 1×1 game trivially has an equilibrium point, thus by Lemma 2.2, a 1×2 game has an equilibrium point, and a $1 \times k$ game has an equilibrium point if a $1 x (k - 1)$ game has one. Using similar reasoning, any $m \times 1$ game has an equilibrium point. By induction, a 2×2 game has an equilibrium point (because all its subgames have one), and by induction games that are $2 \times n$ and $m \times 2$ have equilibrium points. Continuing in the same manner, any $m \times n$ game has an equilibrium point.   QED

Theorem 2.1 was originally proved by von Neumann (1928). His proof is quite long and difficult; however, the brief and simple proofs of Lemma 2.2 and Theorem 2.1 are due to Owen (1967).

2.4   Constant-sum versus zero-sum games

A finite two-person game is *constant sum* if the payoff matrix for player 1 is A and, corresponding to a_{ij}, the payoff to player 2 is $-a_{ij} + c$ for some constant c and all i and j. Just as a two-person, zero-sum game is characterized by the payoff matrix A, a two-person, constant-sum game is characterized by (A, c) where A is, as before, the pure strategy payoff matrix for player 1 and c is the constant to which payoffs must sum. It is left to the reader to prove the following corollary to Theorem 2.1.

COROLLARY   *Let* (A, c) *be a two-person, constant-sum game. Then* $t = (t_1, t_2)$ *is an equilibrium point of* (A, c) *if and only if it is an equilibrium point of the two-person, zero-sum game* A.

At the beginning of this section, it was said that two-person, zero-sum games would be discussed without direct reference to Assumptions 2.1 to 2.3. It is helpful now to check that these games actually satisfy the assumptions. Assumption 2.1 asserts that S_i is compact and convex. For two-person, zero-sum games, $S_1 = \{s_1 \in R^m \mid s_{1i} \in [0, 1] \text{ and } \sum_{i=1}^{m} s_{1i} = 1\}$. The reader can easily verify that S_1 is closed and bounded (hence compact), as well as convex. S_2 satisfies parallel conditions. $P_i(s)$ is defined for all $s \in S_1 \times S_2$, continuous, and bounded. Finally, $P_i(s \backslash t_i)$ is linear in t_i; therefore, it is concave in t_i, and Assumption 2.3 is met.

3   Strictly competitive two-person games

Two-person, zero-sum situations are a rarity in practice, particularly recalling that payoffs are utilities to the players and not money amounts. Consider a parlor game played for money in which the two players care only about how much money they win or lose and, apart from that, do not care about winning or losing as such. Suppose that the utility of each player is normalized so that $U_i(0) = 0$, $i = 1, 2$, where $U_i(x_i)$ is the utility function of player i and x_i is the amount of money he wins. By hypothesis $x_2 = -x_1$; however, it does not follow that $U_1(x_1) + U_2(-x_1) = 0$. Assuming that $U_i(x_i)$ is strictly increasing in x_i, the salient feature of the game is that any change that aids one player will, of necessity, hurt the other. In this sense, the interests of the players are perfectly opposed. Such games are more easily imagined than zero-sum games. For example, in a two-candidate electoral race, each candidate wants to win, and by the largest margin possible; however, there is no reason to suppose the candidates' utilities are related by a zero (or, equivalently, constant) sum condition. Games of this variety, which include zero-sum games as a subclass, are called *strictly competitive games*.

3.1 Properties of equilibrium points for strictly competitive games

Two-person strictly competitive games are defined below in terms of Assumptions 2.1 to 2.3 and Rules 2.1 and 2.2. Thus, they are a subset of noncooperative games in which $n = 2$ and $P_1(s') \geq P_1(s'')$ if and only if $P_2(s') \leq P_2(s'')$. Although some finite games are included among strictly competitive games, attention is not restricted to such games.[2] After strictly competitive two-person games are formally defined, three of their interesting features are proved: (a) Any two equilibrium points, s' and s'', yield precisely the same payoffs. That is, $P_i(s') = P_i(s'')$, $i = 1, 2$. (b) If s' and s'' are equilibrium points, then (s_1', s_2'') and (s_1'', s_2') are also equilibrium points. Another way to state this condition is that each player i has a set of equilibrium strategies S_i^0 and any combination s for which $s_1 \in S_1^0$ and $s_2 \in S_2^0$ is an equilibrium point. Thus the *set of equilibrium points* is $S^0 = S_1^0 \times S_2^0$. This is sometimes called the *interchangeability property*. (c) The set of equilibrium points is convex.

DEFINITION 2.6 *A **strictly competitive game** is a two-person game of complete information that satisfies Assumptions 2.1 to 2.3 and Rules 2.1, 2.2, and in which, for all $s, s' \in S$, $P_1(s) \geq P_1(s')$ if and only if $P_2(s) \leq P_2(s')$.*

When the rules and information conditions are completely specified, all that remains to characterize a game is N, the set of players, S, the strategy space, and P, the payoff functions; hence, with rules and information understood, $\Gamma = (N, S, P)$ may, without ambiguity, be called a game. This notation is used in this section, and frequently in the remainder of the chapter. Of course, in this section $N = \{1, 2\}$. Theorem 2.2 establishes the properties (a) and (b) above: all equilibrium points yield the same payoffs and satisfy the interchangeability property.

THEOREM 2.2 *Let $\Gamma = (N, S, P)$ be a strictly competitive game and let $S^0 \subset S$ be the set of equilibrium points of Γ. If $s', s'' \in S^0$ then $P_i(s') = P_i(s'')$, $i = 1, 2$, $(s_1', s_2'') \in S^0$, and $(s_1'', s_2') \in S^0$.*

Proof Suppose that $s', s'' \in S^0$, and $P_1(s') \leq P_1(s'')$. Then $P_2(s'') \leq P_2(s')$ because the game is strictly competitive and $P_2(s'') \leq P_2(s_1'', s_2)$ because $P_2(s'') = \max_{s_2 \in S_2} P_2(s_1'', s_2)$. The latter inequality, along with the definition of a strictly competitive game, implies that $P_1(s_1'', s_2') \geq P_1(s'')$ and $P_1(s') = \max_{s_1 \in S_1} P_1(s_1, s_2')$ implies that $P_1(s') \geq P_1(s_1'', s_2')$; therefore, $P_1(s') \geq P_1(s'')$ and $P_1(s') \leq P_1(s'')$, which establishes that $P_i(s') = P_i(s'')$, $i = 1, 2$. Additionally, the latter, together with $P_1(s') \geq P_1(s_1'', s_2') \geq P_1(s'')$, implies that

$(s_1'', s_2') \in S^0$. A parallel argument can be made to show that $(s_1', s_2'') \in S^0$. QED

Convexity of S^0, the set of equilibrium points, is established in Theorem 2.3. Lemma 2.3, which appears prior to the theorem, is used in its proof.

LEMMA 2.3 *Let $\Gamma = (N, S, P)$ be a strictly competitive game, $s' \in S^0$ and $u \notin S^0$. Then, either $max_{s_1 \in S_1} P_1(s_1, u_2) > P_1(s')$ or $max_{s_2 \in S_2} P_2(u_1, s_2) > P_2(s')$.*

Proof The lemma holds trivially for the case where $P_1(s') \neq P_1(u)$, because either $P_1(s') < P_1(u)$ or $P_2(s') < P_2(u)$. Consider the remaining case where $P_i(s') = P_i(u)$, $i = 1, 2$. If $max_{s_1 \in S_1} P_1(s_1, u_2) = P_1(s')$ and $max_{s_2 \in S_2} P_2(u_1, s_2) = P_2(s')$, then $u \in S^0$, which is a contradiction; hence, the lemma follows. QED

THEOREM 2.3 *Let $\Gamma = (N, S, P)$ be a strictly competitive game whose set of equilibrium points is S^0. Then S^0 is convex.*

Proof It suffices to show that, for any $s', s'' \in S^0$, $s' \neq s''$, and $\lambda \in [0, 1]$, that $s^\lambda = \lambda s' + (1 - \lambda)s''$ is an equilibrium point. Suppose that $s^\lambda \notin S^0$. Then, by Lemma 2.3, either $max_{s_1 \in S_1} P_1(s_1, s_2^\lambda) = P_1(t_1, s_2^\lambda) > P_1(s') = P_1(s'')$ or a parallel condition holds for player 2. Without loss of generality, suppose the condition holds for player 1. Then $P_2(t_1, s_2^\lambda) < P_2(s') = P_2(s'')$. By concavity of P_2 in s_2, $P_2(t_1, s_2^\lambda) \geq \lambda P_2(t_1, s_2') + (1 - \lambda) P_2(t_1, s_2'')$; therefore, $P_2(t_1, s_2') \leq P_2(t_1, s_2^\lambda)$ or $P_2(t_1, s_2'') \leq P_2(t_1, s_2^\lambda)$. If the latter holds, then $P_1(t_1, s_2'') \geq P_1(t_1, s_2^\lambda) > P_1(s'')$, which implies that s'' is not an equilibrium point and is a contradiction. If the former holds, then $P_2(t_1, s_2') \leq P_2(t_1, s_2^\lambda) < P_2(s')$, and a similar argument leads to a contradiction; thus S^0 is convex. QED

3.2 Equilibrium characteristics of strictly competitive games that do not generalize

Taking Theorems 2.2 and 2.3 together, the equilibrium points of strictly competitive games (a) all have the same payoffs, (b) form a convex subset of the strategy space, and (c) have the interchangeability property (i.e., if s' and s'' are equilibrium points, then (s_1', s_2'') and (s_1'', s_2') are also). Interchangeability implies that S^0 is the Cartesian product of sets $S_1^0 \subset S_1$ and $S_2^0 \subset S_2$. Thus, each player i has a set of equilibrium strategies S_i^0 and, for any $t_1 \in S_1^0$ and $t_2 \in S_2^0$, the combination $t = (t_1, t_2)$ is an equilibrium point that affords exactly the same payoffs as any other equilibrium point. This remarkable fact means that no coordination is required for two players to choose equilibrium strategies. Contrast this with general n-person noncooperative games in which there may be multiple equilibrium points, but interchangeability does not generally hold. Then, for a general n-person noncooperative game, if $s', s'' \in S^0$ and the players choose (s_1', s_2''), the result need not be an equilibrium point. This suggests that where neither interchangeability nor uniqueness of equilibrium holds, the players must coordinate their strategy choices if an equilibrium point is to be achieved with certainty.

For two-person, zero-sum games, Theorem 2.2 appears in Section 17 of von Neumann and Morgenstern (1944), and, although they do not mention Theorem 2.3, it follows easily from the linear structure of the game. For strictly competitive two person games, Harsanyi (1977:170) asserts Theorem 2.2 as if it were well known. A proof of Theorems 2.2 and 2.3 is in Friedman (1984). That Theorems 2.2 and 2.3 do not extend to general two-person noncooperative games or to games of three or more persons that retain an appropriately modified condition of strict competitiveness can be illustrated by a pair of examples. Table 2.3 contains a two-person noncooperative game that has two equilibrium points: (1, 1) and (3, 3). At the former, player 1 receives 10 and player 2 receives 8, and, at the latter, the payoffs are 12 and 25, respectively. These two equilibria are the only pure strategy equilibrium points of the game, their payoffs are not the same, they do not obey the interchangeability condition, and the set of equilibria is not convex. All of these assertions are easily verified. That the two equilibria yield different payoffs is readily seen from Table 2.3. The failure of interchangeability is verified by noting that (1, 3) is not an equilibrium point. To see that S^0, the set of equilibria, is not convex, recall that S_1 is the unit simplex in R^3; that is, $S_1 = \{s_1 \in R^3 \mid s_1 \geq 0, \sum_{i=1}^{3} s_{1i} = 1\}$. S_2 is similarly defined. Let $s' = [(1, 0, 0), (1, 0, 0)]$ and $s'' = [(0, 0, 1), (0, 0, 1)]$. These are, of course, the two pure strategy equilibrium points. Now consider $s^0 = s'/2 + s''/2$. The payoff to player 1 for s^0 is $(10 + 4 + 3 + 12)/4 = 7.25$. The combination $s^0 = [(\frac{1}{2}, 0, \frac{1}{2}), (\frac{1}{2}, 0, \frac{1}{2})]$, and player 1 would fare better with $(0, 0, 1)$: the payoff to player 1 for $[(0, 0, 1), (\frac{1}{2}, 0, \frac{1}{2})]$ is 8.

The natural extension of strict competitiveness to three or more players is to stipulate that, for $s', s'' \in S$, if $P_i(s') > P_i(s)$ for a player i, then there is at least one other player j for whom $P_j(s') < P_j(s'')$. This preserves the condition that, in comparing s' to s'', if some player i is better off at s', then some other player is better off at s''. Obviously n-person, zero-sum games obey this condition. Table 2.4 illustrates a game in which there are just two pure strategy equilibrium points; (1, 1, 1) and (3, 3, 1). This game is zero

TABLE 2.3 A two-person noncooperative game with two equilibrium points

		Strategies of player 2		
		1	2	3
Strategies of player 1	1	10, 8	4, 4	3, 2
	2	6, 10	14, 15	9, 20
	3	4, 10	8, 20	12, 25

TABLE 2.4   A three-person, zero-sum game with two equilibrium points

		Payoffs when player 3 chooses his strategy 1 strategies of player 2		
		1	2	3
Strategies of player 1	1	8, 6, −14	2, 2, −4	1, 0, −1
	2	4, 8, −12	12, 13, −25	7, 18, −25
	3	2, 8, −10	6, 18, −24	10, 23, −33

		Payoffs when player 3 chooses his strategy 2 strategies of player 2		
		1	2	3
Strategies of player 1	1	10, 8, −18	4, 4, −8	3, 2, −5
	2	6, 10, −16	14, 15, −29	9, 20, −29
	3	4, 10, −14	8, 20, −28	12, 25, −37

sum; however, just like the game in Table 2.3, it satisfies none of the conditions proved in Theorems 2.2 and 2.3.

4   Existence of equilibrium points for n-person noncooperative games

The principal purpose of this section is to prove that all n-person noncooperative games of complete information that satisfy Assumptions 2.1 to 2.3, and Rules 2.1 and 2.2 have equilibrium points. Throughout this section, any game $\Gamma = (N, S, P)$ is understood to satisfy all the preceding conditions and is referred to, simply, as a noncooperative game.[3] The first existence proof for equilibrium points in n-person noncooperative games is due to Nash (1951). The concept of equilibrium point is a natural, although not obvious, generalization of von Neumann's (1928) saddle point equilibrium for zero-sum games. In his generalization, Nash had the insight to abandon the minimax approach of von Neumann. In von Neumann's context, a player who strives to increase her own payoff is necessarily striving to decrease the payoff of the other player. Outside two-person, strictly competitive games, this is not true in general; hence, for player i to act as if other players in an n-person noncooperative game wish to minimize her payoff is, usually, incorrect and excessively pessimistic. As the Cournot oligopoly example in Section 7 makes clear, Nash was generalizing the Cournot (1838) oligopoly equilibrium as well as generalizing von Neumann's (1928) saddle point equilibrium. Nash dealt with finite games; important generalizations of the Nash model appear in Nikaido and Isoda (1955) and Berge (1957).

The reader who is totally uninterested in existence proofs is urged, nonetheless, to read enough of this section to become acquainted with *best reply mappings* and their relationship to equilibrium points. The best reply concept lends a great intuitive appeal to the method of proof, and, more importantly, is very useful and widely used. It is introduced and discussed next, after which existence of equilibrium points is proved. The existence argument is that any noncooperative game has at least one equilibrium point; however, nothing is said concerning either the number of equilibrium points or about how such equilibria might be related. Without making further restrictions on the model, nothing more can be said.

4.1   Best reply mappings and their relationship to equilibrium points

The best reply mapping might better be called the optimal strategy mapping; however, the former usage is firmly entrenched and is followed here. Suppose player i performs the following thought experiment. He contemplates a particular strategy assignment to the other players—$(s'_1, s'_2, \ldots, s'_{i-1}, s'_{i+1}, \ldots, s'_n)$—and wonders what strategy choice on his own part would maximize P_i given the $s'_j (j \neq i)$. It is this thought experiment that defines the best reply mapping for player i. In Definition 2.7, the best reply mapping is defined as a mapping from S (rather than from $S_1 \times \cdots \times S_{i-1} \times S_{i+1} \times \cdots \times S_n$) to subsets of S_i. This is merely a technical convenience. The best replies to s are the same as the best replies to $s \setminus t_i$ for player i.

DEFINITION 2.7   *The* **best reply mapping for player** i *is a set-valued relationship associating each strategy combination $s \in S$ with a subset of S_i according to the following rule:* $r_i(s) = \{t_i \in S_i \mid P_i(s \setminus t_i) = max_{s'_i \in S_i} P_i(s \setminus s'_i)\}$.

The strategy t_i is a best reply for player i to the strategy combination s if t_i maximizes the payoff of player i, given the strategy choices of the others. In general, t_i need not be unique. The strategy combination $t \in S$ is a (joint) best reply to $s \in S$ if each component, t_i, of t is a best reply for player i.

DEFINITION 2.8   *The* **best reply mapping** *is a set valued relationship associating each strategy combination $s \in S$ with a subset of S according to the rule $t \in r(s)$ if and only if $t_i \in r_i(s)$, $i \in N$. Thus $r(s)$ is the Cartesian product $r_1(s) \times r_2(s) \times \cdots \times r_n(s)$.*

The best reply mapping provides a natural way to think about equilibrium points, because all equilibrium points satisfy the condition that s^* is an equilibrium point if and only if $s^* \in r(s^*)$. That is, an equilibrium point is a best reply to itself, and any strategy combination that is a best reply to itself is an equilibrium point. Thus

LEMMA 2.4   *Let* $\Gamma = (N, S, P)$ *be a noncooperative game.* $s \in S$ *is an equilibrium point of* Γ *if and only if* $s \in r(s)$.

Proof   First it is shown that if s^* is an equilibrium point, then $s^* \in r(s^*)$. Recall the definition of equilibrium point. s^* is an equilibrium point if $s^* \in S$ and $P_i(s^*) = \max_{s_i \in S_i} P_i(s^* \backslash s_i)$, $i \in N$. The latter condition is precisely the condition for $s_i^* \in r_i(s^*)$.

Now suppose that $s^* \in r(s^*)$. To see that s^* must be an equilibrium point, refer to the definition of the best reply mapping: $s_i^* \in r_i(s^*)$ if $P_i(s^*) = \max_{s_i \in S_i} P_i(s^* \backslash s_i)$, $i \in N$. But the latter condition states that no player could achieve a greater payoff by using a different strategy, given the strategies of the other players. This, of course, is what defines an equilibrium point.   QED

4.2   Fixed points of functions and correspondences

When $s \in r(s)$, s *is called a* **fixed point** *of* r, and Lemma 2.4 can be restated by saying that the set of fixed points of r coincides with the set of equilibrium points. This allows the question of existence of equilibrium to be stated in terms of the existence of fixed points of the best reply mapping r. Before this is directly addressed, some facts about set valued mappings are stated, and a theorem relating to the existence of fixed points is introduced. *For mappings from* R^n *to* R^m *it is customary in the economics literature to call a set valued mapping, such as the best reply mapping, a* **correspondence** *and to save the word* **function** *for mappings which associate a point in* R^m *with a point in the domain. For example, the payoff* mappings, P_i, are functions. This custom is followed here.

DEFINITION 2.9   *Let* A *be a subset of* R^n *and* B *be a subset of* R^m. *Suppose the correspondence* $\phi(x)$ *is defined for any* $x \in A$ *and that* $\phi(x) \subset B$. *Then* ϕ *is* **upper semicontinuous** *if* $y^0 \in \phi(x^0)$ *whenever* (a) $x^0 \in A$, (b) $x^k \in A$, $k = 1, 2, \ldots$, (c) $\lim_{k \to \infty} x^k = x^0$, (d) $y^k \in \phi(x^k)$, $k = 1, 2, \ldots$, *and* (e) $\lim_{k \to \infty} y^k = y^0$.

Thus a correspondence ϕ is upper semicontinuous if, for any convergent sequence in the domain of ϕ whose limit is also in the domain of ϕ, and any convergent companion sequence of points, y^k in the image sets $\phi(x^k)$, the limit of the companion sequence, y^0, is in the set $\phi(x^0)$. *An equivalent definition of upper semicontinuity is that the* **graph of** ϕ **is closed**. That is, ϕ, whose domain is $A \subset R^n$ and whose range is subsets of $B \subset R^m$, is upper semicontinuous if the set $\{(x, y) \in R^{n+m} \mid y \in \phi(x), x \in A\}$ is closed. Examples are shown in Figure 2.2. Note that in Figure 2.2c the sets $\phi(x)$ are always convex; whereas, in Figure 2.2a and b, they are not. Convexity of the image sets, $\phi(x)$, is required for the following remarkable theorem that gives conditions guaranteeing existence of a fixed point.

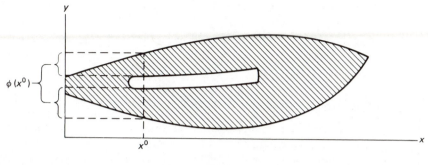

$\phi(x^0)$

x^0

(a)

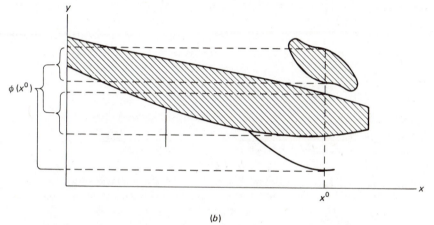

$\phi(x^0)$

x^0

(b)

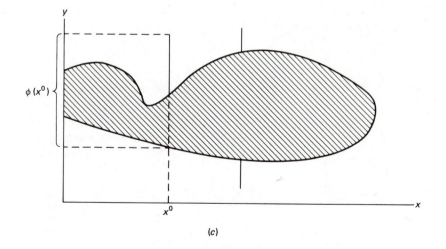

$\phi(x^0)$

x^0

(c)

FIGURE 2.2 Upper semicontinuous correspondence.

KAKUTANI (1941) FIXED POINT THEOREM.   *Let $\phi(x)$ be an upper semicontinuous correspondence, defined for $x \in A \subset R^n$, with $\phi(x) \subset A$ for all $x \in A$. If A is compact and convex and, for all $x \in A$, $\phi(x)$ is nonempty and convex, then ϕ has a fixed point. That is, there is $x^* \in \phi(x^*)$ for some $x^* \in A$.*

4.3   Continuity properties of the best reply mapping

It is readily apparent that the best reply correspondence r satisfies many of the conditions of the Kakutani theorem. The domain of r is S, which is a compact and convex subset of the Euclidean space R^{nm}. $r(s)$ is nonempty for each s because $r_i(s)$ is the set of payoff maximizing values of s_i (given the $s_j, j \neq i$), and a continuous function (the payoff function) defined on a compact set (S_i) must achieve a maximum on that set. Furthermore, $r(s)$ is convex and contained in S for all $s \in S$. It is convex because each $r_i(s)$ is convex due to each P_i being concave in s_i, and it is contained in S by the very definition of $r(s)$. The one requirement that is not obviously satisfied is upper semicontinuity of r; however, that is proved in Lemma 2.5. The other properties are established in Theorem 2.4.

LEMMA 2.5   *Let $\Gamma = (N, S, P)$ be a noncooperative game of complete information that satisfies Assumptions 2.1 to 2.3 and Rules 2.1 and 2.2. The best reply correspondence of Γ, $r : S \to S$, is upper semicontinuous.*

Proof   Let (a) $\{s^k\}_{k=1}^\infty \subset S$ be any convergent sequence of points in S, (b) s^0 be the limit of the sequence, (c) $t^k \in r(s^k)$, $k = 1, 2, \ldots$ be a convergent companion sequence of points, and (d) t^0 be the limit of the $\{t^k\}_{k=1}^\infty$. $r(s)$ is upper semicontinuous if, for any such $\{s^k\}_{k=1}^\infty$, s^0, $\{t^k\}_{k=1}^\infty$, and t^0, the limit point of the companion sequence is in the image set of the limit of the original sequence. That is, $t^0 \in r(s^0)$. The lemma is proved by showing that, for arbitrary i, $t_i^0 \in r_i(s^0)$, and noting that the same argument applies for all $i \in N$.

Select an element of $r_i(s^0)$ and denote it t_i'. Then $P_i(s^0\backslash t_i^0) > P_i(s^0\backslash t_i')$ is impossible for it contradicts the best reply property of t_i'. If $P_i(s^0\backslash t_i^0) = P_i(s^0\backslash t_i')$, then $t_i^0 \in r_i(s^0)$; therefore, it remains to show that $P_i(s^0\backslash t_i^0) < P_i(s^0\backslash t_i')$ is impossible. To show this, assume for the moment that it is true (i.e., that $P_i(s^0\backslash t_i^0) < P_i(s^0\backslash t_i')$) and let $P_i(s^0\backslash t_i') - P_i(s^0\backslash t_i^0) = \varepsilon > 0$. From the continuity of P_i, for any $\delta > 0$ there is finite k_δ such that, if $k > k_\delta$, $|P_i(s^k\backslash t_i^k) - P_i(s^0\backslash t_i^0)| < \delta$ and $|P_i(s^k\backslash t_i') - P_i(s^0\backslash t_i')| < \delta$. Choose $\delta < \varepsilon/4$. Then

$$P_i(s^k\backslash t_i') > P_i(s^0\backslash t_i') - \varepsilon/4 > P_i(s^0\backslash t_i') - 3\varepsilon/4 = P_i(s^0\backslash t_i^0) + \varepsilon/4 > P_i(s^k\backslash t_i^k)$$

(2.3)

which implies that $t_i^k \notin r_i(s^k)$ for $k > k_\delta$ because $P_i(s^k\backslash t_i') - P_i(s^k\backslash t_i^k) > \varepsilon/2$. But $t_i^k \notin r_i(s^k)$ is a contradiction; therefore, $P_i(s^0\backslash t_i^0) = P_i(s^0\backslash t_i')$ and r is upper semicontinuous.   QED

4.4 Existence of an equilibrium point

In view of Lemmas 2.4 and 2.5 it is easy to prove that a noncooperative *n*-person game has an equilibrium point.

THEOREM 2.4 *Let* $\Gamma = (N, S, P)$ *be a game of complete information that satisfies Assumptions 2.1 to 2.3 and Rules 2.1 and 2.2.* Γ *has at least one equilibrium point.*

Proof By Lemma 2.4, the set of equilibrium points of Γ is identical with the set of fixed points of the best reply correspondence, $r(s)$; therefore, the theorem is proved if it can be shown that r has a fixed point (i.e., shown that there is some $s^* \in S$ for which $s^* \in r(s^*)$). This is established by Kakutani fixed point theorem if $r(s)$ (a) is a correspondence whose domain, S, is compact and convex, (b) is defined for all $s \in S$, (c) has image sets, $r(s)$, that are contained in S for all s, (d) has convex image sets, and (e) is upper semicontinuous. (a) is satisfied by Assumption 2.1 and the fact that the Cartesian product of n convex sets is convex. To see (b) and (c), note that for any $s \in S$

$$r_i(s) = \{t_i \in S_i \mid P_i(s \backslash t_i) \geqslant P_i(s \backslash t_i') \text{ for all } t_i' \in S_i\} \qquad (2.4)$$

Such t_i exist because they are the maximizers of a continuous function (P_i) defined over a compact set (S_i), and, by construction, they are in S_i. If $t \in r(s)$, then $t_i \in r_i(s)$, $i \in N$; therefore, $r(s)$ is defined for all $s \in S$ and $r(s) \subset S$. (d) follows easily from Assumption 2.3. Suppose that t_i, $t_i' \in r_i(s)$. Then, for $\lambda \in [0, 1]$, let $t_i^\lambda = \lambda t_i + (1 - \lambda)t_i'$, and recall that concavity of P_i in s_i means that $P_i(s \backslash t_i^\lambda) \geqslant \lambda P_i(s \backslash t_i) + (1 - \lambda)P_i(s \backslash t_i')$. Strict inequality implies that t_i, $t_i' \notin r_i(s)$, a contradiction; hence equality holds and $t_i^\lambda \in r_i(s)$. Therefore, $r_i(s)$ is convex for $i \in N$ and $r(s)$, being the Cartesian product of convex sets, is also convex. (e) is established by Lemma 2.5, so the theorem is proved. Γ has an equilibrium point. QED

Theorem 2.4 is an existence theorem that sheds no light on the multiplicity of equilibrium, and, the possibility of multiple, separated equilibria is illustrated by the game in Table 2.4, and by the following infinite game. Let $N = \{1, 2\}$, $S_1 = S_2 = [-150, 150]$, $P_1(s) = 2{,}720{,}000s_1 - 33{,}600s_1s_2 - s_1^4$, and $P_2(s) = 2{,}720{,}000s_2 - 33{,}600s_1s_2 - s_2^4$. Equilibrium points of this game include $(20, 80)$, $(80, 20)$, $(-59.139, 105.576)$, $(105.576, -59.139)$, and $(57.875, 57.875)$.[4] Uniqueness of equilibrium is addressed below in Section 5.

There is a corollary, due to Debreu (1952), which extends Theorem 2.4 to pseudogames in which the payoff function of a player is not defined on the whole of S. With each P_i defined on only a subset of S, the model is called a *pseudogame*, because the model is not completely well defined. There is, in fact, an unsatisfactory element present when some $s' = (s_1', \ldots, s_n')$ can be chosen by the players, yet at least one payoff $P_i(s')$ is not defined. Surely it is superior to specify the payoffs to all players corresponding to all choices that can actually be made.

Imagine a duopoly market in which the firms sell differentiated products.

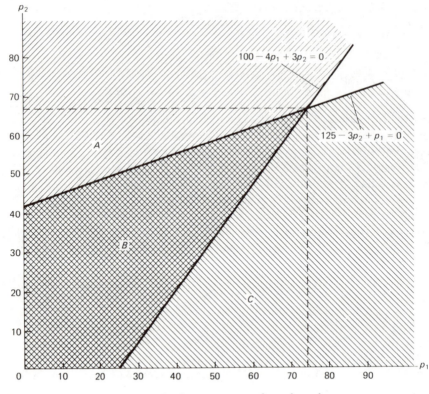

FIGURE 2.3   Strategy spaces for a duopoly.

Suppose firm 1 has a demand function $q_1 = 100 - 4p_1 + 3p_2$, where p_i is the price of the ith firm and q_i is its output level (which is assumed equal to both demand and sales). Let the demand function of firm 2 be $q_2 = 125 - 3p_2 + p_1$. One may say that demand is defined for firm 1 on the set of prices given by $\{(p_1, p_2) \in R_+^2 \mid 100 - 4p_1 + 3p_2 \geq 0\}$, and for firm 2 on the set $\{(p_1, p_2) \in R_+^2 \mid 125 - 3p_2 + p_1 \geq 0\}$. These sets are illustrated in Figure 2.3. Note that $q_1 = q_2 = 0$ at $p_1 = 75$ and $p_2 = 66\frac{2}{3}$. The economically interesting prices are in the set comprising regions A, B, and C, which correspond to $\{(p_1, p_2) \in R_+^2 \mid p_1 \leq 75 \text{ and } p_2 \leq 66\frac{2}{3}\} = S$. Let $S_1 = [0, 75]$ and $S_2 = [0, 66\frac{2}{3}]$. $S = S_1 \times S_2 = A \cup B \cup C$; however, within S, the demand for firm 1 is defined only on $T_1 = A \cup B$, and for firm 2 on $T_2 = B \cup C$. To complete the description of the pseudogame, suppose that both firms produce at zero cost, so that their payoffs equal their respective revenues. Thus, letting $p = (p_1, p_2)$, $P_1(p) = 100p_1 - 4p_1^2 + 3p_1p_2$ and $P_2(p) = 125p_2 - 3p_2^2 + p_1p_2$.

In such a market as this, is there any assurance that an equilibrium point exists? Indeed, in allowing that P_i is defined only on a subset, T_i, of S, is there any assurance that S has a region on which all strategies are

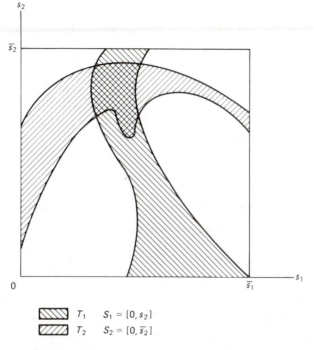

FIGURE 2.4   Strategy combinations for which payoff functions are defined.

simultaneously defined? An affirmative answer can be given to both questions if the sets, T_i, are suitably restricted.

ASSUMPTION 2.2' $P_i(s)$ *is defined, continuous, and bounded for all $s \in T_i \subset S$ and all $i \in N$. For each $i \in N$, T_i is closed and for each $s \in S$ and $i \in N$, the set $\tau_i(s) = \{t_i \in S_i \mid (s \backslash t_i) \in T_i\}$ is nonempty, closed, and convex.*

Figure 2.4 illustrates the restrictions placed on the sets T_i. Each T_i is closed, and for any choice of $s_j \in S_j$ $(j \neq i)$, there is a (nonempty) set of strategies s_i from which player i can choose. This set is closed because T_i is closed, and it is also convex. Note, however, that T_i is not required to be convex, as Figure 2.4 shows. Assumption 2.3 must be modified in the light of Assumption 2.2'.

ASSUMPTION 2.3' $P_i(s \backslash t_i)$ *is concave with respect to $t_i \in \tau_i(s)$ for all $s \in S$ and all $i \in N$.*

COROLLARY.   *Let $\Gamma = (N, S, P)$ be a pseudogame of complete information that satisfies Assumptions 2.1, 2.2', and 2.3', and Rules 2.1 and 2.2. Γ has at least one equilibrium point.*

Proof   To prove the corollary, the best reply mapping must be correctly defined. To that end, let

$$r_i(s) = \{t_i \in \tau_i(s) \mid P_i(s \backslash t_i) \geq P_i(s \backslash t_i') \text{ for all } t_i' \in \tau_i(s)\}, s \in S, i \in N$$

$$(2.5)$$

$r(s) = \times_{i \in N} r_i(s)$. $r(s)$ is defined for all s because $\tau_i(s)$ is nonempty and closed for all i and s; hence, a fixed point of r is an element of $\bigcap_{i \in N} T_i$. By parallel argument to that used in the proof of Theorem 2.3, $r(s)$ satisfies the Kakutani fixed point theorem; hence, it has a fixed point that is an equilibrium point of the game.   QED

Note that, of necessity, the equilibrium point, s^*, satisfies $s_i^* \in \tau_i(s^*)$, so that $s^* \in T_i$ for all i.

In this section, existence of equilibrium points has been studied for a standard model satisfying Assumptions 2.1 to 2.3. In addition, a model has been examined for which the payoff functions are not defined on all of S and also incomplete information games are investigated below in Section 6. Other interesting variations, not covered here, are games with an infinite number of players. Peleg and Yaari (1973) cover the case where the number of players is countably infinite and Schmeidler (1973) covers the uncountably infinite case. Another variation of the assumptions is obtained by relaxing the concavity requirement. All the theorems of the present chapter go through as they are if concavity is replaced with quasi-concavity; however, to see that even quasi-concavity can be relaxed, look at Nishimura and Friedman (1981).

5   Uniqueness of equilibrium points

Multiple equilibria are troublesome from more than one standpoint. First, it is not clear that players can be expected to coordinate to play an equilibrium strategy combination when there is more than one equilibrium point; if they have no means of communication, even if each one selects a strategy associated with an equilibrium point, the resulting combination may not be an equilibrium. Were the players able to communicate, then they could agree on a particular equilibrium point, but we are then left with the problem of figuring out which equilibrium point they would be expected to choose. The situation is much happier if equilibrium is unique. Then it is reasonable to view all players as being able to calculate the equilibrium and to presume the equilibrium is the only reasonable outcome. Furthermore, in many applications, the particular restrictions that imply a unique equilibrium are reasonable assumptions to make; however, that must always be judged case by case.

5.1   Some additional restrictions needed to ensure uniqueness

Two theorems on uniqueness are given below. Neither is a special case of the other; so both are useful to have in one's arsenal. Both require that

Assumption 2.3 be modified so that the best reply mapping is a (single-valued) function. The first theorem requires, furthermore, that the best reply function be a contraction. The second theorem, by contrast, does not restrict the best reply function in this way, but it requires differentiability and places some additional restrictions that are explained below. Taken as given in this section are Assumptions 2.1 and 2.2, Rules 2.1 and 2.2, complete information and

ASSUMPTION 2.3″ $P_i(s \backslash t_i)$ *is strictly concave with respect to* $t_i \in S_i$ *for all* $i \in N$.

Strict concavity means that, for any $s \in S$, any $t_i, t_i' \in S_i$ with $t_i \neq t_i'$, and any $\lambda \in (0, 1)$, that

$$P_i(s \backslash (\lambda t_i + (1 - \lambda)t_i')) > \lambda P_i(s \backslash t_i) + (1 - \lambda)P_i(s \backslash t_i') \qquad (2.6)$$

The key feature of using Assumption 2.3″ in place of Assumption 2.3 is stated in Lemma 2.6.

LEMMA 2.6 *For a game* $\Gamma = (N, S, P)$ *satisfying Assumptions* 2.1, 2.2, *and* 2.3, *the set*

$$\{t_i \in S_i \mid P_i(s \backslash t_i) \geq P_i(s \backslash t_i') \text{ for all } t_i' \in S_i\} \qquad (2.7)$$

consists of exactly one element for each $s \in S$.

Proof Suppose that t_i^0 and t_i^1 both maximize $P_i(s \backslash t_i)$. Then, by Assumption 2.3, if $t_i^0 \neq t_i^1$ and $t_i' = (t_i^0 + t_i^1)/2$,

$$P_i(s \backslash t_i') > P_i(s \backslash t_i^0) = P_i(s \backslash t_i^1) \qquad (2.8)$$

however, the latter inequality contradicts the optimality of t_i^0 and t_i^1. Thus $t_i^0 = t_i^1$. QED

For the remainder of this section, $r(s)$ is understood to be single valued; hence, the best reply function can be stated as $t = r(s)$.

LEMMA 2.7 *The best reply function,* $r(s)$, *is continuous.*

Proof This is implied by the upper semicontinuity of the best reply correspondence. A proof could be directly given by writing a proof parallel to the proof of Lemma 2.5. QED

5.2 Uniqueness of equilibrium—contraction mapping formulation

Preparing for the first uniqueness theorem, definitions are needed for *distance between two points of* R^m and *contraction.*

DEFINITION 2.10 *Let* $x, y \in R^m$. *The* **distance from** x **to** y, *denoted either* $d(x, y)$ *or* $\|x - y\|$, *is* $d(x, y) = max_i |x_i - y_i|$.

DEFINITION 2.11 *Let* $f(x)$ *be a function with domain* $A \subset R^m$ *and range* $B \subset R^n$. *If there is a positive scalar* $\lambda < 1$ *such that for any* $x, x' \in A$, $d(f(x), f(x')) \leq \lambda d(x, x')$, *then* $f(x)$ *is a* **contraction**.

Simply put, a contraction leaves the images of two points closer than were the original points themselves. When $f(x)$ is a differentiable function, the contraction condition in Definition 2.11 is equivalent to $\sum_{i=1}^{m} |\partial f_j(x)/\partial x_i| \leq \lambda$ for each component $f_j(x)$ of $f(x) = (f_1(x), \ldots, f_n(x))$. For example, $y = .3x_1 - .2x_2 + .4x_3$ satisfies the contraction condition for $\lambda = .9$.

THEOREM 2.5   *Let $\Gamma = (N, S, P)$ be a game of complete information that satisfies Assumptions 2.1, 2.2, and 2.3, and Rules 2.1 and 2.2. If the best reply function, $r(s)$, is a contraction, then Γ has exactly one equilibrium point.*

Proof From Theorem 2.4, the game is known to have at least one equilibrium point. Suppose that $s', s'' \in S$ are equilibrium points (i.e., $s' = r(s')$ and $s'' = r(s'')$). Then $d(r(s'), r(s'')) = d(s', s'')$, but r being a contraction means that $d(r(s'), r(s'')) \leq \lambda d(s', s'')$ for $\lambda < 1$. The latter can only hold for $s' = s''$, which implies that the equilibrium point is unique.   QED

5.3   Uniqueness of equilibrium—Univalent mapping approach

The second uniqueness theorem is not restricted to games in which $r(s)$ is a contraction, but it does need differentiability of the payoff functions. Let $\overset{\circ}{S}$ denote the *interior* of S.

DEFINITION 2.12 $\Gamma = (N, S, P)$ *is a **smooth game** if the following derivatives exist and are continuous on $\overset{\circ}{S}$: $\partial P_i/\partial s_{jk}$, $k = 1, \ldots, m, j \in N$ and $\partial^2 P_i/\partial s_{ik}\, \partial s_{jl}, k, l = 1, \ldots, m, i, j \in N$.*

DEFINITION 2.13 $\Gamma = (N, S, P)$ *is a **strictly** smooth game if it is a smooth game, and for each s' on the boundary of S (i.e., $s' \in S$, $s' \notin \overset{\circ}{S}$)*

$$\frac{\partial P_i(s')}{\partial s_{ik}} = \lim_{t \to s'} \frac{\partial P_i(t)}{\partial s_{ik}}, \qquad k = 1, \ldots, m, \quad i \in N \tag{2.9}$$

$$\frac{\partial^2 P_i(s')}{\partial s_{ik}\, \partial s_{jl}} = \lim_{t \to s'} \frac{\partial^2 P_i(t)}{\partial s_{ik}\, \partial s_{jl}}, \qquad k, l = 1, \ldots, m, \quad i, j \in N \tag{2.10}$$

exist for all sequences of points in $\overset{\circ}{S}$ converging to s' on the boundary of S.

The second partial derivatives that exist everywhere in S for a strictly smooth game are precisely the derivatives that appear in the Jacobian of the system

$$\frac{\partial P_i}{\partial s_{ik}} = 0, \qquad k = 1, \ldots, m, \quad i \in N \tag{2.11}$$

This Jacobian, denoted $J(s)$, is a square matrix with $m \times n$ rows and columns. Its elements are $\partial^2 P_i/\partial s_{ik}\, \partial s_{jl}$ ($i, j \in N$ and $k, l = 1, \ldots, m$). It is the Jacobian of the implicit form of the best reply function, which must obey a special condition everywhere on its domain, S. Recall that *a square symmetric matrix A is **negative semidefinite** if all principal minor sub-*

determinants of odd order are negative and those of even order are positive. A related condition for nonsymmetric square matrices is *quasi-negative definiteness*.

DEFINITION 2.14   *Let A be an m × m matrix. A is* **negative quasi-definite** *if $B = A + A^T$ is negative definite.*

At a glance, it may appear that a negative quasi-definite matrix differs only trivially from a negative definite matrix; however, an example can illuminate the difference. Suppose that

$$A = \begin{bmatrix} -1 & a \\ a & -1 \end{bmatrix} \tag{2.12}$$

Then the determinant of A is $|A| = 1 - a^2$ and $|A| > 0$ is required for negative definiteness. This, in turn, means that $|a| < 1$. Now consider

$$A^* = \begin{bmatrix} -1 & a \\ b & -1 \end{bmatrix} \tag{2.13}$$

and

$$B = A^* + A^{*^T} = \begin{bmatrix} -2 & a+b \\ a+b & -2 \end{bmatrix} \tag{2.14}$$

Then $|B| = 4 - (a + b)^2$ and negative quasi-definiteness requires $(a + b)^2 < 4$. a and b are not constrained to be less than 1 in absolute value, but the sum of their absolute values must be less than 2. So $a = 98.5$ and $b = -100$ satisfies negative quasi-definiteness. To see the connecting link between these concepts from another angle, let A be an $m \times m$ matrix and x be a vector in R^m. A is negative quasi-definite if, for all $x \neq 0$, $xAx^T < 0$; however, A is negative definite if A is both negative quasi-definite and symmetric.

The uniqueness theorem requires that $J(s)$ be negative quasi-definite for all $s \in S$, and the theorem allowing the proof of uniqueness is the following theorem:

GALE–NIKAIDO (1965) UNIVALENCE THEOREM   *Let $f(x)$ be a function from a convex set $X \subset R^m$ to R^m. If the Jacobian of f is negative quasi-definite for all $x \in X$, then f is one to one. (That is, if $f(x') = y'$, then, for all $x \neq x'$, $f(x) \neq y'$.)*

THEOREM 2.6   *Let $\Gamma = (N, S, P)$ be a smooth game of complete information that satisfies Assumptions 2.1, 2.2, and 2.3″, and Rules 2.1 and 2.2. Assume that $J(s)$, the Jacobian of the implicit form of the best reply function, is negative quasi-definite for all $s \in \overset{\circ}{S}$, and that, for any $s \in S$, $r(s) \in \overset{\circ}{S}$. Then Γ has a unique equilibrium point.*

Proof   The theorem is a direct consequence of Theorem 2.4 and the Gale–Nikaido univalence theorem. From the former, equilibria are known to exist, and, by the condition that $r(s) \in \overset{\circ}{S}$, there are no equilibrium points on the boundary of S. Thus all equilibrium points must satisfy conventional first-order conditions: $\partial P_i(S^*)/\partial s_{jk} = 0$, $k = 1, \ldots, m$, $i, j \in N$. Denote the system of first derivatives of all the P_i with respect to the s_{ik} by $P'(s)$.[5] An equilibrium point s^* corresponds to $P'(s) = 0$. $P'(s)$ is a function from $\mathring{S} \subset R^{nm}$ to R^{nm}. Its Jacobian is $J(s)$, which is negative quasi-definite; therefore $P'(s)$ is univalent and takes on the value $P'(s) = 0$ only once, establishing uniqueness of equilibrium.   QED

A stronger result is

ROSEN (1965) UNIQUENESS THEOREM   *Let* $\Gamma = (N, S, P)$ *be a strictly smooth game of complete information that satisfies Assumptions 2.1, 2.2, and 2.3″, and Rules 2.1 and 2.2. If $J(s)$ is negative quasi-definite for all $s \in S$, then Γ has a unique equilibrium point.*

   In comparing Theorem 2.6, and the Rosen uniqueness theorem, the latter is based on an extension of the differentiability and quasi-definiteness conditions from $\mathring{S}$ to S. This permits a global uniqueness theorem that is not hampered by restriction to models in which all equilibria must be in $\mathring{S}$. These two theorems are closer to each other than is either one to Theorem 2.5. As between Theorem 2.5 and Rosen uniqueness theorem, neither one is a generalization of the other, because each requires an assumption which is stronger than the other theorem requires. Theorem 2.5 does not require differentiability of the payoff functions, while the other two theorems require continuous second partial derivatives. But, for differentiable payoff functions, the contraction condition of Theorem 2.4 is much more confining than the negative quasi-definiteness of the Jacobian, $J(s)$. If $r(s)$ is a differentiable contraction, then $J(s)$ is always negative quasi-definite and obeys the dominant diagonal condition $P_i^i(s) + \sum_{j \neq i} |P_i^j(s)| < 0, i \in N$, but negative quasi-definiteness does not imply the dominant diagonal condition, as the 2×2 example with $a = 99.5$ and $b = -100$ clearly demonstrates. In practice it is useful to have all of these uniqueness theorems available.

5.4   *Examples of games with unique equilibrium points*

These theorems on uniqueness are easily illustrated with simple examples. Suppose $S_1 = [-10, 0]$, $S_2 = [-3, 0]$,

$$P_1(s) = 10s_1 + 7s_1s_2 - s_1^2$$
$$P_2(s) = 15s_2 + 5s_1s_2 - s_2^2$$

The first-order conditions for an interior equilibrium point are

$$10 + 7s_2 - 2s_1 = 0 \tag{2.15}$$

$$15 + 5s_1 - 2s_2 = 0 \tag{2.16}$$

Equations (2.15) and (2.16) are solved at $(-280/31, -80/31)$. In addition to this interior equilibrium, there is a boundary equilibrium: $(0, 0)$. Checking for negative quasi-definiteness, the Jacobian of equations (2.15) and (2.16) is

$$\begin{bmatrix} -2 & 7 \\ 5 & -2 \end{bmatrix} = J(s) \tag{2.17}$$

and $J(s) + J^T(s)$ is

$$\begin{bmatrix} -4 & +12 \\ +12 & -4 \end{bmatrix} \tag{2.18}$$

The determinant of equation (2.18) is $16 - 144 = -128$. To satisfy negative quasi-definiteness requires the diagonal elements to be negative, which they are, and the determinant to be positive. Furthermore, the best reply mapping is not a contraction. Solving for $r(s)$ from equations (2.15) and (2.16) yields

$$s_1 = 5 + 3.5s_2 \tag{2.19}$$

$$s_2 = 7.5 + 2.5s_1 \tag{2.20}$$

Neither equation (2.19) nor (2.20) is a contraction. For example, $\partial s_1 / \partial s_2 = 3.5 > 1$.

Consider a slight variant of this example: S_1, S_2, and P_2 are as before, but

$$P_1(s) = 10s_1 - 7s_1s_2 - s_1^2 \tag{2.21}$$

The first-order condition for an interior equilibrium are equation (2.16) and

$$10 - 7s_2 - 2s_1 = 0 \tag{2.22}$$

These are not simultaneously satisfied anywhere on S; however, there is a unique equilibrium at $(0, 0)$. The Jacobian of this system is

$$\begin{bmatrix} -2 & -7 \\ 5 & -2 \end{bmatrix} \tag{2.23}$$

and $J(s) + J^T(s)$ is

$$\begin{bmatrix} -4 & -2 \\ -2 & -4 \end{bmatrix} \tag{2.24}$$

This matrix is negative definite, thus the quasi-negative definiteness conditions are met: $-4 < 0$ and the determinant of equation (2.24) is $16 - 4 = 12 > 0$. If the example were changed again by letting $S_2 = [-3, +3]$ with S_1, P_1, and P_2 unchanged, there would be a unique equilibrium at $(-85/39, 80/39)$. It can be easily verified that the best reply function is not a contraction for the second and third examples as well. Thus the uniqueness theorems in Section 5 give sufficient, but not necessary, conditions for uniqueness. It is left as an exercise to the reader to suggest modifications to one of the examples that change the best reply function into a contraction.

6 Noncooperative games under incomplete information

It is possible to specify an equilibrium concept for some incomplete information games by making assumptions on the way that incompleteness enters into the game. The following treatment is based on Harsanyi (1967, 1968a, 1968b). It is assumed that each player i knows the set N of players and each of the strategy sets $S_j, j \in N$; however, players do not know the correct payoff functions for the game. Instead, each player knows the set of possible payoff functions, and has a subjective probabilty distribution over that set. The players' subjective probability distributions differ from one another, because each one has some private information, but the distributions are consistent with one another in a sense made clear by Definitions 2.18 and 2.19. Associated with each player i is an integer $\beta_i \in V = \{1, \ldots, v\}$. $\beta = (\beta_1, \ldots, \beta_n) \in V^n$ indexes the set of possible payoff functions for all players in that, given some $\beta \in V^n$, the payoff functions $P_{i\beta}, i \in N$, are precisely determined.

DEFINITION 2.15 $P_i^* = \{P_{i\beta}\}_{\beta \in V^n}$ *is the* **set of potential payoff functions for player** $i \in N$.

DEFINITION 2.16 $P^* = \times_{i \in N} P_i^*$ *is the* **set of potential payoff functions** *for an incomplete information game* Γ_I. $P^* = \{(P_{1\beta}, \ldots, P_{n\beta}) \mid P_{i\beta} \in P_i^*, i \in N, \beta \in V\}$.

An element of P^* is a vector of payoff functions $(P_{1\beta}, \ldots, P_{n\beta}) = P_\beta$.

ASSUMPTION 2.4 $P_{i\beta}(s)$ *is defined and continuous on* $s \in S$, *and concave in* s_i, *for all* $i \in N$ *and all* $\beta \in V^n$.

From Assumption 2.4, the strategy sets are identical for all possible payoff functions of the ith player, and the payoff functions satisfy Assumptions 2.2 and 2.3.

6.1 Definition of a game of incomplete information

Differing information among the players arises because each player i is assumed to know the true value of β_i, and to have a subjective probability distribution over $\beta^i = (\beta_1, \ldots, \beta_{i-1}, \beta_{i+1}, \ldots, \beta_n)$, the values of the β_j pertaining to the other players.

DEFINITION 2.17 π_i *is a* **subjective probability distribution for player** i. *It satisfies* $\pi_i(\beta^i) \geqslant 0$ *for each* $\beta^i \in V^{n-1}$ *and* $\sum_{\beta^i \in V^{n-1}} \pi_i(\beta^i) = 1$.

Letting $\pi = (\pi_1, \ldots, \pi_n)$, a game of incomplete information is denoted $\Gamma_I = (N, S, V, P^*, \pi)$.

DEFINITION 2.18   *A* **noncooperative game of incomplete information** $\Gamma_I = (N, S, V, P^*, \pi)$ *satisfies Assumptions 2.1 and 2.4, Rules 2.1 and 2.2, and is a game in which each player* i *knows* (a) *all the strategy sets* $S_j, j \in N$, (b) *all the* *possible payoff functions $P_{j\beta}, j \in N, \beta \in V^n$, (c) the true value of β_i, and (d) has her own subjective probability distribution π_i over $\beta^i \in V^{n-1}$. Each player knows the nature of the information in the possession of all players and is aware that all players are thus informed.*

Note that the players are unable to calculate equilibrium points on their own if each player i is ignorant of the subjective probability distributions of the others. It is not reasonable to suppose they would get together and exchange this information, for, even if they could communicate, there is no reason to think that a player would be truthful nor that he would be believed. By contrast, in a complete information game, each player has the information needed to calculate all of the equilibrium points. To define equilibrium points for Γ_I, the technique is to assume each player does have some information concerning the subjective probability distributions of the others, although this information is not entirely complete. Then it is shown that the incomplete information game has an identical mathematical structure to a complete information game, and the equilibrium points of the complete information game are defined to be the equilibrium points of the incomplete information game. This identification of equilibrium points is done in a natural way.

6.2 Consistency of players' subjective beliefs

Now suppose the subjective probability distributions are mutually consistent in the sense that there is a probability distribution $\theta(\beta)$ satisfying Assumption 2.5.

ASSUMPTION 2.5 *Suppose $b \in V^n$ is the true state and $\theta(\beta)$ is a probability distribution over V^n that is known to all players and that satisfies*

$$\pi_i(\beta^i) = \theta(\beta^i \mid b_i) = \frac{\theta(\beta \backslash b_i)}{\sum_{k^i \in V^{n-1}} \theta(k \backslash b_i)} \tag{2.25}$$

The beliefs each player i has concerning the subjective probability distributions π_j $(j \neq i)$ are that $\pi_j(\beta^j) = \theta(\beta^j \mid \beta_j)$.

Although technically $\theta(\beta)$ is a probability distribution over V^n, it implies a distribution over P^*, and it should not cause confusion to refer to it as a distribution over P^*. In Assumption 2.5, $\theta(\beta^i \mid \beta_i)$ is the conditional distribution of β^i given β_i, and $\pi^i(\beta^i)$ is required to equal this conditional distribution for $\beta_i = b_i$. In addition, θ embodies the beliefs that each player holds concerning the subjective probability distributions of the others. Thus, if player i believes the correct value of β_j (for $j \neq i$) is β_j', then player i supposes that the subjective probability distribution of player j is $\theta(\beta^j \mid \beta_j')$.

DEFINITION 2.19 *A **consistent game of incomplete information** $\Gamma_I = (N, S, V, P^*, \theta)$ is a game of incomplete information that satisfies Assumption 2.5.*

6.3   A complete information companion game

It is now possible to look for equilibrium points in consistent games of incomplete information. These games satisfy Assumptions 2.1, 2.4, and 2.5, and Rules 2.1 and 2.2, as well as the information conditions stated in Definition 2.18. The technique is to specify a mathematically equivalent complete information game and assume that the equilibrium points of the complete information game are the equilibrium points of the incomplete information game. To define the complete information game, suppose that there are nv players in a game in which a chance move occurs after the players select their strategies. The players fall into n groups, with v players in each group. Player (i, β_i) is the β_ith player in group i, $i \in N$, $\beta_i \in V$. The chance move is the choice of $\beta \in R^n$ where $\beta = (\beta_1, \ldots, \beta_n)$. Informally, if β is selected, the active players designated by β, namely $(1, \beta_1), \ldots, (n, \beta_n)$, may be thought of as the active players in the game. An active player has the payoff function $\bar{P}_{i\beta_i}$, and any player (j, k_j) who is not active has the payoff function $P'_{jk_j}(s) = 0$. Technically, the payoff function of a player must depend on the strategy choices of all nv players. The random mechanism that selects β has the distribution $\theta(\beta)$. The set of players is $N \times V$ and a single player is denoted (i, β_i). Let $\sigma_{i\beta_i}$ denote a strategy selected by player (i, β_i). The strategy space of this player, $T_{i\beta_i}$ is the same for all $\beta_i \in V$ and is $T_{i\beta_i} = S_i$. The joint strategy space of the nv player game is $\times_{(i, \beta_i) \in N \times V} T_{i\beta_i} = \times_{i \in N} S_i^v = S^v$. An element of S^v is denoted σ. Let $\sigma_\beta = (\sigma_{1\beta_1}, \ldots, \sigma_{n\beta_n}) \in S$ and let $\delta_{k_i\beta_i}$ be the Kronecker delta (i.e., $\delta_{k_i\beta_i} = 1$ if $k_i = \beta_i$ and $\delta_{k_i\beta_i} = 0$ if $k_i \neq \beta_i$). Then the payoff function of active player (i, β_i) is

$$\bar{P}_{i\beta_i}(\sigma) = \sum_{k \in V^n} \delta_{k_i\beta_i}\theta(k)P_{ik}(\sigma_k) = \sum_{k^i \in V^{n-1}} \theta(k \mid \beta_i)P_{ik\setminus\beta_i}(\sigma_{k\setminus\beta_i}) \qquad (2.26)$$

Letting $\bar{P} = (\bar{P}_{11}, \ldots, \bar{P}_{1v}, \ldots, \bar{P}_{n1}, \ldots, \bar{P}_{nv})$, the complete information game corresponding to $\Gamma_I = (N, S, V, P^*, \theta)$ is $\Gamma_C = (N \times V, S^v, \bar{P})$, and Γ_C is called the *companion game of Γ_I*.

THEOREM 2.7   *The complete information game $\Gamma_C = (N \times V, S^v, \bar{P})$ which is the companion game to the consistent incomplete information game $\Gamma_I = (N, S, V, P^*, \theta)$ has a noncooperative equilibrium point.*

Proof   It suffices to show that Γ_C satisfies Assumptions 2.1 to 2.3. Clearly, each $T_{i\beta_i}$ is compact and convex because each is one of the original compact, convex sets S_i. Therefore S^v is compact, because it is a v-fold product of the set S. $\bar{P}_{i\beta_i}$ is continuous and bounded because it is the sum of a finite number of continuous and bounded functions. Similarly, $\bar{P}_{i\beta_i}$ is concave in $\sigma_{i\beta_i}$ because it is a sum of concave functions.   QED

6.4   Existence of equilibrium points for incomplete information games

The equilibrium points of Γ_I are defined to be those of Γ_C. Recall that in Γ_I each player knows which type she is. That is, there is $b \in V$, which is the true player specification. Now suppose that player i selects s_i to maximize his expected payoff, and, although player i does know b_i, he does not know $b_j (j \neq i)$. Indeed, $\pi_i(\beta^i)$ is his subjective probability distribution over the possible payoff functions of the other players. Player i recognizes that another player j will choose s_j differently according to the true value of β_j, so player i will think of player j actually choosing $u_j = (u_{j1}, \ldots, u_{jv}) \in S_j^v$ where $u_{j\beta_j}$ is the strategy choice of player j contingent on $\beta_j = b_j$, and $u^i = (u_1, \ldots, u_{i-1}, u_{i+1}, \ldots, u_n)$. Thus player i views his payoff function as the expected payoff

$$F_{ib_i}(s_i, u^i) = \sum_{\beta^i \in V^{n-1}} \pi_i(\beta^i) P_{i\beta \backslash b_i}(u_{1\beta_1}, \ldots, u_{i-1,\beta_{i-1}}, s_i, u_{i+1,\beta_{i+1}}, \ldots, u_{n\beta_n})$$

(2.27)

Player i chooses s_i to maximize equation (2.27), given the values of $u_{j\beta_j}$ which player i expects. Note that equations (2.26) and (2.27) are equivalent.

DEFINITION 2.20 $s^* \in S$ *is an* **equilibrium point relative to** b *for the consistent noncooperative incomplete information game* $\Gamma_I = (N, S, V, P^*, \theta)$ *if there is* $u^* \in S^v$ *such that* $u_{ib_i}^* = s_i^*$ *and*

$$\max_{s_i \in S_i} F_{ib_i}(s_i, u^{*i}) = F_{ib_i}(s_i^*, u^{*i})$$

(2.28)

for all $i \in N$.

Under Definition 2.20, each player i has a system of expectations π^i concerning what the true payoff functions will be for the other players and concerning the strategy choices the other players will make as a function of the various payoff functions. These expectations are consistent in the sense that all the $\pi^i = (\pi_1, \ldots, \pi_{i-1}, \pi_{i+1}, \ldots, \pi_n)$ are conditional distributions for a common $\theta(\beta)$ and all players $i, i' \neq j$ expect, in common, that player j will select $u_{j\beta_j}$ if his payoff function is $\bar{P}_{j\beta_j}$.

DEFINITION 2.21 $u^* \in S^v$ *is* **an equilibrium point for the consistent noncooperative incomplete information game** $\Gamma_I = (N, S, V, P^*, \theta)$ *if*

$$\max_{s_i \in S_i} F_{i\beta_i}(s_i, u^{*i}) = F_{i\beta_i}(u_{i\beta_i}^*, u^{*i})$$

(2.29)

for all $i \in N$ *and* $\beta_i \in V$.

Definition 2.21 specifies a u^* that satisfies Definition 2.20 for all possible $k \in V^n$.

THEOREM 2.8 *Let* $\Gamma_C = (N \times V, S^v, P)$ *be the companion game to* $\Gamma_I = (N, S, V, P^*, \theta)$. *Then* $\sigma^* \in S^v$ *is an equilibrium point of* Γ_C *if and only if it is an equilibrium point of* Γ_I.

Proof The games and the definitions of their respective equilibrium points are mathematically equivalent.   QED

A generalization of this model can be obtained easily by allowing the strategy set of player i to be different for each value of β_i, giving each player (i, β_i) his own distinct strategy space.

6.5 A numerical example

An example of a consistent noncooperative incomplete information game is presented in Table 2.5 for two players and two states per player. The payoff functions for the complete information companion game are

$$F_{11}(u) = .2P_{111} + .8P_{112} = 20u_{11} - u_{11}^2 + .2u_{21}^2 - u_{11}u_{21} - .8u_{22}^2 - .8u_{11}u_{22} \tag{2.30}$$

$$F_{12}(u) = .6P_{121} + .4P_{122} = 12u_{12} - u_{12}^2 + 1.8u_{12}u_{21} + .4u_{12}u_{22} \tag{2.31}$$

$$F_{21}(u) = .25P_{211} + .75P_{221} = 12.5u_{21} - u_{21}^2 + 2.5u_{11}u_{21} - 3.75u_{12}u_{21} \tag{2.32}$$

$$F_{22}(u) = \tfrac{2}{3}P_{212} + \tfrac{1}{3}P_{222} = 20u_{11} - u_{22}^2 - 6\tfrac{2}{3}u_{11}u_{22} + 6\tfrac{2}{3}u_{12}u_{22} \tag{2.33}$$

TABLE 2.5   A game of incomplete information

		States for player 2	
		1	2
States for player 1	1	.1	.4
	2	.3	.2

Conditional distributions (Subjective Probability Assessments)

For player 1

	$\beta_2 = 1$	$\beta_2 = 2$
If $\beta_1 = 1$	.2	.8
If $\beta_1 = 2$	.6	.4

Strategy Spaces $S_1 = [-15, 25]$

For player 2

	$\beta_1 = 1$	$\beta_1 = 2$
If $\beta_2 = 1$	.25	.75
If $\beta_2 = 2$	$\tfrac{2}{3}$	$\tfrac{1}{3}$

$S_2 = [-100, 80]$

Payoff functions for each player, conditional on the state

State	for player 1	for player 2
(1, 1)	$P_{111}(u_{11}, u_{21}) = 100u_{11} - u_{11}^2 + u_{21}^2 - 5u_{11}u_{21}$	$P_{211}(u_{11}, u_{21}) = 50u_{21} - u_{21}^2 + 10u_{11}u_{21}$
(1, 2)	$P_{112}(u_{11}, u_{22}) = -u_{11}^2 - u_{22}^2 - u_{11}u_{22}$	$P_{212}(u_{11}, u_{22}) = 30u_{11} - u_{22}^2 - 10u_{11}u_{22}$
(2, 1)	$P_{121}(u_{12}, u_{21}) = -u_{12}^2 + 3u_{12}u_{21}$	$P_{221}(u_{12}, u_{21}) = -u_{21}^2 - 5u_{12}u_{21}$
(2, 2)	$P_{122}(u_{12}, u_{22}) = 30u_{12} - u_{12}^2 + u_{12}u_{22}$	$P_{222}(u_{12}, u_{22}) = -u_{22}^2 + 20u_{12}u_{22}$

An equilibrium point is a solution to the equation system

$$\frac{\partial F_{11}}{\partial u_{11}} = 20 - 2u_{11} - u_{21} - .8u_{22} = 0 \tag{2.34}$$

$$\frac{\partial F_{12}}{\partial u_{12}} = 12 - 2u_{12} + 1.8u_{21} + .4u_{22} = 0 \tag{2.35}$$

$$\frac{\partial F_{21}}{\partial u_{21}} = 12.5 - 2u_{21} + 2.5u_{11} - 3.75u_{12} = 0 \tag{2.36}$$

$$\frac{\partial F_{22}}{\partial u_{22}} = -2u_{22} - 6\tfrac{2}{3}u_{11} + 6\tfrac{2}{3} - u_{12} = 0 \tag{2.37}$$

The equilibrium point is $u^* = (12.05, 8.49, 5.41, -11.89)$ and the associated expected payoffs are 37.98, 72.10, 29.34, and 381.82.

It is interesting to consider a variant of the example in Table 2.5. Suppose that the true state is $\beta_1 = 1$ and $\beta_2 = 1$. Of course, player 1 is unaware of the true value of β_2, just as player 2 is unaware of the true value of β_1. Say that the two players' subjective probability assessments are as shown in Table 2.5. That is, player 1 places .2 as the probability that $\beta_2 = 1$ and .8 that $\beta_2 = 2$; while player 2 believes $\beta_1 = 1$ with probability .25 and $\beta_1 = 2$ with probability .75. A large family of probability distributions θ are consistent with these subjective distributions; that is, all the distributions shown in Table 2.7 for $0 \leqslant a \leqslant .125$. In Table 2.5, $a = .1$. Table 2.6 displays the equilibrium strategies and payoffs for several values

TABLE 2.6 Equilibrium strategies and payoff for a game of incomplete information

a	u_{11}	u_{12}	u_{21}	u_{22}	F_{11}	F_{12}	F_{21}	F_{22}
0	11.30	−3.75	24.70	−37.50	−847.2	14.06	807.6	1406.3
.001	11.36	−3.77	27.53	−37.82	−1551.0	−270.1	814.1	−4286.4
.05	20.53	−7.87	46.67	−84.67	−4878.0	61.89	228.6	7325.9
.1	12.05	8.49	5.41	−11.89	37.98	72.10	89.34	381.8
.125	−10.98	−2.94	−1.96	54.90	−2289.9	8.64	−51.05	2684.6

TABLE 2.7 Probability distribution over states for a game of incomplete information

		States of player 2	
		1	2
States of player 1	1	a	$4a$
	2	$3a$	$1 - 8a$

of a. Clearly, both u^* and equilibrium payoffs are very sensitive to the value of a, which is not surprising. Many complete information games are compatible with this incomplete information game in the sense that they can be companion games, and, although each complete information game has a unique Nash equilibrium, the equilibrium changes rapidly as a is changed. Merely imposing mutually consistent beliefs on the players does not bring determinateness to the outcome.

7   Applications of noncooperative games

Three examples of noncooperative games are sketched in this section. The first is the Cournot (1838) oligopoly, the classic instance of a non-cooperative game in economics. The second is a model of general equilibrium, and the third is the free rider problem. These examples are by no means exhaustive, but they illustrate the underlying principles of noncooperative games, bring out some interesting special problems, and give some indication of the scope of noncooperative games for economics.

7.1   *Cournot oligopoly*

Suppose a single market in which n firms, offering a homogeneous good, sell to a very large number of consumers whose willingness to purchase the product is summarized by the inverse demand function $p = f(Q)$ where p is the market price and Q is the total output in the industry. The set of firms is $N = \{1, \ldots, n\}$ and the output of firm $i \in N$ is q_i. Thus, $Q = \sum_{i \in N} q_i$. Firms produce output, all of which is sold at whatever price will clear the market. Each firm faces a cost of production, $C_i(q_i)$; hence, letting $q = (q_1, \ldots, q_n)$, the profit to firm i is $\pi_i(q) = q_i f(Q) - C_i(q_i)$.

Common, although not universal, assumptions placed on the model are as follows

CONDITION 2.1   *The inverse demand function is finite valued, nonnegative, defined for all $Q \in [0, \infty)$, and twice continuously differentiable wherever $f(Q) > 0$. In addition, $f(0) > 0$, and, if $f(Q) > 0$, then $f'(Q) < 0$.*

CONDITION 2.2 $C_i(q_i)$ *is defined for all $q_i \in [0, \infty)$, nonnegative, convex, twice continuously differentiable, and $C_i'(q_i) \geq \varepsilon > 0$.*

CONDITION 2.3 $Qf(Q)$ *is bounded and is strictly concave for all q such that $f(Q) > 0$.*

For the most part, these assumptions have natural economic interpreta-tions. Condition 2.1 stipulates a demand function that is downward sloping, starting from a point on the price axis. Condition 2.2 specifies nonnegative fixed cost $(C_i(0) \geq 0)$ and positive, nondecreasing marginal cost $(C_i'(q_i) > 0)$. These stem from C_i being nonnegative, increasing, and convex. Condition 2.3 asserts concavity of $Qf(Q)$, total industry revenue. This, in turn, implies concavity of $q_i f(\sum_{j \in N} q_j)$ with respect to q_i. Therefore, $\pi_i(q)$ is concave in q_i for all q such that $f(Q) > 0$, because it is a sum of two concave functions: $q_i f(Q)$ and $-C_i(q_i)$.

On the Cournot model, see his own description (1838: Chapter 7), and more recent expositions such as Fellner (1949: Chapter 2) and Friedman (1977: Chapter 2, 1983: Chapter 2). In time-honored fashion, Cournot discussed stability in a way that helped confuse later readers about whether he was dealing with a strictly static, one-shot model or a multiperiod model. For our present purpose, I treat the model as strictly one period. Thus, each firm knows the inverse demand function and the cost functions of all firms. For each firm i, strategy is simply an output level, q_i. In principle, the firm's strategy set can be $[0, \infty)$; however, in practice, a finite upper bound can be invoked. The market operates very simply: The n firms simultaneously choose output levels $q_1, \ldots, q_n$. These determine the profits of all firms. There is no past history of behavior to guide the firms, nor is there any future to concern them. *Cournot's concept of equilibrium* in this market is characterized by an output vector q^c such that no single firm could have greater profits by having selected an output level different from q_i^c, given the output levels of the others. That is, $\pi_i(q^c) \geqslant \pi_i(q^c \backslash q_i)$ for all admissible q_i and all $i \in N$. Clearly, this is the Nash equilibrium in a game where each firm is a player, the π_i are the payoff functions, q_i is the strategy of player i, and some subset of $[0, \infty)$ is each firm's strategy set.

From the foregoing description, it may not be evident that this model actually has a Nash equilibrium. To verify existence of equilibrium, it is sufficient to prove that the model satisfies the assumptions of an existence theorem such as the corollary to Theorem 2.4. To this end, the firms' strategy spaces must be carefully defined. The strategy space of each firm i will consist of an interval $[0, q_1^0]$ where $q_i^0 < \infty$. Although a firm can, in principle, select any nonnegative output level, there are output levels so high that they cannot, under any circumstances, be best replies. Thus q_i^0 must be chosen so that any larger output level would never be a best reply. By Condition 2.3, $Qf(Q)$ is bounded above; therefore, let z^* be its least upper bound. Now let q_i^0 be defined by $z^* = q_i^0 \varepsilon$ or $q_i^0 = z^*/\varepsilon$, where ε is the lower bound on marginal cost. Then clearly for $q_i > q_i^0$, the firm's revenue must fall short of its total variable cost and the firm would never, in equilibrium, choose such a large output. Because z^* is finite and $\varepsilon > 0$, q_i^0 is finite.

Some demand functions touch the quantity axis. That is, there may be a finite output level, Q^*, for which $f(Q^*) = 0$ and $f(Q) > 0$ if $Q < Q^*$. Clearly, $q_i^0 \leqslant Q^*$. If $f(Q) > 0$ for all positive Q, then $Q^* = \infty$.

Therefore, it is reasonable to take $S_i = [0, q_i^0]$ as the strategy set of player i and to let $S = \times_{i \in B} S_i$. Now suppose that $\pi_i(q)$ is defined for all $q_i \in T_i = S \cap \{q \in R^n \mid \sum_{i \in N} q_i \leqslant Q^*\}$. Figure 2.5 illustrates possible sets T_i. Clearly, Assumptions 2.1, 2.2', and 2.3' are satisfied: $S_i = [0, q_i^0]$ is compact and convex, $\pi_i(q)$ is defined, continuous, and bounded for all $q \in T_i$, and $\tau_i(q) = \{t_i \in S_i \mid (q \backslash t_i) \in T_i\}$ is nonempty, closed, and convex for all $q \in S$. Finally, $\pi_i(q \backslash t_i)$ is concave in $t_i \in \tau_i(q)$ for all $q \in S$. Therefore, from the corollary to Theorem 2.4, the market has a Cournot equilibrium.

As a numerical example, let $n = 2$, $p = 100 - 4Q + 3Q^2 - Q^3$, $C_1(q_1) =$

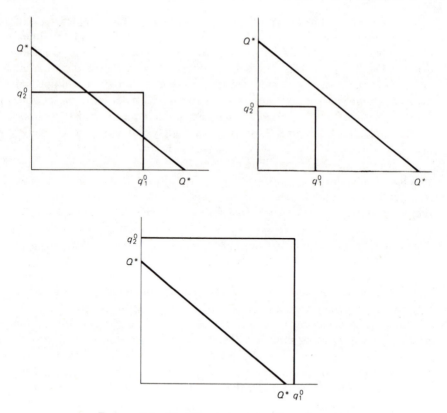

FIGURE 2.5   Possible strategy sets for a duopoly.

$4q_1$, and $C_2(q_2) = 2q_2 + .1q_2^2$. Then,

$$\pi_1(q) = 96q_1 - 4q_1(q_1 + q_2) + 3q_1(q_1 + q_2)^2 - q_1(q_1 + q_2)^3 \qquad (2.38)$$
$$\pi_2(q) = 98q_2 - 4q_1q_2 - 4.1q_2^2 + 3q_2(q_1 + q_2)^2 - q_2(q_1 + q_2)^3 \qquad (2.39)$$

As the reader can verify, the Cournot equilibrium occurs at the solution of the equations

$$\frac{\partial \pi_1}{\partial q_1} = 96 - 8q_1 - 4q_2 + 6q_1(q_1 + q_2) + 3(1 - q_1)(q_1 + q_2)^2 - (q_1 + q_2)^3 = 0$$
$$(2.40)$$

$$\frac{\partial \pi_2}{\partial q_2} = 98 - 4q_1 - 8.2q_2 + 6q_2(q_1 + q_2) + 3(1 - q_2)(q_1 + q_2)^2 - (q_1 + q_2)^3 = 0$$
$$(2.41)$$

which is $q^c = (2.028, 2.081)$.

There is a second way that Cournot oligopoly could be treated; however, it requires replacing Assumption 2.3' (the concavity of P_i in s_i) with a weaker statement: quasiconcavity of P_i in s_i. $P_i(s)$ is a *quasiconcave function* of s_i if the set

$$\{t_i \in S_i \mid P_i(s \backslash t_i) = \max_{t_i' \in S_i} P_i(s \backslash t_i')\} \qquad (2.42)$$

is convex for any $s \in S$. Then a theorem based on assumptions 2.1 and 2.2 and quasiconcavity can be used (see Friedman, 1977, Theorem 7.1). It is understood that $f(Q) = 0$ for $Q > Q^*$ and the strategy sets are $S_i = [0, q_i^0]$ for all i. Profit functions are defined everywhere on S.

7.2 General competitive exchange equilibrium

Now a Walrasian model of a general competitive exchange economy is analyzed as a noncooperative pseudogame. In brief, a Walrasian pure trade model is made of the following ingredients: There is a set $N' = \{1, \ldots, n\}$ of consumers. Each consumer is endowed with a bundle of consumption goods $w^i \in R^m_+$. Markets exist in which consumers can trade, selling any portion of their endowments in exchange for whatever they wish, at fixed prices $p \in R^m_{++}$. Letting x^i denote the final consumption bundle of consumer i, trading is limited by the conditions $x^i \geq 0$ and $pw^i = px^i$. The former requires that quantities be nonnegative, and the latter is the conventional budget constraint. Equilibrium is characterized by a price vector p^* such that, at p^*, $\sum_{i \in N'} w^i = \sum_{i \in N'} x^i$, and the consumption bundle x^i maximizes the utility of each consumer $i \in N'$, relative to his budget constraint (i.e., markets clear in equilibrium, and each consumer has optimized).

Approaching this model as a noncooperative pseudogame is natural in one respect, yet strange in another. In a competitive economy, each agent is assumed to choose her action (strategy) from her set of available alternatives so as to maximize her objective function (payoff). This is clearly noncooperative. A pillar of competitive economics, indeed the element defining the term *competitive*, is that the actions of one agent have no effect on the opportunities facing any other agent. In a pure trade model, such as that examined below, having no effect on the opportunities of others means that (a) the endowment of a consumer is fixed, independently of the actions of others, and (b) no single agent can affect prices. Thus, the player interactions that are generally present in non-cooperative games, which many regard as a distinguishing characteristic of such games, are absent. Nonetheless, a competitive economy can certainly be regarded as a noncooperative pseudogame, although in certain respects, a simple one. The model set out below and the game theoretic approach are based on the classic article by Arrow and Debreu (1954).

Approaching a competitive economy as a noncooperative pseudogame provides another means of proving existence of equilibrium; however, in taking this approach, a means must be built into the pseudogame for price determination. This is done by the addition of another player, player 0, whose objective function and strategy space are described below. Thus, the set of players becomes $N = \{0, 1, \ldots, n\}$. Before describing player 0, the consumers' payoff functions and strategy sets are described. The preferences of consumer i are represented by the utility function $u_i(x^i)$ where $u_i(x^i)$ is scalar valued and $x^i \in R^m_+$ is a commodity bundle. The utility function u_i is defined for all $x^i \in R^m_i$ and, if $x^i, y^i \in R^m_+$ then $u_i(x^i) \geq u_i(y^i)$ means that x^i

is preferred or indifferent to y^i. Suppose, further, that u_i is concave, continuous, and finite valued for finite x^i. The vector $w^i \in R_+^m$ is the endowment of player i, and $w^0 = \sum_{i \in N} w^i$ is the total endowment of the economy. The individual consumer, facing prices $p \in R_{++}^m$, is regarded as having a budget set $B(p, w^i) = \{x^i \in R_+^m \mid px^i \le pw^i\}$. Thus, $B(p, w^i)$ is the set of commodity bundles costing no more than the value of player i's endowment when prices are p.

Player 0, the price chooser, is fictitious in the sense that he does not correspond to an actual maximizing economic agent in the usual Walrasian model, but he is a useful artifact. Player 0 chooses a price vector $p \in \Phi = \{p \in R_{++}^m \mid \sum_{i \in N} p_i = 1\}$ and wishes to minimize the extent to which the economy is out of equilibrium. If $(x^1, \ldots, x^n)$ are chosen by the consumers, $x^0 = \sum_{i \in N} x^i$ is the aggregate demand of consumers. Excess supply of good j in the economy is $w_j^0 - x_j^0$. The sum of the value of (positive) excess supplies in the economy is $\sum_{j=1}^m p_j \max\{w_j^0 - x_j^0, 0\}$. It is this value that player 0 seeks to minimize. An alternative version of the objective function of player 0 is $\sum_{j=1}^m p_j \min\{(x_j^0 - w_j^0), 0\}$. This is the negative of the preceding formulation (i.e., it is the negative of the value of aggregate excess supplies), and player 0 would wish to maximize it.

Returning to the consumers, it is well known that for any $p \gg 0$, there is a solution to the following consumer's problem: $\max u_i(x^i)$ subject to $x^i \in B(p, w^i)$. If u_i is strictly concave, the x^i that achieves the maximum is unique. If weak concavity holds, then, for a given (p, w^i), there is a nonempty, convex set of consumption bundles, denoted $d^i(p, w^i)$, which maximize utility. $d^i(p, w^i)$ is called the *demand correspondence*. Thus, $d^i(p, w^i) \subset R_+^m$ and $y^i \in d^i(p, w^i)$ if and only if $u_i(y^i) = \max_{x^i \in B(p, w^i)} u_i(x^i)$.

The purpose of the following formulation is to use the noncooperative equilibrium concept and the corollary to Theorem 2.4 as tools to prove existence of a competitive equilibrium. The pseudogame is defined by Conditions 2.4 to 2.6.

CONDITION 2.4 $u_i(x^i)$ *is a concave and strictly increasing utility function defined on R_+^m and satisfying nonsatiation. Let $d^i(p, w^i)$ be the demand correspondence for consumer i, defined for all $p \in \Phi$, and let $z_j^i(p, w^i) = \inf\{y_j \mid y \in d^i(p, w^i)\}$. $z_j^i(p, w^i)$ is the greatest lower bound on the demand for good j by consumer i when prices are p and endowment is w^i. For any $\{p^l\} \in \Phi$ such that $p^l \to p^0$ and $p_j^0 = 0$, $z_j^i(p^l, w^i) \to +\infty$ as $l \to \infty$.*

This condition establishes two things. First, the payoff function of player i ($\ne 0$) is continuous in all strategies and concave in the strategy of player i. The continuity with respect to other players' strategies is trivial because these other strategies do not enter the payoff function. Second, the demand for a good goes to infinity as the price of that good goes to zero, which ensures that individual prices close to zero need not be considered. They can never arise in equilibrium because markets cannot clear. This is important in assuring compact strategy sets, as seen in Condition 2.6. Let $z_j^0(p, w) = \sum_{i \in N'} z_j^i(p, w^i)$ where $w = (w^1, \ldots, w^n)$ and let $\varepsilon > 0$ satisfy

$z_j^0(p, w) > w_j^0$ if $p \in \Phi$ and $p_j < \varepsilon$, for $j = 1, \ldots, m$. That is, if $p_j < \varepsilon$ then the aggregate demand for good j must exceed the aggregate endowment of that good, and the market for good j cannot clear. Condition 2.4 guarantees that such an ε can be found.

CONDITION 2.5 *The strategy set of player 0 is* $S_0 = \{p \in \Phi \mid p_j \geq \varepsilon, j = 1, \ldots, m\}$, *and his payoff function is* $\sum_{j=1}^m p_j \min\{(x_j^0 - w_j^0), 0\}$.

CONDITION 2.6 *The strategy set of player* $i > 0$ *is* $S_i = \bigcup_{p \in S_0} B(p, w^i)$. *The payoff function of player* $i > 0$, $P_i(p, x^1, \ldots, x^n)$, *is defined on the set* $T_i = \{(p, x^1, \ldots, x^n) \mid p \in S_0, x^i \in B(p, w^i)\}$, *and* $P_i(p, x^1, \ldots, x^n) = u_i(x^i)$.

A pseudogame satisfying Conditions 2.4 to 2.6 also satisfies Assumptions 2.1, 2.2′, and 2.3′; hence the corollary to Theorem 2.4 can be applied, and an equilibrium point to this game is a competitive equilibrium. The converse is also true: A competitive equilibrium in this model is an equilibrium point to the game. To see the latter, suppose that $(p, y^1, \ldots, y^n)$ is a competitive equilibrium. Then, $u_i(y^i) = \max_{x^i \in B(p, w^i)} u_i(x^i)$ for $i \in N$. This may also be stated in the form $y^i \in d^i(p, w^i)$, $i \in N$. The demand correspondence d^i is, of course, the best reply mapping of player $i > 0$. Because markets clear at a competitive equilibrium, $x_j^0 = w_j^0$ for all j and $\sum_{j=1}^m p_j \min\{(x_j^0 - w_j^0), 0\} = 0$, which is clearly the maximum value of player 0's payoff function. Now, to see that an equilibrium point is a competitive equilibrium, suppose that $(p, y^1, \ldots, y^n)$ is an equilibrium point. Then, clearly $y^i \in d^i(p, w^i)$, otherwise, consumer i would not be choosing a best reply. Let $y^0 = \sum_{i=1}^n y^i$, and suppose that $\sum_{j=1}^m p_j \min\{(y_j^0 - w_j^0), 0\} < 0$. Then, for at least one value of j, say j^*, $y_{j^*}^0 < w_{j^*}^0$. This follows from Walras' law, which states that $\sum_j p_j(y_j^0 - \omega_j^0) = \sum_j p_j(\sum_i y_j^i - \sum_i w_j^i) = \sum_i [\sum_j (p_j y_j^i - p_j w_j^i)] = 0$. Note that if $y_j^0 = w_j^0$ does not hold for all j, then there must be at least one market j^* in which $y_{j^*}^0 < w_{j^*}^0$ and at least one j^{**} in which $y_{j^{**}}^0 > w_{j^{**}}^0$. Furthermore, $p_{j^*} > \varepsilon$ due to Condition 2.4. Therefore, p is not a best reply to $(y^1, \ldots, y^n)$. The price vector p' yields a higher value of the payoff function of player 0 than does p, where $p_j' = p_j$ for $j \neq j^*, j^{**}$, $p_{j^*}' = \varepsilon$, and $p_{j^{**}}' = p_{j^*} + p_{j^{**}} - \varepsilon$. Thus, if $(p, y^1, \ldots, y^n)$ is an equilibrium point, it is also a competitive equilibrium. For a general treatment of competitive equilibrium see Hildenbrand and Kirman (1976) or Debreu (1959).

As a numerical example, imagine an economy with two commodities, apples and oranges, and 10 consumers. Table 2.8 gives the utility functions and endowments for the consumers. The typical consumer, holding w_1^i of apples and w_2^i of oranges, seeks to maximize the utility function $u_i(x_1^i, x_2^i) = x_1^i(x_2^i)^a$ subject to the budget constraint $p_1 w_1^i + p_2 w_2^i = p_1 x_1^i + p_2 x_2^i$. From the budget constraint, $x_1^i = w_1^i + (w_2^i - x_2^i)p_2/p_1$. Using this in the utility function, consumer i wishes to maximize

$$[w_1^i + (w_2^i - x_2^i)p_2/p_1][x_2^i]^a \qquad (2.43)$$

TABLE 2.8   A competitive economy

Consumer	Utility	Endowment		Demand at $(\frac{1}{3}, \frac{2}{3})$	
		Apples	Oranges	Apples	Oranges
1	$x_1 x_2^{10}$	5	3	1	5
2	$x_1 x_2^{8}$	6	6	2	8
3	$x_1 x_2^{5}$	8	2	2	5
4	$x_1 x_2^{3}$	6	1	2	3
5	$x_1 x_2^{3/2}$	16	2	8	6
6	$x_1 x_2^{2/3}$	16	2	12	4
7	$x_1 x_2^{1/3}$	2	7	12	2
8	$x_1 x_2^{1/5}$	8	5	15	1.5
9	$x_1 x_2^{1/8}$	4	7	16	1
10	$x_1 x_2^{1/10}$	9	1	10	.5

with respect to x_2^i. Solving this gives

$$x_1^i = \frac{1}{1 + a}\,(w_1^i + p_2 w_2^i / p_1) \tag{2.44}$$

$$x_2^i = \frac{a}{1 + a}\,(p_1 w_1^i / p_2 + w_2^i) \tag{2.45}$$

It is easily verified that $p = (\frac{1}{3}, \frac{2}{3})$ is an equilibrium price vector. Demands at this price vector are shown in the last two columns of Table 2.8. At $p = (\frac{1}{3}, \frac{2}{3})$ the objective function of player 0 is equal to zero, but, away from an equilibrium, her objective function would be strictly negative.

7.3   The free rider problem

The free rider problem concerns a conflict between individual incentives and Pareto optimality. This conflict arises when a group of people are concerned with the provision of a public good, and each person knows only her own preferences. No one knows the preferences of any other person; hence, each is dependent on the information that others voluntarily provide concerning the value to them of the public good and concerning their willingness to pay toward its cost.

Consider the following example: Twenty neighbors jointly own a piece of land on which they may build a swimming pool. Suppose that the pool must, of necessity, be open for all 20 to use (exclusion is impossible), and that it is sufficiently large that there are no congestion effects. Assume that the pool will cost $200,000 and that each person i has a value V_i which he or she attaches to the pool. That is, person i is indifferent between (a) his or her original income and no pool, and (b) a diminution in his or her income of V_i and obtaining the pool. Clearly, if $\sum_{i=1}^{n} V_i > 200,000$, it would be possible to build the pool with person i contributing w_i toward its cost and leave everyone better off than they would be without the pool. This requires that $w_i < V_i$ for all i and $\sum_{i=1}^{n} w_i = 200,000$. Each person knows that $V_i \geq 0$ for all persons, and w_i must be nonnegative.

Now imagine that each person actually values the pool at $V_i = \$15,000$, that each is asked to state a valuation, w_i, and the pool is built if and only if $\sum_i w_i \geq \$200,000$. Thus, the total true valuation of $300,000 greatly exceeds its cost. Imagine now the position of one person i. If $\sum_{j \neq i} w_j \geq 200,000$, then the pool is built no matter what value player i announces for w_i, and the optimal value for player i is $w_i = 0$. Similarly, if $\sum_{j \neq i} w_j < 185,000$ the person cannot cause the pool to be built unless he or she announces a contribution high enough to make himself worse off, and $w_i = 0$ is still optimal. If $185,000 \leq \sum_{j \neq i} w_j < 200,000$, then the ideal amount for person i to announce is $w_i = 200,000 - \sum_{j \neq i} w_j$, just enough to ensure that the pool is built. In general, this amount is less than V_i, thus the narrowly selfish incentive of each person is almost surely to understate the true value the pool has for him.

This can be illustrated with an elaboration of the pool example. Suppose person i regards the total bids of the others $(\sum_{j \neq i} w_j)$ as a random variable that has a rectangular distribution over the interval from a to $a + b$. Suppose, too, that the cost of the pool is $a + kb$, where $k \in (0, 1)$, and the value of the pool to person i, V_i, is independent of his or her income level. Then person i's subjective probability estimate that the pool will be built, as a function of his or her own bid, w_i, is $[(1 - k)b + w_i]/b$. If u_i^* is the utility he or she achieves with no pool and $u_i^* + V_i - w_i$ is his or her utility if the pool is built and he or she pays w_i, then person i's expected utility is

$$u_i^* + \frac{(1 - k)bV_i + [V_i - (1 - k)b]w_i - w_i^2}{b} \tag{2.46}$$

If $V_i \leq (1 - k)b$, the optimal value of w_i is zero. Otherwise it is $w_i = [V_i - (1 - k)b]/2$. Note that $(1 - k)b$ is the difference between the cost of the pool $(a + kb)$ and the largest aggregate amount that person i believes the others would bid $(a + b)$. Thus, even with $k = 1$, the highest bid that would be rational for person i is $V_i/2$. While this is merely a simple example, not a general theory, it illustrates the force of the free rider problem.

Ideally, a solution to this problem would be a means, or mechanism, of decision that would encourage each person to truthfully state her valuation of the pool and, along with this, devise a schedule of contributions (taxes) t_i such that $t_i \leq V_i$ for all i and $\sum_{i=1}^{20} t_i = 200,000$. All this is too much to ask; however, some limited progress is described below.

Imagine the following variant of the swimming pool situation described above: $N = \{1, \ldots, n\}$ is the set of economic agents (e.g., the neighbors).

Each person i announces a valuation $s_i \in S_i = R$. The valuation is for a specific proposal consisting of the swimming pool plus a system of taxes $t = (t_1, \ldots, t_n)$ to pay for it. The aggregate tax, $\sum_{i \in N} t_i$ is just equal to the cost of the public good. Supposing that V_i is the value of the pool to person i, then her or his value for the proposal (pool with tax plan t) is $v_i = V_i - t_i$. Clearly, the situation here is a noncooperative game of incomplete information. It remains to describe the payoff functions of the players. These will specify actual payments and a decision on the public project as functions of the strategies chosen by the players. These payoff functions, along with the decision and tax rules, embody a *Groves mechanism*, which is a structure under which telling the truth is always a best choice. Consequently, announcing v_i will maximize the utility of player i, no matter what other players select. On Groves mechanisms and incentive compatibility, see Green and Laffont (1979, part II), Tideman and Tullock (1976), or Groves and Ledyard (1977). Thus, $v = (v_1, \ldots, v_n) \in S$ is a Nash equilibrium for the game, no matter how each player contemplates the payoff functions of the others. That is, there are special features of the game that make it irrelevant to the analysis that there is incomplete information. In essence, this is achieved by making the payoff of a player dependent on the way her or his actions affect the others.

There are two caveats concerning Groves mechanisms. First, the sum of revenues collected for a project need not equal the cost of the project. The dominant strategy property (that truth telling is best) is lost if budget balance is forced to occur. The second is that truth telling need not remain optimal if two or more players can collude.

Specifically, let $f_i(s)$ be a function such that, for all $s \in S$ and all $s_i' \in S_i, f_i(s) = f_i(s \backslash s_i')$. In other words, f_i depends on all the s_j $(j \neq i)$, but does not vary with s_i. The project is adopted if and only if $\sum_{j \in N} s_j \geq 0$; hence the payoff function of player i is

$$P_i(s) = f_i(s) + v_i + \sum_{j \neq i} s_j \qquad \text{if } \sum_{j \in N} s_j < 0$$

$$= f_i(s) \qquad\qquad\qquad \text{if } \sum_{j \in N} s_j < 0 \qquad (2.47)$$

The game, then, is described by (N, S, P). Interestingly, v_i is a best reply to any $s \in S$. That is, $P_i(s \backslash v_i) \geq P_i(s)$ for all $s \in S$ and all $i \in N$. Such a strategy is called a *dominant strategy*. To see that v_i is a best reply under all circumstances, consider the best reply mapping of player i:

$$r_i(s) = \left\{ s_i' \in S_i \mid s_i' \geq -\sum_{j \neq i} s_j \right\} \qquad \text{if } v_i + \sum_{j \neq i} s_j \geq 0$$

$$= \left\{ s_i' \in S_i \mid s_i' < -\sum_{j \neq i} s_j \right\} \qquad \text{if } v_i + \sum_{j \neq i} s_j < 0 \qquad (2.48)$$

Clearly, $v_i \in r_i(s)$ in either case; therefore, $v \in S$ is an equilibrium point of the game.

There are several ways in which this model fails to satisfy the usual assumptions for noncooperative games. (a) the strategy sets are not compact, (b) the payoff functions P_i are discontinuous at $s_i = -\sum_{j \neq i} s_j$, and (c) each player knows nothing about the payoff functions of the other players. These three differences do not prevent the model from having at least one equilibrium point due to the special structure of the model.

It is interesting to examine more closely the utility functions appearing in the free rider game just discussed. To do this, a slightly more general approach is now taken. Suppose that there are m private goods, $1, \ldots, m$, and that good 0 is the swimming pool. Let $x^i = (x_1^i, \ldots, x_n^i)$ so that the complete consumption bundle for consumer i is (x_0, x^i) where $x_0 = 1$ or 0 according to whether the pool is $(x_0 = 1)$ or is not $(x_0 = 0)$ obtained. Suppose $p = (p_1, \ldots, p_m)$, the prices of private goods, are unaffected by the swimming pool decision. In general, the representation of preferences would be by means of a utility function, $U_i(x_0, x^i)$ that depended on the commodity bundle that a player actually consumed; however, the requirement that the value of the pool to person i is independent of the rest of his or her consumption bundle places additional restrictions on the form of U_i. To make these restrictions clear, an indirect utility function is first derived. Suppose x_0, p, and income M_i is given. The consumer then seeks to maximize $U_i(x_0, x^i)$ with respect to x^i and subject to a conventional budget constraint: $M_i = px^i$. A result of this process is that, for each (x_0, p, M_i) there is a maximum attainable utility level summarized in the indirect utility function $u_i(x_0, p, M_i)$. Supposing U_i to be strictly concave and letting $d^i(x_0, p, M_i)$ denote the consumer's demand system, then the functions U_i and u_i are related by

$$U_i(x_0, d^i(x_0, p, M_i)) = u_i(x_0, p, M_i) \tag{2.49}$$

The value of the swimming pool to consumer i, given prices p and an income M_i, where M_i is the income that the consumer will have available for spending on private goods if there is no pool, is $\phi_i(p, M_i)$, defined by

$$u_i(0, p, M_i) = u_i(1, p, M_i - \phi_i(p, M_i)) \tag{2.50}$$

On the left in equation (2.50) is the utility level that the consumer will achieve in the absence of a pool. On the right is the same utility level, which is achieved at an income of $M_i - \phi_i(p, M_i)$. Thus, if the consumer pays $\phi_i(p, M_i)$ for the pool, he or she is indifferent between the two situations. Suppose that the form of u_i is

$$u_i(x_0, p, M_i) = a_i x_0 + M_i \theta_i(p) \tag{2.51}$$

Then the equation defining $\phi_i(p, M_i)$ is

$$M_i \theta_i(p) = a_i + [M_i - \phi_i(p, M_i)]\theta_i(p) \tag{2.52}$$

or

$$\phi_i(p, M_i) = \frac{a_i}{\theta_i(p)} \tag{2.53}$$

If ϕ_i is to be independent of income, which is all we require, then equation

(2.51) puts sufficient restrictions on the utility functions. Utility in the form of equation (2.51) is a rather strong assumption. Since prices are constant throughout this discussion, let $a_i/\theta_i(p) = V_i$. V_i is the value of the pool. Recalling that a utility function will continue to represent the same preferences when divided by a positive constant, equation (2.51) can be divided by $\theta_i(p)$ leaving $u_i(x_0, p, M_i) = V_i x_0 + M_i$ as the utility function.

Now consider a proposal to build the swimming pool and to finance it with payments $t = (t_1, \ldots, t_n)$. The sum $\sum_{i \in N} t_i$ is the cost of the pool. Each person i is asked to state an amount w_i with the understanding that the project will be undertaken if $\sum_{i \in N} w_i \geq 0$, and that each person i will receive $\sum_{j \neq i} w_j$ if the project is undertaken. Thus the utility function of person i is

$$
\begin{aligned}
&M_i && \text{if} \sum_{j \in N} w_j < 0 \\
&M_i + (V_i - t_i) + \sum_{j \neq i} w_j && \text{if} \sum_{j \in N} w_j \geq 0
\end{aligned}
\tag{2.54}
$$

That is, the status quo is entirely maintained if $\sum_{j \in N} w_j < 0$ and the project is not undertaken; however, if the project is undertaken, person i receives the benefit of it (V_i) minus his preassigned tax (t_i) and plus another sum determined by the strategies announced by the other players.

The interesting feature of this scheme is that player i can do no better than to announce $w_i = V_i - t_i$, which is the true net benefit to him of the project. To see this, note that player i's utility does not depend on w_i, except with respect to whether the project is undertaken. That is, for all w_i such that $\sum_{j \in N} w_j \geq 0$, the utility is $M_i + (V_i - t_i) + \sum_{j \neq i} w_j$. Player i benefits from having the project undertaken if and only if $M_i + (V_i - t_i) + \sum_{j \neq i} w_j > M_i$ or $V_i - t_i > -\sum_{j \neq i} w_j$. If w_i is chosen larger than $V_i - t_i$, then the project might be undertaken in circumstances that are worse for player i than no project. Conversely, if $w_i < V_i - t_i$, the project could fail to be adopted in circumstances where player i is better off with it being carried out. Only $w_i = V_i - t_i$ is foolproof.

8   Concluding comments

In this chapter, the basic analytical tool is the noncooperative equilibrium, which is defined for games in which each player knows the payoff functions and strategy spaces of all players. In this setting, equilibrium is characterized by a strategy combination under which each player is maximizing his payoff given the strategies of the other players.

The assumption of complete information is used virtually throughout the chapter; even in the section on incomplete information, the incomplete information equilibrium is found by defining a complete information game whose equilibria have obvious analogues in the incomplete information game. Then these analogue-equilibria are taken to be the equilibrium points of the incomplete information game. Advantages of these incomplete information equilibria are that they are clearly related to the noncooperative equilibrium (for complete information games) and the players have, at equilibrium, beliefs that are mutually consistent. Yet there may be other ways of defining such equilibria that appear equally appealing.

The complete information condition itself may be criticized as being unrealistic; however, complete information is a natural starting point for the investigation of noncooperative games. It is easier to deal with conceptually than incomplete information, the condition is bound to be met in some instances of interest, and it provides a natural benchmark against which to measure incomplete information game equilibria.

Finally, if the assumption of complete information is accepted, at least provisionally, one can question whether the noncooperative equilibrium is appealing in such games. A clear point in its favor is that it is defined by a condition of internal consistency: If the players in a game choose a noncooperative equilibrium point combination, then no player, ex post, will see that she could have gotten a larger payoff by selecting a different strategy. This is good, and, indeed, in many particular games, it may be an overriding concern. But note that the attractiveness of the equilibrium rests, in part, on the confidence that each player must have that every other player will (a) approach the game in the same way and (b) believe that all players believe that they will all approach the game this way. The Nash approach looks less appealing if players have reason to think that other players may violate either (a) or (b). This issue is addressed in Section 4, Chapter 4.

Another issue arises, even when noncooperative equilibrium behavior is accepted as reasonable, if a game lacks a unique equilibrium point. Supposing that the players cannot meet and discuss which equilibrium to select, there is no reason to suppose they would select a noncooperative equilibrium strategy combination; each player may choose a strategy assuming a different equilibrium point as the outcome. This problem is absent when the equilibrium is unique or when the game is a strictly competitive two-person game; however, many games fail to fall into either of these categories.

In summary, the noncooperative equilibrium is not free from disadvantages, but, at the same time, it has appealing characteristics. In this, it is like most of what is best in economic theory; it is a useful and interesting tool that provides genuine, important insights, but, at the same time, there is considerable scope to improve on or supplement it.

Exercises

1. For the following two-person, zero-sum games, find the value and the equilibrium strategies.

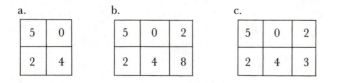

a.

5	0
2	4

b.

5	0	2
2	4	8

c.

5	0	2
2	4	3

2. The "Prisoners' Dilemma" is a game in which each of two players has two pure strategies, confess (C) and maintain innocence (I). The two players are criminals who have committed a crime together and who are being separately grilled by the police. Thus, they are moving simultaneously in a game having one move per player. If both choose I, their payoffs are 15 each (in utility terms), corresponding to conviction on a minor charge. If both confess, they get quite harsh treatment, receiving 5 utility units each. If one confesses and the other does not, the payoffs are 20 and 0, respectively. In this case, the police will let the confessor off free and throw the book at the other. Make a game tree for this game.

3. In the following bimatrix game, player one chooses the row and receives the first payoff in a payoff pair. Find an equilibrium point for the game.

5, 0	0, 8
2, 6	4, 5

4. Suppose a game in strategic form is given by (N, S, P) where $N = \{1, 2\}$, $S_1 = [0, 100]$, $S_2 = [0, 100]$, $P_1(s) = 25s_1 - 4s_1^2 + 15s_1s_2$, and $P_2(s) = 100s_2 - 50s_1 - s_2^2 - s_1s_2$. What is the best reply mapping? Find an equilibrium point for the game.

5. Suppose the conditions in problem 4, except that $S_1 = [0, 30]$. Find an equilibrium point for the game.

6. Suppose a game (N, S, P) given by $N = \{1, 2\}$, $S_1 = [10, 20]$, $S_2 = [0, 15]$, $P_1(s) = 40s_1 + 5s_1s_2 - 2s_1^2$, and $P_2(s) = 50s_2 - 3s_1s_2 - s_2^2$. What is the best reply mapping? Find an equilibrium point.

7. Can any of the theorems on the uniqueness of noncooperative equilibrium be used to prove uniqueness in problems 4, 5, or 6?

Notes

1. Although game theory books usually include a treatment of the expected utility theorem due to von Neumann and Morgenstern, I am taking that material for granted here. On the one hand, the theorem is of great interest apart from its uses in game theory and is commonly taught in microeconomics courses. On the other hand, finite games, where the theorem mainly comes into play, are a minor part of this book. Readers wishing to refresh their memories on the expected utility theorem could read Luce and Raiffa (1957, Chapter 2), Varian (1978, Sections 3.13 to 3.15), or Arrow (1971).

2. A finite two-person, strictly competitive game is a *bimatrix game* and is characterized by a pair of $m \times n$ payoff matrices A and B. A is the payoff matrix of player 1, and B is the payoff matrix of player 2. The requirement of strict competitiveness takes the form $a_{ij} \geqslant a_{kl}$ if and only if $b_{ij} \leqslant b_{kl}$ for all $i, k = 1, \ldots, m$ and all $j, l = 1, \ldots, n$.

3. It goes without saying that one may contemplate noncooperative games in which (a) N is not finite, (b) the $P_i(s)$ are defined on only a (proper) subset of S, (c) the P_i are not concave in s_i, or (d) the game is one of incomplete information. These relaxations of assumptions are discussed in Section 4.

4. I am uncertain whether this game has other equilibrium points than the five listed here; however, I strongly suspect these are all of them.
5. That is,

$$P'(s) = \begin{bmatrix} \partial P_1/\partial s_{11} \\ \vdots \\ \partial P_1/\partial s_{1m} \\ \vdots \\ \partial P_n/\partial s_{n1} \\ \vdots \\ \partial P_n/\partial s_{nm} \end{bmatrix}$$

3

Multiperiod noncooperative games without time dependence

The strategic form of a noncooperative game tends to obscure interesting aspects of how the game is played, aspects that are of paramount importance in many applications. For example, in an infinite horizon oligopoly, economists want to understand what determines the individual choices of the firms within each time period. While it is important to know equilibria exist, it is also important to understand characteristics of equilibrium behavior. Indeed, our usual conception of a game is something like, say, a single hand of poker where a sequence of moves is played, the game ends, and then payoffs are realized. It is a short step from a single hand of poker to a sequence of hands. The sequence itself ought to be viewed as a game, or supergame, whose component parts are games, each having its own structure of moves and payoffs. Naturally, an astute poker player will adopt a strategy that takes account of the connections between distinct poker hands. How one plays in a particular hand (game) can influence the way opponents play in subsequent hands, thus one's play in one hand can affect one's payoffs in later hands.

Two points emerge from this illustration. First, it is not desirable to analyze each hand as if it were totally independent of all others. Second, it is natural to be curious about how the optimal play of a single hand will differ according to whether the single play is the whole game or is one of a long sequence of plays.

1 Introduction

The games studied in this chapter and in Chapter 4 are often called supergames. The word is intended to suggest a sequence of games, finite or infinite in number, that are played by a fixed set of players. A *repeated game* is a supergame in which the same (ordinary) game is played at each iteration. It is central to the study of supergames that all players realize they will play a sequence of games and know that this is common knowledge. Various classes of supergames are investigated in the sections that follow and in Chapter 4. It is clearly possible to model such a sequence in a strategic form and obscure the underlying structure of individual component games; however, it is interesting to retain explicit knowledge of these component games and of the choices made within them. Thus, we are left with a *semiextensive* form in which the move structure is not totally obscured.

The difference between extensive and semiextensive forms lies in the way simultaneous moves are modeled. In the extensive form, players are modeled as if no two players move at the same moment and information sets are used to preserve the appropriate information conditions. In the semiextensive form, the simultaneous moves of the players are modeled as a game in strategic form. Thus, there is a succession of points in time ($t = 0, 1, 2, \ldots$). At each point each player makes a choice. The simultaneous choices at one such time are represented within a (component) game in strategic form and the (super) game is the sequence of these games.

The particularly fascinating feature of supergames is that the set of equilibria in them is greatly, and interestingly, enlarged as compared with the single play of a component game. In particular, the set of noncooperative equilibria of, say, a repeated game, will often include realizations on the payoff possibility frontier which are, in general, unobtainable as equilibrium outcomes in the ordinary game that is being repeated. Luce and Raiffa (1957) noticed this in connection with the Prisoner's Dilemma.

1.1 The repeated prisoners' dilemma

Table 3.1 shows a Prisoners' Dilemma game in which the players are the robbers Bonnie and Clyde. After each robbery, the police bring the two in for questioning, and the table shows their utilities associated with each possible pair of actions they can take. As a game to be played just once, there is a unique equilibrium point: Both players choose *confess* and each receives a payoff of 5. Now consider the repeated game based on Table 3.1, repeated infinitely many times, and suppose each player discounts future payoffs using a discount parameter of .9. To always confess is still an equilibrium point, yielding a supergame payoff of $5(1 + .9 + .9^2 + \ldots) = 50$ to each player. Contrast this with a strategy for Bonnie under which she refuses to confess at the first iteration and continues to refuse in each later

TABLE 3.1 A prisoner's dilemma

Bonnie \ Clyde	Confess	Not confess
Confess	5, 5	15, 0
Not confess	0, 15	10, 10

period if both have in the past also always refused. But if Clyde fails even once to cooperate, Bonnie will revert forever to the safe policy of confessing. If Clyde adopts a parallel strategy, then they can reap 10 units per period and obtain a supergame payoff of 100 each. If Clyde takes advantage of Bonnie's willingness to cooperate, he can get 15 in the first period and will receive 5 in each later period for a supergame payoff of $15 + 5(.9 + .9^2 + ...) = 60$. Clearly it is not in Clyde's interest to follow the latter strategy.

Note that the ability to condition choice in period t on the observed actions of past periods allows Bonnie and Clyde to achieve in a noncooperative equilibrium an outcome normally associated with cooperation (i.e., with collusion and binding agreements). In principle, it is not even necessary that they discuss plans in advance. If each presumes the other will have the good sense to act in this quasi-coopertaive way, their presumptions will be correct, they will be at a noncooperative equilibrium, and they will each receive a payoff of 10 per period.

The first systematic study of these equilibria was done by Aumann (1959, 1961) who proved that *core* (see Chapter 6) outcomes are attainable as noncooperative equilibrium points in repeated games. An earlier qualitative insight into the driving force behind these equilibria comes from David Hume (1739–1740) who writes that

> we can better satisfy our appetites in an oblique and artificial manner, than by their headlong and impetuous motion. Hence I learn to do a service to another, without bearing him any real kindness; because I forsee, that he will return my service, in expectation of another of the same kind, and in order to maintain the same correspondence of good offices with me or with others. And accordingly, after I have serv'd him, and he is in possession of the advantage arising from my action, he is induc'd to perform his part, as foreseeing the consequences of his refusal.

And in describing why people are quite reliable about keeping promises when no legal sanction requires them to do so, and when keeping them is inconvenient or costly, Hume comments

> After these signs [i.e., promises] are instituted, whoever uses them is immediately bound by his interest to execute his engagements, and must never expect to be trusted any more, if he refuse to perform what he promis'd.

1.2 Outline of the chapter

Section 2 is devoted to setting up a basic framework for the study of multiperiod games and to the exposition of some refinements of the noncooperative equilibrium. With respect to the former, information conditions, strategy spaces, and other aspects of multiperiod game models are spelled out, both in strategic and semiextensive forms. Refinements to the equilibrium point have been proposed because there are certain clear-cut circumstances in which games can have intuitively unreasonable, or unacceptable, equilibria. The refinements that are examined below are *subgame perfect equilibrium*, *perfect equilibrium*, and *sequential equilibrium*.

The next several sections deal, in turn, with the models of Section 2, but in semiextensive form. Thus, it will be possible to gain some insight into optimal behavior within individual component games. Section 3 is devoted to *repeated games* and the most straightforward generalization of them. The results of the Bonnie and Clyde example are obtained formally, along with some additional results, for a large class of repeated games.

Section 4 is devoted to repeated games that are repeated only a finite number of times. It has long been thought that such games are inherently the same as single period games (i.e., the games of Chapter 2) in the sense that the only equilibrium points of such a repeated game would necessarily be restricted to repetitions of equilibrium points of the individual game being repeated. In the Prisoners' Dilemma, for example, that would mean the only equilibrium point would be for both players to confess in each iteration of the game. In fact, this long-held belief is not true in general, although it is true for some games. Thus, equilibria like those of Section 3 can occur in some finite horizon repeated games. In addition, Section 4 examines approximate equilibria (ε-equilibria) and it is seen that virtually all finite horizon repeated games can have ε-equilibria that approximate the equilibria of Section 3. Section 5 has a brief description of the recent literature in which the results of Section 3 and 4 are generalized by means of very complicated strategies. Section 6 contains several related applications to oligopoly theory and Section 7 contains concluding comments.

2 Multistage noncooperative games, the strategic form, and refinements of noncooperative equilibrium

The connection between *games* and *supergames*, and the relationship between *extensive* and *semiextensive* forms requires clarification. The names *supergames* and *repeated games* have arisen due to historical accident. The accident is that certain one-move-per-player situations, such as the Cournot oligopoly, have been regarded as games, while multiperiod versions of the same situation have only recently been formally studied. The result is that people think of the single move version as "a game," and the infinite period counterpart becomes labeled as "an infinitely repeated game" or a "supergame." In fact, the single-move Cournot market is one game, and the countably infinite Cournot market is merely another game. Developments in what are called supergames are very important to economists, because the supergame models have often been inspired by, and developed with an eye toward, interesting economic applications. Furthermore, specific results have been obtained that go beyond existence of equilibrium points and specify some characteristics of equilibrium.

The desire to know more than merely whether equilibrium exists has led to using a *semiextensive form* of a game. Recall that the extensive form details the game in a move by move way, so that each individual move appears to take place at a different point in time. No two players move simultaneously; however, the device of information sets allows an extensive form to be logically equivalent to a game in which some moves are simultaneous. Recall, too, that the extensive form is not usually helpful for other than very small, simple games. The semiextensive form utilized below is based on stating strategies in terms of individual moves and on writing payoff functions in terms of individual moves. In the material that follows in this chapter and Chapter 4, the *individual move of player i at time t* is the same as the *ordinary game strategy of player i at time t*. Reference is made to "time t" because the games under study are assumed to have an explicit temporal structure. In each time period, the n players simultaneously select moves. These moves can be interpreted as strategies in a game confined to the current time period. That is, each time period has associated with it a payoff function for each player and a strategy set (set of available moves) for each player. A *repeated game* is a game in which the circumstances of the initial time period (payoff functions and sets of available moves) repeat themselves identically in each succeeding period. Of course, the player does not merely consider each occurrence in isolation; he is interested in his overall payoff over the whole time horizon, and he considers strategies that direct the choices of each individual period's action from this global perspective. These strategies are called supergame strategies to distinguish them from the single period actions.[1]

The definitions pertaining to the structure of supergames are collected in Section 2.1, along with some basic results on existence of equilibrium. The many-move nature of the game introduces a need to refine the Nash equilibrium because certain conceivable Nash equilibria are not plausible. The fundamental refinement, called *perfect equilibrium*, applies to both single-period and many-period games and is discussed in Section 2.2. *Sequential equilibrium*, an interesting relative of perfect equilibrium, is discussed in Section 2.3. Some further refinements of the noncooperative equilibrium are briefly mentioned as well.

2.1 Supergame definitions and a few results

The main purpose of this section is to introduce basic definitions that are used in supergames. Four categories of supergames are distinguished, all of which are supergames without time-dependent structures. The absence of *structural time dependence* means that the payoff associated with a particular time period depends only on the actions of that time period, as in the Bonnie and Clyde example. Note that the absence of structural time dependence does not preclude strategic time dependence. *Strategic time depencence* is present when the action taken in a time period by a player depends on the history of actions in the game to that time.[2] Again, this is illustrated in the Bonnie and Clyde example where the *action* taken at any time can depend on the past actions of all players. The four categories of supergames are the combinations obtainable from finite versus infinite horizons, and from repeated versus nonrepeated games. Clearly, infinite horizon nonrepeated supergames contain the other three categories as special cases. In addition to distinguishing these types of supergame, the role of the information flow in the game is discussed and a basic existence of equilibrium theorem is established.

2.1.1 Repeated games and information rules

Suppose that $\Gamma = (N, S, P)$ is a game in strategic form satisfying Assumptions 2.1 to 2.3, and Rules 2.1 and 2.2 and imagine that the players will engage in this game in each of the time periods $t = 0, 1, 2, \ldots, T$. Assume, too, that each player $i \in N$ discounts the future using the discount parameter $\alpha_i = 1/(1 + r_i)$, where $r_i > 0$ is the discount rate. Letting s_{it} be the strategy chosen by player i in the tth play of the game, and $s_t = (s_{1t}, \ldots, s_{nt})$, the discounted payoff stream to player i is

$$G_i(\sigma) = \sum_{t=0}^{T} \alpha_i^t P_i(s_t), \qquad i \in N \tag{3.1}$$

Allowing the possibility that $T = \infty$, the number of plays can be finite or infinite.

DEFINITION 3.1 *A* **repeated game** *is* $\Gamma = (N, S, P, \alpha, T)$ *where* (N, S, P) *satisfies Assumptions 2.1 to 2.3 and Rules 2.1 and 2.2,* $\alpha = (\alpha_1, \ldots, \alpha_n)$ *satisfies* $\alpha_i \in (0, 1]$ *for all* $i \in N$ *and* T *is nonnegative.* T *can be finite or equal to* $+\infty$.

Something must be specified concerning the flow of information over the time horizon. The player is not actually committed to s_{it} until time t occurs. That is, even if a sequence, $s_{i0}, s_{i1}, s_{i2}, \ldots$ is decided at time 0, the player retains the right at any time t to select *at that moment* any element of S_{it}. Two natural assumptions are: (a) At each play of the game, Rule 2.2 holds and, after s_{it} is chosen for all $i \in N$, then all players are informed of s_t. (b) s_{it} must be chosen for all $i \in N$ and $t = 0, 1, \ldots, T$ before any player is informed of the choices made by the other players. These two assumptions are stated as Rules 3.1 and 3.1', respectively.

RULE 3.1 *At each time* t, *the* s_{it} $(i \in N)$ *are chosen simultaneously; however, for* $t > 0$, s_τ, $\tau = 0, 1, \ldots, t - 1$ *is known to all players.*

RULE 3.1' *At each time* t, *the* s_{it} $(i \in N)$ *are chosen simultaneously. For* $t > 0$, *player* i *knows* $s_{i\tau}$ *but does not know* $s_{j\tau}$ $(j \neq i)$, $\tau = 0, 1, \ldots, t - 1$. *The realized values of* $P_i(s_t)$ *are not revealed to the players until after all choices are made.*

Rules 3.1 and 3.1' have different implications regarding the way the players' strategy spaces should be modeled. Under Rule 3.1', a player accumulates no information as time passes, therefore, her choice at any time t cannot be a function of the previous actions of the other players. Thus, her strategy space is naturally $\mathcal{S}_i = \times_{t=0}^{T} S_{it}$. Let elements of $\mathcal{S}_i$ be denoted σ_i and let $\sigma = (\sigma_1, \ldots, \sigma_n) \in \mathscr{S} = \times_{i \in N} \mathscr{S}_i$. Recalling that the discounted payoff stream in equation (3.1) is denoted $G_i(\sigma)$, $G = (G_1, \ldots, G_n)$, and $(N, \mathscr{S}, G)$ can be used as an alternate notation for (N, S, P, α, T). Under Rule 3.1, the information revealed to each player is the past component game pure strategy combination that was chosen; however, in most games of this chapter, the players do not choose mixed strategies.

THEOREM 3.1   *A repeated game* $\Gamma = (N, S, P, \alpha, T)$ *satisfying Rule 3.1' has a noncooperative equilibrium.* $\sigma^* = (s_0^*, s_1^*, \ldots, s_T^*)$ *is a noncooperative equilibrium of* Γ *if and only if* s_t^* *is a noncooperative equilibrium for the game* (N, S, P), $t = 0, \ldots, T$.

Proof (N, S, P) has an equilibrium point; therefore the theorem is proved if it is shown that σ^* is an equilibrium point of Γ if and only if s_t^* is an equilibrium point of (N, S, P) for all t.

Suppose that s_t^* is an equilibrium point of (N, S, P), $t = 0, \ldots, T$. Let $\sigma_i' \in \mathscr{S}_i$, $\sigma_i' \neq \sigma_i^*$. Then, $P_i(s_t^* \backslash s_{it}') \neq P_i(s_t^*)$ only if $s_{it}' \neq s_{it}^*$. Because the individual iterations of (N, S, P) are structurally independent (i.e., the action of one period s_t does not enter into the payoff functions of any period other than period t), $P_i(s_t^* \backslash s_{it}') \neq P_i(s_t^*)$ means $P_i(s_t^* \backslash s_{it}') < P_i(s_t^*)$. Thus σ^* is an equilibrium point of Γ.

Suppose now that σ^* is an equilibrium point of Γ. If s_t^* were not an equilibrium point of (N, S, P) for some value of t, then there would be a player i who could choose σ_i' with $s_{i\tau}' = s_{i\tau}^*$ for $\tau \neq t$, $P_i(s_t^* \backslash s_{it}') > P_i(s_t^*)$, and $P_i(s_\tau^* \backslash s_{i\tau}') = P_i(s_\tau^*)$ for all $\tau \neq t$. Thus, if s_t^* were not an equilibrium point for (N, S, P) for all t, then σ^* could not be an equilibrium point for $(N, \mathscr{S}, G)$.   QED

This theorem is certainly not surprising; indeed it is trivial. In a supergame composed of independent plays of a game, and with players receiving no information as the game progresses, it is clear that a supergame equilibrium must, of necessity, be a sequence of plays of individual game equilibria. Note that s_t^* need not equal $s_{t'}^*$ as long as both are equilibrium points of (N, S, P). It is interesting to note that an equilibrium point for a game, such as Γ in Theorem 3.1, is still an equilibrium point for an otherwise identical game in which Rule 3.1' is replaced with Rule 3.1. To see why this is true, it is first necessary to contemplate strategy spaces for games under Rule 3.1.

2.1.2 Strategies and strategy spaces for supergames

The most appropriate way to define strategy spaces for the players takes into account all the information the players will have at each decision point and assumes this information will be utilized. Under Rule 3.1, the players will accumulate information on the history of actual period by period choices. Let h_t be the *history of the game* at time t. Then, $h_t = (s_0, s_1, \ldots, s_{t-1})$

where s_τ, $\tau = 0, \ldots, t-1$, is understood to be the actual game move combination chosen in time τ. Then a player i can select her own action in period t as a function of the history of the game to that time. Any *decision function* $v_{it}(h_t)$ is suitable as long as it is defined for all $h_t \in S^t = \times_{\tau=0}^{t-1} S_\tau$ and has values in S_i.

DEFINITION 3.2 *The* **set of decision functions for player** i *at time* $t > 0$ *is* $V_{it} = \{ v_{it} \mid v_{it} : S^t \to S_i \}$.

DEFINITION 3.3 *A* **complete memory supergame strategy** $\sigma_i = (v_{i0}, v_{i1}, v_{i2}, \ldots, v_{iT})$ *is a strategy that satisfies* $v_{i0} \in S_i$, *and* $v_{it} \in V_{it}$, $t = 1, \ldots, T$. *The set of such strategies for player* i *is denoted* $\mathscr{S}_i^*$.

Aside from some self-contained material that deals explicitly with finite games (Sections 2.2.3 and 2.3 of Chapter 3, and Sections 3 and 4 of Chapter 4), the models of Chapter 3 and 4 are based on assumptions under which mixed strategies need not be considered. Thus, it is reasonable to assume that s_{jt} is observable, after it is played, by players $i \neq j$. If mixed strategies were used, then it would be appropriate to define h_t as the history of actual pure moves that were played and to assume that the underlying distributions governing the selection of moves were not observable by other players. The virtue of the space $\mathscr{S}_i^*$ is that it is the natural (pure) strategy space under the information conditions specified in Rule 3.1. In period 0, there is no past history; hence, all a player can do is choose some $s_i \in S_i$. In a later period $t > 0$, a player has seen $(s_0, \ldots, s_{t-1}) = h_t$. Clearly, any function associating h_t with an element of S_i, defined for all $h_t \in S^t$, is imaginable and should not be ruled out. That is, no such function should be thought technically beyond the player's reach.

The elements of the strategy space $\mathscr{S}_i^*$ are often called *closed loop strategies* to connote that the action taken in a period will, in general, depend on information which has become available after the beginning of play. This contrasts with elements of $\mathscr{S}_i$, which are called *open loop strategies*, under which the action chosen by a player i for some period t does not depend on any information that might become available as the game progresses from period 0 to period $t-1$. Of course, under Rule 3.1' no such information accumulates; however, it is possible to contemplate both open and closed loop strategies under Rule 3.1.

DEFINITION 3.4 σ_i *is a* **closed loop strategy** *if* $\sigma_i = (v_{i0}, \ldots, v_{iT})$ *where* $v_{it} \in V_{it}$ *for* $t = 0, \ldots, T$.

Note that $\mathscr{S}^*$ is the largest set of closed loop strategies compatible with Rule 3.1. It is clearly possible to contemplate smaller sets of closed loop strategies that are subsets of $\mathscr{S}^*$ but are larger than $\mathscr{S}$, the set of open loop strategies.

DEFINITION 3.5 σ_i *is an* **open loop strategy** *if* $\sigma_i = (v_{i0}, \ldots, v_{iT})$ *and* $v_{it}(h_t) = v_{it}(h_t')$ *for all* $h_t, h_t' \in S^t$ *and* $t = 0, \ldots, T$.

Open loop strategies are defined here as a special (degenerate) case of closed loop strategies.

DEFINITION 3.6 $\Gamma^* = (N, \mathscr{S}^*, G)$ *is a* **repeated game with closed loop strategies** *if the game* $\Gamma = (N, \mathscr{S}, G)$ *is a repeated game (as given by Definition 3.1),* $\mathscr{S} \subset \mathscr{S}^*$, *and Rule 3.1 holds.*

On the face of it, restricting attention to strategies in $\mathscr{S}$ (i.e., to open loop strategies) when Rule 3.1 holds seems unreasonably restrictive. The player is being prevented from taking explicit advantage of information that will come into his possession; however, for games satisfying Assumptions 2.1 to 2.3 and Rules 2.1, 2.2, and 3.1, a noncooperative equilibrium with the strategy space restricted to $\mathscr{S}$ is still a noncooperative equilibrium when the enlarged strategy space $\mathscr{S}^*$ is considered.

COROLLARY.   *Let* $\Gamma = (N, \mathscr{S}, G)$ *and* $\Gamma^* = (N, \mathscr{S}^*, G)$ *satisfy Assumptions 2.1 to 2.3 and Rules 2.1 and 2.2. Let* Γ *satisfy Rule 3.1' and* Γ^* *satisfy Rule 3.1. Then if* $\sigma^* \in \mathscr{S}$ *is an equilibrium point of* Γ, *it is also an equilibrium point of* Γ^*.

Proof   It suffices to note that, given the σ_j^* $(j \neq i)$, player i could not alter her strategy from σ_i^* and increase her payoff, $i \in N$.   QED

It is vital to this corollary that the players know in advance what the exact payoff functions will be in each future period, and that the intended strategy of each player can be carried out precisely as he plans. If, in each period, a player might face either P_i^0 or P_i^1 as a single-period payoff function, with the realization being randomly determined and announced at the start of each period before that period's action is selected, then an open loop strategy combination would not, in general, be an equilibrium point in a game allowing closed loop strategies. A player could improve on an open loop strategy by selecting a strategy that directed, say $s_{it} = s_i^0$ when P_i^0 is the tth-period payoff function and $s_{it} = s_i^1$ when P_i^1 is the tth-period payoff function.

2.1.3   Existence of equilibrium in supergames

Sections 3 and 4 contain results that are mainly concerned with various special closed loop equilibria. Before turning to these sections, a general theorem on open loop equilibria is stated in a parallel fashion to Theorem 2.4. Theorem 3.2 is stated for a class of games that includes *general supergames without time dependence*. The latter class of games is similar to repeated games with the essential change being that the fixed set of players engages in an arbitrary sequence of ordinary games and the discount rate between two adjacent periods need not be constant over time. Thus, S_{it} need not be the same as $S_{it'}$, $P_{it}(s_t)$ need not be the same function as $P_{it'}(s_{t'})$, and the objective function of the ith player is

$$G_i(\sigma) = \sum_{t=0}^{\infty} \alpha_{it} P_{it}(s_t) \tag{3.2}$$

where α_{it} is the discounted value at $t = 0$ of a unit of payoff from period t.

ASSUMPTION 3.1 *S_{it} is a compact, convex subset of R^{m_i} for $t = 0, 1, \ldots$ and $\mathscr{S}_i$ is the product set $\times_{t=0}^{\infty} S_{it}$. $\mathscr{S} = \times_{i \in N} \mathscr{S}_i$. $S_t = \times_{i \in N} S_{it}$. Based on the topology generated by the norm $\|\sigma_i\| = \Sigma_{t=0}^{\infty} \alpha_{it} \|s_{it}\|$, $\mathscr{S}_i$ is compact.*[3]

ASSUMPTION 3.2 *$G_i(\sigma)$ is a bounded and continuous function from $\mathscr{S}$ to R.*

ASSUMPTION 3.3 *$G_i(\sigma \backslash \sigma_i)$ is concave in σ_i.*

DEFINITION 3.7 *Let $\Gamma = (N, \mathscr{S}, G)$ be a game satisfying Assumptions 3.1 to 3.3 with $N = \{1, \ldots, n\}$ being finite, and $G_i(\sigma)$ defined by equation (3.2) with $\alpha_{it} \in [0, 1)$, $i \in N$, $t = 1, \ldots, \infty$, and $\alpha_{i0} = 1$, $i \in N$. Then Γ is a* **general supergame without time dependence.**

Clearly a supergame satisfying Definition 3.7 consists of a sequence of ordinary games (N, S_t, P_t) with ordinary game payoffs discounted by the elements of $\{\alpha_{it}\}$. This class of games includes finite horizon supergames as a subset (let $\alpha_{it} = 0$ for $i \in N$ and $t > T$), as well as repeated games: Let $P_{it} = P_{i0}$ and $S_{i0} = S_{it}$ for all i and t, and let $\alpha_{it} = \alpha_i^t$ for all i and t if the horizon is infinite; the game is now reduced to a repeated game. For a finite horizon repeated game, the same conditions are used as for an infinite horizon repeated game except that $\alpha_{it} = 0$ for all i and for $t > T$. It is immediate that noncooperative equilibria exist for these games. If s_t^* is an equilibrium point for (N, S_t, P_t), then $\sigma^* = (s_0^*, s_1^*, s_2^*, \ldots)$ is an equilibrium point for a supergame based on $\{(N, S_t, P_t)\}_{t=0}^{\infty}$.

THEOREM 3.2 *A game $\Gamma = (N, \mathscr{S}, G)$ satisfying Assumptions 3.1 to 3.3 has a noncooperative equilibrium.*

A proof can be stated along the lines of the proof of Theorem 2.4 using the fixed point theorem of Fan (1952).

The appropriate strategy space to consider is, of course, the space of closed loop strategies, which are defined by Definitions 3.2 and 3.3. It was remarked in connection with these definitions that such a strategy space as this is too large to work with; however, interesting closed loop equilibria are found in Sections 3 and 4.

2.2 Perfect equilibrium points

There are certain equilibrium points that, on examination, appear implausible. In games where each player has more than one move, some unsatisfactory equilibrium points can be interpreted as utilizing threats that are not credible. In games in strategic form or games of one move per player, an equilibrium point may appear unsatisfactory, because the equilibrium strategy of (at least) one player would be far from optimal if the game were perturbed in a very slight way. To avoid such equilibria, Selten (1975) has proposed a refinement of the Nash equilibrium called *perfect equilibrium*. A perfect equilibrium point is a Nash equilibrium that satisfies some additional properties. Two versions of perfect equilibrium are discussed below. The first, called *subgame perfection*, applies to games of more than one move per player and is covered in Section 2.2.2. The second, sometimes called *trembling hand perfection*, is discussed in Section 2.2.3. The two are related in that a (trembling hand) perfect equilibrium point is always subgame perfect. The converse is not true. Section 2.2.1 contains an example.

2.2.1   *An example illustrating an unsatisfactory equilibrium point*

Consider a two-period repeated game (without discounting) based on the game in Table 3.2. The single period game has one equilibrium point, (a_1, b_1) at which the payoff is 12 to each player. The two-period game is shown in Table 3.3 in strategic form, and the table also lists the complete description of all of the pure strategies of both players. Note that the game in Table 3.3 has six pure strategy equilibrium points. Denoting the kth strategy of player 1 by α_k and the kth strategy of player 2 by β_k, these equilibrium points are (α_1, β_1), (α_2, β_1), (α_1, β_2), (α_2, β_2), (α_3, β_5), and (α_3, β_6). The first four of these points yield payoffs of $(24, 24)$ and the realized actions are (a_1, b_1) in both periods. The last two equilibrium points yield payoffs of $(27, 22)$ and the realized actions are (a_1, b_2) in the first period, followed by (a_1, b_1) in the second.

TABLE   3.2   A   single
stage of a repeated game

	b_1	b_2
a_1	12, 12	15, 10
a_2	9, 5	8, 8

But look closer at these last two equilibrium points. In each, the strategy of player 1, α_3, is *choose a_1 at time 1; in time 2 choose a_1 if player 2 has chosen b_2 for time 1, but choose a_2 if player 2 has chosen b_1 for time 1.* This is an unreasonable outcome, even though it is an equilibrium point, because it could have player 1 behaving against his own interests in the second period. Suppose that player 2 does not select b_2 in the initial period but instead chooses b_1 as the first move of β_1. At the close of period 1, the two players each collect 12, and, for period 2 they face the game displayed in Table 3.2. Even though player 1 has supposedly chosen α_3, if player 2 chooses b_1 in period 1, player 1 will not rationally wish to continue with α_3. She will want to modify her strategy midstream, changing it into α_1. This is because (α_3, β_1) is not an equilibrium strategy combination for the part of the game (the *subgame*) that begins at the end of period 1. Thus neither (α_3, β_5) nor (α_3, β_6) is subgame perfect.

TABLE 3.3   A two-period repeated game in strategic form

	β_1	β_2	β_3	β_4	β_5	β_6	β_7	β_8
α_1	24, 24	24, 24	27, 22	27, 22	27, 22	27, 22	30, 20	30, 20
α_2	24, 24	24, 24	27, 22	27, 22	24, 15	24, 15	23, 18	23, 18
α_3	21, 17	21, 17	20, 20	20, 20	27, 22	27, 22	30, 20	30, 20
α_4	21, 17	21, 17	20, 20	20, 20	24, 15	24, 15	23, 18	23, 18
α_5	21, 17	24, 15	21, 17	24, 15	20, 20	23, 18	20, 20	23, 18
α_6	21, 17	24, 15	21, 17	24, 15	17, 13	16, 16	17, 13	16, 16
α_7	18, 10	17, 13	18, 10	17, 13	20, 20	23, 18	20, 20	23, 18
α_8	18, 10	17, 13	18, 10	17, 13	17, 13	16, 16	17, 13	16, 16

Strategies for Player 1

		Second-period choice if player 2 chose	
Strategy	First-period choice	b_1	b_2
α_1	a_1	a_1	a_1
α_2	a_1	a_1	a_2
α_3	a_1	a_2	a_1
α_4	a_1	a_2	a_2
α_5	a_2	a_1	a_1
α_6	a_2	a_1	a_2
α_7	a_2	a_2	a_1
α_8	a_2	a_2	a_2

Strategies for Player 2

		Second-period choice if player 1 chose	
Strategy	First-period choice	a_1a_1	a_2
β_1	b_1	b_1	b_1
β_2	b_1	b_1	b_2
β_3	b_1	b_2	b_1
β_4	b_1	b_2	b_2
β_5	b_2	b_1	b_1
β_6	b_2	b_1	b_2
β_7	b_2	b_2	b_1
β_8	b_2	b_2	b_2

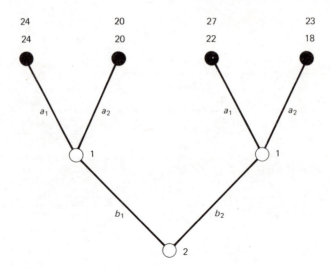

FIGURE 3.1   A game with reasonable and unreasonable Nash equilibria.

This example and the lesson associated with it can be illustrated in a simplified version of the game, shown in extensive form in Figure 3.1. In the figure, only the first move of player 2 and the second move of player 1 are shown. The first move of player 1 is assumed to be a_1 and the second move of player 2 is taken to be the choice that maximizes player 2's payoff.

In this abbreviated version of the game, the strategy of player 1 that incorporates a noncredible threat is play a_2 if b_1 was selected by player 2 and play a_1 if b_2 was selected. Given this strategy for player 1, player 2 is better off with b_2, yielding him 22, than with b_1, yielding him 20. Likewise, for player 1, given that player 2 selects b_2, her strategy nets her 27, the highest payoff available to her. Now note the situation from the vantage point of player 1 if player 2 chooses b_1. Her equilibrium strategy directs her to choose a_2, but the selection of b_1 is a fait accompli and she will attain a larger payoff with a_1 than she will with a_2. Thus the plan to choose a_2 in response to b_1 is not credible because it would not be in the interest of player 1 to do this in the prescribed circumstances. The strategy of player 1 that is intended to result in the payoffs $(27, 22)$ contains a provision that looks like a threat. One can almost hear player 1 saying to player 2. "Choose b_2 in your first move and I will choose a_1 in my second. If you don't do this, I'll punish you by choosing a_2 in my second move." To carry out this threat in the face of player 2 choosing b_1 is like locking the barn after the horse is stolen; it is costly and cannot bring a return to compensate for the cost. As a threat, it is not credible.

2.2.2   Subgame perfect equilibrium points

To avoid such noncredible threats, Selten (1975) has proposed that the strategies of the players should be best replies to one another for each subgame in the game, and a strategy combination obeying this condition is called a *subgame perfect equilibrium*. In playing out a game, there are certain moments such that, from that moment onward, the remainder of the game is, itself, a game. Such a game is a *subgame* of the original game. More formally:

DEFINITION 3.8 *Let* $\Gamma = (N, \mathscr{S}^*, G)$ *be a supergame with a closed loop strategy set and for $t \geq 0$ let b_t be the history of the game through period t. Then the* **subgame of Γ at time t with history** h_t *is described by* (a) *the set of players N,* (b) *the strategy spaces* $\mathscr{S}^*_{ih_t} = \times^\infty_{\tau=t} V_{i\tau}, i \in N$, (c) *the payoff functions* $G_{ih_t} = \Sigma^\infty_{\tau=t} \alpha_{i\tau} P_{i\tau}(s_\tau)$, *and* (d) *the history h_τ. This subgame is denoted* $\Gamma_{h_t} = (N, \mathscr{S}^*_{h_t}, G_{h_t})$.

For example, there are five subgames in the game consisting of two plays of the game in Table 3.2—the original game and four additional games. Each additional subgame is defined relative to the four possible histories (a_1, b_1), (a_1, b_2), (a_2, b_1), and (a_2, b_2).

For $\sigma_i \in \mathscr{S}^*_i$, to say that player i uses $\sigma_i = (v_{i0}, v_{i1}, v_{i2}, \ldots)$ in the subgame Γ_{h_t} means that he chooses $v_{i\tau}(h_\tau)$ for $\tau = t+1, \ldots, \infty$. An alternate terminology is that the strategy combination σ *induces* a strategy combination on the subgame Γ_{h_t}. The induced strategy combination for Γ_{h_t} is $(v_t(h_t), v_{t+1}(h_{t+1}), v_{t+2}(h_{t+2}), \ldots)$.

DEFINITION 3.9 $\sigma^* \in \mathscr{S}^*$ *is a* **subgame perfect equilibrium point** *of Γ if σ^* is an equilibrium point of Γ_{h_t} for $t = 0, 1, \ldots, \infty$ and for all $h_t \in S^t$.*

Under Definition 3.9, σ^* is subgame perfect if it is an equilibrium point for any possible subgame of the original game. That is, the strategy combination induced on Γ_{h_t} by σ^* must be an equilibrium point in each subgame Γ_{h_t}, even if the subgame Γ_{h_t} would never be encountered when σ^* is actually played. This characteristic shows up in the example. Recall that (α_3, β_5) is unsatisfactory because it does not induce equilibrium strategies on the subgame starting from $h_1 = (a_1, b_1)$. On this subgame, (α_3, β_5) calls for (a_2, b_1) to be played, but (a_1, b_1) is the only equilibrium for the subgame. This is important even though the history $h_1 = (a_1, b_1)$ will not be seen if (α_3, β_5) is actually played ($h'_1 = (a_1, b_2)$ will be observed).

It may be of interest to see how one can be at a decision point of a game when the game, from that decision point on, is not a subgame. Recall the way that simultaneous moves are handled in the extensive form: One player is treated as if he moves first, another second, etc. Any player after the first is at an information set that makes it impossible for him to tell what moves were made by the players before him. In terms of the extensive form, the game from one particular decision node (call it the *selected node*) onward is a subgame (a) if the selected node constitutes an information set and (b) if a given node of the game can be reached starting from the selected node, then all nodes in the same information set as the given node can be reached from the selected node. Figure 3.2 provides an illustration. The game from node A is not a subgame because node A is not an information set all by itself. A simultaneous-move, many-period game is at

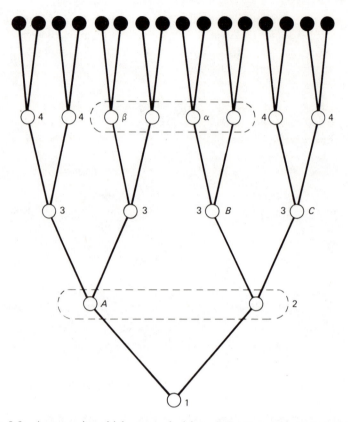

FIGURE 3.2   A game in which some decision nodes are not starting points of subgames.

a node similar to A that violates condition (a) if it is time t and some players have moved while others have not. The game from node B is not a subgame because node α is reachable from B, but node β, in the same information set, is not reachable from B. The game from node C onward is a subgame.

2.2.3   *Trembling-hand, perfect equilibrium points*

Perfect equilibrium points, defined in Selten (1975) for finite games, are sketched only briefly here, because finite games play only a small role in this book and, for the games mainly studied, subgame perfection seems the more useful concept. To see the way that perfection is framed, imagine that a finite game is perturbed so that each player in it selects a strategy, pure or mixed, and that there is a small probability that the actual strategy played will not be the one intended. Thus, no matter what strategy a player selects, there is a small probability that this selection is ignored and that any of the player's pure strategies is chosen instead. This chance of error in executing a strategy is the source of the name *trembling-hand perfect equilibrium*. For a strategy combination in the original game (i.e., the game without errors in strategy selection) to be perfect requires that as the error probability becomes very small, the strategy combination becomes an equilibrium point in the perturbed game.

To be more precise, suppose a finite game in strategic form, Γ_0, in which player i has k_i pure strategies and let S_i be the k_i-dimensional unit simplex representing the player's mixed strategy set. All games are assumed to be games with *perfect recall*. Roughly speaking, this means that the information sets are consistent with a player never forgetting his own past moves. The practical importance of perfect recall is that one need only consider a narrow class of strategies, called *behavior strategies*. These are strategies in which the choice of move by a player depends only on the current information set. Thus, in the extensive form, a strategy for a player is described by a collection of independent probability distributions, one for each of the player's information sets. Strategic form strategies are constructed from these behavior strategies in the obvious way. Perfect recall and behavior strategies are discussed in Kuhn (1953). See also Selten (1975). The error probability attaching to pure strategy k of player i is $\lambda \pi_{ik}$ where $\pi_{ik} > 0$ for $k = 1, \ldots, k_i$, $\lambda \geq 0$, and $\sum_k \pi_{ik} = 1$. Letting $\pi_i = (\pi_{i1}, \ldots, \pi_{ik_i})$, the *perturbed game* Γ_λ has the same payoff function as Γ_0, but the ith player's strategy set consists of all strategies of the form $u_i^\lambda = (1 - \lambda)s_i + \lambda \pi_i$ with $s_i \in S_i$.

Now select a particular collection of errors π_i ($i \in N$) and let u^λ be an equilibrium point of the game Γ_λ that is based on these errors. Next choose a sequence of values for λ that converges to zero. The sequence of λ values has a companion sequence of equilibrium strategy combinations, u^λ. Then, s^* is a perfect equilibrium point in the original game Γ_0 if there is a collection of errors and a corresponding sequence of equilibrium points $\{u^\lambda\}$ such that s^* is the limit of the sequence $\{u^\lambda\}$ as λ goes to zero.

With this definition in mind, examine the game in Table 3.3. Suppose that all the π_{ik} are equal and examine the pure strategy equilibria to see if they are perfect. Let ε ($= \lambda \pi_{ik}$ for all i and k) be the probability of selecting one of the unintended pure strategies, let p ($= 1 - 7\varepsilon$) be the probability that player 1 select the intended strategy, and let q ($= 1 - 7\varepsilon$) be the probability that player 2 selects the intended strategy. (Note that $\varepsilon = \lambda/8$.) Then, for the intended strategy combination (α_3, β_5), the payoff to player 1 is $1063\varepsilon^2 + 149\varepsilon q + 169\varepsilon p + 27qp$. For the intended strategy combination (α_1, β_5) the payoff of player 1 is $1043\varepsilon^2 + 149\varepsilon q + 189\varepsilon p + 27qp$. As ε goes to zero, the latter becomes larger than the former. This would hold true for any selection of the π_i; therefore, (α_3, β_5) is not a perfect equilibrium point of the original game. The equilibrium point (α_3, β_6) can be ruled out in a parallel fashion.

The semiextensive form of this game has four subgame perfect pure strategy equilibrium points corresponding to the four ways that the two players could select their first and second pure strategies. When these are checked similarly, it is found that the only perfect pure strategy equilibrium is (α_1, β_2). For small, positive ε, the intended strategy α_1 is superior to α_2 when the intended strategy of player 2 is either β_1 or β_2, and similarly, β_2 is superior to β_1 when the intended strategy of player 1 is either α_1 or α_2. Thus, the perfect equilibrium in this example is subgame perfect, but not all the subgame equilibria are perfect.

2.3 Sequential equilibrium

Sequential equilibrium, due to Kreps and Wilson (1982b), is related to both Selten's (1975) perfect equilibrium and to Harsanyi's (1967, 1968a, 1968b) treatment of games with incomplete information. A (trembling hand) perfect equilibrium is always a sequential equilibrium, but some sequential equilibria are not perfect. With respect to incomplete information games, the players in the Kreps and Wilson formulation have some scope for selecting probability beliefs, akin to the subjective probability assignments made by the players in incomplete information games. That scope is limited by certain consistency requirements that are sketched below.

Imagine a finite, n-person game with perfect recall, Γ. Now suppose player i is checking out whether a particular strategy of hers, s_i, appears optimal, and assume she is using two other pieces of information: (a) she has in mind for each of the other players, j, a particular strategy, s_j, and (b) for each information set in the game at which she would move, she has a probability assignment to each of the nodes. That is, within information set k that has, say l_k nodes, player i assigns probability $\mu_{1i}^k \geq 0$ to node 1, $\mu_{2i}^k \geq 0$ to node 2, and so forth. The sum of the probabilities assigned to the nodes in a single information set is unity. Denote by μ_i the probability assignments made in this way by player i. It is reasonable for player i to choose a strategy, s_i, that maximizes her expected payoff, contingent on the strategies she believes the other players will use $(s_j, j \neq i)$ and her own beliefs (μ_i), when calculated from each information set at which she moves. At a sequential equilibrium, each player is maximizing in the sense described above, subject to some consistency conditions. These consistency conditions are discussed next.

The first consistency condition is that all players have in mind the same strategy combination, s. The remaining conditions relate to the beliefs, μ_i. Let $\mu = (\mu_1, \ldots, \mu_n)$, the collection of probability assignments of all the players. μ is called a *system of beliefs*. A pair (s, μ) is called an *assessment*, and an assessment is a sequential equilibrium if (a) μ satisfies the appropriate consistency properties and (b) from each information set at which each player i moves, expected payoff is maximized by s_i, given both μ_i and the s_j $(j \neq i)$. If condition (b) holds, s is called a *sequential best reply against* (s, μ).

As a starting point in seeing the consistency conditions on μ, let s be an arbitrary strategy combination. The s_i are, of course, mixed strategies. A mixed strategy, s_i, is called *completely mixed* if $s_i \gg 0$; that is, a completely mixed strategy places strictly positive probability on each of the pure strategies of the game. If all the s_i in the equilibrium combination are completely mixed, then it follows that there is a strictly positive probability of reaching each decision node of the game when s is played. Given such an s, the probability of reaching each node can be calculated; thus, s can be used to assign a conditional probability to each node within any of the player's information sets that is conditional on the node being reached. One consistency requirement on μ is that it assign the probabilities that are implied by s to the extent that such probabilities are, in fact, implied. When s is completely mixed, then s determines μ entirely. When s is not completely mixed, there may be some information sets that would not, in fact, be reached. On these sets, consistency requires that the probability assignments be determined in a way analogous to the way the (trembling hand) perfect equilibrium is defined.

Suppose that (s, μ) is an assessment for the game Γ_0. Now, form a family of games Γ_λ precisely as in Section 2.2.3. Let the strategy combination u^λ be related to s as in Section 2.2.3 and let μ^λ be the system of beliefs implied by u^λ. Then (s, μ) is *consistent* if μ equals the limit of μ^λ as λ goes to zero. The assessment (s, μ) is a *sequential equilibrium* if s is a sequential best reply against (s, μ) and μ is consistent. For many games, the set of sequential equilibria and the set of perfect equilibria coincide; however, there are games in which some sequential equilibria are not perfect.

The reader interested in delving deeper into perfect equilibrium and related concepts is referred to Selten (1975) where perfection and subgame perfection are discussed, to Kreps and Wilson (1982b) where sequential equilibrium is discussed, to Myerson (1978) and Kalai and Samet (1982) who propose alternate concepts, and to van Damme (1983) who discusses these notions as well.

3 Infinite horizon supergames

This section is divided further into Sections 3.1 and 3.2. Section 3.1 deals exclusively with infinite horizon repeated games, and, in Section 3.2, some results are generalized to infinite horizon supergames without time dependence.

3.1 Trigger strategy equilibria in repeated games

Trigger strategy equilibria allow players to achieve cooperative outcomes in games that are (structurally) noncooperative. The essence of such an equilibrium is that all players can choose moves resulting in an outcome on the payoff possibility frontier. Players expect these precise moves to be repeated as long as all players have, in past periods, chosen them. The players' strategies contain provisions to "punish" a player who is seen to deviate from this expected pattern of behavior. The punishment is to change the chosen moves to ones corresponding to a single-period equilibrium point. This punishment punishes the faithful as well as the deviator, but the deterrent effect of the punishment is great enough that no one would deviate anyway. The punishment is credible because it is Nash equilibrium behavior; thus the supergame trigger strategies are subgame perfect.

To explain all this in sufficient detail, Section 3.1.1 contains further discussion of trigger strategy equlibria, Section 3.1.2 provides an example, and conditions for existence of these equilibria are found in Section 3.1.3.

3.1.1 *A brief description of a trigger strategy equilibrium*

All equilibria in Section 3.1 are subgame perfect Nash noncooperative equilibria; however, they divide into two subtypes. The first is simply a supergame equilibrium that is compounded of equilibria of the individual game that is being repeated. That such equilibria exist is already established by Theorem 3.1 and its corollary above; and the equilibria of this type are really only recalled to mind now to serve as a benchmark against which to compare the second category of equilibria.

The second sort of equilibrium is based on a closed loop strategy combination of a special type. Informally, it can be thought to characterize a joint agreement among the players under which they are to choose a particular move combination in each period, s^*, which is not an ordinary game noncooperative equilibrium; however, the arrangement also provides an automatic punishment if any player i ever deviates from the behavior expected of him. The punishment is that the other players $(N - \{i\})$ switch to choosing $s_j^c (j \neq i)$ in each future period. The combination s^c is a noncooperative equilibrium for the game that is being repeated. The payoff levels associated with s^* are higher for all players than payoffs at s^c. Thus, should some player i in some period t choose $s_i' \neq s_i^*$, then, from period $t + 1$ onward the other players will choose $s_j^c (j \neq i)$. In the circumstances following the choice of s_i', player i can do no better than to choose s_i^c, and, likewise for any other player j. If all players $k \neq j$ are expected to choose s_k^c, then player j can do no better than to choose s_j^c. Such strategies have been known at least since they were discussed by Luce and Raiffa (1957) with respect to repeated games based on the Prisoners' Dilemma. Radner (1980) has aptly named them *trigger strategies*, because the deviation by one player from a prescribed pattern of behavior triggers a change in the behavior of the other players.

The most interesting s^* are those for which $P_i(s^*) > P_i(s^c)$ for all $i \in N$, so that each player would strictly gain by the choice of s^* over s^c. The strategy of choosing s_i^* in the first period, then continuing to choose s_i^* as long as all other players have chosen $s_j^* (j \neq i)$ in the past, and switching to s_i^c if someone deviates from s_j^* does provide a means of achieving payoffs larger than those of the single-shot noncooperative equilibria. Any time a trigger strategy combination is being followed, it is possible for at least one player to obtain a payoff larger than $P_i(s^*)$ in one period. This is achieved by choosing s_i' to maximize $P_i(s^* \backslash s_i')$, and it is possible as long as s^* is not a single-period equilibrium point. No player will wish to collect this extra single period payoff if the future decline in payoff, from $P_i(s^*)$ to $P_i(s^c)$, is sufficiently large. If no player can increase the value of his discounted payoff stream by deviating from his trigger strategy, then the trigger strategy combination is a noncooperative equilibrium.

3.1.2 An example of a cooperative outcome supported by noncooperative equilibrium strategies

Trigger strategy equilibria explain how people who place no value on one another's welfare, each only caring about himself, can cooperate to attain Pareto efficient outcomes when binding agreements between them are not possible. For example, imagine a lake around which are located rental cottages, the cottages are in five clusters with each cluster having a single owner, each summer season is a single time period, and at the start of each season the five cottage owners choose rental rates for their cabins that must remain in effect for the duration of the season. Let s_{it} be the (scalar) rental rate chosen by owner i for season t, and suppose that

$$P_i(s_t) = 180s_{it} - 6s_{it}^2 + s_{it} \sum_{j=1}^{5} s_{jt}, \qquad i = 1, \ldots, 5 \qquad (3.3)$$

It is easily seen that if each period is regarded as a separate noncooperative game, the choice of $s_{it} = 30$ for all i will be an equilibrium point, and each player's payoff will be 4500 per period. If all players choose trigger strategies with $s_{it} = 90$ being selected in each period, and with the understanding that the players will switch to $s_{i,t+1} = 30$ if, in some period t, a choice other than 90 is observed, then the payoff per period will be 8100.

The choice of $s_{it} = 30$ by all players may be thought to cause very high occupancy rates, while $s_{it} = 90$ yields only a moderate occupancy rate coupled with a very high price per unit. Under a trigger strategy, a single firm can take advantage of the high prices of the others and, for one period only, attain an extraordinary payoff. Given $s_{jt} = 90$ for the others, owner i will maximize her single-period payoff by choosing $s_{it} = 54$ and will receive 14,580. This may be thought to couple a very high occupancy rate with a moderately high price. The fact that one owner can obtain 14,580 by choosing 54 when all others choose 90 shows that the choice of 90 by all owners is not an equilibrium point for the single-period game. Now suppose that all owners except owner i are using trigger strategies, and consider the alternatives facing owner i. If she also uses a trigger strategy she receives 8100 in each period or $8100/(1 - \alpha_i)$ for the supergame, where α_i is her discount parameter. If she maximizes her first-period gain, then she gets 14,580 in period 1 and the best she can do in the subsequent periods is 4500. The discounted value of this course of action is $14,580 + 4500\alpha_i/(1 - \alpha_i)$. It is easily seen that the trigger strategy is superior if $\alpha_i > 9/14$, it is inferior if $\alpha_i < 9/14$, and the two strategies yield equal supergame payoffs if $\alpha_i = 9/14$. When the trigger strategies form a noncooperative equilibrium, the extra gain available by maximizing against $s_{jt} = 90$ $(14,580 - 8100 = 6480)$ is smaller than the future discounted losses suffered by reverting to the single-period noncooperative equilibrium $([8100 - 4500]\alpha_i/[1 - \alpha_i])$.

3.1.3   Conditions for subgame perfect trigger strategy equilibria

Trigger strategy equilibria may be considered self-enforcing agreements where the enforcement mechanism is a threat made by all players that, in the event that the agreement is violated, they will change their actions to actions which correspond to a single-period noncooperative equilibrium whose associated payoffs are worse for every player than are the agreed-on payoffs. Because the threat involves playing noncooperative equilibrium strategies, it is perforce credible. If all owners say they will choose 30, then no single owner can find a better alternative. The two pillars supporting the trigger strategy equilibrium are (a) a credible threat and (b) no player can deviate from the trigger strategy and increase his own supergame payoff, given that the other players are following their trigger strategies. Condition (b) is the requirement that the trigger strategies are a noncooperative equilibrium, and condition (a) is the further stipulation that the equilibrium is subgame perfect. In the remainder of this section, results on trigger strategy equilibria are formally developed.

DEFINITION 3.10 $\phi_i(s)$ *is the* **best reply payoff of player** i **relative to** s *in the game* (N, S, P) *if* $\phi_i(s) = max_{s'_i \in S_i} P_i(s \backslash s'_i)$.

Clearly the function ϕ_i is defined everywhere on S.

DEFINITION   3.11 $\sigma_i = (v_{i0}, v_{i1}, v_{i2}, \dots) \in \mathscr{S}_i^*$ *is a* **stationary trigger strategy for player** i *if* (a) $v_{i0}(h_0) = s_i^i \in S_i$, (b) *for* $t \geq 1$, $v_{it}(h_t) = s_i^i \in S_i$ *if* $h_t = (s^i, \dots, s^i)$ *and* $v_{it}(h_t) = s_i^c \in S_i$ *otherwise.*

Thus for a player i, a trigger strategy is characterized by $s^i \in S$ and $s_i^c \in S_i$. Player i chooses the ith component of s^i as his period 0 move and continues to choose s_i^i as long as s^i has been the joint choice of all players in all past periods. If at least one player j in at least one past period deviated from s_j^i, then player i changes to choosing s_i^c forever. It is obvious that if $s^i \neq s^j$ for any pair of players, then only s^c will be chosen from period 1 onward when all players are using trigger strategies; therefore, trigger strategies are of interest only when $s^* = s^1 = \cdots = s^n$. (s^*, s^c) characterizes a *trigger strategy combination*.

THEOREM 3.3   *Let* $\Gamma = (N, S, P, \alpha, \infty)$ *be a repeated game satisfying Rule 3.1,* $s^c \in S$ *be an equilibrium point of* (N, S, P), *and* $(s^*, s^c) \in S \times S$ *be a trigger strategy combination. If*

$$\alpha_i > \frac{\phi_i(s^*) - P_i(s^*)}{\phi_i(s^*) - P_i(s^c)}, \qquad i \in N \tag{3.4}$$

then (s^*, s^c) *is a subgame perfect equilibrium point of* Γ.

Proof It is first shown that (s^*, s^c) is an equilibrium point; then that the equilibrium point is subgame perfect. Suppose all players except player i are using their trigger strategies. By using his trigger strategy, player i achieves a payoff of $P_i(s^*)/(1 - \alpha_i)$. If he follows the trigger strategy until period t, then in period t chooses something other than s_i^*, the largest possible payoff he can obtain is

$$(1 + \alpha_i + \cdots + \alpha_i^{t-1})P_i(s^*) + \alpha_i^t \phi_i(s^*) + (\alpha^{t+1} + \alpha^{t+2} + \cdots)P_i(s^c)$$

$$= \frac{1 - \alpha_i^t}{1 - \alpha_i} P_i(s^*) + \alpha_i^t \phi_i(s^*) + \frac{\alpha_i^{t+1}}{1 - \alpha_i} P_i(s^c) \quad (3.5)$$

To see that this is the largest possible payoff, given $s_{it} \neq s_i^*$, note that the first term is fixed by the stipulation that the trigger strategy is followed until period t, the second term is the largest possible payoff that player i can receive in period t, given the choices of the other players, and the third term is the optimum for player i, given that the other players are committed to choosing $s_j^c (j \neq i)$ after time t. If $P_i(s^*)/(1 - \alpha_i)$ exceeds equation (3.5), then the trigger strategy of player i is a best reply to the trigger strategies of the others; however, this is precisely the condition given in equation (3.4). Thus, when equation (3.4) holds, the trigger strategy combination (s^*, s^c) is an equilibrium point.

Turning now to subgame perfectness, (s^*, s^c) is subgame perfect if its projection onto any possible subgame induces an equilibrium point for that subgame. An arbitrary subgame is obtained by selecting a value for t and some $h_t \in S^t$. Denote this subgame by Γ_{h_t}, and consider the strategies that will be followed in this subgame, given h_t and given (s^*, s^c). Because of the special nature of trigger strategies, all subgames can be partitioned into two sets. The first consists of those subgames in which $h_t = (s^*, \ldots, s^*)$ for $t \geq 1$ or in which $t = 0$. The second set contains all other subgames. For a subgame in the first set, following the trigger strategies will yield payoffs of $P_i(s^*)$ in each period, and, by the same reasoning establishing that (s^*, s^c) is an equilibrium point of the original game, (s^*, s^c) induces an equilibrium point on the subgame. For a member of the second set of subgames, because $s_{i\tau} \neq s_i^*$ was selected by some player in a past period, all players j will choose s_j^c in all periods. This, again, is an equilibrium point for the subgame; hence, (s^*, s^c) is subgame perfect.   QED

COROLLARY.   *Under the conditions of Theorem 3.3 if $P(s^*) \gg P(s^c)$ then there are $\alpha_i \in (0, 1), i \in N$, such that (s^*, s^c) is a trigger strategy noncooperative equilibrium.*

Proof   Because $\phi_i(s^*) \geq P_i(s^*) > P_i(s^c)$, it is immediate that

$$\alpha_i^* = \frac{\phi_i(s^*) - P_i(s^*)}{\phi_i(s^*) - P_i(s^c)} \in (0, 1), \qquad i \in N \tag{3.6}$$

Choosing $\alpha_i \in (\alpha_i^*, 1), i \in N$, completes the proof.   QED

Aumann (1959, 1961) provides the first systematic study of cooperative

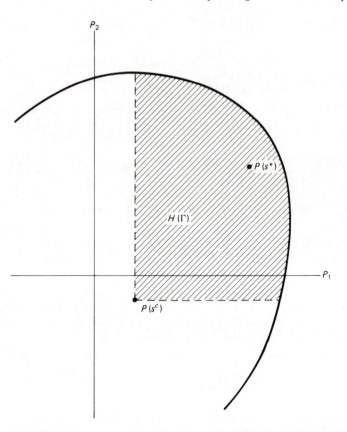

FIGURE 3.3   Supergame outcomes that dominate the single-shot Nash equilibrium.

equilibria in repeated games that are achieved by means of noncooperative behavior.[4]

Figure 3.3 illustrates the relationship of s^* and s^c for a two-player example. Any payoff in the shaded region above and to the right of $P(s^c)$ could be $P(s^*)$. This region is denoted $H(\Gamma)$. Depending on the values of the discount parameters, there are a large number of potential equilibria; therefore, it is appealing to look for ways to select among them. One obvious technique is to eliminate dominated equilibria. That is, let $E(\Gamma)$ denote the set of trigger strategy equilibrium points for the game Γ, and let $E^*(\Gamma)$ denote those that are locally efficient. Then $(s^*, s^c) \in E(\Gamma)$ if s^c is a single-period Nash equilibrium and $P(s^*) \gg P(s^c)$. Thus,

$$E^*(\Gamma) = \{(s^*, s^c) \in E(\Gamma) \mid P(s) \gg P(s^*)$$

$$\text{does not hold for any } (s, s^c) \in E(\Gamma)\} \quad (3.7)$$

The criterion of local efficiency is that the single-period payoffs under the trigger strategy lie on the payoff possibility frontier of (N, S, P). That local efficiency does not imply global efficiency may be seen by examining Figure

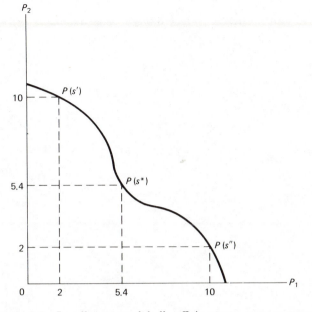

FIGURE 3.4 Locally versus globally efficient supergame outcomes.

3.4. Note that $P(s^*)$ is locally efficient but the discounted payoffs of both players can be increased by selecting s' in odd numbered periods and s'' in even-numbered periods. The trigger strategy specification must be restated to require this alternation, along with reversion to s^c if a player violates the prescribed alternation between s' and s''. Supposing the payoffs to be those shown in Figure 3.4 and assuming the discount parameters of the two players to be .9, the trigger strategy based on s^* gives a discounted payoff of 54 to each player, while the trigger strategy based on alternating between s' and s'' gives player 1 a payoff of 57.89 and player 2, 62.11. If $(s^*, s^c) \in E(\Gamma)$ and $P(s^*)$ lies on the payoff possibility frontier, then supergame payoffs under (s^*, s^c) will certainly be Pareto optimal if the payoff possibility frontier is concave. This condition is violated in Figure 3.4. A weaker condition is that $P(s^*)$ lie on the upper right boundary of the convex hull of $H(\Gamma)$. Figure 3.5 repeats Figure 3.4 with the boundary of the convex hull drawn solid and the rest of the boundary of $H(\Gamma)$ drawn as a broken curve.

Even restricting attention to globally efficient trigger strategies, it is clear that there are a great many possible equilibrium points, particularly if the discount parameters are close to unity. While there is no a priori reason to eliminate any of these efficient subgame perfect equilibrium points, it is nonetheless desirable to single out a small number of these equilibria if an appealing criterion can be found for doing so. One proposal is the *balanced temptation equilibrium*, found in Friedman (1971). Basically, the idea is to select a point s^* such that α_i^* in equation (3.6) has the same value for all i.

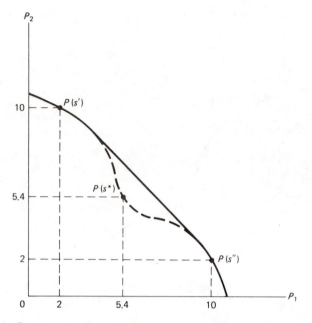

FIGURE 3.5   In a repeated game the set of attainable payoffs is approximately convex.

This can be expressed equally well by

$$\frac{\phi_i(s^*) - P_i(s^*)}{P_i(s^*) - P_i(s^c)} = \frac{\phi_j(s^*) - P_j(s^*)}{P_j(s^*) - P_j(s^c)}, \qquad i, j \in N \qquad (3.8)$$

The numerator in equation (3.8) is the single-period gain to defecting from the trigger strategy and the denominator is the per period loss that will be sustained following defection. The ratio of the two can be thought to measure the temptation to defect, with a higher rate meaning a smaller temptation. At a balanced temptation equilibrium, all players' temptations are equalized. Exact conditions for existence of this equilibrium can be found in Friedman (1971) or (1977: Chapter 8).

3.2   Trigger strategy equilibria in supergames without time dependence

Theorem 3.3 can be extended to general supergames that lack time dependence. The class of games $\Gamma = (N, \mathscr{S}^*, G)$ has closed loop strategy sets $\mathscr{S}_i^*$ given by Definition 3.9, the objective functions $G_i(\sigma)$ are given by equation (3.2), and a game satisfies Assumptions 3.1 to 3.3. It is appropriate to think of the supergame as consisting of the playing of the games $\{(N, S_t, P_t)\}_{t=0}^{\infty}$ by a fixed set, N, of players. Each game (N, S_t, P_t) satisfies the usual conditions imposed in Chapter 2: Assumptions 2.1 to 2.3 and Rules 2.1 and 2.2. Additionally, equation (3.2) specifies the way that players discount period by period payoffs, and Rule 3.1 is in force. Using Rule 3.1 rather than Rule 3.1', of course, allows the possibility of complete memory, or closed loop, strategies, which include trigger strategies.

Theorem 3.4, which generalizes Theorem 3.3, is conceptually quite straightforward; the mechanisms at work are unchanged. There is really only one difference: The supergames in Section 2.1 have a stationary structure. That is, the payoff functions are identical from period to period and the way that players discount between periods t and $t + 1$ does not depend on t. Therefore, a subgame beginning at t is identical to a subgame beginning at time t'; thus, if it is worthwhile for a player to use s_i^* at time $t = 0$, it will be worthwhile at all other periods. Put another way, if it is better to defect from a trigger strategy than to continue with it, then the earlier the player defects, the better. The value of defection at any time t is constant; however, discounting means that the value of defection at t, discounted to time 0, declines as t increases. By contrast, in the general supergame, it may be profitable to defect in some periods and unprofitable in others; therefore, each individual time period must be checked. Of course, for a trigger strategy equilibrium, it must be worse to defect than to stay with the trigger strategy in each period.

DEFINITION 3.12 $\Gamma = (N, \mathcal{S}^*, G)$ *is a* **general supergame without time dependence and with closed loop strategies** *if $N = \{1, \ldots, n\}$, $\mathcal{S}^*$ is defined by Definition 3.3, G is given by equation (3.2), and satisfies Assumptions 3.1 to 3.3 and Rule 3.1.*

DEFINITION 3.13 $\sigma_i = (v_{i0}, v_{i1}, v_{i2}, \ldots) \in \mathcal{S}_i^*$ *is a* **trigger strategy for player** i *if (a)* $v_{i0}(h_0) = s_{i0}^i \in S_{i0}$, *(b) for $t \geqslant 1$, $v_{it}(h_t) = s_{it}^i$ if $h_t = (s_0^i, \ldots, s_{t-1}^i)$ and $v_{it}(h_t) = s_{it}^c \in S_t$ otherwise.*

Trigger strategy combinations are interesting when the cooperative behavior is based on the same choices for all players (i.e., $s_t^i = s_t^j$ for all $i, j \in N$ and all t), the actions taken following defection (s_t^c) are non-cooperative equilibria for the game of the individual period, and adhering to the trigger strategy is superior in each individual period for each player to the single period equilibrium point. Such trigger strategies are called *admissible*.

DEFINITION 3.14 σ *is an* **admissible trigger strategy combination** *if it is a trigger strategy satisfying (a) s_t^c is an equilibrium point of (N, S_t, P_t), $t = 0, 1, \ldots$, (b) $s_t^i = s_t^*, i \in N$, $t = 0, 1, \ldots$, and (c) $P(s_t^*) \gg P_t(s_t^c)$, $t = 0, 1, \ldots$.*

Following Definition 3.10, $\phi_{it}(s_t)$ is the best reply *payoff of player i in the game* (N, S_t, P_t).

THEOREM 3.4 *Let $\Gamma = (N, \mathcal{S}^*, G)$ be a general supergame without time dependence and with closed loop strategies, and let σ be an admissible trigger strategy* *combination. Then, σ is a subgame perfect equilibrium point of* Γ *if*

$$\sum_{\tau=t}^{\infty} \alpha_{i\tau} P_{i\tau}(s_{\tau}^{*}) > \alpha_{it} \phi_{it}(s_{t}^{*}) + \sum_{\tau=t+1}^{\infty} \alpha_{i\tau} P_{i\tau}(s_{\tau}^{c}), \quad i \in N, \quad t = 0, 1, \ldots \quad (3.9)$$

Proof It is immediate that if equation (3.9) holds, then no player could alter her strategy unilaterally and increase her supergame payoff. The right-hand side of equation (3.9) gives the largest payoff player i can achieve from period t onward, given that she defects in period t from the trigger strategy σ_i. That σ is subgame perfect follows from an argument parallel to the one used in the proof of Theorem 3.3.   QED

4   Finite horizon supergames

There is a well-known result that trigger strategies are not viable if the players have a finite horizon. The result is proved by a backward induction argument in the manner of dynamic programming. This result, which is elaborated below, brings to light a strange discontinuity in behavior: Trigger strategies are possible with an infinite horizon, but a finite horizon of any length, no matter how long, will not support them. This result is actually false in general. Following Friedman (1985), conditions are shown under which finite horizon trigger strategies will exist. Where trigger strategies do not exist, the discontinuity as between infinite and finite horizons can be smoothed if the players no longer seek perfect optimization in their strategies. Following Radner (1980), it is seen that if players are content to use strategies that are within ε of being best replies, then trigger strategy ε-equilibria are possible in games having sufficiently long, but finite, horizons. Settling for strategies that are within some tolerance of being best replies is an instance of *bounded rationality*.

The bounded rationality approach to modeling human behavior is characterized by compromise between purely instinctive and/or traditional behavior on one hand and full rationality on the other. Fully rational modeling in the social sciences usually presumes that decision makers possess large amounts of information and that they incur no costs or significant time delays in processing information. While it is obvious that these information and processing cost conditions are not really met in practice, it remains an open question whether assuming they are met is the most fruitful method of modeling. Any of countless real-life decisions made by individual consumers or businesses is based on far less information than the total relevant information available. For example, a person purchasing an automatic clothes washer is unlikely to obtain and study carefully the specifications of any, much less all, available brands. Roughly speaking, the cost of doing so is unlikely to be less than the expected cost of making a less than optimal choice. Avoiding an extra hundred hours of studying and evaluating information will provide the resources needed to buy a large amount of repair service. Recognizing this, there are two ways to proceed formally. One is to insist that the cost of obtaining and processing information be incorporated explicitly into the model. This approach would preserve full optimization; however, the conditions of the model would be altered to recognize that information itself is not free, and the optimal amount would presumably be bought and used in the best possible way. This route suffers from adding great complications to the model, making it likely to be analytically intractible. The second approach, that of bounded rationality, resorts to objective functions that are admittedly shortcuts, employing approximations and/or rules of thumb. Such models can preserve greater analytical manipulability. These models always look a bit unsatisfactory, because one can see ways that the decision makers in the model could use information they have in order to make better decisions. The rules of the model disallow the decision makers from doing this, because the bounded rationality approach has explicitly limited the avenues open to the decision makers for choosing actions. This can be defended on two grounds. First, if bounded rationality models were to yield better empirical predictions than other models, the approach would be vindicated. Second, it can be argued that decision makers do not make an exhaustive study of the optimal amount of information or of the optimal amount of information processing. Introspection and observation of others suggests that people do use intuition and rules of thumb. Set against these two grounds are that the former has not yet been established, and the apparent use of intuition may be best approximated by a model that explicitly allows for full optimization.

4.1 Trigger strategy equilibrium based on multiple single-shot equilibrium points

In this section, the *backward induction* argument, proving that trigger strategy equilibria are impossible when the horizon is finite, is first presented. This result holds for repeated games when the game being repeated has only one equilibrium point. Then a model is presented in which the game being repeated has at least two equilibrium points. If one of these equilibrium points strongly dominates the other, then trigger strategy equilibria are possible with a finite horizon. Both Theorems 3.5 and 3.6 gives sufficient conditions for their results and do not exhaustively characterize the possibilities.

Turning now to the backward induction argument, everything is stated in terms of repeated games. The generalization to other finite horizon supergames should be obvious. Theorem 3.5 gives conditions under which trigger strategy equilibria are impossible when the horizon is finite, while Theorem 3.6 gives conditions under which trigger strategy equilibria remain possible despite a finite horizon.

THEOREM 3.5 *Let* $\Gamma = (N, S, P, \alpha, T)$ *be a repeated game with finite T and satisfying Rule 3.1, and let $s^c \in S$ be the unique equilibrium point of (N, S, P). Then, the only equilibrium point of Γ is* $\sigma = (s^c, s^c, \ldots, s^c)$.

Proof Suppose that $\sigma^* = (v_0, \ldots, v_T)$ is an equilibrium point of the game. Clearly, $v_T(h_T) = s^c$ for all h_T. If this were not true, then for any h_T such that $v_T(h_T) \neq s^c$, there would be at least one player who could improve her period T payoff without any effect on the payoffs of earlier periods. Therefore, $v_T(h_T) = s^c$ for all h_T, which means that the final period choices are independent of all the previous choices of all players. Looking now at period $T-1$, the choice of s_{T-1} will not affect s_T; hence, the same argument may be applied again to conclude that an equilibrium strategy combination requires that $v_{T-1}(h_{T-1}) = s^c$. This argument may be repeated period by period to complete the proof.   QED

The backward induction argument, used to prove Theorem 3.5, does not hold for Theorem 3.6, because the basic game in Theorem 3.6 has more than one equilibrium point. As a result, $v(h_T)$ has more than one possible value, and this fact can allow finite horizon trigger strategies. Suppose that s' and s'' are equilibrium points of the game that is being repeated, and that $P(s') \gg P(s'')$. The trigger strategies specify a path to which each player continues to adhere as long as all players have adhered in the past. Denote that path $\{s_t^*\}_{t=0}^T$. The last element in the path, s_T^*, is s'. Because s' is an equilibrium point of the single-period game, there is no incentive for any player i to choose differently from s_i' if he has reason to suppose the others will choose s_j' $(j \neq i)$ in period T. Thus it is impossible to obtain an extra payoff in period T by deviating from the trigger strategy, but, because $P(s') \gg P(s'')$, it is possible to discourage such deviation in period $T-1$: If deviation occurs, then s'' is chosen in time T instead of s'.

In fact, the foregoing conditions can be made somewhat less stringent. Let S^c denote the noncooperative equilibria of a single-period game (N, S, P), let $s^i \in S^c$, and let $s^0 \in S^c$ satisfy $P_i(s^0) > P_i(s^i)$ for all $i \in N$. In Definition 3.15, a *discriminating trigger strategy* for each player is defined that is based partly on these single-period equilibria.

Note that s^i need not be unique and the members of $\{s^1, \ldots, s^n\}$ need not be distinct. For a T-period repeated game, a trigger strategy for player i, based on $(s^0, s^1, \ldots, s^n, s^*, t^*)$, is defined below and denoted by $\sigma_i(s^0, s^1, \ldots, s^n, s^*, t^*)$. The gist of the strategy is this: If no player j ever deviates from playing s_j^* in periods $0, \ldots, t^*$, and s_j^0 in periods $t^* + 1, \ldots, T-1$, then player i will select s_i^* for $t = 0, \ldots, t^*$ and s_i^0 for $t = t^* + 1, \ldots, T-1$. If a player j defects at some time t, then player i will choose s_i^j in all periods $t + 1, \ldots, T-1$. Finally, if two or more players defect in the same period, then j is selected to be the defector whose index is smallest. The choice of s^j is a way to punish player j for defecting. The threat to punish this way is credible because s^j is an equilibrium point of (N, S, P). This strategy $\sigma_i(s^0, s^1, \ldots, s^n, s^*, t^*)$ is called a *discriminating trigger strategy* because the action following a defection depends on who defected.

DEFINITION 3.15   *A* **discriminating trigger strategy for player** i, *based on* $(s^0, \{s^i\}_{i \in N}, s^*, t^*)$ *for the game* Γ *is denoted* $\sigma_i(s^0, \{s^i\}_{i \in N}, s^*, t^*)$ *and is given* *by:*

(a) $s_{i0} = s_i^*$;

(b) $s_{it} = s_i^*$ if $s_{j\tau} = s_j^*, j \in N, \tau = 0, \ldots, t-1, t = 1, \ldots, t^*$; *otherwise let* t' *and* j' *satisfy* (i) $s_{j't'} \neq s_{j'}^*$, (ii) $s_{jt'} = s_j^*, j < j'$, *and* (iii) $s_{jt} = s_j^*, j \in N, t < t'$; *then* $s_{it} = s_i^{j'}, t = t', \ldots, t^*$;

(c) $s_{i,t^*+1} = s_i^0$ if $s_{j\tau} = s_j^*, j \in N, \tau = 0, \ldots, t^*$, *otherwise let* t' *and* j' *satisfy* (i) *to* (iii) *above and then* $s_{i,t^*+1} = s_i^{j'}$;

(d) $s_{it} = s_i^0$ if $s_{j\tau} = s_j^0, j \in N, \tau = t^*+1, \ldots, t-1, t = t^*+2, \ldots, T$; *otherwise let* t' *and* j' *satisfy* (i) $s_{j't'} \neq s_{j'}^0$, (ii) $s_{jt'} = s_j^0, j < j'$, *and* (iii) $s_{jt} = s_j^0, j < N, t^*+1 \leq t < t'$; *then* $s_{it} = s_i^{j'}, t = t^*+2, \ldots, T$.

Theorem 3.6 gives sufficient conditions for a finitely repeated game to have a trigger strategy equilibrium and the equilibrium strategies are characterized.

THEOREM 3.6 *Let:* (a) $\Gamma = (N, S, P, \alpha, T)$ *be a finitely repeated game that satisfies Rule 3.1,* (b) $s^0 \in S^c, s^i \in S^c, i \in N, s^* \in S$, *and* (c) $P_i(s^0) > P_i(s^i), i \in N$. *Then there exists a positive integer* $\gamma(\alpha)$ *such that the trigger strategy combination* $\sigma(s^0, s^1, \ldots, s^n, s^*, t^*)$ *is a subgame perfect equilibrium of* Γ *for all* $T \geq t^* + \gamma(\alpha)$ *and all* $t^* = 1, 2, \ldots$, *if for all* $i, P_i(s^*) \geq P_i(s^i)$ *and, either*

$$\alpha_i > \frac{\phi_i(s^*) - P_i(s^*)}{\phi_i(s^*) - P_i(s^*) + P_i(s^0) - P_i(s^i)} \quad for \quad P_i(s^*) > P_i(s^0) \quad (3.10)$$

or

$$\alpha_i > \frac{\phi_i(s^*) - P_i(s^*)}{\phi_i(s^*) - P_i(s^i)} \quad for \quad P_i(s^*) \leq P_i(s^0) \quad (3.11)$$

Proof Suppose all players $j \neq i$ to be using $\sigma_j(s^0, s^1, \ldots, s^n, s^*, t^*)$ and consider the payoff to player i supposing each of the following: (i) player i uses $\sigma_i(s^0, s^1, \ldots, s^n, S^*, t^*)$; (ii) player i follows $\sigma_i(s^0, s^1, \ldots, s^n, s^*, t^*)$ for periods $0, \ldots, t_0 - 1$, for period $t_0 \leq t^*$, player i chooses $s_{it} \neq s_i^*$ and then he chooses s_i^i in periods $t_0 + 1, \ldots, T$. Under (i) the payoff is

$$\sum_{t=0}^{t^*} \alpha_i^t P_i(s^*) + \sum_{t=t^*+1}^{T} \alpha_i^t P_i(s^0) \quad (3.12)$$

Under (ii) the payoff is

$$\sum_{t=0}^{t_0-1} \alpha_i^t P_i(s^*) + \alpha_i^{t_0}\phi_i(s^*) + \sum_{t=t_0+1}^{T} \alpha_i^t P_i(s^i) \quad (3.13)$$

No alternative to $\sigma_i(s^0, s^1, \ldots, s^n, s^*, t^*)$ will deliver a higher payoff than the best alternative under (ii). It remains to compare equations (3.12) and (3.13) to show

$$\sum_{t=0}^{t^*} \alpha_i^t P_i(s^*) + \sum_{t=t^*+1}^{T} \alpha_i^t P_i(s^0) > \sum_{t=0}^{t_0-1} \alpha_i^t P_i(s^*) + \alpha_i^{t_0}\phi_i(s^*) + \sum_{t=t_0+1}^{T} \alpha_i^t P_i(s^i)$$
$$(3.14)$$

Equation (3.14) is equivalent to

$$\alpha_i > \frac{\phi_i(s^*) - P_i(s^*)}{\phi_i(s^*) - P_i(s^i) - \alpha_t^{t^*-t_0}(P_i(s^*) - P_i(s^0)) - \alpha_i^{T-t_0}(P_i(s^0) - P_i(s^i))}$$

$$\text{for} \quad t_0 < t^* \quad (3.15)$$

and

$$\alpha_i > \frac{\phi_i(s^*) - P_i(s^*)}{\phi_i(s^*) - P_i(s^*) + P_i(s^0) - P_i(s^i) - \alpha_i^{T-t_0}(P_i(s^0) - P_i(s^i))} \quad \text{for} \quad t_0 = t^*$$

$$(3.16)$$

For arbitrary large T, the right-hand sides of equations (3.15) and (3.16) are bounded above by equation (3.10) for $P_i(s^*) > P_i(s^0)$ and they are bounded above by equation (3.11) for $P_i(s^*) \leqslant P_i(s^0)$, for any $t^* - t_0 \geqslant 0$. For given t_0 and t^*, let δ_i be the smallest integer value of $T - t^*$ that satisfies either equation (3.15) or equation (3.16), whichever is appropriate, and let $\gamma(\alpha) = \max_{i \in N} \delta_i$. Then $\sigma(s^0, s^1, \ldots, s^n, s^* t^*)$ is a noncooperative trigger strategy equilibrium for Γ if $t^* \geqslant 0$ and $T \geqslant t^* + \gamma(\alpha)$.

Concerning subgame perfection, choose $t \leqslant T$ and note that all past histories of the game at time t (i.e., actual choices $s_0, s_1, \ldots, s_{t-1}$) fall into two disjoint sets: The first are all histories such that the trigger strategy calls for choosing one of the s^i, and the second is the unique history that does not call for choosing any of the s^i (but rather for s^* if $t \leqslant t^*$ or s^0 if $t > t^*$). If $t = 0$, the first set is empty and the (null) history is taken to be in the second set. In either case, the trigger strategy used from t onward forms an equilibrium point for the subgame at time t with the given history.   QED

From the proof of the theorem, it is clear that the equilibrium point $\sigma(s^0, s^1, \ldots, s^n, s^*, t^*)$ could easily yield efficient realizations during part of the game and the inefficient realizations could be limited to the last $\gamma(\alpha)$ periods. This and two additional points are established in the following corollary.

COROLLARY.   *If the conditions of Theorem 3.6 hold, then (a) for suitable T, trigger strategy equilibria exists with s* on the payoff possibility frontier. (b) As T → ∞, the fraction of periods allowing realizations on the payoff possibility frontier goes to one. (c) Restricting α so that $\alpha_i \in (0, 1), i \in N$, and $T \geqslant 1$, a (possibly degenerate) trigger strategy equilibrium exists.*

Proof   For (a) there are two cases: $P(s^0)$ is on the payoff possibility frontier, or it is not. In the former case, let $s^* = s^0$ and apply the theorem. In the latter case, there must be s^* such that $P(s^*)$ dominates $P(s^0)$. Again, using this s^*, apply the theorem. Point (b) follows easily from the observation that γ does not change as T increases. Thus $t^* = T - \gamma$ is permissible and the fraction of periods allowing a realization on the payoff possibility frontier is $1 - \gamma/(T + 1)$. Point (c) follows from the theorem by allowing $s^* = s^0$. (This is a degenerate trigger strategy equilibrium.)   QED

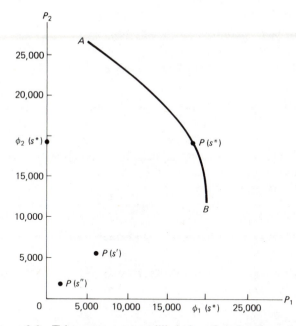

FIGURE 3.6 Trigger strategy equilibria in a finitely repeated game.

Note that the key to Theorem 3.6 is that $s^0, s^1, \ldots, s^n$ are single-shot equilibrium points and $P_i(s^0) > P_i(s^i)$ for all $i \in N$. Nothing would change if $s^1 = s^2 = \cdots = s^n$. The following example may serve to illuminate the theorem. Let $n = 2$, $S_1 = [0, 20]$, $S_2 = [0, 25]$, $\alpha_1 = \alpha_2 = .9$, and let the single-period payoff functions be

$$P_1(s) = -825s_1 - 15s_1^2 + 135s_1s_2 - 5s_1^3 \tag{3.17}$$

$$P_2(s) = -200s_2 - 5s_2^2 + 100s_1s_2 - \tfrac{2}{3}s_2^3 \tag{3.18}$$

The single-period payoff functions are illustrated in Figure 3.6. The payoffs associated with the two single-period equilibrium points are for $s'' = (5, 10)$ the payoffs are $(1625, 1833\tfrac{1}{3})$ and for $s' = (8, 15)$ they are $(6080, 5625)$.[5] The curve marked AB is the profit possibility frontier and a trigger strategy equilibrium can be based on the frontier point $s^* = (15, 25)$ whose associated payoffs are $(18000, 18958\tfrac{1}{3})$. The trigger strategy calls for letting $s_t^* = (15, 25)$ for $t = 0, \ldots, T-1$, $s_T^* = s' = (8, 15)$, and $s_t^c = s'' = (5, 10)$ for $t = 0, \ldots, T$. The gains to short-run maximization for a player when the other player is using the trigger strategy are for player 1, $\phi_1(15, 25) = 19801.15$, which is achieved at $s_1 = 12.0767$, and, for player 2, $\phi_2(15, 25) = 19144.37$, which is achieved at $s_2 = 23.1174$. If player 1 opts for the extra single-period gain of 1801.15 ($= 19801.15 - 18000$), he loses 16375 ($= 18000 - 1625$) in the next period alone if the time of defection is $t < T - 1$, and, if it is $T - 1$, the loss is 4455 ($= 6080 - 1625$). With a discount parameter of .9, this is clearly not worthwhile. Similarly, for player 2, the short-term gain is 186.04 ($= 19144.37 - 18958.3$) and the loss in the next period alone is 17125 ($= 18958.3 - 1833.3$) or 3791.7 ($= 5625 - 1833.3$), depending on which period the defection occurs.

4.2 Epsilon-equilibria in finite horizon games using trigger strategies

Radner (1980) approaches the finitely repeated game using bounded rationality. His players differ from fully rational players by being unable to distinguish between supergame strategies falling within a margin ε of being best replies. Such strategies may be called ε-best replies and the resulting equilibrium, an ε-equilibrium. That is, σ_i is an ε-*best reply* to σ' if the payoff to i from $\sigma'\backslash\sigma_i$ is within ε of the payoff associated with the best reply of i to σ. Similarly, σ is an ε-*equilibrium* if, for each $i \in N$, σ_i is an ε-best reply to σ. Formal definitions are given in Definitions 3.16 and 3.17. The player's objective function is his or her average payoff over the remaining horizon: $G_i^*(\sigma) = 1/\sum_{t=0}^{T} P_i(s_t)/(T+1)$ as of time zero.[6]

DEFINITION 3.16   *In a game* $\Gamma = (N, \mathcal{S}^*, G^*)$ *the strategy* $\sigma_i \in \mathcal{S}^*$ *for player* i *is an* ε-**best reply** *to* σ' *if* $G_i^*(\sigma'\backslash\sigma_i) \geq G_i^*(\sigma'\backslash\sigma_i'') - \varepsilon$ *for all* $\sigma_i'' \in \mathcal{S}^*$, *and for* $\varepsilon \geq 0$.

DEFINITION 3.17 $\sigma \in \mathcal{S}^*$ *is an* ε-**equilibrium** *for the game* $\Gamma = (N, \mathcal{S}^*, G^*)$ *if, for* $\varepsilon \geq 0$, σ_i *is an* ε-*best reply to* σ *for each* $i \in N$.

Why a player is going to be as content with somewhat less than a best reply is not immediately clear, unless costs of calculation are assumed to lurk in the background. If such costs are presumed, then the bounded rationality approach can be taken as an approximation to optimal behavior in the presence of these costs. An ε-equilibrium σ^* is subgame perfect if σ^* induces an ε-equilibrium on each subgame.

The main result in this section is that trigger strategy equilibria remain viable even when the game is of finite length. Under these trigger strategy ε-equilibria, the collusive move is repeated for a while, then, for a duration of several periods at the end of the game, play reverts to a single-period equilibrium point move. The number of periods at the end depends on the payoff functions and the two single-period moves on which the trigger strategy is based; therefore, as the horizon of the game is allowed to grow, the span of time during which cooperation takes place grows at an equal rate.

DEFINITION 3.18 $\sigma = (s^*, s^c, t^*)$ *is a* **finite duration trigger strategy combination.** *Player* i *chooses* s_i^* *in period 0 and on through period* t^* *except if some player* j *deviates from* s_j^* *at time* $t' < t^*$; *however, player* i *chooses* s_i^c *from period* $t^* + 1$ *onward. If some player* j *deviates from* s_j^* *in a period* $t' < t^*$, *then player* i *reverts to* s_i^c *in period* $t' + 1$ *and continues to choose* s_i^c *in all remaining periods.*

THEOREM 3.7   *Let* $(N, \mathcal{S}^*, G^*)$ *be a repeated game with finite* T *that satisfies Rule 3.1 and has a period* t *objective function of* $\sum_{\tau=t}^{T} P_i(s_\tau)/(T+1-t)$, $i \in N$, $t = 0, \ldots, T$. *Let* $\varepsilon > 0$, $s^*, s^c \in S$, *with* $P(s^*) \gg P(s^c)$ *and with* s^c *being an* *equilibrium point of* (N, S, P). *Then the finite duration trigger strategy combination* (s^*, s^c, t^*) *is a subgame perfect ε-equilibrium if*

$$\frac{\phi_i(s^*) - P_i(s^*)}{T + 1 - t^*} \leqslant \varepsilon, \qquad i \in N \tag{3.19}$$

Proof Suppose that the trigger strategy combination is being followed by all players except player i. Obviously, player i can do no better than to choose s_i^c from period $t^* + 1$ onward. But suppose that player i deviates from the trigger strategy in some period $t \leqslant t^*$. Then his payoff for periods t through T is, at best,

$$\frac{\phi_i(s^*) + (T - t)P_i(s^c)}{T + 1 - t} \tag{3.20}$$

but, by following the trigger strategy, it would be

$$\frac{(t^* + 1 - t)P_i(s^*) + (T - t^*)P_i(s^c)}{T + 1 - t} \tag{3.21}$$

The trigger strategy is an ε-best reply for player i if equation (3.20) minus equation (3.21) is less than ε. This difference is

$$\frac{[\phi_i(s^*) - P_i(s^*)] - [t^* - t][P_i(s^*) - P_i(s^c)]}{T + 1 - t} \leqslant \frac{\phi_i(s^*) - P_i(s^*)}{T + 1 - t}$$

$$\leqslant \frac{\phi_i(s^*) - P_i(s^*)}{T + 1 - t^*}$$

$$\leqslant \varepsilon \tag{3.22}$$

The same argument applies to all players $i \in N$; hence, (s^*, s^c, t^*) is an ε-equilibrium. Because it is an ε-equilibrium at each stage of the game, it is subgame perfect. QED

COROLLARY. *Given s^* and s^c, the maximum value for t^* under which (s^*, s^c, t^*) is an ε-equilibrium is given by equation (3.19) and by the condition that*

$$\frac{\phi_i(s^*) - P_i(s^*)}{T - t^*} > \varepsilon \tag{3.23}$$

for at least one player $i \in N$.

Proof The corollary follows obviously from the proof of Theorem 3.7. QED

As an example, consider the single-period payoff functions in equation (3.3) depicting the five owners of rental cottages. Recall that, using $s_i^* = 90$ and $s_i^c = 30$, $i \in N$, $P_i(s^*) = 8100$, $P_i(s_i^c) = 4500$, and $\phi_i(s^*) = 14,580$. Letting $\varepsilon = 100$, it is possible to find $T = t^*$ by solving the equation

$$\frac{\phi_i(s^*) - P_i(s^*)}{T - t^*} = \varepsilon \tag{3.24}$$

Doing so yields $T - t^* = (14{,}580 - 8100)/100 = 64.8$. Thus, the critical value of $T - t^*$ is 64. If, for example, $T = 1000$, a trigger strategy based on $s_i^* = 90$ and $s_i^c = 30$ is viable with t^* equal to 936 or smaller. Note that ε can be any positive number, no matter how tiny, and the critical value of $T - t^*$ will still be finite; thus, if the horizon is sufficiently long, although finite, trigger strategies are possible. Furthermore, for fixed s^*, s^c, and ε, the minimal number of end game periods when s^c must be chosen is constant—it does not grow as T grows. Thus, as T goes to infinity, the number of periods in which s^* can be chosen goes to infinity at the same rate.

Using average payoff over the remaining horizon as the player's objective function plays a crucial role in the proof of Theorem 3.7 as compared with using discounted payoff. This may be seen by supposing that player i faces finite duration trigger strategies on the part of the other players under which s^* is called for in periods 0 through t^*, with s^c called for thereafter. Consider the position of player i in period t^*: If he adheres to the trigger strategy, his discounted payoff stream is

$$P_i(s^*) + P_i(s^c)(\alpha_i + \alpha_i^2 + \cdots + \alpha_i^{T-t^*}) \tag{3.25}$$

and if he maximizes aginst the trigger strategies of the others in period t^*, player i's discounted payoff stream is

$$\phi_i(s^*) + P_i(s^c)(\alpha_i + \alpha_i^2 + \cdots + \alpha_i^{T-t^*}) \tag{3.26}$$

Obviously, equation (3.26) is larger than equation (3.25) by $\phi_i(s^*) - P_i(s^*)$; therefore, the trigger strategy is not an ε-best reply if ε is smaller than this difference. For small ε, the trigger strategy must break down no matter what the length of the (finite) horizon. There is a way to make the average payoff per period criterion and a discounting criterion commensurate. Choose a value for ε and, using a discounting criterion, apply the rule that an ε-best reply must come within $(T + 1 - t)\varepsilon$ of being a best reply in time period t when the end period of the game is period T. With $\alpha_i = 1$, this is equivalent to the formulation used in Theorem 3.7.

Another variant of bounded rationality is obtained by assuming that, in each period, the player looks ahead T periods. That is, as of period t, the objective function is

$$\sum_{\tau=t}^{T+t-1} \alpha_i^{\tau-t} P_i(s_t) \tag{3.27}$$

Bounded rationality is present because, although the game actually continues for infinitely many periods, the players consistently act as if the end point is finitely many periods ahead. Rather than presume the players do not realize the truth, it makes more sense to assume that costs of calculating optimal behavior are eased by looking only a finite distance into the future. The results of Theorem 3.5 to 3.7 can be applied to such a model. If a subgame perfect noncooperative equilibrium is sought, then there are two possibilities: First, if the single-period game has a unique equilibrium point, then a subgame perfect trigger strategy equilibrium cannot exist. The players will perform the backward induction argument at any period t starting from the period they regard as the last one, period $T + t - 1$. Second, if there are two single-shot equilibrium points satisfying the conditions of Theorem 3.6, then a trigger strategy equilibrium is possible; however, if T exceeds 2, then the actual path of observed moves will be stationary. That is, the players never reach a last period in which the better of the two single-shot equilibria is chosen. Similarly, if the ε-equilibrium concept used in Theorem 3.7 is followed, it is utilized in a moving way. The trigger strategy will, in any period t, call for choosing s^* for the next t^* periods; that is, until period $t + t^* - 1$, and the time of the planned reversion to s^c, period $t + t^*$ never actually arrives.

5 Outcomes supported by other than trigger strategies

In Section 3, it was shown that payoff vectors that give each player more than she can achieve at a single-period Nash equilibrium can be supported by a subgame perfect Nash equilibrium trigger strategy combination, and in Section 4 the results of Section 3 were extended to finite horizon games. An appealing feature of trigger strategies is that they are very simple; however, by the use of less simple strategies it is possible to extend the results of these sections to include all payoff vectors that are *individually rational*. A payoff for a player is called individually rational if it is not smaller than a payoff that the player can guarantee to himself. Thus imagine a two-person, zero-sum game in which player i is one player and the remaining $n - 1$ players are the second player. Player i's payoff function is $P_i(s)$ and the payoff function of the other player is $-P_i(s)$. In this game, let u_i' be the security level of player i, and let $u' = (u_1', \ldots, u_n')$. Then, a payoff vector y is *individually rational* if $y \geqslant u'$.

According to Aumann (1981), it has been known since the middle to late 1960s that any individually rational payoff vector can be supported as a Nash equilibrium outcome in an infinitely repeated game where there is no discounting (where the α_i all equal 1), and it is this result that he dubs the *Folk Theorem* because the source of the result is not known. An important aspect of the Folk Theorem, perhaps the most important aspect, is that outcomes usually associated with cooperation can be supported by noncooperative equilibrium strategies. Thus it is useful to think of the Folk Theorem in both narrow and broad senses. The narrow version is the result just cited by Aumann and the broad version is the collection of results on games with and without discounting that relate to attaining through noncooperative means the kind of outcomes usually associated with collusion, cooperation, and binding agreement. Rubinstein (1979) has shown that individually rational payoffs can be supported as outcomes of subgame perfect Nash equilibria in the class of games addressed by the Folk Theorem, and, apparently Rubinstein's results were also found by Aumann and Shapley (see Aumann (1981:17)).

This line of work has been furthered in several directions. Abreu (1983) was able to characterize a class of strategies that support the Folk Theorem in games with discounting. That is, Abreu's strategies can be used to construct a subgame perfect Nash equilibrium that has as its achieved payoff vector any individually rational outcome. Fudenberg and Maskin (1983) have extended Abreu's results for infinite horizon repeated games with discounting and have extended them to games of incomplete information, and Benoit and Krishna (1985) have extended Abreu's work to finite horizon repeated games.

Roughly speaking, a player i who defects from the cooperative move can be punished by forcing him to a payoff of u_i' (or, for finite horizon games, a payoff arbitrarily close to u_i') for a long time. Inflicting this payoff on the defector may require that one or more of the other players have a payoff per period that is below the payoff associated with any of the single-period Nash Equilibria; therefore, the punishment specification must provide for a second phase where the nondefectors have large enough gains to bring their payoffs above the level of the worst single-period Nash equilibrium. It is possible to do this while still keeping the overall ("average" per period) payoff of the defector essentially at u_i'; however, were this not feasible, then it would not be possible to construct subgame perfect Nash equilibria in which defectors could be so severely punished.

Of course, the interested reader is urged to look at the papers cited above. This work fills out and greatly expands the Folk Theorem result cited by Aumann (1981), and it clarifies the role of trigger strategies in supporting cooperative outcomes by means of noncooperative equilibrium strategy combinations. From Friedman (1985), it is obvious that trigger strategies can support in finite horizon repeated games the same sort of outcomes that they can support in infinite horizon games: those that give to each player a payoff no lower than the worst payoff he can receive under a single-period Nash equilibrium. To support lower payoffs, one must have resort to the more complex strategies found by Abreu (1983). Interestingly, these more complex strategies are of no avail in either finite or infinite horizon games having only one single-period Nash equilibrium. (See Benoit and Krishna (1984).) For finite horizon games with unique single-period Nash equilibria, there are no trigger strategy equilibria.

6   Applications of supergames

As with Chapter 2, a prime application of supergames is to oligopoly, and several applications below are variants of a particular oligopoly model that is introduced in Section 6.1. This model is of n firms in an infinitely repeated market under Rule 3.1. In Section 6.2, the same model is retained, and n, the number of firms, is allowed to increase without bound. An interesting question is whether trigger strategy equilibria can be maintained both for large n and in the limit. In Section 6.3, the model of Section 6.1 is used again; the number of firms is fixed, but Rule 3.1 is relaxed. A firm never observes rival decisions; yet it is still possible to maintain trigger strategy equilibria, because a firm remains able to tell whether any firm has defected from the cooperative action. The last section discusses the concept of *altruism*, and it is seen that trigger strategy equilibria provide a means by which ordinary selfish behavior would look altruistic.

6.1 A model of differentiated products oligopoly

In this section, a general model of differentiated products oligopoly is described to provide an idea of the scope of such models. Then, a numerical example from this class is specified. This example and variants of it are the main vehicles of Sections 6.1 to 6.3. Suppose a market in which there are n producers of a differentiated product. Because of differentiation, the demand function facing one firm i is a continuous function of the prices of all n firms in each time period $t : q_{it} = f_i(p_t)$ where $p_t = (p_{1t}, \dots, p_{nt}) \in R_+^n$ is the price vector and q_{it} is the output and demand of firm i in period t. The ith firm's total cost function is $C_i(q_{it}) = C_i(f_i(p_t))$, and the single-period profit function is

$$\pi_i(p_t) = p_{it} f_i(p_t) - C_i(f_i(p_t)) \tag{3.28}$$

The conditions imposed on the profit functions are stated below.

CONDITION 3.1 *The demand function* $q_i = f_i(p)$ *is nonnegative and continuous for* $p \in R_+^n$. *For* $p \gg 0$ *and* $f_i(p) > 0$, $f_i(p)$ *is twice continuously differentiable,* $f_i^j(p) > 0, j \neq i$, *and* $\sum_{j=1}^n f_i^j(p) \le \varepsilon < 0$. *There is* $p^+ \in R_+^n$ *such that* $f_i(p^+) = 0, i \in N$.

CONDITION 3.2 *The cost function* $C_i(q_i)$ *is convex for* $q_i \ge 0$. *For* $q_i > 0$, $C_i(q_i)$ *is twice continuously differentiable and* $C_i'(q_i) \ge 0$. $C_i(0) \ge 0$.

CONDITION 3.3 *For any* $p \gg 0$ *at which* $f_i(p) > 0$ *and* $p_i - C_i'(f_i(p)) \ge 0$, *the profit function* $\pi_i(p) = p_i f_i(p) - C_i(f_i(p))$ *is concave in* p_i.

CONDITION 3.4 *There is* $p^c \in R_{++}^n$ *such that* $\pi_i^i(p^c) = f_i(p^c) + [p_i - C_i'(f_i(p^c))] f_i^i(p^c) = 0, i \in N$.

Condition 3.1 places conventional restrictions on the demand functions: As a firm's price rises, its sales decline; as the price of a rival firm rises, the firm's sales increase; the effect of changes in the firm's own price is larger in absolute value than the effects of all rival firms combined, and there are prices so high that firms sell nothing. Condition 3.2 requires nonnegative fixed and marginal costs, and stipulates that marginal cost is not falling as output rises. Condition 3.3, concavity of π_i with respect to p_{it} (for price vectors where price exceeds marginal cost), is a technical assumption in the sense that economic considerations do not call for it. It is a restriction that assures the existence of a single-period Nash equilibrium. Condition 3.4 is merely a convenience in the present exposition; it asserts existence of an interior Nash equilibrium (i.e., one at which all firms are active; their output levels are strictly positive). For a more detailed exposition of these models see Friedman (1983).

It is easily seen that single-period payoffs at p^c are inside the payoff possibility frontier, and it is possible to find $p^* \gg p^c$ such that $\pi_i(p^*) > \pi_i(p^c)$, $i \in N$. To see this, examine π_i^i and π_i^j evaluated at p^c:

$$\pi_i^i(p^c) = f_i(p^c) + [p_i^c - C_i'(f_i(p^c))]f_i^i(p^c) = 0 \qquad (3.29)$$

$$\pi_i^j(p^c) = [p_i^c - C_i'(f_i(p^c))]f_i^j(p^c) \qquad (3.30)$$

At p^c, $\pi_i^i = 0$ and $f_i(p^c) > 0$. In addition, $f_i^i < 0$ everywhere; hence, $p_i^c > C_i'(f_i(p^c))$. Using this information in equations (3.24), and recalling that $f_i^j > 0$ $(j \neq i)$, it is clear that $\pi_i^j > 0$ for all $i, j \in N$ $(i \neq j)$, evaluated at p^c. Thus, by continuity of the first derivatives, it is possible to find $p^* \gg p^c$ for which all firms have larger profits $(\pi_i(p^*) > \pi_i(p^c), i \in N)$.

Suppose now that the discount parameter of firm i is α_i, making its objective function

$$\sum_{t=0}^{\infty} \alpha_i^t \pi_i(p_t) \qquad (3.31)$$

Characterizing a trigger strategy equilibrium is very easy. Let $\phi_i(p^*) = \max_{p_i \in [0, p_i^+]} \pi_i(p^* \backslash p_i)$. Then, for p^* such that $\pi_i(p^*) > \pi_i(p^c), i \in N$, a trigger strategy combination, σ, based on p^* and p^c would be defined in accordance with Definition 3.11. That is, player i would let $p_{i0} = p_i^*$ and would choose $p_{it} = p_i^*$ if $p_\tau = p^*$ for all $\tau < t$. Otherwise, $p_{it} = p_i^c$ would be selected. This combination σ is a trigger strategy equilibrium if

$$\alpha_i > \frac{\phi_i(p^*) - \pi_i(p^*)}{\phi_i(p^*) - \pi_i(p^c)} \qquad (3.32)$$

which is the condition given in Theorem 3.3.

Turning to a numerical example, suppose $n = 3$, costs are nil, and demand functions for the firms are

$$q_i = 100 - 3p_i + \sum_{j \neq i} p_j \qquad (3.33)$$

Then the single-period profit function of each firm i is

$$\pi_i(p) = 100p_i - 3p_i^2 + p_i \sum_{j \neq i} p_j \qquad (3.34)$$

Because the model is symmetric, all firms have the same prices, output levels, and profits at the single-period Nash equilibrium. These are $p_i = 25$, $q_i = 75$, and $\pi_i = 1875$. A reasonable trigger strategy outcome to examine is the joint profit maximum, at which $p_i = 50$, $q_i = 50$, and $\pi_i = 2500$. Finally, $\phi_i(50, 50, 50)$, the profit that one firm can achieve in just one period by maximizing against joint maximum prices for the others, is $3333\frac{1}{3}$. This profit is achieved at a price of $33\frac{1}{3}$ and an output level of 100. It is easily seen that the right-hand side of equation (3.32) is, in this case, 4/7 which indicates that the trigger strategy combination is an equilibrium point if all firms have discount parameters of $\alpha_i = 4/7$ or more.

6.2 Oligopoly for large and increasing n

In this section, the model of Section 6.1 is examined as n is allowed to grow. As Green (1980) has shown, an infinite number of firms is compatible with trigger strategy equilibria. Sufficient conditions are that (1) equation (3.32) remains satisfied and (2) each firm remains aware in each period t of the price choices of all other firms in all past periods. The former means that following the trigger strategy is superior to defecting from it for each firm, and the latter means that each firm can see the defection of any other firm in the period following the defection. While the information conditions of the model guarantee that defection will be promptly spotted by all players, there is no guarantee that equation (3.32) will remain satisfied as n increases. In fact, it is easy to make up examples of either sort. This is done below to show that the same three-firm model can be a special case of two different n-firm models that differ in the way that they change as n grows. These examples stem from the work of Lambson (1984), who has studied extensively the conditions under which trigger strategy equilibria remain viable as the number of players in a game increases.

For the first example, let the demand and single-period profit functions be

$$q_i = 100 - 3p_i + \frac{2}{n-1} \sum_{j \neq i} p_j \qquad (3.35)$$

$$\pi_i = 100p_i - 3p_i^2 + \frac{2p_i}{n-1} \sum_{j \neq i} p_j \qquad (3.36)$$

If $n = 3$, the model reduces to the model of Section 6.1. For any value of n, price, output, and single-period profit for the single-period Nash equilibrium are $p_i = 25$, $q_i = 75$, and $\pi_i = 1875$; for the joint profit maximum, $p_i = 50$, $q_i = 50$, and $\pi_i = 2500$; and for the single period of defection, $p_i = 33\frac{1}{3}$, $q_i = 100$, and $\pi_i = 3333\frac{1}{3}$. Thus, nothing is changed as n grows, and there are trigger strategy equilibria for all values of n.

For the second example, demand and single-period profits are

$$q_i = \frac{400 - 4np_i + 4 \sum_{j \neq i} p_j}{n+1} \qquad (3.37)$$

$$\pi_i = \frac{400p_i - 4np_i^2 + 4p_i \sum_{j \neq i} p_j}{n+1} \qquad (3.38)$$

The demand system in equation (3.37) is based on the inverse demand functions

$$p_i = 100 - \tfrac{1}{2}q_i - \tfrac{1}{4} \sum_{j \neq i} q_j, \qquad i \in N \qquad (3.39)$$

If equation (3.39) is taken to be the correct structure for all n, and then these inverse demand functions are inverted to express output as a function of prices, one obtains equation (3.37). The single-period noncooperative equilibrium data in this model are $p_i = 100/(n + 1)$, $q_i = 400n/(n + 1)^2$, and $\pi_i = 40,000n/(n + 1)^3$; the joint maximum data are $p_i = 50$, $q_i = 200/(n + 1)$, and $\pi_i = 10,000/(n + 1)$; and the period of defection data are $p_i = 25(n + 1)/n$, $q_i = 100$, and $\pi_i = 2500(n + 1)/n$. The right-hand side of equation (3.32) is

$$\frac{\dfrac{2500(n + 1)}{n} - \dfrac{10,000}{n + 1}}{\dfrac{2500(n + 1)}{n} - \dfrac{40,000n}{(n + 1)^3}} = \frac{1 - 4n/(n + 1)^2}{1 - 16n^2/(n + 1)^3} \tag{3.40}$$

Obviously, equation (3.40) converges to 1 as n goes to infinity; therefore, for any fixed value of $\alpha_i < 1$, as n grows there will come a value of n beyond which the inequality in equation (3.32) will cease to hold; it will be better to defect than to adhere to a trigger strategy. Thus, trigger strategy equilibria will not be possible for fixed α_i and arbitrarily large n. Of course, equation (3.40) is calculated for a particular trigger strategy; however, a similar expression and result would obtain in this example for any point on which one chose to base a trigger strategy.

6.3 Trigger strategy equilibria when firms cannot observe prices

Suppose that the market is characterized by the model in Section 6.1, but that Rule 3.1 does not hold. In particular, a firm never observes the actual prices choices made by the other firms. It is clear in this case that trigger strategy equilibria are still possible because the firms remain able to tell whether their rivals are sticking to the trigger strategy prices or are defecting. The means for this observation is the firm's own output level. In each period, firms simultaneously select prices, following which each firm observes its own output level. If any firm defects from its trigger strategy price, other firms will find their demand and output differ from what they expected. No firm can tell which rival defected, but that knowledge is not necessary for it to get the signal that it should switch to its single-period Nash equilibrium price.

Porter (1983) analyzes a model in which firms do not observe the choices made by rivals, as above, and in which randomness enters the demand functions. The distribution of the random variable is known; however, its presence means that all firms can be following trigger strategies and, at the same time, a firm will have lower sales than expected. Again, it remains possible to have trigger strategy equilibria, but two alterations are called for in those strategies. Assume that the random variable in demand, u_t, is additive and the mean of its distribution is zero. Then the firm's demand function is

$$q_{it} = 100 - 3p_{it} + \sum_{j \neq i} p_{jt} + u_t \tag{3.41}$$

This is the demand function from the example in Section 6.1 with the random variable u_t added. All firms are subject to the same realization of the random variable.

The first alteration in the trigger strategy is to lower the trigger output level to something below the expected output level. Suppose that the firms had determined on prices of 50 for each to achieve the joint profit maximum. The associated expected output levels are 50 each. To state the trigger strategy so that a firm reverts to a price of 25 in the period after observing an output level below 50 is unduly stringent, because it makes no allowance for the random variable ever being negative. Assuming a symmetric distribution, there is a probability of .5 that the random variable is negative in period 0 and a probability of $1 - .5^{t+1}$ that it will have been negative at least once by the end of period t. This standard is clearly too severe; the firms are better off to choose a trigger output level of something less than 50. They face a dilemma: A trigger of 50 leaves little room for a firm to choose a price below 50 and go undetected, but output levels below the trigger will appear very quickly from a negative realization of the random variable. A trigger very far below 50 will ensure that a random variable realization is unlikely to send output below the trigger, but it gives lots of room for firms to cheat without detection. These considerations call for a carefully calculated intermediate value for the trigger that balances off these two elements. A second approach is to do a statistical analysis of the supposed values of the sequence of random variables. If firms are adhering to the trigger strategies, then, in each period a firm can infer the value of the random variable. The value inferred by firm i is $\bar{u}_{it} = q_{it} - 50$. Over time, firm i observes $(\bar{u}_{i0}, \bar{u}_{i1}, \ldots, \bar{u}_{it})$, and at each time t it can test the hypothesis that the observed sequence is drawn from a population with mean 0 and the known variance of u_t. If the standards for that test are agreed on in advance by all firms, then all firms adhering to the trigger strategy will come to identical conclusions in each period.

The second alteration in the trigger strategy is that the firms should, when reverting to single-period equilibrium point prices, only revert for a finite time. Clearly this length of reversion, T, must be the same for all firms and known to all. The reason for using a finite length is that, no matter what positive trigger value is chosen for output, if all firms always adhere to choosing prices of 50, there will still be a time when the trigger level is reached and the firms revert to choosing prices of 25. The only way to have the higher prices continuing into the distant future is to use finite period reversions. Doing this, of course, increases the value of defection, but the choice of T, the duration of the reversion, and of the trigger value of output would be made jointly.

6.4 Altruism and supergames

The Oxford English Dictionary defines *altruism* as "Devotion to the welfare of others, regard for others, as a principle of action; opposed to egoism or selfishness." In a world of rational people who choose their actions according to a plan to maximize the value of an objective function, devising an operational definition of altruism can be difficult. For example, suppose there are two people in a world of m commodities and no production. Suppose that person 1 has an endowment of $w^1 \in R^m$, and person 2 has $w^2 \in R^m$. Now assume that $w^1 \gg 0$ and $w^2 = 0$; hence, person 2 will be miserable unless person 1 gives him part of his endowment. Say person 1 divides his endowment into $y^1 \gg 0$ and $y^2 \gg 0$ where $y^1 + y^2 = w^1$, and he reserves y^1 for his personal consumption while giving y^2 to person 2. To complete the picture, let this whole situation be a one-shot thing and assume that, of all choices open to person 1, the division into y^1 and y^2 is what he decides is best. This is easily explained with conventional consumer choice theory: Person 1 has preferences over commodity allocations $(x^1, x^2) \in R^{2m}$ where x^1 will be consumed by person 1 and x^2 by person 2. Under suitable assumptions (see Green (1976) or Hildenbrand and Kirman (1976), a continuous utility function $u_1(x^1, x^2)$ can represent the preferences of person 1.

The preceding illustration leads to a definition of altruism under which a person is altruistic if increases in the consumption bundles of (some) other people will increase the satisfaction of the person. It is natural to state a companion definition of a selfish person as one whose satisfaction depends only on her own personal consumption bundle. One may wish to argue that a person cannot be altruistic when choosing actions that maximize her own utility, and the fact that x^2 enters the utility function of person 1 merely means that person 1 is being selfish when giving something to person 2. Her motive is to suit herself.

A second definition of altruism, proposed by Kurz (1976), is that a person is altruistic if her satisfaction does not depend on the consumption of others and she gives valuable commodities to another person without having a binding agreement under which she will receive something of value in return. Kurz shows that altruistic behavior can be characteristic of trigger strategy equilibria.

My purpose here is not to settle the question of how best to define altruism within the context of economics; rather, I wish only to indicate briefly two possible definitions and to draw on Kurz (1976) to show the connection between trigger strategy equilibria and the second definition. Suppose there are two people in a trading situation as depicted in Figure 3.7. Their initial endowment of goods is, in each period, at the point E. Player 1 receives $w^1 = (w^1_1, w^1_2)$ and the player 2 receives $w^2 = (w^2_1, w^2_2)$. Now suppose a trigger strategy σ_1 for player 1 under which he gives player 2 $\delta_1 = w^1_1 - y^1_1$ units of good 1 in the initial period. In each subsequent period, he gives the same to player 2 if player 2 has, in all past periods, given player 1 $\delta_2 = w^2_2 - y^2_2$ units of good 2. Otherwise, player 1 gives player 2 nothing. Let σ_2 be defined in a parallel way for player 2. Each player is engaging in voluntary gifts—there is no binding contract between them. Of course, to say no strings are attached goes too far, but, nonetheless, either player in any period is perfectly free to give nothing or

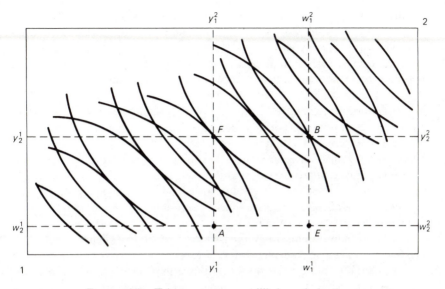

FIGURE 3.7   Trigger strategy equilibria and altruism.

to give any gift falling within his endowment. If, for example, player 1 gave nothing in a particular period, the two players' consumption bundles would be at B in Figure 3.7. Following σ, ever after this act neither player would give any gifts and they would consume at E. On the other hand, if they follow their trigger strategies $\sigma = (\sigma_1, \sigma_2)$ indefinitely, they will consume at F in Figure 3.7. Letting $u_i(x^i)$ be the single-period utility (payoff) function of player i and α_i his discount parameter, σ is a trigger strategy equilibrium if

$$\alpha_1 > \frac{u_1(w_1^1, y_2^1) - u_1(y^1)}{u_1(w_1^1, y_2^1) - u_1(w^1)} \tag{3.42}$$

$$\alpha_2 > \frac{u_2(y_1^2, w_2^2) - u_2(y^2)}{u_2(y_1^2, w_2^2) - u_2(w^2)} \tag{3.43}$$

both hold. This is an equilibrium with behavior that is altruistic under the Kurz definition.

7   Concluding comments

The models studied in this chapter bear out three very important points. First, the Nash noncooperative equilibrium remains the equilibrium concept that is appropriate in supergames; however, a supergame non-cooperative equilibrium need not merely be a sequence of single-shot Nash equilibria. The journals abound with the mistaken view that the Nash equilibrium is myopic in the sense that it merely is the equilibrium of a single-shot game. That is clearly not the intent of Nash (1951) nor is it the understanding of game theorists generally. It is intended that payoff functions and strategy sets be formulated in a very abstract and general way so that a wide variety of circumstances can be encompassed. By moving in the present chapter to a semiextensive form, individual moves are emphasized rather than obscured and the strategic interconnections between the choices at various points in time are seen more clearly.

The second point is that the noncooperative equilibrium can be unsatisfactory by leading to intuitively objectionable outcomes. The faulty outcomes generally incorporate noncredible threats. Literally, these strategies contain provisions that can be interpreted as noncredible threats; however, in game theoretic terms, these objectionable equilibria are not subgame perfect. There are subgames in which the behavior induced by the equilibrium strategies is not equilibrium behavior for the subgame. A way around this difficulty is to require that only subgame perfect noncooperative equilibria be accepted.

The third point stems from the strategic time dependence of players' behavior. In a sense, the line separating cooperative and noncooperative games is slightly blurred by the possibilities that open up in supergames. As the preceding sections show, outcomes are possible as noncooperative equilibria that yield the same actual moves and payoffs as could be obtained using binding agreements, and these noncooperative equilibria are usefully regarded as stemming from self-enforcing agreements. They are agreements because it is difficult to imagine the prescribed behavior resulting from other than an agreement among the players. They are self-enforcing because, being noncooperative equilibria, no player possesses an incentive to deviate from the agreed upon behavior. These quasi-cooperative outcomes have special interest for oligopoly theory, and for the concept of competition in economics.

Regarding oligopoly, many writers have taken the view that oligopolists will necessarily collude and achieve profits on the profit possibility frontier; however, a noncooperative equilibrium in a single-period model is nearly always inside, rather than on, that frontier. The latter point suggests that collusion to reach frontier profits is not possible if contractual agreements are not possible. The two sides of this dispute are able to come together in the face of trigger strategy equilibria, because these equilibria permit payoff possibility frontier realizations resulting from Nash equilibrium behavior.

Concerning competition, it has long been thought that very large numbers of relatively small participants in markets assure that competitive behavior must result. *Competitive* is meant here in the economists' usual sense that each participant is unable to have any effect on other players through her actions and players do not cooperate. Where numbers are large and individual actors small, competition may, in fact, be the norm; however, as Green (1980) ably demonstrates, these conditions do not by themselves rule out noncompetitive outcomes. Probably the information conditions required for these noncompetitive outcomes with large numbers of participants are, in practice, too stringent.

Before turning to Chapter 4, it is well to remember that the results of this chapter assume no structural time dependence. In general, it is sufficient to merely have independent repetitions of a game. Chapter 4 deals with supergames in which there is structural time dependence—the payoffs of a given period depend on past as well as present period choices.

Exercises

1. A finite two-person bimatrix game is given by

5, 9	5, 7	−3, 0	20, 5
3, 10	2, 20	4, 5	15, 17
−4, 1	10, 3	2, 2	0, −5
0, 1	8, −2	6, 4	10, 0

  a. What are the pure strategy equilibrium points of this game?
  b. Based on pure strategies, is there a finitely repeated game equilibrium point that is subgame perfect if the game is repeated T times? Can such a strategy have the pure strategies $(2, 4)$, with payoff realization $(15, 17)$, for part of the game?
  c. For the trigger strategy in b, what is the minimum number of periods during which pure strategy $(2, 4)$ cannot be selected?
  d. For part c, what are the lower bounds for the discount parameters such that the trigger strategy combination you have named is an equilibrium point?
2. Assume that the finite game in problem 1 is to be infinitely repeated. Name a subgame perfect trigger strategy combination and give the associated minimum values of the discount parameters for which this trigger strategy combination is an equilibrium point.
3. Suppose that a game (N, S, P) given by $N = \{1, 2\}$, $S_1 = [0, 50]$, $S_2 = [0, 50]$, $P_1(s) = 100s_1 - 10s_1^2 + 10s_1s_2$, $P_2(s) = 200s_2 - 15s_2^2 + 10s_1s_2$.
  a. What is an equilibrium point of this game? Is it unique? What are the equilibrium payoffs?
  b. What payoffs would the players obtain if they chose s^* in order to maximize $P_1(s) + P_2(s)$? Can these payoffs be supported as a subgame perfect trigger strategy noncooperative equilibrium point? If the answer is yes, with what range of values for the discount parameters?

Notes

1. From an analytical standpoint, it does not matter whether the action taken in a single time period is a *move* in the sense of game theory or a *strategy* that involves several moves. Either way, the actions and payoffs within one time period constitute a game, and the sequence of actions and payoff functions constitute another game—the supergame. The latter is built out of the former. It does happen that the single-period actions are moves (single-move strategies) in many applications of these models.
2. When the concept "strategy" was first introduced, it was emphasized that the move of a player at a particular node would generally depend on the information

the player would have at that point in the game. To allow time dependent strategies is merely to allow this same property to apply.

3. Letting $\|s_{it}\|$ be the norm on S_{it}, with G_i defined by equations (3.2), $\mathcal{S}_i$ is compact if $\sum_{t=0}^{\infty} \alpha_{it} \|s_{it}\|$ is bounded.

4. Propositions like the corollary are related to the *Folk Theorem*, an aspect of which is that an outcome $P(s^*)$ in a (single-period) game can be a noncooperative equilibrium outcome if (a) the game is repeated infinitely often and (b) $P(s^*)$ gives each player a higher payoff than the player could secure for himself. The earliest source I know of for a written statement along the lines of the Folk Theorem is Luce and Raiffa (1957) in their discussion of the repeated prisoner's dilemma. Section 5 has further comments on this topic.

5. There is one other equilibrium: $(0, 0)$ with associated payoffs of zero for each player. For my example, I use the two interior equilibria; however, any two of the three equilibria are suitable for the illustration.

6. Although Radner mentions the objective function used here (average payoff over the remainder of the horizon; $\sum_{\tau=t}^{T} P_i(s_\tau)/(T - t + 1)$ at time t), he actually uses average payoff from the beginning; that is $\sum_{\tau=0}^{T} P_i(s_\tau)/(T + 1)$ at time t. His formulation is easier to work with but is not as reasonable. It is intuitively more appealing that players would, from any time t onward, seek to maximize their average payoffs from that time on; however, both formulations lead to qualitatively similar results.

4

Time-dependent supergames, limited information, and bounded rationality

The models studied in this chapter range over several topics that come under the heading of games in semiextensive or extensive form. The first of these, supergames with time-dependent structures, covered in Section 1, is a straightforward generalization of the infinite horizon models of Chapter 3. The single-period payoff function for a player in time t depends on the actions of all players in the previous period (s_{t-1}) as well as on their current actions (s_t). Most of Section 1 is devoted to models with a stationary structure; that is, the single-period payoff function, $P_i(s_{t-1}, s_t)$, does not change over time. Existence of an equilibrium point is straightforward, but, additionally, conditions are given under which any path of equilibrium actions must converge to a unique steady state. These models and the associated convergence results can be generalized to nonstationary payoff structures.

Section 2 takes up another sort of generalization of the infinite horizon models of Chapter 3—in this case to stochastic games. The setup involves a fixed set of players (N) who play an ordinary single-shot game in each time period; however, the game they play at time t is randomly selected from a finite set of games. When the game of time t is to be played, all players know which game has been chosen. Time dependence enters in the specification of the random process by which the next game is chosen. The probability of playing game Γ_t in time t depends on which game Γ_{t-1} was played in time $t-1$ and on the actions, s_{t-1}, chosen in period $t-1$. Thus the payoff function of time t depends on s_{t-1} through the stochastic mechanism that selects which game is played. The results in this section draw heavily on techniques of stochastic dynamic programming, as the game is essentially made up of n interconnected stochastic dynamic programming problems.

Section 3 is concerned with a bounded rationality approach to an infinite horizon game of incomplete information; in this case, a large number of players are divided into pairs with each pair playing a two-person noncooperative game. This process is repeated indefinitely often with each player knowing very little about the past play of his present opponent and having limited information about the payoff structure of the current game. Each player can be assumed to undertake a full Bayesian analysis of the game. Then, at each play, a player attempts to identify his current opponent by the available information and guesses how the player will act on the basis of this individual evaluation. This approach requires an extremely elaborate set of computations by each player in each period. Instead of using the full rationality Bayesian approach, a bounded rationality method is used that has each player treating the possible opposing players in a statistical fashion. The player knows some characteristics of the opposing set of players, and treats each individual opponent actually faced as being a random draw from this population. The opponent's play can depend on some current, specific information.

Section 4 is concerned with an apparent paradox that is related to finite-period supergames, and with games in which there is an obvious Nash equilibrium that one would not expect players to choose. Common sense suggests an outcome that appears at variance with the non-cooperative equilibrium. Section 5 contains some applications of models in Sections 1 and 2, and Section 6 has concluding comments.

1 Time-dependent supergames

In practice, it is easy to cite examples where the payoffs received by the players in a game for time period t depend not only on the actions taken in that period, but on actions taken in one or more past periods as well. For example, imagine an election campaign in which the candidates' actions are to name positions on issues of public interest. Supposing this election to be one period of an ongoing political game, the credibility of a candidate's announcement of position would naturally depend on the positions she has taken in the past, and, consequently, the relationship between the payoff received in the current period and the positions announced in the current period is affected by the past announcements of positions by the players. To announce extreme departures from past positions is likely to deprive a person of votes. Short- and long-run tradeoffs occur when, for example, a candidate who has been, say, far to the left of the political spectrum and who sees the whole country moving to the right, starts an orderly, slow change of her own position toward the right. This may deprive her of votes in the short run by disappointing her usual constituency, but it may greatly strengthen her position several years hence by keeping her nearer the national mainstream. A member of the House of Representatives who has been winning by a wide margin and who looks to win higher office may make such a trade.

A second example is a market for a durable good. The demand facing any supplier in a given time period will depend on the size and age profile of the stock of the good held by consumers. If a large number of households purchased new refrigerators in 1980, then these people can be pretty well ruled out as potential buyers in 1981 or 1982.

The remainder of this section is divided into three sections, the first of which describes the stationary model and has some basic results that help to characterize equilibria. Section 1.2 examines the existence and stability of steady-state equilibria in the stationary model. In Section 1.3, the nonstationary model is described, and it is seen how the results of Sections 1.1 and 1.2 generalize.

1.1 The stationary model

In Section 1.1.1, the assumptions used for the stationary time-dependent supergame model are given and the class of games is defined. These games fall within the games covered by Theorem 3.2; hence, it is noted that open loop equilibrium points must exist for them. Section 1.1.2 is concerned with the interpretation of a time-dependent supergame as a sequence of single-shot games. There may be many ways to make such an interpretation, but not all of them will be fruitful; however, a particular interpretation is suggested that is intimately connected to the characterization of equilibrium points in the supergame, and that connects them to a sequence of equilibrium points in the (appropriately defined) single-shot games.

1.1.1 Definition of stationary time-dependent supergames and existence of open loop equilibria

Formulating a stationary infinite horizon game model is quite straightforward: The single-period payoff is written as $P_i(s_{t-1}, s_t)$. More than one past period could be incorporated, but the basic principles are illustrated in the simpler situation. Assumption 2.1 is retained and Assumptions 2.2 and 2.3 are suitably modified:

ASSUMPTION 4.1 $P_i(s_{t-1}, s_t) \in R$ is bounded and continuous for all $(s_{t-1}, s_t) \in S \times S$.

ASSUMPTION 4.2 $P_i(s_{t-1}, s_t)$ is a concave function of $(s_{i,t-1}, s_{it}) \in S_i \times S_i$.

DEFINITION 4.1 A **stationary time-dependent supergame**, $\Gamma = (N, S, P, \alpha)$, satisfies Assumptions 2.1, 4.1, and 4.2, and Rules 2.1, 2.2, and 3.1. For all $i \in N$, $\alpha_i \in [0, 1)$. The players' payoff functions are

$$\sum_{t=1}^{\infty} \alpha_i^{t-1} P_i(s_{t-1}, s_t) = G_i(\sigma) \tag{4.1}$$

and an open loop strategy $\sigma_i = (s_{i0}, s_{i1}, \ldots)$ satisfies $s_{it} \in S_i$, $t > 0$, and $s_{i0} = s_i^0, i \in N$.

The condition that s_{i0} has a single possible value merely means that the action in the game begins in period 1, and that s_0 is an initial condition at that time. That a stationary time-dependent supergame has an equilibrium point follows almost immediately from Theorem 3.2. Restricting attention to open loop strategies, $G_i(\sigma)$ is a concave function of σ_i, and, as the other conditions stated for Theorem 3.2 are met, the following corollary is justified:

COROLLARY   *A stationary time-dependent supergame has an equilibrium point in open loop strategies.*

1.1.2   On the interpretation of a time-dependent supergame as a sequence of one-shot games

Three interesting questions relating to stationary supergame equilibrium points are (a) whether the single-period actions, are, in some sense, equilibrium points of single-shot games, (b) whether the supergame has a steady-state equilibrium, and (c) whether a steady-state equilibrium is stable. To be more precise, let $\sigma^* = (s_0^*, s_1^*, s_2^*, \ldots)$ be an equilibrium point of the supergame. Question (a) asks whether there is a natural, reasonable way to form payoff functions for each individual period t so that s_t^* is an equilibrium point for the individual period t game. Question (b) inquires whether there is some special $s^* \in S$ such that, if the initial condition is $s_0 = s^*$, then $s_t^* = s^*, t = 0, 1, 2, \ldots$ is an equilibrium point of the super-game. Question (c), stability of σ^*, can be posed this way: Suppose that s_0^*, the initial condition, is an arbitrary member of S. Then, for the equilibrium sequence of actions $\{s_t^*\}$, must s_t^* converge independently of s_0^* to a steady-state s^* as t goes to infinity?

Question (a) is answered in the remainder of this section. The most obvious candidate for a single-shot game is a game using the single-period payoff functions as payoff functions, but this is not a fruitful approach, as an example demonstrates. After the example, an interesting definition of single-shot games is given and then it is proved that a supergame equilibrium strategy combination must induce a sequence of equilibrium points in each member of this family of single-shot games. Questions (b) and (c) are taken up in Section 1.2.

Returning to question (a), it is definitely not true that $s_t = s^*$ (the supergame steady-state equilibrium value) is an equilibrium point of the single-shot game $(N, S, P(s_{t-1}^*, s_t))$. This point can be illustrated by an example. Suppose that

$$P_1(s_{t-1}, s_t) = s_{1,t-1}^2 - s_{1,t-1}s_{2t} + 3s_{1t} - s_{1,t-1}s_{1t}^2 \qquad (4.2)$$

$$P_2(s_{t-1}, s_t) = s_{2,t-1}^2 - s_{2,t-1}s_{1t} + 3s_{2t} - s_{2,t-1}s_{2t}^2 \qquad (4.3)$$

and $\alpha_1 = \alpha_2 = .5$. Then, for player 1,

$$G_1(\sigma) = \sum_{t=1}^{\infty} .5^{t-1} P_1(s_{t-1}, s_t) \qquad (4.4)$$

and an equilibrium strategy for player 1 will satisfy

$$.5^{t-1}\left[\frac{\partial P_1(s_{t-1}, s_t)}{\partial s_{1t}} + .5\frac{\partial P_1(s_t, s_{t+1})}{\partial s_{1t}}\right]$$

$$= .5^{t-1}[3 - 2s_{1,t-1}s_{1t} + .5(2s_{1t} - s_{2,t+1} - s_{1,t+1}^2)] = 0, \qquad t = 1, 2, \ldots \quad (4.5)$$

If $s_{10} = s_{20} = 1.2$ and $s_{2t} = 1.2$ for $t = 1, 2, \ldots$ then the optimal strategy for player 1 is $\sigma_1^* = (1.2, 1.2, 1.2, \ldots)$. Due to the symmetry of the model, if player 1 uses σ_1^*, the best reply of player 2 is $\sigma_2^* = (1.2, 1.2, 1.2, \ldots)$. Now suppose that $s_\tau = (1.2, 1.2)$, $\tau = 0, \ldots, t-1$ and that player 1 believes that $s_{2t} = 1.2$ will be chosen by player 2. What would player 1 select if he wished to maximize $P_1(s_{t-1}, s_t)$? Clearly, this is determined by

$$\frac{\partial P_1(s_{t-1}, s_t)}{\partial s_{1t}} = 3 - 2s_{1,t-1}s_{1t} = 3 - 2.4s_{1t} = 0 \tag{4.6}$$

or $s_{1t} = 1.25$. Thus, the equilibrium supergame strategy combination $\sigma^* = (s_0^*, s_1^*, \ldots)$ is not composed of actions s_t^* that are equilibrium points for the myopic games $(N, S, P(s_{t-1}^*, s_t))$.

In other words, equilibrium behavior does not mean, in general, that a player maximize the payoff in each period by their choice for that period. The reason, of course, is that the choice in period t will affect the payoff in period $t+1$ as well as that of period t, which suggests that s_t^* is an equilibrium point of some speciality formed myopic game that takes into account the payoffs of periods t and $t+1$. This is stated as Lemma 4.1 where, as the foregoing numerical example indicates, the relevant payoff functions are seen to be

$$P_i(s_{t-1}^*, s_t) + \alpha_i P_i(s_t, s_{t+1}^*) = P_i^*(s_{t-1}^*, s_t, s_{t+1}^*).$$

LEMMA 4.1 $\sigma^* = (s_0^*, s_1^*, s_2^*, \ldots)$ *is an open loop equilibrium point of the stationary time-dependent supergame* (N, S, P, α) *if and only if* s_t^* *is an equilibrium point of the game* $(N, S, P^*(s_{t-1}^*, s_t, s_{t+1}^*))$ *for* $t = 1, 2, \ldots$.

Proof It is first shown that if σ^* is an equilibrium point of (N, S, P, α), then s_t^* is an equilibrium point of $(N, S, P^*(s_{t-1}^*, s_t, s_{t+1}^*))$. If, for some t, s_t^* is not an equilibrium point, then there is at least one player i who can choose $s_{it}' \neq s_{it}^*$ and increase his payoff. Look at the supergame payoff function in detail, evaluated at $\sigma^* \backslash s_{it}'$:

$$G_i(\sigma^* \backslash s_{it}') = P_i(s_0^*, s_1^*) + \cdots + \alpha_i^{t-2} P_i(s_{t-2}^*, s_{t-1}^*) + \alpha_i^{t-1} P_i(s_{t-1}^*, s_t^* \backslash s_{it}')$$
$$+ \alpha_i^t P_i(s_t^* \backslash s_{it}', s_{t+1}^*) + \alpha_i^{t+1} P_i(s_{t+1}^*, s_{t+2}^*) + \cdots$$
$$= P_i(s_0^*, s_1^*) + \cdots + \alpha_i^{t-2} P_i(s_{t-2}^*, s_{t-1}^*) + \alpha_i^{t-1} P_i^*(s_{t-1}^*, s_t^* \backslash s_{it}', s_{t+1}^*)$$
$$+ \alpha_i^{t+1} P_i(s_{t+1}^*, s_{t+2}^*) + \cdots$$

By selecting s_{it}', player i increases his payoff for the combined periods t and $t+1$, but payoffs are unchanged for all remaining periods; thus, if s_t^* is not an equilibrium point for $(N, S, P^*(s_{t-1}^*, s_t, s_{t+1}^*))$ then σ^* is not an equilibrium point for (N, S, P, α).

Thus, if σ^* is an equilibrium point of (N, S, P, α), s_t^* is an equilibrium point of $(N, S, P^*(s_{t-1}^*, s_t, s_{t+1}^*))$ for all $t > 1$. If s_t^* is an equilibrium point of $(N, S, P^*(s_{t-1}^*, s_t, s_{t+1}^*))$ for $t = 1, 2, \ldots$ then σ_i^* is a local maximum of G_i; however, a local maximum of a concave function is a global maximum (see Roberts and Varberg (1973:123)). Therefore, σ^* is an equilibrium point of (N, S, P, α) and the theorem is proved. QED

Lemma 4.1 allows a simple way of describing the open loop equilibrium points of (N, S, P, α) by means of the equilibrium points of the games $(N, S, P^*(s_{t-1}, s_t, s_{t+1}))$. For any $s_{t-1}, s_{t+1} \in S \times S$, there is a nonempty set of equilibrium points of $(N, S, P^*(s_{t-1}, s_t, s_{t+1}))$. This set of equilibrium points is denoted $\psi(s_{t-1}, s_{t+1})$ and ψ is called the *equilibrium correspondence*. More formally:

DEFINITION 4.2 *The* **equilibrium correspondence** *of* (N, S, P, α) *is denoted* $\psi(s', s'')$ *and is defined by the conditions that* $\psi(s', s'') \subset S$ *and,* $s^* \in \psi(s', s'')$ *if and only if* s^* *is an equilibrium point of* $(N, S, P^*(s', s, s''))$.

In view of Definition 4.2, the content of Lemma 4.1 can be stated as follows: $\sigma^* = (s_0^*, s_1^*, \ldots)$ is an open loop equilibrium point of the time-dependent supergame if and only if $s_t^* \in \psi(s_{t-1}^*, s_{t+1}^*)$ for $t = 1, 2, \ldots$.

1.2 Existence and stability of a steady-state equilibrium

The assumptions made thus far, Assumptions 2.1, 4.1, and 4.2, are not sufficient to ensure existence of a steady-state equilibrium. In Section 1.2.1, where existence of equilibrium points is proved, an additional assumption is made that places restrictions on the equilibrium correspondence. It is seen in Section 1.2.2 that these same conditions guarantee stability of the open loop equilibria of time-dependent supergames.

1.2.1 Existence of a unique steady-state equilibrium

Whether there is a steady-state equilibrium, that is, an equilibrium $\sigma^* = (s_0^*, s_1^*, \ldots)$ where $s_t^* = s_{t'}^*$ for all t and t', can be stated in terms of the equilibrium correspondence: There is a steady-state equilibrium point if and only if there is some s^* such that $s^* \in \psi(s^*, s^*)$. This, however, is a fixed point problem; there is a steady-state equilibrium if and only if the equilibrium correspondence has a fixed point. The following assumption is one which assures that there is a fixed point and, in addition, that starting from any initial condition s_0, an equilibrium is both unique and converges to the steady state.[1]

ASSUMPTION 4.3 *The equilibrium correspondence* $\psi(s', s'')$ *is a single-valued function that obeys the following Lipschitz condition:*

$$\|\psi(s_{t-1}, s_{t+1}) - \psi(s'_{t-1}, s'_{t+1})\| \leqslant k_1 \|s_{t-1} - s'_{t-1}\| + k_2 \|s_{t+1} - s'_{t+1}\| \quad (4.8)$$

where $k_1 + k_2 \leqslant k < 1$ *for all* $s_{t-1}, s'_{t-1}, s_{t+1}, s'_{t+1} \in S$.

This assumption restricts the equilibrium correspondence in two ways. First, the condition that ψ is a function satisfying a Lipschitz condition k, with $k < 1$, means that the game $(N, S, P^*(s_{t-1}^*, s_t, s_{t+1}^*))$ has a unique equilibrium point. Second, this equilibrium point, which changes as s_{t-1}^* and s_{t+1}^* change, cannot change very fast. In particular, suppose S is a subset of R^m and suppose that the equilibrium correspondence is differentiable. Then Assumption 4.3 would require

$$\sum_{j=1}^{m} \sum_{i=1}^{n} \left| \frac{\partial \psi}{\partial s_{ij,t-1}} \right| \leqslant k_1 \qquad \sum_{j=1}^{m} \sum_{i=1}^{n} \left| \frac{\partial \psi}{\partial s_{ij,t+1}} \right| \leqslant k_2 \qquad (4.9)$$

A function that satisfies the inequalities in equations (4.8) or (4.9) is called a *contraction*. A useful fact about contractions is that a contraction never has more than one fixed point, and, if the contraction maps a set into itself, it has a fixed point (see Bartle (1964:170)).[2]

LEMMA 4.2 *If a stationary time-dependent supergame satisfies Assumption 4.3, then there is a unique steady-state equilibrium. That is, there is a unique $s' \in S$ such that, if $s_0 = s'$, then $\sigma' = (s', s', \ldots)$ is an equilibrium point.*

Proof If s_{t-1} is required to equal s_{t+1}, then $\psi(s,s)$ can be treated as a function from S to S. A fixed point of this mapping is a steady-state equilibrium. Such a fixed point exists and is unique because ψ is a contraction. QED

1.2.2 Stability of open loop equilibria

Showing stability of steady-state equilibria is not nearly as short and easy as proving existence of a unique steady state. Suppose that $\sigma^* = (s_0^*, s_1^*, \ldots)$ is an equilibrium point of a supergame and that s' is the unique steady state. To prove stability is to prove that s_t^* converges to s' as t goes to infinity. In other words, no matter what the initial condition s_0^*, eventually any (open loop) equilibrium behavior will have the players choosing actions arbitrarily close to s'.

THEOREM 4.1 *Let (N, S, P, α) be a stationary time-dependent supergame satisfying assumption 4.3, let $\sigma^* = (s_0^*, s_1^*, \ldots)$ be an open loop equilibrium of that game, and let s' be the (unique) steady-state equilibrium action. Then $\lim_{t \to \infty} s_t^* = s'$.*

Proof The basic fact exploited in the proof is that ψ obeys the contraction conditions in Assumption 4.3. A sequence of functions, $g_t(s_{t+1}, s_0)$, $t = 1, 2, \ldots$, is defined using ψ and having the property that $s_t^* = \psi(s_{t-1}^*, s_{t+1}^*)$ implies $s_t^* = g_t(s_{t+1}^*, s_0^*)$. The functions g_t are all shown to be contractions, which, in turn, allows the theorem to be proved.

Define g_1 by $s_1 = \psi(s_0, s_2) = g_1(s_2, s_0)$. To define g_t for $t > 1$ when g_{t-1} is known, let

$$s_t = \psi(s_{t-1}, s_{t+1}) = \psi(g_{t-1}(s_t', s_0), s_{t+1}) \qquad (4.10)$$

Holding fixed the values of s_0, and s_{t+1}, the function $s_t = \psi(g_{t-1}(s_t', s_0), s_{t+1})$ is a mapping of s_t' into s_t. It is the fixed point of this mapping, shown below to be unique, which defines $g_t(s_{t+1}, s_0)$. From Assumption 4.3, ψ is a contraction, and this implies both that g_t exists and is also a contraction. Suppose that g_{t-1} exists and is a contraction obeying the Lipschitz condition λ_{t-1} with respect to s_t and μ_{t-1} with respect to s_0. Then, by way of deriving g_t, let $s'_t = \psi(g_{t-1}(s^1_t, s^1_0), s^1_{t+1})$ and $s''_t = \psi(g_{t-1}(s^2_t, s^2_0), s^2_{t+1})$ and note that

$$
\begin{aligned}
\|s'_t - s''_t\| &= \|\psi(g_{t-1}(s^1_t, s^1_0), s^1_{t+1}) - \psi(g_{t-1}(s^2_t, s^2_0), s^2_{t+1})\| \\
&\leq k_1 \|g_{t-1}(s^1_t, s^1_0) - g_{t-1}(s^2_t, s^2_0)\| + k_2 \|s^1_{t+1} - s^2_{t+1}\| \\
&\leq k_1(\lambda_{t-1}\|s^1_t - s^2_t\| + \mu_{t-1}\|s^1_0 - s^2_0\|) + k_2\|s^1_{t+1} - s^2_{t+1}\| \quad (4.11)
\end{aligned}
$$

If $\lambda_{t-1} < 1$, then g_t is well defined. That is, equation (4.10) as a function of s'_t into s_t is a contraction; hence it has a fixed point. Suppose this contraction condition holds for $t-1$ (it surely holds for $t-1 = 1$), and let us see if it holds for t. Using the fact that g_t is well defined, s'_t may be set equal to s^1_t and s''_t to s^2_t. Doing this and rearranging equation (4.11) gives

$$
\|s^1_t - s^2_t\| \leq \frac{\|s^1_0 - s^2_0\| k_1\mu_{t-1} + \|s^1_{t+1} - s^2_{t+1}\| k_2}{1 - k_1\lambda_{t-1}} \tag{4.12}
$$

If $\lambda_{t-1} + \mu_{t-1} \leq k$ (which holds for $t-1 = 1$) then, because $\lambda_t = k_2/(1 - k_1\lambda_{t-1})$ and $\mu_t = k_1\mu_{t-1}/(1 - k_1\lambda_{t-1})$, it follows that

$$
\lambda_t + \mu_t = \frac{k_2 + k_1\mu_{t-1}}{1 - k_1\lambda_{t-1}} \leq k_1 + k_2 \leq k < 1 \tag{4.13}
$$

Thus, g_t is a contraction, and, by induction, $g_t(s_{t+1}, s_0)$ is well defined and is a contraction obeying the Lipschitz conditions λ_t, μ_t where $\lambda_t + \mu_t \leq k$ for all $t \geq 1$.

Thus, the contractions g_t also have the properties, inherited from ψ, that $s^*_t = g_t(s^*_{t+1}, s^*_0)$ for all $t \geq 1$ if $\sigma^* = (s^*_0, s^*_1, \ldots)$ is an equilibrium point, and that $s' = g_t(s', s')$ for all $t \geq 1$ where $s' = \psi(s', s')$ is the steady-state equilibrium action. It remains to use the sequence of functions $\{g_t\}$ to show that s^*_t converges to s'. Define $\delta_t = \|s^*_t - s'\|$, $t = 0, 1, 2, \ldots$, and use

$$
\begin{aligned}
\|s^*_t - s'\| &= \|g_t(s^*_{t+1}, s^*_0) - g_t(s', s')\| \leq \lambda_t\|s^*_{t+1} - s'\| + \mu_t\|s^*_0 - s'\| \\
&= \lambda_t\delta_{t+1} + \mu_t\delta_0
\end{aligned}
$$

to see that

$$
\delta_1 \leq \lambda_1\delta_2 + \mu_1\delta_0 \leq \lambda_1(\lambda_2\delta_3 + \mu_2\delta_0) + \mu_1\delta_0 \leq \delta_{T+1}\prod_{t=1}^{T}\lambda_t + \delta_0\sum_{t=1}^{T}\mu_t\prod_{\tau=0}^{t-1}\lambda_\tau \tag{4.15}
$$

where λ_0 is defined to be unity. Clearly, the first term in equation (4.15) goes to zero as T goes to infinity, because the δ_t are bounded due to S being compact, and the λ_t are less than $k < 1$. Therefore,

$$
\delta_1 \leq \delta_0\sum_{t=1}^{\infty}\mu_t\prod_{\tau=0}^{t-1}\lambda_\tau \leq k\delta_0 \tag{4.16}
$$

Thus, in general, $\delta_t \leq k\delta_{t-1}$ and by induction, $\delta_t \leq k^t\delta_0$, which goes to zero as t goes to infinity, which completes the proof. QED

While the assumption restricting ψ to be a function satisfying a Lipschitz condition is rather strong, it does permit quite an interesting result in Theorem 4.1. Furthermore, as an example in Section 5 illustrates, this result can be useful in applications to economics. The open loop equilibria of Theorem 4.1 are clearly not perfect equilibria. To see this, suppose that $\sigma^* = (s_0^*, s_1^*, \ldots)$ is an equilibrium point and assume that the history of the game at time t is $h_t = (s_0', s_1', \ldots, s_{t-1}')$ where $s_{t-1}' \neq s_{t-1}^*$. In general, the subgame strategy combination $\sigma_t^* = (s_{t-1}', s_t^*, s_{t+1}^*, \ldots)$ for the subgame starting in period t with an initial condition s_{t-1}' is not an equilibrium point; for $s_t^* \in \psi(s_{t-1}', s_{t+1}^*)$ would not usually hold. Although these equilibria are not perfect, they are not faulty or intuitively unacceptable in the sense of incorporating noncredible threats. Insofar as one is dealing with completely rational players who hold complete information and who are capable of carrying out the actions they plan, these equilibria have no fault.

1.3 Brief remarks on nonstationary supergames and on trigger strategy equilibria

A further note on Theorem 4.1 is that it can be generalized to nonstationary time-dependent supergames. The payoff function of player i in period t is written $P_{it}(s_{t-1}, s_t)$, and the equilibrium correspondence is no longer stationary. Letting $P_{it}^*(s_{t-1}, s_t, s_{t+1}) = P_{it}(s_{t-1}, s_t) + \alpha_i P_{i,t+1}(s_t, s_{t+1})$, $\psi_t(s_{t-1}, s_{t+1})$ is the set of equilibrium points for (N, S, P_t^*). In allowing a different single-period payoff function for each time period, it is necessary to assure that the supergame payoffs are bounded. Lemma 4.1 takes an appropriately different form: σ^* is an open loop equilibrium for the supergame, if and only if $s_t^* \in \psi_t(s_{t-1}^*, s_{t+1}^*)$ for all $t \geq 1$. Finally, Assumption 4.3 must be restated so that each ψ_t obeys Lipschitz conditions k_{1t} and k_{2t} with $k_{1t} + k_{2t} \leq k < 1$. Because the payoff functions can change arbitrarily from period to period, there is no hope of finding a steady state to which any equilibrium converges; however, a turnpike result is possible. That is, all equilibria converge to the same ultimate path: if σ' and σ'' are any two equilibria, then $\|s_t' - s_t''\|$ goes to zero as t goes to infinity. Details may be found in Friedman (1981).

It is natural to inquire about trigger strategy equilibria in time-dependent supergames. There is no difficulty in stating conditions for them. As long as an open loop equilibrium for the supergame has the property that s_t^* is not on the payoff possibility frontier of P_t^*, and the difference between P_t^* at equilibrium and the frontier is appropriately bounded away from zero, there is clearly room to show the existence of such equilibria. Even without such a condition, criteria that are sufficient for trigger strategy equilibria are easy to state in a way that is obviously analogous to their statement in Chapter 3; however, it is difficult to give conditions ensuring that a trigger strategy equilibrium is on the global payoff possibility frontier of the supergame, as opposed to its being merely on the frontiers of the P_i^* (see Friedman (1974)). These trigger strategy equilibria will not be subgame perfect for the same reason that the open loop equilibria are not subgame perfect: although trigger strategies are closed loop by definition, under certain conditions the trigger strategies can give rise to subgames in which the players follow open loop equilibrium strategies. Because these open loop equilibria are not subgame perfect, the trigger strategy equilibria of which they are part cannot be subgame perfect. Again, despite the absence of perfectness, these equilibria contain no threats that are noncredible.

2   Stochastic games

The basic feature that distinguishes stochastic games from other games is that, in each time period, the particular payoff functions to be faced by the players are chosen randomly, and the exact probability distribution depends on the actions of the players in the previous period as well as on the particular payoff functions that were drawn at that time. The treatment below follows the line of development started by Shapley (1953a) and carried further by Rogers (1969) and Sobel (1971). The specific model developed below is found in Friedman (1977: Chapter 10) and is a slight variant of Sobel's model. Essentially, the situation is that there is a fixed group of n players and a fixed collection of K ordinary one-shot games. At the start of each time period, one of the K games is selected at random. The selection is made known to the players; then they make their choices for the period.

2.1   The transition mechanism and the conditions defining a stochastic game

The probability distribution governing the choice among the K games to be played in period $t + 1$ depends on the actual game played in period t and on the actions selected by the players in period t. This probability distribution, called the *transition mechanism*, is defined in Definition 4.3. An individual single-shot game is also called a *state*; thus, to say that game k was encountered (or played) at time t is exactly the same as to say the state at time t was state k.

ASSUMPTION 4.4   *The set of states $\Omega = \{1, \ldots, K\}$ is finite.*

DEFINITION 4.3   *The **transition mechanism** is $q(k' \mid k, s)$, which is the probability that the next state will be state k' when the current state is k and the current action is s.*

ASSUMPTION 4.5   *The transition mechanism satisfies the following conditions: (a) $q(k' \mid k, s) \geq 0$ for all $k, k' \in \Omega$ and all $s \in S_k$; (b) $\sum_{k' \in \Omega} q(k' \mid k, s) = 1$; and (c) for any $s', s'' \in S_k$, $k', k \in \Omega$, and $\lambda \in [0, 1]$,*

$$q(k' \mid k, \lambda s' + (1 - \lambda)s'') = \lambda q(k' \mid k, s') + (1 - \lambda)q(k' \mid k, s'') \quad (4.17)$$

Conditions (a) and (b) in Assumption 4.5 are usual conditions requiring probabilities to be nonnegative and sum to 1; however, condition (c) bears a closer examination. It states that probabilities are linear in s, the actions of the players. Although this condition is rather strong and is not explicitly stated in the earlier literature (Sobel (1971) and earlier work), it is implicitly assumed there as well. For example, Sobel (1971) deals with finite single-period games and, of course, allows mixed strategies. As a consequence, his framework implies condition (c).

DEFINITION 4.4 *A* **stochastic game** *is denoted* $\Gamma = (N, \Omega, \{S_k\}, \{P_k\}, q, \alpha)$ *where* (N, S_k, P_k) *is, for each* $k \in \Omega$, *a game satisfying Assumptions 2.1 to 2.3 and Rules 2.1 and 2.2.* Γ *has* q *as its transition mechanism,* Γ *satisfies Assumptions 4.4 and 4.5, as well as Rule 4.1, and, for each player* $i \in N$, *the objective function is expected discounted payoff using the discount parameter* $\alpha_i \in [0, 1)$.

2.2 Existence of equilibrium

Tackling existence of equilibrium points is done in several stages. The first of these, carried out in Section 2.2.1, is to define *policies*, which are essentially closed loop strategies under which the move of a player in each period is a function of the current state. It is known from stochastic dynamic programming that the set of optimal rules for a decision maker in a stationary decision problem includes one or more policies. This result can be applied to the stochastic game model to allow attention to be restricted to strategies that are policies. Then, in Section 2.2.2, the transition probabilities and payoff functions are formulated for the case where all players use policies. Following that, in Section 2.2.3, the decision problem facing a single player is examined, and finally, in Section 2.2.4, existence of equilibrium is proved.

2.2.1 Policies, strategies, and Blackwell's lemma

In a stochastic game, the history as of period t consists of the actual state and action for every past period plus the state for period t. It might be thought that the whole history would, at any time, be relevant for a decision; however, that need not be so. Under reasonable and interesting conditions, it is possible to restrict attention to strategies that are *policies*. These are defined, after which the needed conditions are stated.

DEFINITION 4.5 *A* **policy for player** i, θ_i, *is a function from* Ω *to* $X_{k \in \Omega} S_{ik}$. Θ_i *is the set of policies for player* i. $\theta = (\theta_1, \ldots, \theta_n)$, *and* $\Theta = \times_{i \in N} \Theta_i$. *The distance between two policies,* $d(\theta, \theta')$, *is defined by* $d(\theta_i, \theta_i') = max_{k \in \Omega} d(\theta_i(k), \theta_i(k))$ *and* $d(\theta, \theta') = max_{i \in N} d(\theta_i, \theta_i')$.

Thus, a policy for player i is a rule that picks out a particular action (single-shot game strategy) $s_{ik} \in S_{ik}$ for each state $k \in \Omega$. There is no time dependence in the sense that the value of t does not help determine the chosen action. Only the current state matters, and any time that a particular state k is encountered, the same action s_{ik} is taken. Now consider the situation of player i when all other players are known to be choosing policies. It turns out that among the best replies of player i, when any history dependent strategy is available, is a policy. In other words, if attention is restricted to policies and an equilibrium point in policies is found, then this strategy combination is still an equilibrium when more general strategies are allowed. This result is due to Blackwell (1965) and is stated, but not proved, as follows:[3]

BLACKWELL'S LEMMA. *Let* $\Gamma = (N, \Omega, \{S_k\}, \{P_k\}, q, \alpha)$ *be a stochastic game and let* $\theta \in \Theta$. *If player i has a best reply to θ when she is allowed to choose from the set of all history dependent strategies, then one of the best replies is an element of* Θ_i.

2.2.2   Transition probabilities and the payoff functions when players use policies

Given a policy combination $\theta \in \Theta$, the transition probabilities are exactly determined. q_θ denotes the $K \times K$ transition matrix that governs the stochastic game when the players choose θ.[4]

$$q_\theta = \begin{bmatrix} q(1 \mid 1, \theta(1)) \cdots q(K \mid 1, \theta(1)) \\ \cdot \\ \cdot \\ \cdot \\ q(1 \mid K, \theta(K)) \cdots q(K \mid K, \theta(K)) \end{bmatrix} = \begin{bmatrix} q(1, \theta(1)) \\ \cdot \\ \cdot \\ \cdot \\ q(K, \theta(K)) \end{bmatrix} \qquad (4.18)$$

To formulate the expected payoff of a player, let

$$F_{i\theta} = [P_{i1}(\theta(1)), \ldots, P_{iK}(\theta(K))] \qquad (4.19)$$

$F_{i\theta}$ is a single-period payoff vector for player i in which the first coordinate, $P_{i1}(\theta(1))$, is the payoff that player i receives when the game is in state 1 and the policy (strategy) combination θ is being followed. Suppose now that the state in time zero is k. Then the expected discounted payoff of player i, given the policy combination θ, is

$$P_{ik}(\theta(k)) + \alpha_i q(k, \theta(k))F_{i\theta} + \alpha_i^2 q(k, \theta(k))q_\theta F_{i\theta} + \cdots$$
$$+ \alpha_i^t q(k, \theta(k))q_\theta^{t-1}F_{i\theta} + \cdots \qquad (4.20)$$

and

$$G_{i\theta} = F_{i\theta} + \alpha_i q_\theta F_{i\theta} + \alpha_i^2 q_\theta^2 F_{i\theta} + \cdots + \alpha_i^t q_\theta^t F_{i\theta} + \cdots = [I - \alpha_i q_\theta]^{-1}F_{i\theta} \qquad (4.21)$$

is the vector of expected discounted payoffs for player i. $[I - \alpha_i q_\theta]$ has an inverse because it is a strictly dominant diagonal matrix. The kth component of equation (4.21) is the expected discounted payoff for player i, given that the initial state is state k.

2.2.3 The decision problem of a single player

The decision problem faced by one player when the policies of the other players are given, or, to put it another way, finding a best reply for a player to a policy combination θ, is an exercise in stochastic dynamic programming. A maximum of

$$G_{i\theta\backslash\theta_i} = [I - \alpha_i q_{\theta\backslash\theta_i}]^{-1} F_{i\theta\backslash\theta_i} \qquad (4.22)$$

over $\theta_i \in \Theta_i$ is sought; however, this maximum is of a different character than the best replies seen earlier: Ideally, we seek a best reply θ_i' to θ such that θ_i' leads to a maximum expected payoff *irrespective of the initial state*. On the face of it, there should be no surprise if the optimal policy were different according to what the initial state happened to be, but a result from stochastic dynamic programming establishes that a best reply exists that is best no matter what the initial state. This is proved in Denardo (1967) and can also be seen in Friedman (1977: Chapter 10).

DENARDO'S LEMMA. *In a stochastic game* Γ, *the set of policies for player i that are best replies to a policy combination* θ, *denoted* $r_i(\theta)$, *is nonempty. If* $\theta_i' \in r_i(\theta)$, *then* $G_{i\theta\backslash\theta_i'} \geq G_{i\theta\backslash\theta_i''}$ *for all* $\theta_i'' \in \Theta_i$.

2.2.4 Equilibrium in the stochastic game

The lemmas of Blackwell and Denardo assure that $r(\theta) = \times_{i \in N} r_i(\theta)$ is nonempty for all $\theta \in \Theta$ and that r maps Θ into Θ. Proving that the stochastic game has an equilibrium point is, of course, done if $r(\theta)$ can be shown to have a fixed point. This, in turn, can be based on the Kakutani fixed point theorem if (a) Θ is compact and convex, (b) $r(\theta)$ is upper semicontinuous, and (c) the image sets, $r(\theta)$, are nonempty and convex. These properties are true and are established in the following three lemmas.

LEMMA 4.3 *In a stochastic game* Γ, *the policy space* Θ *is compact and convex.*

Proof A policy can be thought of as a point in a Euclidean space of finite dimension. The dimension is $K \times m$ where K is the number of states and m is the dimensionality of S_{ik} for all i and k.[5] Thus, Θ is compact if it is closed and bounded. Boundedness follows from $K \times m$ being finite and from the boundedness of each S_{ik}. Similarly, closedness follows from the closedness of each S_{ik}. Finally, convexity of Θ follows from convexity of S_{ik}. That is, if $\theta_i'(k)$ and $\theta_i''(k)$ are both in S_{ik}, then $\lambda\theta_i'(k) + (1 - \lambda)\theta_i''(k)$ is also in S_{ik} for all i and k.   QED

As to upper semicontinuity of $r(\theta)$, this follows directly if $G_{i\theta}$ is continuous with respect to θ for each i.

LEMMA 4.4 $G_{i\theta}$ *is continuous with respect to* θ.

Proof Continuity of $G_{i\theta}$ is implied by continuity of $[I - \alpha_i q_\theta]^{-1}$ with respect to $(s_{11}, \ldots, s_{1K}, \ldots, s_{n1}, \ldots, s_{nK})$ and continuity of $P_{ik}(s_{1k}, \ldots, s_{nk})$

with respect to $(s_{1k}, \ldots, s_{nk})$ for all k. Continuity of the P_{ik} is Assumption 2.2, while continuity of $[I - \alpha_i q_\theta]^{-1}$ follows from $[I - \alpha_i q_\theta]$ being continuous in θ and nonsingular for all $\theta \in \Theta$.   QED

DEFINITION 4.6   *Let $f(x)$ be a function from $A \subset R^n$ to R^m. Then $f(x)$ is* **quasiconcave** *if, for any $x \in A$, the set $\{y \in A \,|\, f(y) \geq f(x)\}$ is convex.*

LEMMA 4.5 $G_{i\theta}$ *is quasiconcave in θ_i, and $r(\theta)$ is convex for all $\theta \in \Theta$.*

Proof   If $G_{i\theta}$ is quasiconcave in θ_i, then $r_i(\theta)$ is convex; hence $r(\theta)$ is also convex. Thus, all that remains to show is that $G_{i\theta}$ is quasiconcave in θ_i. Suppose that $\theta \backslash \theta_i'$ and $\theta \backslash \theta_i''$ are any two policy combinations such that $G_{i\theta\backslash\theta_i'} = G_{i\theta\backslash\theta_i''}$, and let $\theta_i^* = \lambda\theta_i' + (1 - \lambda)\theta_i''$ for $\lambda \in [0, 1]$. Then, $G_{i\theta}$ is quasiconcave if

$$G_{i\theta\backslash\theta_i^*} \geq \lambda G_{i\theta\backslash\theta_i'} + (1 - \lambda) G_{i\theta\backslash\theta_i''} \tag{4.23}$$

for any such choice of θ, θ_i', θ_i'', and λ. To simplify notation, let $q' = q_{\theta\backslash\theta_i'}$, $q'' = q_{\theta\backslash\theta_i''}$, $q^* = q_{\theta\backslash\theta_i^*}$, $F_i' = F_{i\theta\backslash\theta_i'}$, $F_i'' = F_{i\theta\backslash\theta_i''}$, and $F_i^* = F_{i\theta\backslash\theta_i^*}$. Recalling that $[I - \alpha_i q']^{-1}F_i' = G_{i\theta\backslash\theta_i'} = G_{i\theta\backslash\theta_i''} = [I - \alpha_i q'']^{-1}F_i''$, it follows that

$$F_i'' = [I - \alpha_i q''][I - \alpha_i q']^{-1}F_i' \tag{4.24}$$

and defining F_i^ε by the relation

$$F_i^* = \lambda F_i' + (1 - \lambda)F_i'' + F_i^\varepsilon \tag{4.25}$$

it follows from Assumption 2.3 that $F_i^\varepsilon \geq 0$. Now, using equation (4.25)

$$G_{i\theta\backslash\theta_i^*} = [I - \alpha_i q^*]^{-1}F_i^* = [I - \alpha_i q^*]^{-1}[\lambda F_i' + (1 - \lambda)F_i'' + F_i^\varepsilon] \tag{4.26}$$

and using equation (4.24)

$$\begin{aligned}
G_{i\theta\backslash\theta_i^*} &= [I - \alpha_i q^*]^{-1}\{\lambda F_i' + (1 - \lambda)[I - \alpha_i q''][I - \alpha_i q']^{-1}F_i'\} \\
&\quad + [I - \alpha_i q^*]^{-1}F_i^\varepsilon = [I - \alpha_i q^*]^{-1}\{\lambda[I - \alpha_i q'] \\
&\quad + (1 - \lambda)[I - \alpha_i q'']\}[I - \alpha_i q']^{-1}F_i' + [I - \alpha_i q^*]^{-1}F_i^\varepsilon \\
&= [I - \alpha_i q^*]^{-1}\{\lambda[I - \alpha_i q'] + (1 - \lambda)[I - \alpha_i q'']\}G_{i\theta\backslash\theta_i'} + [I - \alpha_i q^*]^{-1}F_i^\varepsilon
\end{aligned} \tag{4.27}$$

From condition (c) of Assumption 4.5,

$$\lambda[I - \alpha_i q'] + (1 - \lambda)[I - \alpha_i q''] = [I - \alpha_i q^*] \tag{4.28}$$

therefore, equation (4.27) becomes

$$G_{i\theta\backslash\theta_i^*} = G_{i\theta\backslash\theta_i'} + [I - \alpha_i q^*]^{-1}F_i^\varepsilon \tag{4.29}$$

$G_{i\theta}$ is quasiconcave in θ_i if $[I - \alpha_i q^*]^{-1}F_i^\varepsilon \geq 0$. Because $F_i^\varepsilon \geq 0$, it remains to point out that $[I - \alpha_i q^*]^{-1} \geq 0$. The latter holds because $[I - \alpha_i q^*]$ is a dominant diagonal matrix whose principal diagonal elements are positive and whose off-diagonal elements are nonpositive. From McKenzie (1960), it is known that the inverse of such a matrix has all nonnegative elements; therefore, the lemma is proved.   QED

THEOREM 4.2   *A stochastic game has an equilibrium point.*

Proof   The proof follows from Lemmas 4.3 to 4.5.   QED

3   Supergames with incomplete information

There is one model examined in this section, due to Rosenthal (1979), and utilizing an equilibrium concept that is computationally simpler than Harsanyi's (1967, 1968a, 1968b) equilibrium, with the players' choices based on relatively little information. An equilibrium concept is proposed that differs from the noncooperative equilibrium but that retains some resemblance to it. Section 3.1 describes the structure of the game, Section 3.2 contains the equilibrium notion and a proof of existence of equilibrium, and Section 3.3 comments on the model.

3.1   Description of the game

Suppose a collection of players, divided into two subsets, are to play a sequence of two person games. Each such game is finite—that is, each player possesses a finite number of pure strategies. In each time period, the players are randomly matched into pairs, one member of the pair coming from subset I, the other from subset II. Each player knows her own payoff function, but is ignorant of the payoff function of any other player. Unlike the Harsanyi (1967, 1968a, 1968b) modeling of incomplete information games, the player does not possess a subjective probability distribution over a family of payoff functions for the other players.

The player does have one piece of useful information: At each time t, the player knows what pure strategy was played in period $t - 1$ by her current opponent, although the opponent is not identified. If the opponent used a mixed strategy in period $t - 1$, the player knows the pure strategy realization that was selected by use of the mixed strategy. She does not know the mixed strategy itself. Although the single-period payoff function of a player is the same in all periods, the behavior to be expected from opponents need not be the same in all periods, because different opponents will have different payoff functions. The player is assumed to approach the game as a problem in stochastic dynamic programming under which the behavior expected by her in period t depends on the information commonly available to her and her opponent—the pair of actions which the two of them realized, respectively, in their period $t - 1$ games. An equilibrium, called a *Markovian equilibrium point*, is characterized by strategies fulfilling two kinds of conditions. First, the players all have emprically testable beliefs concerning how they will be paired over time and what behavior they will see from opponents. The evidence they observe must be consistent with these beliefs. Second, given those beliefs, it must be impossible to increase a player's payoff by means of another strategy.

The assumptions on which the model is based are described in Section

3.1.1. These assumptions describe the structure of the game; then in Section 3.1.2 the information conditions under which the players operate and the belief systems ascribed to them are described. Section 3.1.3 describes the players' strategies, and their payoff functions are formulated in relation to these strategies. Finally, in Section 3.1.4 the formal definition of the game is given.

3.1.1   Assumptions of the model

The main outlines of the structure are that there are two pools of players, with the same (finite) number in each pool. In each time period, the players from the first pool are randomly paired into two-player games with players of the second pool. The games played in each period are finite (i.e., they have a finite number of pure strategies available to each player).

ASSUMPTION 4.6   *There are two types of players, denoted I and II; the set of players of each type is $V = \{1, \ldots, v\}$. Type j players have pure strategy sets $M_j = \{1, \ldots, m_j\}$ where m_j is finite and $j = I, II$. The payoff matrix for player $(j, i), j \in \{I, II\}, i \in V$, is A_{ji}, with m_I rows and m_{II} columns. The matrix entry $a_{ji}(k, l)$ is the payoff to player (j, i) when the type I player chooses pure strategy k and the type II player chooses pure strategy l. The only payoff matrix known to player (j, i) is A_{ji}.*

ASSUMPTION 4.7   *In each period t, a permutation of the type II players, $(\phi(1), \ldots, \phi(v))$, is chosen. Each of the $v!$ permutations has a probability of $1/v!$ of being chosen, and the pairing into two-person games is $\{i, \phi(i)\}, i \in V$.*

Assumptions 4.6 and 4.7 set up the basic structure concerning the single-period games and the pairing of players. A player of type I has equal probability of being paired with any type II player in each period. Each period the players engage in finite two-person noncooperative games of incomplete information. The players may use mixed strategies; however, it is convenient to defer their formal introduction until the players' beliefs are sketched.

3.1.2   Information conditions and the players' beliefs

The beliefs of the player must, of course, be described in relation to the information that they possess and that will come to them in the course of the play of the game. Denote by u_{jit} the actual pure strategy played by player $(j, i), (j \in \{I, II\}, i \in V)$ at time t. Thus, if a mixed strategy were used, $u_{jit} \in M_j$ would be the realization of the random process that the mixed strategy describes.

DEFINITION 4.7   *The **immediate history** for two players (I, i) and (II, i') who are paired together at time t in a single-period game is $(u_{Ii,t-1}, u_{IIi',t-1}) = \mu = (\mu_I, \mu_{II})$.*

From the vantage point of the paired players, μ is, in effect, a state variable. It is denoted below in the simple form $\mu = (\mu_I, \mu_{II})$ to avoid unnecessary notational baggage.

A player of one type will have beliefs about two aspects of the game that concern the players of the other type. First, at time t, anticipating the state that will prevail, a player i of type I will, of course, know $u_{Ii,t-1} = \mu_I$, but, prior to being told μ_{II}, he will have beliefs given by the probability distribution $\pi_I = (\pi_I(1), \ldots, \pi_I(m_{II}))$. That is, $\pi_I(k)$ is the probability that the next opponent will have $\mu_{II} = k$. The distribution π_I is identical for all type I players and is a belief of those players. Similarly, there is a distribution π_{II} describing the common beliefs of the type II players. The reason for all players of one type having the same beliefs is that their beliefs must be consistent with the available evidence, and, as they all have the same evidence, they are led to the same beliefs. How this works is spelled out below.

DEFINITION 4.8 π_j *is the* **player selection belief** *of all players of type j.* $\pi_j(k) \geq 0$ *for* $j \in \{I, II\}$ *and all k, and* $\sum_{k=1}^{m_{II}} \pi_I(k) = \sum_{k=1}^{m_I} \pi_{II}(k) = 1$.

The second element of the players' beliefs is the pair of probability distributions $p_I = (p_I(1 \mid \mu), \ldots, p_I(m_{II} \mid \mu))$ and $p_{II} = (p_{II}(1 \mid \mu), \ldots, p_{II}(m_I \mid \mu))$. $p_I(k \mid \mu)$ is the probability belief of a type I player that his current opponent will select $k \in M_{II}$ given that their immediate history is μ.

DEFINITION 4.9 p_j *is the* **player action belief** *of all players of type j.* $p_j(k \mid \mu) \geq 0$ *for* $j \in \{I, II\}$ *and all k, and* $\sum_{k=1}^{m_{II}} p_I(k \mid \mu) = \sum_{k=1}^{m_I} p_{II}(k \mid \mu) = 1$ *for all* $\mu \in \{M_I \times M_{II}\}$.

DEFINITION 4.10 *Letting* $\pi = (\pi_I, \pi_{II})$ *and* $p = (p_I, p_{II})$, (π, p) *is the* **belief structure of the game** *and* (π_j, p_j) *is the* **belief structure of the type j players.**

3.1.3 *Players' strategies and the payoff function*

Based on Blackwell's lemma and on Denardo's lemma, if all players other than player (j, i) use policies that choose mixed strategies for each individual time period, contingent on only the immediate history, then among the discounted payoff maximizing strategies open to player (j, i) will be a policy of the same simple sort. Therefore, attention is restricted to these policies. In this interpretation of the game, it is assumed that each player has forgotten her own past history further than one period back.

DEFINITION 4.11 *A* **policy for player** (j, i), θ_{ji}, *is an array having* $m_j \times m_I \times m_{II}$ *elements. An individual element is denoted* $\theta_{ji}(k \mid \mu)$ *where* $k \in M_j$ *and* $\mu \in M_I \times M_{II}$.

ASSUMPTION 4.8 θ_{ji} *satisfies the following conditions:* $\theta_{ji}(k \mid \mu) \geq 0$, $k \in M_j$, $\mu \in M_I \times M_{II}$; $\sum_{k=1}^{m_j} \theta_{ji}(k \mid \mu) = 1$, $\mu \in M_I \times M_{II}$; *and* θ_{ji} *is defined for all* $j \in I, II$ *and* $i \in V$.

The policy combination for all type j players is $\theta_j = (\theta_{j1}, \ldots, \theta_{jv})$, the policy combination for all players is $\theta = (\theta_I, \theta_{II})$, the set of policies for player (j, i) is denoted Θ_{ji}, the set of policy combinations for type j players is $\Theta_j = \times_{i \in V} \Theta_{ji}$, and the set of policy combinations for all players is $\Theta = \Theta_I \times \Theta_{II}$.

The single-period payoff functions for the players are given by

$$P_{Ii}(\theta_{Ii}, p_I \mid \mu) = \sum_{k \in M_I} \sum_{l \in M_{II}} \theta_{Ii}(k \mid \mu) p_I(l \mid \mu) a_{Ii}(k, l) \qquad (4.30)$$

$$P_{IIi}(\theta_{IIi}, p_{II} \mid \mu) = \sum_{k \in M_I} \sum_{l \in M_{II}} \theta_{IIi}(l \mid \mu) p_{II}(k \mid \mu) a_{IIi}(k, l) \qquad (4.31)$$

Let $P_{ji}(\theta_{ji}, p_j) = (P_{ji}(\theta_{ji}, p_j \mid (1, 1)), \ldots, P_{ji}(\theta_{ji}, p_j \mid (m_I, m_{II})))$ be the single-period payoff vector for player (j, i). That is, it shows the single-period expected payoff associated with every state. The decision problem of a single player, say (I, i), with (π_I, p_I) specified, looks like a straightforward stochastic dynamic programming exercise. Note that the single-period payoff, conditional on the state μ, depends on the player's policy θ_{Ii} and her beliefs about opponents' actions p_I. The transition mechanism for this player is defined by

$$q_{Ii}(\mu' \mid \mu, \theta_{Ii}) = \theta_{Ii}(\mu_I' \mid \mu) \pi_I(\mu_{II}') \qquad (4.32)$$

which depends on the current state, μ, the player's own policy, θ_{Ii}, and her beliefs about how her opponents are selected, π_I. $q_{Ii}(\mu' \mid \mu, \theta_{Ii})$ is the probability that today's state for player (I, i) will be μ', given that yesterday's state was μ and the player's policy is θ_{Ii}. The transition mechanism itself is a square array of $m_I \times m_{II}$ rows and columns. Each row is a probability distribution over today's states, contingent on yesterday's state and the policy. The mechanism is denoted

$$q_{Ii\theta} = \begin{bmatrix} q_{Ii}((1, 1) \mid (1, 1), \theta_{Ii}), \ldots, q_{Ii}((m_I, m_{II}) \mid (1, 1), \theta_{Ii}) \\ \cdot \qquad\qquad\qquad \cdot \\ \cdot \qquad\qquad\qquad \cdot \\ \cdot \qquad\qquad\qquad \cdot \\ q_{Ii}((1, 1) \mid (m_I, m_{II}), \theta_{Ii}), \ldots, q_{Ii}((m_I, m_{II}) \mid (m_I, m_{II}), \theta_{Ii}) \end{bmatrix}$$
$$(4.33)$$

Denoting the discount parameters by α_{ji}, the (discounted, expected) supergame payoff for a type I player is

$$\sum_{t=0}^{\infty} \alpha_{Ii}^t q_{Ii\theta} P_{Ii}(\theta_{Ii}, p_I) = G_{Ii}(\theta_{Ii}, p_I, \pi_I, \alpha_{Ii}) \qquad (4.34)$$

Analogous expressions to equations (4.32) to (4.34) can be written for type II players.

3.1.4 Defining the game

With the material developed in Sections 3.1.1 to 3.1.3, it is possible to complete the description of the game. To that end, *a stationary two-person, incomplete information supergame* is defined in Definition 4.11. Note that, in one sense, this game has $2v$ players, but, in each time period, a player is in a two-person, single-shot game.

DEFINITION 4.12 *A* **stationary two-person, incomplete information supergame**, $\Gamma = (M_I, M_{II}, V, \{A_{ji}\}, \{\alpha_{ji}\})$ *is defined by Assumptions 4.6 to 4.8, Definitions 4.7 to 4.11, and the information conditions*: (1) *all players know* M_I, M_{II}, *and* V, (2) *only player* (j, i) *knows* A_{ji} *and* α_{ji}, *and* (3) *a player knows she is always paired with a player of the other type, but never is informed which player*.

3.2 Existence of equilibrium

In order to prove existence of equilibrium, the equilibrium concept itself must first be carefully specified. This is done in Section 3.2.1, and then existence is proved in Section 3.2.2.

3.2.1 Markovian beliefs and the definition of a Markovian equilibrium

Two sorts of conditions, outlined in the following two definitions, are required. The first set of conditions defines consistency of beliefs with observed phenomena; the second is a best reply condition.

DEFINITION 4.13 (p, π) *is a* **rational Markovian belief relative to** θ *if*

$$w_{Ii}(k) = \sum_{\mu_I \in M_I} w_{Ii}(\mu_I) \sum_{\mu_{II} \in M_{II}} \theta_{Ii}(k \mid \mu) \pi_I(\mu_{II}), \qquad i \in V \quad (4.35)$$

$$w_{IIi}(k) = \sum_{\mu_{II} \in M_{II}} w_{IIi}(\mu_{II}) \sum_{\mu_I \in M_I} \theta_{IIi}(k \mid \mu) \pi_{II}(\mu_I), \qquad i \in V \quad (4.36)$$

$$\pi_{II} = \frac{1}{v} \sum_{i \in V} w_{Ii} \quad (4.37)$$

$$\pi_I = \frac{1}{v} \sum_{i \in V} w_{IIi} \quad (4.38)$$

$$p_{II}(k \mid \mu) \sum_{i \in V} w_{Ii}(\mu_I) = \sum_{i \in V} w_{Ii}(\mu_I) \theta_{Ii}(k \mid \mu), \qquad \mu \in M_I \times M_{II} \quad (4.39)$$

$$p_I(k \mid \mu) \sum_{i \in V} w_{IIi}(\mu_{II}) = \sum_{i \in V} w_{IIi}(\mu_{II}) \theta_{IIi}(k \mid \mu), \qquad \mu \in M_I \times M_{II} \quad (4.40)$$

Equations (4.35) to (4.36) define the steady-state distributions of the observed pure strategy plays of each player. The equilibrium concept is defined only with respect to long-run, steady-state conditions. Equation (4.37) requires that the beliefs of type II players about the distribution of player selections conform to the actual distribution of the choices of type I players. Any discrepancy could, in fact, be detected. Equation (4.38) is a parallel requirement concerning the beliefs of type I players. Equation (4.39) is a consistency requirement that the player action beliefs of type II players are the same as the frequencies that are actually observed, given the policies and steady-state distributions of the type I players. Again, a discrepancy could be detected if a game were moving over time in a steady state. Equation (4.46) is a parallel statement concerning the beliefs of the type I players.

DEFINITION 4.14 (θ, p, π) *is a* **Markovian equilibrium point** *if* (p, π) *is a rational Markovian belief relative to* θ, $\theta \in \Theta$, *and*

$$G_{ji}(\theta_{ji}, p_j, \pi_j, \alpha_{ji}) = \max_{\theta'_{ji} \in \Theta_{ji}} G_{ji}(\theta'_{ji}, p_j, \pi_j, \alpha_{ji}), \qquad i \in V, \qquad j \in \{\text{I, II}\} \quad (4.41)$$

Clearly Definition 4.14 is a best reply condition. No single player could alter his behavior and increase his payoff.

3.2.2   *The existence of Markovian equilibrium*

Existence of a Markovian equilibrium is proved in the following theorem.

THEOREM 4.3   *A stationary two-person, incomplete information supergame* $\Gamma = (M_I, M_{II}, V, \{A_{ji}\}, \{\alpha_{ji}\})$ *has a Markovian equilibrium point.*

Proof   The proof proceeds by means of a standard fixed point argument using the Kakutani theorem. A correspondence is described below whose fixed points are the equilibria whose existence is to be shown. Let $w(\mu) = (w_I(\mu_I), w_{II}(\mu_{II}))$ where $w_j(\mu_j) = (w_{j1}(\mu_j), \ldots, w_{jv}(\mu_j))$. Equations (4.35) to (4.41) define a correspondence, $f(w, p, \pi, \theta)$, which maps a compact, convex domain into itself. Letting an image of $f(w, p, \pi, \theta)$ be denoted by (w', p', π', θ'), the image elements are obtained as follows: w' is defined by equations (4.35) and (4.36). Clearly, w'_{ji} is always a probability distribution with nonnegative entries that sum to 1, and $f_w(w, \pi, \theta) = w'$, given by equations (4.35) and (4.36), is a continuous function. $p' \in f_p(w, \theta)$ is defined using equations (4.39) and (4.40) as follows:

$$p'_{II}(k \mid \mu) = \frac{\sum\limits_{i \in V} w_{Ii}(\mu_I) \theta_{Ii}(k \mid \mu)}{\sum\limits_{i \in V} w_{Ii}(\mu_I)}, \qquad i \in V, \qquad \mu \in M_I \times M_{II}, \qquad k \in M_I$$

$$(4.42)$$

when $\sum_{i \in V} w_{Ii}(\mu_I) > 0$. Otherwise, $(p'_{II}(1 \mid \mu), \ldots, p'_{II}(v \mid \mu))$ takes on any values satisfying the conditions $p'_{II}(k \mid \mu) \geqslant 0$ and $\sum_{k \in M_I} p'_{II}(k \mid \mu) = 1$. That is, when $\sum_{i \in V} w_{Ii}(\mu_I) = 0$, then any probability distribution is in the image set. $p'_I(k \mid \mu)$ is defined analogously. The correspondence f_p is clearly upper semicontinuous and has convex image sets. Finally, from Lemma 4.5, it is clear that $f_\theta(p, \pi)$, defined by equation (4.41), is upper semicontinuous and has convex image sets. Here, f corresponds to the best reply mapping r, in Lemma 4.5. The mapping f is

$$f(w, p, \pi, \theta) = f_w(w, \pi, \theta) \times f_p(w, \theta) \times f_\pi(w) \times f_\theta(p, \pi) \quad (4.43)$$

and it clearly satisfies the Kakutani fixed point theorem; therefore, the game has an equilibrium point.   **QED**

3.3 Comments on the model

In commenting on this interesting model, there are two directions in which I particularly wish to go. The first, in Section 3.3.1, is to note directions in which the work might be extended, and the second, in Section 3.3.2, is to make some comparisons of Rosenthal's model with Harsanyi's (1967, 1968a, 1968b), because Harsanyi's work also deals with incomplete information.

3.3.1 Extensions

One generalization is certainly easy to make: To allow for n different types of player rather than only two. Under this arrangement, there would be v players of each type. They would be randomly grouped into v-different, n-person games in each period with each individual game having one player of each type. It is a straightforward matter to reformulate equations (4.35) to (4.41) to define rational Markovian beliefs for such a game, to define the Markovian equilibrium point, and to use essentially the same existence proof.

Straying from the finite game formulation to allow the single-period games the same structure as that allowed by Assumptions 2.1 to 2.3 may not be so easy. The difficulty lies in moving from discrete to continuous probability distributions. Doing so might prove analytically difficult. Also, it becomes less plausible to argue that the players, in a steady state, could obtain enough evidence to see that their conjectures are correct. Although the accumulating evidence need not contradict the conjectures, it would be insufficient to give strong confirmation to them.

3.3.2 Comparison to Harsanyi's incomplete information model

It is interesting to compare this game to Harsanyi's incomplete information games and also to compare the Markovian equilibrium point with a Nash noncooperative equilibrium point. Doing the latter first, recall that the game with v players of type I and type II is, in fact, a noncooperative incomplete information game with $2v$ players. The Markovian equilibrium strategy of each player is an approximate best reply for the player, given the level of his information; however, if the information conditions were changed so that a player in each time period knew the identity of his opponent, he could have a strategy conditioned on this. Such a more finely tuned strategy would, in general, be different from the Markovian strategy as it could take advantage of differences in the strategies of the various rival players.

Comparing with Harsanyi's incomplete information games, two differences stand out. First, Harsanyi's game is formulated to be one shot; therefore players have no opportunity to gather information over time and compare it with their beliefs. This frees beliefs in Harsanyi's model from having to conform to experience. Harsanyi's players are assumed to know the list of possible payoff functions their rival players may be endowed with, while, in the Rosenthal model, no such information is assumed. Harsanyi's game is one in which there are truly n players, but the players act as if there are more, while in the Rosenthal model there are, in fact, as many players as the players presume. It is an advantage of the Rosenthal formulation that the players do not make presumptions about rivals' payoff functions that may be arbitrary. Instead, they do not concern themselves with rivals' payoff functions; they follow rules of behavior that are optimal relative to assumptions about how other players will actually behave, and in equilibrium their beliefs about rivals' behavior are consistent with observations.

4   Reputations, rationality, and Nash equilibrium

There are games in which a noncooperative equilibrium outcome appears intuitively unreasonable, and this section is devoted to examining two of them. The first is called the Chain Store Paradox, presented and discussed by Selten (1978). The second, lacking a cute name, is due to Rosenthal (1981). In fact, Rosenthal's paper was apparently inspired by contemplating Selten's work and the related work of others. The common thread running through both is that "irrational" equilibrium outcomes appear superior to strictly "rational" ones. The so-called rational outcome is the Nash noncooperative equilibrium; thus these papers point to deficiencies in the Nash concept.

4.1   Selten's Chain Store Paradox

The Selten (1978) example is presented below in Section 4.1.1, following which Section 4.1.2 describes a way out of the paradox, suggested by Kreps and Wilson (1982a), that is based on altering the information conditions originally used by Selten.

4.1.1   Formulation of the Chain Store example

In this game there are 21 players. Player 0 is called the chain store and it has branches in 20 different cities, numbered $1, \ldots, 20$, Player $i \in \{1, \ldots, 20\}$ is an entrepreneur who could open a competing store in city i. The game goes on for exactly 20 periods. In period i, player i decides whether or not to enter the market in his town. After player i announces his decision, player 0 decides to play either *soft* or *tough*. The single-period payoffs are shown in Table 4.1. In period 2, player 2 makes a similar decision, and the game proceeds in this way through period 20. A single period is shown in Figure 4.1.

Working backward from the final period, it is clear that player 20 should enter and player 0 should play *soft*. Given that plyer 20 decides *in*, player 0

TABLE 4.1 One stage of the Chain
Store Paradox

		Player i	
		In	Out
Player **0**	Soft	2, 2	5, 1
	Tough	0, 0	5, 1

is better off playing *soft*, because her payoff is higher. In period 19, the
situation is the same. Player 0 cannot affect the later period through her
current decision, and player 19 is best off to choose *in*. The backward
induction argument holds, and the only perfect equilibrium point of the
game involves each player $i \in \{1, \ldots, 20\}$ choosing *in*, with player 0
choosing *soft* in each period. The payoff matrix in Table 4.1 is known to all
players, all know the structure of the game, and all know the past choices of
all players.

The source of the paradox is that this (unique) perfect equilibrium point
seems intuitively unreasonable as compared with player 0, the chain store,
playing *tough* in the early periods of the game to scare off later firms from
entering the market. Very likely, by playing *tough* for the first several
periods, many players will decide it is not worthwhile to come into the
market. Players who act near the end of the game (say $i = 18$, 19, and 20)

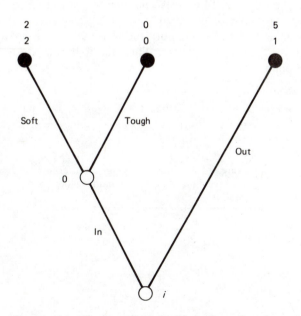

FIGURE 4.1 One round of the Chain Store Paradox.

may be undeterred from entering the market because they may believe that the remaining time is not enough to make it worthwhile for the chain store to attempt to deter entry. The chain store would likely take this view as well, thus entrance in the last few periods, coupled with player 0 choosing *soft* seems reasonable. To summarize, the chain store would play *tough*, in any period a player chose *in*, from the start to the last few periods. In these final periods, the chain store would play *soft* in the face of entry. The other players would either never enter until the last few periods, when a *soft* response could be expected, or, perhaps the first few firms would try *in*, be greeted with *tough*, and convince all but the last few firms to play *out*. The problem is how to formally rationalize the intuitively plausible behavior just described. The method suggested below is appealing, but it does make a change in the structure of the game.

4.1.2 *Escaping the paradox via incomplete information*

Kreps and Wilson (1982a) suggest a way out which requires a change in the information conditions of the game. Suppose the chain store's true payoff structure is not known with certainty to the other players, but instead they know it is either as shown in Table 4.1 or Table 4.2. The original payoff structure is called a *weak chain store* and the payoff structure in Table 4.2 depicts a *strong chain store*. A strong chain store will always play *tough* in the face of entry, because doing so maximizes its single-period payoff and has no adverse long-run consequences. Therefore, a chain store that plays *tough* in the face of entry could be (a) a strong chain store using its dominant strategy or (b) a weak chain store trying to discourage entry by mimicking the behavior expected of a strong chain store. Suppose the players i ($\neq 0$) believe the probability the chain store is weak to be $p < \frac{1}{2}$, and that player 0 is, in fact, weak. Then the following strategies are an equilibrium point:

Player 1 chooses *out*.

Player i chooses *in* if player 0 has chosen *soft* at any past time and chooses *out* otherwise ($i = 2, \ldots, 20$).

TABLE 4.2 A single stage of an alternate version of the Chain Store Paradox

		Player i	
		In	Out
Player 0	Soft	0, 0	4, 1
	Tough	−1, 2	5, 1

Player 0 chooses *tough* in any period 1, ..., 17 during which another
player selects *in* and *soft* in any period 18, 19, 20 during which
another player selects *in*.

Under these strategies, the equilibrium path will be that all players
$i = 1, ..., 20$ choose *out*. None of them can increase expected payoff by
selecting differently. Of course, this version of the game lacks the complete
information assumed in Selten's original specification; therefore, it does not
resolve the paradox on Selten's terms.

4.2 Another view of beneficial "irrational" behavior

The second game, due to Rosenthal (1981), involves a version of the finitely
repeated prisoners' dilemma with sequential decision. Suppose a single-
shot payoff matrix as shown in Table 4.3. The rules of the game are that
player 1 chooses, then his choice is revealed to player 2 who chooses. If one
or both choose *s* (stop), the game ends with the completion of the first
round of play. Otherwise, a second round is played in the same manner as
the first. If both choose *c* (continue), another round is played until a total of
five rounds have been played and the game ends. An abbreviated extensive
form of the five-round game is shown in Figure 4.2. It is assumed that
player 2 would never choose *c* after learning that player 1 has chosen *s*;
therefore, the figure is drawn with this sequence omitted. If player 1
chooses *s*, then player 2 also chooses *s*, but if player 1 chooses *c*, player 2
might choose either *s* or *c*. Now suppose that each player believes that the
other player will choose to continue at each decision point with probability
$\min\{1, .5 + .4D\}$ where D is the difference between the payoff to the player if
he continues and stops. Then, at his last decision point, player 2 would
choose stop with probability .9 and continue with probability .1. At the
next to last decision node, it is the turn of player 1. He chooses to continue
with probability $.5 + .4(.9 \times 7 + .1 \times 10 - 8) = .22$, and his strategy is
$(.78, .22)$. The game is displayed again in Figure 4.3 showing, at each
branch, the probability assigned to it, and at each node, the expected
payoff to the two players conditional on reaching that node and using the

TABLE 4.3   One stage of a sequential game with uncertainty

		Player 2	
		s	*c*
Player 1	*s*	0, 0	3, −1
	c	−1, 3	2, 2

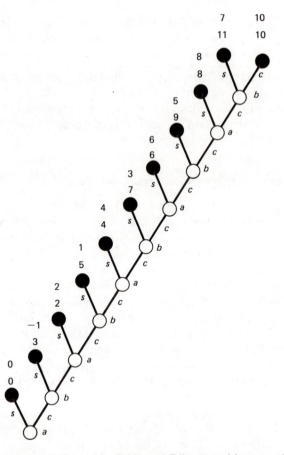

FIGURE 4.2   A game similar to the Prisoners' Dilemma with sequential decision.

strategies just outlined. An asterisk appears next to the payoff of the player who moves at the node. As with the Chain Store Game, the only equilibrium point is for player 1 to choose to stop at the first node. The reasonable solution proposed by Rosenthal rests on a small irrationality or act of faith by the players: Each supposes the other will, with some positive probability, choose to continue the game at each node. I hesitate to use the word "irrational" to describe this behavior, because it prejudges that only best reply behavior is rational. In the present game, at each node, the player who moves enters into a risk: If he continues, the other player can terminate the game immediately, which lowers his payoff one unit, or he can continue, which gives him a payoff two units higher. If the game continues to his own next decision node, then no matter how much further it goes, he must be better off as compared with immediate stopping. To continue and trust to the good sense of the other player to also continue seems a reasonable risk, because both players stand to gain.

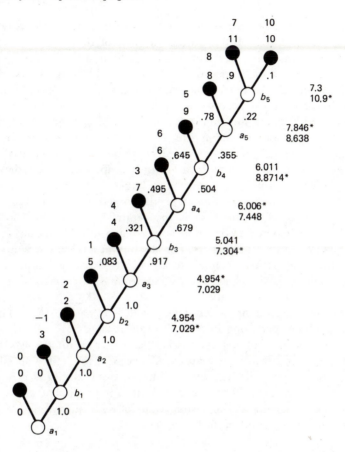

FIGURE 4.3 The effect of some "irrationality" on expected payoffs.

5 Applications of time-dependent supergames

Two oligopoly applications are sketched in this section. The first is one in which the intertemporal link is a firm's capital stock. In the second model, there is a time dependence stemming from advertising. Both of these are simple examples of time-dependent (nonstochastic) supergames.

5.1 A model of oligopoly with capital

Imagine a market in which the firms make differentiated products but are regarded as choosing output levels rather than prices. If one variable is easily changed within a time frame during which the second is not, then it is reasonable to take the second as the decision variable, to assume the time period is long enough that the second can be changed freely in each period, and to suppose the first variable is finely tuned often during the period in response to market conditions. For example, suppose the period is one day, and that the firms are each individual fishermen who fish early in the morning and sell their catch during the rest of the day. Price is easily adjusted throughout the day, but quantity (the number of fish brought to market) is decided once per day. Output would then be the decision variable. Although both variables are decided by the firm, it is really output that has the major strategic importance.

The inverse demand function of a firm is $p_{it} = f_i(q_t)$ where p_{it} is the price of the ith firm in period t and $q_t = (q_{1t}, \ldots, q_{nt})$ is the output vector of the n firms in the market. $f_i(q_t)$ is assumed continuous and differentiable with $f_i^i < f_i^j (j \neq i) < 0$. An increase in any firm's output will lower the market clearing price for firm i, but firm i has a larger effect on p_{it} than any other single firm. Cost of production depends on output and capital, and is denoted by $C_i(q_{it}, K_{it})$ where K_{it} is the capital stock of firm i at time t. $C_i(q_{it}, K_{it})$ is a convex function that is increasing in q_{it}, marginal cost (i.e., $\partial C_i / \partial q_{it} = C_i^1$) declines as K_{it} rises. For any output level, there is an optimal (cost minimizing) level of capital stock. This level rises as output rises. As K_{it} goes to zero, fixed cost goes to zero and marginal cost, $C_i^1(q_{it}, K_{it})$, goes to infinity. Finally, the relationship between K_{it}, $K_{i,t+1}$, and the amount spent on new capital in period t (I_{it}) is $I_{it} = K_{it}g(K_{i,t+1}/K_{it})$. This is a convex function, increasing in $K_{i,t+1}$ and decreasing in K_{it}. That is, given the size of the present capital stock, the higher is tomorrow's level of capital, the more it will cost to attain. Conversely, to attain a specific level of $K_{i,t+1}$, the larger is K_{it}, the less it will cost. Convexity of $K_{it}g(K_{i,t+1}/K_{it})$ means that the cost of adding one more unit to the capital stock rises, or at best, remains constant, as the desired value of $K_{i,t+1}$ increases.

Thus the single-period profit function is

$$\pi_{it} = q_{it}f_i(q_t) - C_i(q_{it}, K_{it}) - K_{it}g\left(\frac{K_{i,t+1}}{K_{it}}\right) \tag{4.44}$$

To see all the details of this model, see Friedman (1983: Chapter 7). Formulating the strategy spaces for the players is cumbersome. In any period t, it is possible to specify an interval for output, $[0, q_i^+]$, where q_i^+ is chosen to be so high that production at this level would never be profitable. For example, q_i^+ might be high enough that $f_i(q \backslash q_i^+) = 0$ for all $q \geq 0$. The situation with $K_{i,t+1}$ is less straightforward. There is an upper bound, K_i^+, so high that it cannot be in a firm's interest to maintain such a large or larger capital stock; however, the minimum value of $K_{i,t+1}$ is not generally 0. It is the level satisfying the condition $0 = K_{it}g(K_{i,t+1}/K_{it})$, because the firm cannot, by assumption, sell off capital and, once bought, it is not in the firm's interest to throw away any capital.

Letting α_i be the ith firm's discount parameter, denoting strategies by $\sigma_i = (q_{i0}, K_{i1}, q_{i1}, K_{i2}, \ldots)$, and letting I' be a fixed start-up cost for the firm that buys an initial capital of $K_{i0} = K'$, the firm's supergame payoff function is

$$G_i(\sigma) = -I' + \sum_{t=0}^{\infty} \alpha_i^t \left[q_{it}f_i(q_t) - C_i(q_{it}, K_{it}) - K_{it}g\left(\frac{K_{i,t+1}}{K_{it}}\right) \right] \tag{4.45}$$

Note that in period t, firm i chooses q_{it} and $K_{i,t+1}$. Choosing $K_{i,t+1}$ is equivalent to choosing I_{it}. Turning to a specific example, let $n = 2$, $\alpha_i = .9$, $i = 1, 2$, and

$$p_{1t} = 140 - 1.5q_{1t} - q_{2t} \tag{4.46}$$

$$p_{2t} = 140 - 1.5q_{2t} - q_{1t} \tag{4.47}$$

$$C_i(q_{it}, K_{it}) = .05K_{it} + \frac{10 + 3q_{it} + q_{it}^2}{K_{it}}, \qquad i = 1, 2 \tag{4.48}$$

$$I_{it} = \frac{K_{i,t+1}^2}{K_{it}} \tag{4.49}$$

Thus, the supergame payoff for player 1 is

$$G_1(\sigma) = -I' + \sum_{t=0}^{\infty} .9^t \left[q_{1t}(140 - 1.5q_{1t} - q_{2t}) - \frac{10 + 3q_{1t} + q_{1t}^2}{K_{1t}} - \frac{K_{1,t+1}^2}{K_{1t}} \right] \tag{4.50}$$

Looking for a steady-state equilibrium, and taking advantage of the symmetry of the model to find a symmetric steady state,

$$\frac{\partial G_1(\sigma)}{\partial q_{1t}} = .9^t \frac{\partial \pi_{1t}}{\partial q_{1t}} = .9^t \left(140 - 3q_{1t} - q_{2t} - \frac{3 + 2q_{1t}}{K_{1t}} \right) = 0 \tag{4.51}$$

$$\frac{\partial G_1(\sigma)}{\partial K_{1t}} = .9^t \left[\frac{-2K_{1t}}{K_{1,t-1}} + .9 \left(-.05 + \frac{10 + 3q_{1t} + q_{1t}^2 + K_{1,t+1}^2}{K_{1t}^2} \right) \right] = 0 \tag{4.52}$$

Denoting steady-state values by q^* ($= q_{1t} = q_{2t}$) and K^* ($= K_{1t} = K_{2t}$), equations (4.51) can be expressed as

$$q^* = \frac{140K^* - 3}{4K^* + 2} \tag{4.53}$$

and equation (4.52) reduces to

$$-2 + .9 \left(-.05 + \frac{10 + 3q^* + q^{*2}}{K^{*2}} + 1 \right) = 0 \tag{4.54}$$

Using equations (4.53) and (4.54), $q^* = 34.438$, $K^* = 31.96$, and steady-state, single-period profits are $\pi^* = 1783.77$.

In this model, the element of time dependence is very restricted in the sense that π_{it} depends only on the firm's own previous choice of capital and on no previous choices of the other firm. In addition, the only variables of other firms that directly enter a firm's payoff function are the q_{jt}. Other models of oligopoly with capital are Prescott (1973), from which the investment function $I_{it} = K_{it} g(K_{i,t+1}/K_{it})$ is borrowed, and Flaherty (1980). The Flaherty model has the unusual feature that it is symmetric in structure, has both symmetric and asymmetric steady states, and only asymmetric steady states are stable.

5.2 *A model of oligopoly with advertising*

The model presented here has considerable similarity to the capital model. Advertising is treated like capital in the sense that an expenditure on advertising from time $t(y_{it})$ affects sales at t and all future periods. The effect is captured in a variable called *goodwill* (Y_{it}) whose value depends on the firm's past path of advertising. Of course, goodwill enters into a firm's demand function rather than its production cost function. An important difference from the capital example is that the demand facing firm i will depend on the goodwill levels of all firms in the market. The effect of an increase in the goodwill of firm j can be either to raise or lower demand. Products and industries seem to differ with regard to whether the advertising of a firm aids or hurts competing firms.

The demand structure is given by an inverse demand function, $p_{it} = f_i(q_t, Y_t)$, cost of production depends on current output only, $C_i(q_{it})$, and the relationship between the current expenditure on advertising (y_{it}), the goodwill level of the preceding period ($Y_{i,t-1}$) and that of the current period (Y_{it}) is $y_{it} = \theta_i(Y_{it}, Y_{i,t-1})$. Analogously to $K_{it}g(K_{i,t+1}/K_{it})$, θ_i is convex, increasing in Y_{it} and decreasing in $Y_{i,t-1}$. In period t, the firm chooses q_{it} and Y_{it}. Single-period profit is

$$\pi_{it} = q_{it}f_i(q_t, Y_t) - C_i(q_{it}) - \theta_i(Y_{it}, Y_{i,t-1}) \tag{4.55}$$

and the supergame payoff, letting $\sigma_i = (q_{i0}, Y_{i0}, q_{i1}, Y_{i1}, q_{i2}, Y_{i2}, \ldots)$, is

$$G_i(\sigma) = q_{i0}f_i(q_0, Y_0) - C_i(q_{i0}) - \theta_i(Y_{i0}, 0)$$

$$+ \sum_{t=1}^{\infty} \alpha_i^t[q_{it}f_i(q_t, Y_t) - C_i(q_{it}) - \theta_i(Y_{it}, Y_{i,t-1})] \tag{4.56}$$

As a specific symmetric example of this model, let $n = 2$, production costs be nil, and

$$p_{1t} = 140 - 1.5q_{1t} - q_{2t} + Y_{1t} + wY_{2t} \tag{4.57}$$

$$p_{2t} = 140 - 1.5q_{2t} - q_{1t} + Y_{2t} + wY_{1t} \tag{4.58}$$

$$y_{it} = Y_{it}^2 + 1.5Y_{it}Y_{i,t-1} + Y_{i,t-1}^2, \quad i = 1, 2 \tag{4.59}$$

Single-period profits for firm 1 are

$$\pi_{1t} = 140q_{1t} - 1.5q_{1t}^2 - q_{1t}q_{2t} + q_{1t}Y_{1t} + wq_{1t}Y_{2t} - Y_{1t}^2 - 1.5Y_{1t}Y_{1,t-1} - Y_{1,t-1}^2 \tag{4.60}$$

The parameter w controls the degree to which the advertising of one firm helps or hurts the rival firm. Two values of w are used for sample computations: $w = +.8$ and $w = -.8$. The first figure causes advertising to be highly cooperative between firms, while the second causes it to be highly predatory. Letting $\alpha_i = .9$, supergame payoffs for firm 1 are

$$G_1(\sigma) = \sum_{t=0}^{\infty} .9^t[(140 - 1.5q_{1t} - q_{2t} + Y_{1t} + wY_{2t})q_{1t}$$

$$- Y_{1t}^2 - 1.5Y_{1t}Y_{1,t-1} - Y_{1,t-1}^2] \tag{4.61}$$

where $Y_{1t} = 0$ for $t = -1$.

The first-order conditions for equilibrium, which define in implicit form the equilibrium correspondence (see Definition 4.2), are

$$\frac{\partial G_1}{\partial q_{1t}} = .9^t[140 - 3q_{1t} - q_{2t} + Y_{1t} + wY_{2t}] = 0 \tag{4.62}$$

$$\frac{\partial G_2}{\partial q_{2t}} = .9^t[140 - 3q_{2t} - q_{1t} + Y_{2t} + wY_{1t}] = 0 \tag{4.63}$$

$$\frac{\partial G_1}{\partial Y_{1t}} = .9^t[q_{1t} - 2Y_{1t} - 1.5Y_{1,t-1} + .9(-1.5Y_{1,t+1} - 2Y_{1t})] = 0 \tag{4.69}$$

$$\frac{\partial G_2}{\partial Y_{2t}} = .9^t[q_{2t} - 2Y_{2t} - 1.5Y_{2,t-1} + .9(-1.5Y_{2,t+1} - 2Y_{2t})] = 0 \tag{4.65}$$

For $w = .8$, the equilibrium correspondence is

$$q_{1t} = 39.7015 - .121Y_{1,t-1} - .0805Y_{2,t-1} - .1089Y_{1,t+1} - .07243Y_{2,t+1} \tag{4.66}$$

$$q_{2t} = 39.7015 - .0805Y_{1,t-1} - .121Y_{2,t-1} - .07243Y_{1,t+1} - .1089Y_{2,t+1} \tag{4.67}$$

$$Y_{1t} = 10.4478 - .4266Y_{1,t-1} - .0212Y_{2,t-1} - .3839Y_{1,t+1} - .01906Y_{2,t+1} \tag{4.68}$$

$$Y_{2t} = 10.4478 - .0212Y_{1,t-1} - .4266Y_{2,t-1} - .01906Y_{1,t+1} - .3839Y_{2,t+1} \tag{4.69}$$

and the steady-state values are $q^* = 37.54$, $Y^* = 5.65$, $p^* = 56.31$, and $\pi^* = 2002.5$. For $w = -.8$, the equilibrium correspondence is

$$q_{1t} = 35.467 - .24276Y_{1,t-1} + .22276Y_{2,t-1} - .21848Y_{1,t+1} + .20048Y_{2,t+1} \tag{4.70}$$

$$q_{2t} = 35.467 + .22276Y_{1,t-1} - .24276Y_{2,t-1} + .20048Y_{1,t+1} - .21848Y_{2,t+1} \tag{4.71}$$

$$Y_{1t} = 9.333 - .45862Y_{1,t-1} + .05862Y_{2,t-1} - .41276Y_{1,t+1} + .052759Y_{2,t+1} \tag{4.72}$$

$$Y_{2t} = 9.333 + .05862Y_{1,t-1} - .45862Y_{2,t-1} + .052759Y_{1,t+1} - .41276Y_{2,t+1} \tag{4.73}$$

and the steady-state values are $q^* = 35.265$, $Y^* = 5.303$, $p^* = 52.9$, and $\pi^* = 1767.03$. As one would expect, where advertising is more cooperative, output, goodwill, price, and profit are all higher. To check whether the equilibrium correspondence is a contraction, add the absolute values of the coefficients of $Y_{1,t-1}$, $Y_{2,t-1}$, $Y_{1,t+1}$, and $Y_{2,t+1}$ for each equation to see if their sum is, in each case, less than 1. These sums are .38283 for equations (4.66) and (4.67), .85076 for equations (4.68) and (4.69), .88448 for equations (4.70) and (4.71), and .98276 for equations (4.72) and (4.73); therefore, the equilibrium correspondence (at least for the chosen parameter values) is a contraction, which means that the steady state is unique and stable. For more detail on this model, see Friedman (1983: Chapter 6).

6   Concluding comments

A connection between the time-dependent supergames of Section 1 and the stochastic games of Section 2 is worth pointing out: If the state space in the stochastic game model were generalized to be an uncountably infinite space, then the model of Section 1 would become a special case of a stochastic game. The state at time t would be defined as s_{t-1}, and the definition of a stochastic game would be satisfied. Such a stochastic game would be degenerate in the sense that there would be no stochastic elements; however, the two sections would then fit within a single framework. This approach is not taken here because Section 1 contains some results on uniqueness and stability of equilibrium that have not been developed, as far as I know, in the stochastic games literature. In addition, where one is dealing with a time-dependent supergame and there are not any stochastic elements, it may be simpler to use an explicitly nonstochastic model.

The stochastic game model has a natural application to oligopoly. Developing such a model sufficiently fully takes too much space for present purposes, but the nature of the model in outline form can easily be given. See Kirman and Sobel (1974) and Miller (1982). The following description is closer to Miller. Suppose there are two firms, and, in each time period, each firm selects its price and its output level. Demand for each firm is subject to random shocks from a distribution known to the firms. Thus, at the start of each period the state is described by two numbers, x_{1t} and x_{2t}. If x_{1t} is positive, it is the starting inventory of firm 1; if it is negative, it is the amount of backlogged orders. A similar interpretation is applied to x_{2t} for firm 2. Both backlogging and carrying inventories are costly; the latter represents storage costs, and the former represents penalties for being unable to satisfy some demand. The realized values of the random variables that affect demand in period t are not known to the firms until after they have chosen their prices and output levels for period t. Miller proves that the model has an equilibrium in which the firms eventually reach a region where the firms choose the same prices in all periods and they choose output levels so that the sum of inventory and production would be the same in all periods. Inventory plus production is the stock available for sale in the period, and the equilibrium policies are constant stock in the sense that this sum is constant.

Bounded rationality has been around for several decades at least; Simon (1957) being an early contributor. The topic is difficult and appealing, and I think it fair to say results have not yet gotten very far. The topics relating to the Chain Store Paradox and reputation are of recent origin and promise to develop quite a bit more in coming years. These investigations promise to resolve some situations in which the noncooperative equilibrium has appeared inappropriate, or in which a conventional application of it has been unsatisfactory.

Exercise

1. Let the single-period payoff functions of two players be

$$P_1(s_t) = -5s_{1,t-1}^2 - 5s_{1,t-1}s_{1t} - 10s_{1t}^2 + s_{2,t-1}s_{1t} + 5s_{1t}$$

$$P_2(s_t) = 10s_{2t} - 5s_{2,t-1}^2 - 4s_{2t}^2 - 6s_{1,t-1}s_{2t} - 2s_{1t}s_{2t}$$

Let the single-period strategy spaces be [0, 1] for both players and suppose that the discount parameter is .8 for both players. What is the equilibrium correspondence? What is the steady-state value of s?

Notes

1. Existence of a steady-state equilibrium, assured by existence of a fixed point of the correspondence $\psi(s', s'')$ when s' and s'' are restricted to equal one another, is implied by a weaker condition than Assumption 4.3. It is enough that ψ satisfy the conditions for the Kakutani fixed point theorem. The only condition not implied already is that the sets $\psi(s, s)$ be convex for all $s \in S$. Note that (s', s'') need not be convex if $s' \neq s''$.
2. The condition that a contraction map a set into itself can be weakened. If a contraction $f(x):A \to B(A, B \subset R^m)$ satisfies a Lipschitz condition with ratio k, and if $\|x^0 - f(x^0)\| \leq \beta$, then any fixed point x^* of f would have to be within a distance $\beta/(1-k)$ of x^0. Therefore, if B, the range of f, contains the set $\{x \in R^m \mid \|x - x^0\| \leq \beta/(1-k)\}$, then f has a fixed point. Note that this result does not require compactness of A or of B. See Dieudonné (1960: 261).
3. Blackwell (1965) is on dynamic programming, not games; however, if all players except player i are using policies, finding a best reply for player i amounts to solving a dynamic programming problem of the sort Blackwell treats. The lemma is stated here in terms of the stochastic game context of this section.
4. Throughout this section, θ_i is referred to as either a policy or a strategy. Literally, θ_i is not a strategy; however, the plan to use the policy θ_i in each and every period is a strategy, and this strategy is meant when θ_i is called a strategy. This slight abuse of terminology eliminates some cumbersome wording and should cause no confusion. In writing column and row vectors, no notational distinction is made. The use of a prime or superscript T would add to an already heavy load of notation, and what is meant should be obvious from the context.
5. It is no restriction to require that $S_{ik} \subset R^m$ for all i and k. Suppose $S_{ik} \subset R^{m_{ik}}$ that m_{ik} is finite for all i and k. Now let $m = \max_{i,k} \{m_{ik}\}$ and, clearly, $S_{ik} \subset R^m$.

5

Two-person cooperative games

This chapter, the first of three devoted to cooperative games, covers two-person cooperative games only. There are two principal ways to simplify the study of cooperative games: One is to limit attention to two persons, which eliminates any complications due to allowing a myriad of coalitions, and the other is to assume *transferable utility*. Transferable utility is explained fully in Chapter 6, which is entirely devoted to *n*-person transferable utility games, but, in brief, the restriction allows a much simpler statement of the relevant aspects of a game. Finally, Chapter 7 takes up *n*-person nontransferable utility games. This chapter begins with a short overview of cooperative games.

1 Introduction to cooperative games

By way of setting the stage for the study of cooperative games, there are two main things to consider: First, how do cooperative and noncooperative games differ? Second, what are the main sorts of cooperative games and/or cooperative game equilibrium concepts? These two topics are discussed in the following two sections.

1.1 Comparison of cooperative and noncooperative games

The fundamental distinction between cooperative and noncooperative games is that cooperative games allow binding agreements while non-cooperative games do not. This distinction is maintained here; however, there are other differences that will emerge, and, in contrast, there are ways that the two categories of games shade into one another. Differences concern (a) the fairness of outcomes, (b) the naturalness of outcomes, (c) the scope for players to make active choices, and (d) the levels on which players can interact. These are briefly discussed in turn.

On fairness, it is not usual for the Nash noncooperative equilibrium to be heralded as a fair outocme; however, various cooperative game solutions are sometimes put forth as being fair outcomes on the assertion that the axioms characterizing them embody fairness. These assertions do not have universal appeal and they often merely reflect the enthusiasm of their inventors and supporters. The lack of consensus about which solution is most desirable stimulates partisans of one or another solution to make claims for their favorites. Explicit concern with fair division schemes is outside the scope of this book; however, the interested reader might look at Crawford (1979, 1980) where additional references can be found.

By the "naturalness" of an outcome, I mean to ask whether it seems reasonable to expect a particular solution or equilibrium to be realized in practice. The noncooperative equilibrium seems natural in the sense that it is an outcome under which each player is, in an appropriate sense, doing the best he can. Put another way, it is intuitively plausible that players would behave in accord with that equilibrium. Regarding cooperative games, it is easy to visualize players agreeing on a *core* outcome, because core outcomes satisfy a set of conditions guaranteeing that no individual or group could possibly fare better. The core, however, can be very large, or it can be empty. A core consisting of one point is unusual.

For other cooperative outcomes, it is not clear how they might naturally occur unless a pregame arrangement is made to select one of them. A pregame agreement that is made for only a single game would be difficult to imagine. Because different solutions generally treat players differently, each player would favor the solution that maximized his own payoff. The situation is different for a group of people who know that, from time to time, subsets of them will be in games, and no one knows in advance which games will arise or who the players will be. Agreeing in advance to use a particular cooperative solution is like establishing a clause in the constitution, or basic legal framework, of the group. If no one knows how and when he will enter a game, then each player can discuss the merits of various solutions from the standpoint of his overall sense of fairness. If an agreement is reached on a solution concept, the individuals reap two advantages compared with playing an unknown sequence of single-period, isolated, noncooperative games. First, they can assure in advance that each game will have a Pareto optimal outcome, which makes it likely that each player will, over time, have a larger total payoff than he would without the agreement. Second, a player's payoffs would be regarded as being ex ante fair. When a cooperative game solution is used by a prearrangement that lies outside the game proper, the solution is called an *arbitration scheme*.

The scope for players to make active choices is always great in noncooperative games. Were there not such scope, a noncooperative game would hold no interest. In cooperative games the situation varies. For example, if the Nash bargaining model is adopted, individual action is precluded. That is, if two players are in a fixed threat game in which they decide to accept the Nash bargaining solution, then there is no further action for either of them to take. Of course, this model can only apply to special situations (see Section 2); however, the Shapely value, which can be used in a large class of games, has the same feature. In contrast, the Nash variable threat solution and the bargaining set, among others, leave scope for individual actions aimed at improving a player's final outcome.

By the levels on which players interact, I mean the scope for various subgroups to discuss possible joint actions. In Chapters 3 and 4, it was seen that all players jointly could make self-enforcing agreements. The possibility of two or more, but fewer than n, players making a self-enforcing agreement is not much discussed; however, there is no reason in principle why such possibilities are not explored. Perhaps the omission is because many interesting results are obtainable without bringing in groups of intermediate size. With cooperative games, it is often of central importance that groups of any size be allowed to form. Again, this is not a difference of principle; it is a difference in emphasis.

1.2 The various kinds of cooperative games

It was noted at the start of the chapter that Chapters 5, 6, and 7 are divided along lines that are pedagogically convenient. Comparing two-person cooperative games with general n-person cooperative games, note the scope for coalition formation that is allowed when there are n players. A *coalition* is simply a subset of N that is allowed to make a binding agreement, and it is usually assumed that any subset of N can form for this purpose; therefore, there are 2^n possible coalitions if the *coalition of the whole* (i.e., the coalition consisting of N itself) and the *empty coalition* (consisting of no one) are allowed. And there are $2^n - 2$ coalitions consisting of between 1 and $n - 1$ players. The number of possible coalitions clearly grows much faster than n.

Intuitively, limiting n to be two would seem to shed some complications, and it is true that certain solution concepts for cooperative games have been developed specifically for $n = 2$. Some of these are examined in this chapter. These solution concepts apply to models with both transferable and nontransferable utility. The latter distinction is, of course, the basis on which the final two chapters are divided. *Transferable utility* means that each coalition can achieve a certain total amount of utility that it can freely divide among its members in any mutually agreeable fashion. The concept is discussed further in Chapters 6 and 7; however, an example should make clear what is involved. Assume that for all individuals utility is proportional to money, and one unit of money equals one unit of utility. Then, in a game where all outcomes are measured in money and any amount of money that is achievable by a coalition can be divided arbitrarily among the coalition members, transferable utility is present. Transferable utility is a very restrictive assumption that forces a strong relationship onto the utility functions of the players in a game.

As with two-person cooperative games, certain solution concepts have been developed for n-person transferable utility games, and, even though some of them can be generalized to nontransferable utility games, there are losses in the process. For example, the uniqueness of a solution may be lost.

Another distinction in cooperative games, cutting across the divisional lines of these chapters, is between core type and value type solutions. This distinction is not always perfectly clear cut; however, it is still useful. The core is a set of payoff vectors that passes a minimal criterion of acceptability: The payoff vector $x \in R^n$ is in the core if it is achievable by the members of N and if no coalition could, on its own, obtain more for all of its members than what it gets under x. The *von Neumann–Morgenstern solution* (also called the *stable set*) is similar to the core in singling out an acceptable set of outcomes, and in rarely achieving a unique outcome. In contrast, the Nash cooperative solution, and the relatives of it that are the subject of the present chapter, and the Shapley and Banzhaf values, and the generalizations of the Shapley values, are all value solutions. For many games, these solution concepts give unique outcomes. It is for this reason that they may be termed *value* solutions. Recall that von Neumann proved that any finite two-person, zero-sum game has a (unique) value. Some of the motivation behind the value solutions appears to have been the desire to find a unique value for each game in a given class.

1.3 Outline of the chapter

In this chapter, two-person cooperative games are covered from several points of view. The (fixed threat) bargaining model of Nash (1950) is discussed in Section 2, following a brief discussion of Edgeworth's early contribution. This model deals with two-person situations in which the players each obtain fixed utility levels if they fail to make an agreement. There is a feasible set of outcomes that they can achieve if they make an agreement; however, in the absence of agreement, there is nothing a player can do to help or hurt either himself or the other player. Section 3 is concerned with precisely the same basic game situation, but the rules defining a solution concept, that is, an appropriate, fair, or desirable agreement, are altered from those proposed by Nash. The models of Sections 2 and 3 do not really examine the bargaining process as such, nor is the element of time considered. These topics are in Section 4 where an explicit bargaining process is outlined that leads to Nash's outcome. A model that places an explicit value on time is also explored. The means of doing this is to suppose that each step of bargaining, offer or counteroffer, takes a fixed length of time and that the value of any particular outcome shrinks with the passing of time. Another model is examined in which players make demands of one another at the first stage of the game, and, in the second, they discover whether their demands are simultaneously feasible. Section 5 takes up variable threat models. In these models the players have strategy sets from which to choose actions in the absence of agreement. Thus the disagreement outcomes are not fixed; they depend on the chosen actions. It is natural to approach this cooperative game by styling it as a noncooperative game in which the disagreement actions determine disagreement payoffs and the disagreement payoffs determine the cooperative agreement. Then a player's choice of a disagreement action is guided by the effect of that action on a final cooperative outcome. Section 6 contains some applications and concluding comments are in Section 7. A good source on the bargaining models in the present chapter is Roth (1979).

2   Fixed threat bargaining—The models of Edgeworth and Nash

Imagine two persons isolated on a desert island. Suppose that each has a fixed supply of various commodities, and each has a utility function assigning a personal value to any conceivable commodity bundle. The two players' utility functions need not be the same, nor need their initial holdings be the same. To think of this situation as a game, a player's payoff is defined as her utility. Suppose they may engage in trade with one another, exchanging anything from their respective holdings that both would agree on. The possibilities for them are depicted in two different

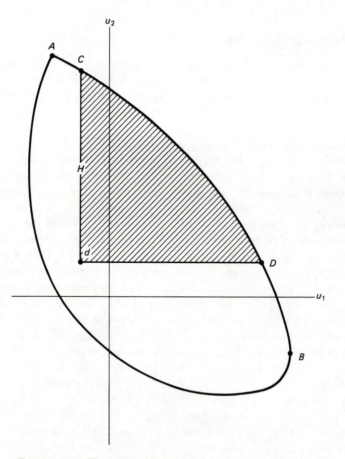

FIGURE 5.1   The attainable payoffs in a fixed threat game.

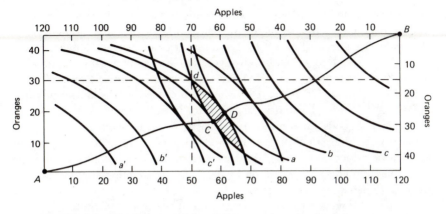

FIGURE 5.2   The Edgeworth box representation of a fixed threat game.

ways in Figures 5.1 and 5.2. In Figure 5.1, the axes are labeled with the two players' utility levels, or payoffs. The point marked d is the outcome that obtains in the absence of trade and the set H is the set of feasible trades (in payoff space), assuming that the two players trade by reallocating their joint total holdings. That is, the possibility of discarding some holdings is not considered, but the possibility that one player gives resources to the other, receiving nothing in return, is allowed. The point d is sometimes called the *status quo* or the *no trade point* or the *threat point.*[1]

2.1   Edgeworth two-person bargaining and the core

This trading situation was first studied by Edgeworth (1881) and Figure 5.2 shows the Edgeworth box, a representation familiar in economics. The dimensionality of the *Edgeworth box* is equal to the number of commodities existing in the two-person society, while Figure 5.1 is applicable for any number of commodities. Figure 5.2, then, shows two goods, apples and oranges, with units of apples measured on the horizontal axis and oranges on the vertical. Curves such as a, b, and c are *indifference curves* for player 1 whose origin is at A, and for whom larger amounts are upward and to the right. An indifference curve for a player is a curve on which each point corresponds to exactly the same payoff for that player as any other point on the curve. The curves labeled a', b', and c' are indifference curves for player 2, whose origin is at B and for whom quantities and utility increase as one moves down and to the left in the diagram. The overall size of the box is determined by the total holdings of the two players. Thus the point d, which shows their initial holdings, indicates that player 1 has 50 apples and 30 oranges while player 2 has 70 apples and 15 oranges.

Edgeworth's analysis of this trading situation is an important forerunner of cooperative game theory. He notes two limitations on any reasonable agreement: (1) Any agreement should be efficient in the sense that no alternative agreement is feasible that yields higher payoffs simultaneously to both players. Such agreements are the points on the curve going from A to B in both Figures 5.1 and 5.2. (2) No player can be expected to agree to a trade that leaves him with a lower payoff than he would get if no trade were made. Such agreements are the shaded regions of Figures 5.1 and 5.2. The curve from C to D in Figure 5.1 satisfies both criteria and is known in game theory as the *core*. The curve from C to D in Figure 5.2 is the set of allocations of goods (in commodity space) that yield payoffs in the core.

Of course, in a game of three or more players, a third limitation would have to be added in defining the core that stipulates that a core outcome would have to give each coalition as much as the coalition could obtain on its own. (See Chapter 6 for details.)

The curve from A to B is, of course, the set of trades yielding outcomes on the payoff possibility frontier. It is often called the *Pareto optimal set* for the obvious reason that each point on the curve is Pareto optimal for the players in the game. The requirement of Pareto optimality is also known in cooperative game theory as *group rationality*, because it seems intuitively unreasonable (irrational) that the set of all players would ever settle for a non-Pareto optimal outcome. Why should they where there is a Pareto optimal outcome available that benefits some or all of them and harms no one?[2] Condition (2) is often called *individual rationality*, because it would be irrational for a single player to agree to a joint outcome under which he receives a lower payoff than he could assure himself by his own individual efforts.

2.2   The Nash fixed threat bargaining model

Frequently, the core consists of many points, as in the illustration in Figures 5.1 and 5.2. The Nash solution, in contrast, always gives a unique outcome. The Nash solution satisfies several conditions that one might find intuitively appealing. In discussing bargaining models, $H \subset R^2$ denotes the set of attainable *payoff pairs* and $d \in H$ denotes the *threat point*. If a payoff point $u = (u_1, u_2) \notin H$, then it is impossible for the players to achieve it, but if $u \in H$, then there are (joint) actions open to them that will result in u being the payoff. The salient feature of the threat point, d, is that the players will receive the payoffs $d = (d_1, d_2)$ if they fail to achieve an agreement. In Sections 2 and 3, the models are all characterized by such fixed threat points. This means that there is no way that one player can take unilateral action that hurts the other. For example, if the game is an Edgeworth game of pure trade in which each player has an endowment of goods and the utility (payoff) of each player depends only on his own personal consumption, then a player cannot be forced to a payoff below the level he achieves by consuming the endowment of goods with which he begins. The present section is further divided. In Section 2.2.1, the Nash bargaining game is defined and the *Nash axioms* that define his bargaining solution are given. In Section 2.2.2, the existence and uniqueness of the solution is proved, and, in the process, a simple characterization of it is provided. Finally, Section 2.2.3 briefly describes a half-century-old model that anticipated Nash in the context of labor-management negotiations.

2.2.1 The game and conditions defining the Nash bargaining solution

The class of games studied in Sections 2 and 3 is characterized by a pair (H, d) and by the rule that the players will attain any single payoff point in H that they jointly agree on. In the absence of an agreement, they attain d. Definitions 5.1 and 5.2 formally describe these games, Definition 5.3 defines the meaning of *solution*, and Conditions 5.1 to 5.4 define the Nash solution to the class of games specified in Definitions 5.1 and 5.2.

DEFINITION 5.1 *The pair* $\Gamma = (H, d)$ *is a* **two-person fixed threat bargaining game** *if* $H \subset R^2$ *is compact and convex,* $d \in H$, *and* H *contains at least one element,* u, *such that* $u \gg d$.

DEFINITION 5.2 *The* **set of two-person fixed threat bargaining games** *is denoted* W.

Parenthetically, recall that the utility axioms of von Neumann and Morgenstern are assumed throughout this book. Consequently, one could have a bargaining game in which there were a nonconvex set (including a finite set) of outcomes. The set H would consist of the utility pairs associated with all possible lotteries defined on elements from the original set of outcomes. Such a set H would be convex. It would also be compact if the set of original outcomes were compact.

A solution to some game $\Gamma = (H, d)$ is a particular element of H which is the payoff pertaining to the solution concept under discussion, for example, the Nash solution. Because (H, d) can be any game drawn from a large set of games, a particular solution concept can be conveniently described as a function of the game, $f(H, d) \in H$.

DEFINITION 5.3 *A* **solution** *to* $(H, d) \in W$ *is a function* $f(H, d)$ *that associates a unique element of* H *with the game* $(H, d) \in W$. $f(H, d) = (f_1(H, d), f_2(H, d))$.

The conditions defining the Nash solution are:

CONDITION 5.1 $f(H, d) \geq d$ *for all* $(H, d) \in W$.

CONDITION 5.2 *Let* $a_1, a_2 \in R_{++}$, $b_1, b_2 \in R$, *and* $(H, d), (H', d') \in W$ *and define* $d'_i = a_i d_i + b_i$, $i = 1, 2$, *and* $H' = \{x \in R^2 \mid x_i = a_i y_i + b_i, i = 1, 2, y \in H\}$. *Then* $f_i(H', d') = a_i f_i(H, d) + b_i$, $i = 1, 2$.

CONDITION 5.3 *If* $(H, d) \in W$ *satisfies* $d_1 = d_2$ *and* $(x_1, x_2) \in H$ *implies* $(x_2, x_1) \in H$, *then* $f_1(H, d) = f_2(H, d)$.

CONDITION 5.4 *If* $(H, d), (H', d') \in W$, $d = d'$, $H \subset H'$, *and* $f(H', d') \in H$, *then* $f(H, d) = f(H', d')$.

Condition 5.1 stipulates that the solution payoff to each player should be at least as large as the payoff the player would get if no agreement were reached. That is, the solution must be *individually rational*.

Condition 5.2 requires that the solution should be invariant to positive affine utility transformations. A *positive affine transformation* of utility is a transformation of the form $x_i = a_i y_i + b_i$, defined for all y_i, that moves the zero point of utility in an arbitrary way (b_i can be positive or negative), and changes the scale of units on which utility is measured (a_i must be strictly positive). The two essential features of such transformations are that (a) if $y_i > y_i'$ then $a_i y_i + b_i > a_i y_i' + b_i$ and (b) if $y_i^0 - y_i^1 > y_i^2 - y_i^3$, then $(a_i y_i^0 + b_i) - (a_i y_i^1 + b_i) > (a_i y_i^2 + b_i) - (a_i y_i^3 + b_i)$. Two games related in the manner of (H, d) and (H', d') in Condition 5.2 are like two games that are identical in terms of physical possibilities but that differ only in an arbitrary aspect of their utility representation. For such a pair of games, their solutions should be related by precisely the same utility transformation that relates the games themselves. If the two games embody the same set of physical outcomes and the two threat points correspond to the same physical outcome, then the same physical outcome is the solution to both. Condition 5.2 also states that the outcome does not depend on which particular von Neumann–Morgenstern utility function is used for a player (among those that, in fact, represent her preferences).

Condition 5.3 imposes symmetry: If the attainable set H is symmetric about a 45° line through the origin and $d_1 = d_2$, then $f_1(H, d) = f_2(H, d)$. This does not imply comparability of the two utility scales. Given symmetry if $f_1(H, d) \neq f_2(H, d)$, it would appear that one player was being favored over the other.

Condition 5.4 is called *independence of irrelevant alternatives*. It compares two games (H, d) and (H', d') that are related in three ways: (1) they have the same threat point ($d = d'$), (2) the attainable set of one game is contained in the attainable set of the other ($H \subset H'$), and (3) the solution of the larger game is an attainable point in the smaller game ($f(H', d') \in H$). Thus the game (H, d) can be regarded as (H', d') with some of the attainable set of (H', d') removed, but with $f(H', d')$ remaining available. Condition 5.4 requires that $f(H', d')$ be the solution to (H, d). The heuristic justification is that, if $f(H', d')$ is to be preferred as the outcome for (H', d'), then it should be preferable to any alternative in $(H, d') = (H, d)$ because $H \subset H'$.

Nash also assumed that $f(H, d)$ is Pareto optimal. That is, if $u \in H$, then $u \not> f(H, d)$; however, Pareto optimality is implied by conditions 5.1 to 5.4, as the following lemma due to Roth (1977) shows:

LEMMA 5.1   *Let $(H, d) \in W$ and let $u^* = f(H, d)$ satisfy Conditions 5.1 to 5.4. Then if $u \in H$ and $u \neq u^*$ either $u_1^* > u_1$ or $u_2^* > u_2$.*

Proof   Without loss of generality, we may let $d = 0$.[3] Assume the lemma false; then there is some $y^* \in H$ such that $y^* > u^*$. Define a game $(H', 0)$ by letting

$$H' = \left\{ x \in R^2 \mid x_1 = \frac{u_1^*}{y_1^*}\, y_1, \qquad x_2 = \frac{u_2^*}{y_2^*}\, y_2, \qquad y \in H \right\} \tag{5.1}$$

Clearly, $H' \subset H$, $H' \neq H$, and $u^* \in H'$, because $y^* \in H$. By Condition 5.4, u^* is the solution to $(H', 0)$, but by Condition 5.2, $[(u_1^*/y_1^*)u_1^*, (u_2^*/y_2^*)u_2^*] \neq u^*$ is the solution to $(H', 0)$. This contradiction implies that the solution of $(H, 0)$ must be Pareto optimal. QED

2.2.2 *Characterization and existence of the Nash solution*

The Nash solution can be characterized in a very simple way: The element of H that maximizes the product of gains from agreement, $(u_1 - d_1)(u_2 - d_2)$, is the unique outcome satisfying Conditions 5.1 to 5.4. This is proved in Theorem 5.1 and the Nash solution is illustrated in Figure 5.3. The shaded area of H is the region of outcomes that are individually rational. A rectangular hyperbola, as shown in Figure 5.3, that is asymptotic to the broken lines through d is a curve along which the product $(u_1 - d_1)(u_2 - d_2)$ is constant; therefore, the point of H at which the product of gains from

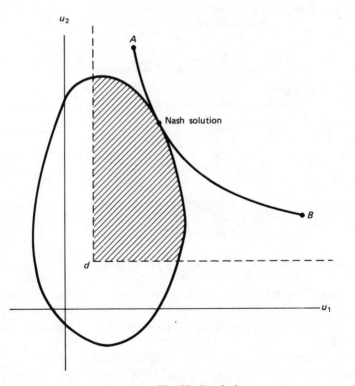

FIGURE 5.3 The Nash solution.

agreement is maximized is the point of tangency between the upper boundary of H and the most highly placed rectangular hyperbola that still touches H. The result is proved in two steps. Lemma 5.2 establishes the result for games with threat points at the origin $(d = 0)$, and Theorem 5.1 generalizes the result to games with arbitrary threat points.

LEMMA 5.2 *Any game $(H, 0) \in W$ has a unique Nash solution $u^* = f(H, 0)$ satisfying Conditions 5.1 to 5.4. The solution u^* satisfies Conditions 5.1 to 5.4 if and only if*

$$u_1^* u_2^* > u_1 u_2 \tag{5.2}$$

for all $u \in H$, $u \geqslant 0$, and $u \neq u^*$.

Proof It is first proved that if $u_1^* u_2^* = \max_{u \in H, u \geqslant 0} u_1 u_2$, then u^* is unique and satisfies Conditions 5.1 to 5.4. Then it is shown that if $u_1' u_2' < u_1^* u_2^*$, u' violates one of the four conditions. That the product maximizer is unique may be seen from a simple algebraic argument. Suppose the utility product is maximized at (u_1, u_2) and also at $(u_1 + \delta, u_2 - \gamma)$ where δ and γ are both positive. Then

$$u_1 u_2 = (u_1 + \delta)(u_2 - \gamma) \tag{5.3}$$

and $u_2 = \gamma + \gamma u_1 / \delta$. Now consider the point $(u_1 + \delta/2, u_2 - \gamma/2)$ which is in H, because H is convex. The utility product for this point is

$$\left(u_1 + \frac{\delta}{2}\right)\left(u_2 - \frac{\gamma}{2}\right) = u_1 u_2 + \frac{\delta u_2}{2} - \frac{\gamma u_1}{2} - \frac{\delta \gamma}{4} = u_1 u_2 + \frac{\delta \gamma}{4} > u_1 u_2 \tag{5.4}$$

Thus, if two distinct points in H achieve the same payoff product, the point halfway between them will achieve a higher product. Because of the convexity of H, the halfway point is in H. A parallel argument can be made when δ and γ are negative. Therefore, the product maximizer is unique.

Turning now to Conditions 5.1 to 5.4, Condition 5.1 is satisfied by definition. For Condition 5.2, let (H', d') be defined by $d_i' = a_i d_i + b_i$, $i = 1, 2$ and $H' = \{y \in R^2 \mid y_i = a_i u_i + b_i, i = 1, 2, u \in H\}$. Let w be an arbitrary element of H', let u be the point in H that transforms into w, and let $w^* \in H'$ be the point to which u^*, the product maximizer for (H, d), transforms. Comparing w^* and w,

$$(w_1^* - d_1')(w_2^* - d_2') - (w_1 - d_1')(w_2 - d_2') = a_1 a_2 (u_1^* u_2^* - u_1 u_2) > 0 \tag{5.5}$$

To see that Condition 5.3 is satisfied, suppose H is symmetric about a 45° line through the origin and let u' be the point in H that is on the 45° line where it intersects the upper right boundary of H. Then $u_1' = u_2'$ and, for any $u \in H$, $u_1 + u_2 \leqslant u_1' + u_2'$. That is, the set H is bounded above by a line of slope -1 passing through u'. The product $u_1' u_2'$ is strictly larger than any product of the form $(u_1' + a)(u_2' - a)$ for $a \neq 0$; hence, u' has a larger product than does any other point in H. Thus, $u^* = u'$.

That Condition 5.4 is satisfied is trivial; for, if u^* is the product maximizer in H, and H' is derived from H by paring away some regions of H, then $u_1^* u_2^*$ must exceed a similar product for any point in H'.

A constructive argument is used to prove that if u' is not the payoff product maximizer, it violates at least one of the four conditions. First, let u^* be the payoff product maximizer for the game $(H, 0)$ and transform $(H, 0)$ into the game $(H', 0)$ by letting $H' = \{y \in R^2 \mid y_1 = u_2^* x_1 / u_1^*$ and $y_2 = x_2$ for $(x_1, x_2) \in H\}$. Thus, the product maximizer in $(H', 0)$ is (u_2^*, u_2^*). From $(H', 0)$, we obtain a third game $(H'', 0)$ by adding points to H': Let

$$H'' = \{y \in R^2 \mid y_1 + y_2 \leqslant 2u_2^* \quad \text{and} \quad |y_1| + |y_2| \leqslant \max_{u \in H'} [|u_1| + |u_2|]\} \quad (5.6)$$

The upper right boundary of H'' is a line of slope -1 through (u_2^*, u_2^*) and H'' contains H'; therefore, by Condition 5.3, symmetry, (u_2^*, u_2^*) is the solution of $(H'', 0)$; by Condition 5.4, independence of irrelevant alternatives, (u_2^*, u_2^*) is also the solution of $(H', 0)$; and by Condition 5.2, invariance to affine transformations, $u^* = (u_1^*, u_2^*)$ is the solution of $(H, 0)$. Thus u' fails to satisfy Conditions 5.1 to 5.4 and only u^*, the product maximizer, can be the solution of the game. QED

THEOREM 5.1 *A game $(H, d) \in W$ has a unique Nash solution $u^* = f(H, d)$ satisfying Conditions 5.1 to 5.4. The solution u^* satisfies Conditions 5.1 to 5.4 if and only if*

$$(u_1^* - d_1)(u_2^* - d_2) > (u_1 - d_1)(u_2 - d_2) \quad (5.7)$$

for all $u \in H$, $u \geqslant d$, and $u \neq u^*$.

Proof Transform (H, d) into $(H', 0)$ by letting $a_1 = a_2 = 1$, $b_1 = -d_1$, and $b_2 = -d_2$. Clearly, $f(H', 0) = (u_1^* - d_1, u_2^* - d_2)$ where u^* is the point in H satisfying equation (5.7). Therefore, by Condition 5.2 and Lemma 5.2, $f(H, d) = u^*$. QED

2.2.3 *Zeuthen's anticipation of the Nash solution*

There is an interesting precursor to the Nash bargaining solution that also attempts to deal with the bargaining process itself. It was proposed by Zeuthen (1930) as a method of resolving labor-management disputes, and Harsanyi (1956) discovered that it yields an outcome formally identical to Nash's solution. Zeuthen envisaged a bargaining process in which each player, at any point in time, had a proposal on the table. Each proposal could be stated as a point on the payoff possibility frontier. Depending on how the two proposals were related, it would be incumbent on one of the two players to replace his proposal with a new one that made a concession. Letting the proposal of player 1 be $u^1 = (u_1^1, u_2^1)$, that of player 2 be u^2, and $d = 0$, the values $(u_1^1 - u_1^2)/u_1^1$ and $(u_2^2 - u_2^1)/u_2^2$ are compared. If the first is smaller than the second, then Zeuthen directed that player 1 should make a concession big enough to reverse the inequality. The reason is the view that $(u_i^i - u_i^j)/u_i^i$ measures the cost to player i of making a concession to player j, and the player facing the smaller cost should make a concession. It is easily seen that $(u_1^1 - u_1^2)/u_1^1 < (u_2^2 - u_2^1)/u_2^2$ is equivalent to $u_1^1 u_2^1 < u_1^2 u_2^2$; therefore, the player whose proposal has the smaller Nash product makes a concession of sufficient size that his Nash product becomes larger than that of the other player. Clearly this process ends at the Nash solution. Although the proposed bargaining process seems ad hoc, it is interesting to see this totally independent route to Nash's outcome.

3   Other approaches to fixed threat bargaining

Several alternatives to the Nash approach have been put forth and a few of them are reviewed in this section. The first of these takes up a suggestion of Raiffa's described briefly in Luce and Raiffa (1957: 136). Raiffa's model has been axiomatized by Kalai and Smorodinsky (1975). The basic intuitive notion is that each player naturally aspires to have the largest payoff available in the game that is consistent with individual rationality. These two individual payoffs are, in general, not attainable simultaneously and the proposed solution is to settle at the largest attainable payoff point that is proportional to them. The Raiffa–Kalai–Smorodinsky model is examined in Section 2.1. The remaining several solutions, reviewed in Section 2.2, are members of a family to which the Nash solution also belongs. In this family, the Condition 5.4, independence of irrelevant alternatives, is replaced with a parallel condition in which the place of the threat point d is taken by another point that lies below the payoff possibility frontier.

3.1   The Raiffa–Kalai-Smorodinsky solution

For the Nash model the threat point, d, is a *reference point* with respect to which the solution is found. All the models in Section 2 and 3 use reference points, but the Raiffa–Kalai–Smorodinsky solution is unique among them, because it is the only solution for which there are two reference points. One is d and the other is above and to the right of the Pareto optimal curve. Exposition of this solution is carried out in three sections. In Section 3.1.1 the solution is described, in Section 3.1.2 existence is established, and in Section 3.1.3 it is compared with the Nash solution.

3.1.1   A description of the Raiffa–Kalai–Smorodinsky solution

As in the discussion of the Nash solution, a game is characterized by (H, d) as specified in Definitions 5.1 and 5.2. The solution concept is easily described with the aid of Figure 5.4. Locate point A where player 1 has a payoff M_1, the highest payoff among all points in H that are individually rational. This payoff of M_1 is regarded as an aspiration level for player 1, at least in the sense that the larger is M_1, the more the player thinks he should obtain at a final settlement. Point B and the amount M_2 are analogously defined for player 2. The point $M = (M_1, M_2)$, which generally lies beyond the attainable set H, is called the *ideal point* and is a reference point. A

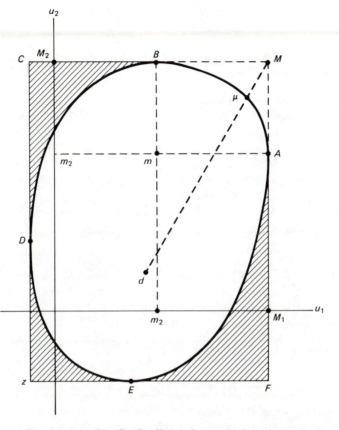

FIGURE 5.4   The Raiffa–Kalai–Smorodinsky solution.

straight line is then drawn from d, the threat point, to (M_1, M_2) and the solution occurs at μ where the straight line intersects the payoff possibility frontier. This simple characterization yields the only outcome that satisfies a set of conditions including Conditions 5.2 and 5.3, Pareto optimality, and monotonicity. These latter two conditions are stated formally, following some definitions.

$$M_1(H, d) = \max\{x_1 \in R \mid (x_1, x_2) \in H \text{ and } x_2 \geq d_2\} \tag{5.8}$$

$$m_2(H, d) = \max\{x_2 \in R \mid (M_1(H, d), x_2) \in H\} \tag{5.9}$$

$$M_2(H, d) = \max\{x_2 \in R \mid (x_1, x_2) \in H \text{ and } x_1 \geq d_1\} \tag{5.10}$$

$$m_1(H, d) = \max\{x_1 \in R \mid (x_1, M_2(H, d)) \in H\} \tag{5.11}$$

$M_1(H, d)$ is the largest payoff in H for player 1 among all outcomes at which player 2 obtains at least d_2. $m_2(H, d)$ is the payoff player 2 receives when player 1 gets $M_1(H, d)$. If the payoff for player 2 corresponding to $M_1(H, d)$ is not unique, then $m_2(H, d)$ is the largest of the corresponding payoffs. $M_2(H, d)$ and $m_1(H, d)$ are analogously defined.

Definition 5.4   *The point $M(H, d) = (M_1(H, d), M_2(H, d))$ is called the* **ideal point.**

Definition 5.5   *The point $m(H, d) = (m_1(H, d), m_2(H, d))$ is called the* **point of minimal expectations.**

Note that, in general, the ideal point is not an element of H. Indeed, if it were, there would be nothing to bargain over (i.e., no conflict in the interests of the two players).

It will prove convenient to work with a set somewhat larger than H that is obtained by adding a *free disposal of utility* assumption to the model. To that end, let $z_i = \min\{y_i \in R \mid (y_1, y_2) \in H\}$ for $i = 1, 2$. Thus z_i is the smallest payoff in H that player i could conceivably receive, and $z = (z_1, z_2)$. The set $\bar{H}$ is defined as the set of payoff points that both weakly dominate z and that are weakly dominated by an element of H. That is,

$$\bar{H} = \{y \in R^2 \mid y \geq z \quad \text{and,} \quad \text{for some} \quad x \in H, \, x \geq y\} \tag{5.12}$$

In Figure 5.4, the set H is the unshaded set enclosed by the curve $ABDEA$, and the set $\bar{H}$ consists of H plus the three shaded areas (i.e., the set enclosed by the curve $ABCzFA$). The Raiffa–Kalai–Smorodinsky (RKS) solution satisfies Conditions 5.5 and 5.6 below.

Condition 5.5   *If $x > f(H, d)$ then $x \notin H$.*

Condition 5.6   *Let (H, d) and (H', d') satisfy (a) $d = d'$, (b) $M_1(H, d) = M_1(H', d')$, and (c) $\bar{H} \subset \bar{H}'$. Then $f_2(H, d) \leq f_2(H', d')$.*

Condition 5.5, *strong Pareto optimality*, states that there is no alternative in H that gives more to one player than $f(H, d)$ without giving less to the other. *Weak Pareto optimality* states that $u \in H$ is Pareto optimal if there is no $u' \in H$ for which $u' \gg u$. That is, a point is not weakly Pareto optimal if there is another point that gives strictly more to each player. Both concepts are used in Chapters 5 to 7, and the choice between them is usually based on mathematical tractability. Condition 5.6, *monotonicity*, states that if two games yield the same maximum payoff to player 1 $(M_1(H, d) = M_1(H', d'))$, the second game affords at least as large a maximum payoff as the first to player 2, they have the same threat point, and the Pareto set of the second game lies on or above the Pareto set of the first game $(\bar{H} \subset \bar{H}')$, then the solution payoff to player 2 in the second game must be at least as large as in the first game. The conditions on M_2 and the payoff frontier can be stated as stipulating that, for fixed x_1, the largest value of x_2 is at least as large in $\bar{H}'$ as in $\bar{H}$. The point here is that the game (H', d') is at least as favorable to player 2 as the game (H, d), while the two games retain the same value of M_1. In this situation, monotonicity requires that player 2 get at least as large a payoff from the second game as from the first.

Figure 5.5 shows an example in which the Nash solution violates Condition 5.6. For both (H, d) and (H', d') the threat point is at d. The set $\bar{H}$ is the four-sided figure whose vertices are at d, A, B, and D. The set $\bar{H}'$

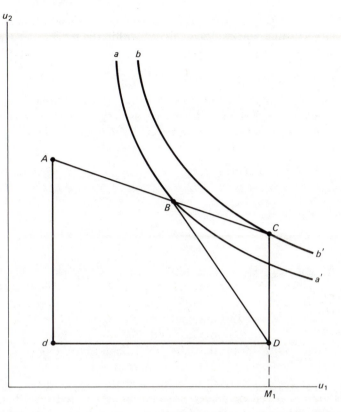

FIGURE 5.5   An example to show the Nash solution can violate Condition 5.6.

is the four-sided figure whose vertices are at d, A, C, and D. Note that $M_1(H, d) = M_1(H', d')$ (marked at M_1 in Figure 5.5), and $\bar{H} \subset \bar{H}'$. The curves aa' and bb' are each curves along which $(u_1 - d_1)(u_2 - d_2)$ is constant; therefore, the Nash solution to (H, d) is at B, the Nash solution to (H', d') is at C, and player 2 receives a smaller Nash solution payoff from (H', d') than from (H, d). This is contrary to Condition 5.6.

    Now let the solution $f(H, d)$ be defined by the following two conditions:
(a)

$$\frac{f_2(H, d) - d_2}{f_1(H, d) - d_1} = \frac{M_2(H, d) - d_2}{M_1(H, d) - d_1} \tag{5.13}$$

(b) if

$$\frac{x_2 - d_2}{x_1 - d_1} = \frac{M_2(H, d) - d_2}{M_1(H, d) - d_1} \tag{5.14}$$

and $x > f(H, d)$, then $x \notin H$. Condition (a) states that the amount each player receives over and above his threat point payoff is proportional to his ideal point payoff with the proportionality constant being parallel for both players. Then condition (b) requires that the proportionality constant must be the largest value that can be achieved within the feasible set H.

3.1.2   Existence of the Raiffa–Kalai–Smorodinsky solution

The main result of Kalai and Smorodinsky (1975) is that the function $f(H, d)$, defined by (a) and (b) above, is well defined and is the only function that satisfies Conditions 5.1 to 5.3, 5.5, and 5.6. This is proved in Theorem 5.2 with the aid of the following two lemmas.

LEMMA 5.3   *A nonnegatively sloped ray (i.e., straight line) through d passes through a strongly Pareto optimal point of H if and only if the slope of the ray lies in the interval*

$$\left[\frac{m_2(H, d) - d_2}{M_1(H, d) - d_1}, \frac{M_2(H, d) - d_2}{m_1(H, d) - d_1} \right] \tag{5.15}$$

Proof   A nonnegatively sloped ray whose slope lies in the interval in equation (5.15) must pass through a point on the (weak) upper right frontier of H. (A point $u \in H$ is on this frontier if there is no $u' \in H$ such that $u' \gg u$.) To fail to do so would contradict the convexity of H, and for the point to fail to be Pareto optimal would, likewise, contradict the convexity of H. A ray of slope steeper than the upper bound in equation (5.15) could only intersect the upper right boundary of H at a point where $x_1 < m_1(H, d)$ and $x_2 \le M_2(H, d)$; therefore, x could not be strongly Pareto optimal. A parallel argument can be made for nonnegatively sloped rays that are too flat to lie in the interval in equation (5.15).   QED

LEMMA 5.4   *The function $f(H, d)$ defined by equations (5.13) and (5.14) has a unique value for every (H, d) and corresponds to a strongly Pareto optimal element of H.*

Proof $f(H, d)$ is that point in H which lies on a ray through d of slope $[M_2(H, d) - d_2]/[M_1(H, d) - d_1]$. This slope lies in the interval in equation (5.15); therefore, it passes through a strongly Pareto optimal element of H. The ray could not pass through two or more Pareto optimal elements, because its slope is positive and, hence, one of the supposed Pareto optimal points would strongly dominate the other.   QED

THEOREM 5.2   *The function $f(H, d)$ is well defined, satisfies Conditions 5.1 to 5.3, 5.5, and 5.6, and is the only function to satisfy these conditions.*

Proof   First it is shown that $f(H, d)$ satisfies the several conditions and is well defined; then it is shown that it is the only function to satisfy the conditions. It is proved in Lemma 5.4 that $f(H, d)$ is well defined and satisfies Condition 5.5. That Condition 5.1 is satisfied is obvious, that Condition 5.2 is satisfied is left as an exercise for the reader, and that Condition 5.3 is satisfied follows from the definition of $f(H, d)$ and the definition of a symmetric game.

To see that Condition 5.6 is satisfied, suppose that (H, d) and (H', d') are two games satisfying $d = d'$, $M_1(H, d) = M_1(H', d')$, and $\bar{H} \subset \bar{H}'$. The latter implies that $M_2(H, d) \leqslant M_2(H', d')$. The ray from a threat point d through a point $f(H, d)$ is called below the *defining ray for $f(H, d)$*. Note the following facts: (a) Because $M_1(H, d) = M_1(H', d')$ and $M_2(H, d) \leqslant M_2(H', d')$, the defining ray for $f(H', d')$ has a slope at least as great as that for $f(H, d)$. (b) The set of Pareto optimal points of H is identical with that of $\bar{H}$, and the same holds for H' and $\bar{H}'$. (c) Let y denote the point on the upper right boundary of $\bar{H}$ that the defining ray of $f(H, d)$ passes through, and let $\bar{y}$ denote the point on the upper right boundary of $\bar{H}$ that the defining ray of $f(H', d')$ passes through. Then $\bar{y}_2 \geqslant y_2$. (d) Let y' denote the point on the upper boundary of $\bar{H}'$ that the defining ray of $f(H', d')$ passes through. Then $y'_2 \geqslant \bar{y}_2$. Now note that y is on the upper right boundary of H; hence $y = f(H, d)$. Similarly, y' is on the upper right boundary of H', implying that $y' = f(H', d')$. Therefore, $f_2(H', d') \geqslant f_2(H, d)$, which establishes that $f(H, d)$ satisfies Condition 5.6.

To see that only $f(H, d)$ satisfies the various conditions, it is first shown to hold for games in which $d = 0$ and $M_1(H, 0) = M_2(H, 0) = 1$. Extension to the full class of games follows from the requirement that the solution satisfy invariance to affine transformations (Condition 5.2). Denote the true solution by $f^*(H, d)$, and let H' be the convex hull of the set of points $\{(0, 0), (0, 1), (1, 0), f(\bar{H}, 0)\}$. Monotonicity requires that $f^*(\bar{H}, 0) \geqslant f^*(H, 0)$ and that $f^*(\bar{H}, 0) \geqslant f^*(H', 0)$, because $H \subset \bar{H}$ and $H' \subset \bar{H}$. At the same time, the definition of $\bar{H}$ and the Pareto optimality of $f(H, 0)$ imply

$$f^*(H, 0) = f^*(\bar{H}, 0) \tag{5.16}$$

Symmetry assures that

$$f^*(H', 0) = f(\bar{H}, 0) \tag{5.17}$$

Meanwhile, $f(\bar{H}, 0)$ is in the Pareto optimal set of both H and $\bar{H}$; hence,

$$f(\bar{H}, 0) = f(H, 0) \tag{5.18}$$

and

$$f^*(\bar{H}, 0) = f^*(H', 0) \tag{5.19}$$

Equations (5.16) to (5.19) imply that $f^*(H, 0) = f(H, 0)$.   QED

3.1.3 A comparison of the Raiffa–Kalai–Smorodinsky and Nash solutions

Before moving on to other bargaining solutions, it is worthwhile to compare Condition 5.4 with Condition 5.6. Nash's condition says that two games sharing the same threat point must have the same solution if one feasible set is contained in the other $(H \subset H')$ and the solution to the larger game is available in the smaller game $(f(H', d') \in H)$. This is like saying that, if the best tennis player in Europe is from Sweden, then the best tennis player in

Europe must be the best tennis player in Sweden. Condition 5.6 says, approximately, that if the payoff frontier is moved outward to increase $M_2(H, d)$ without increasing $M_1(H, d)$, then the solution payoff to player 2 should be increased. The former condition states when a change in the game should have no effect on the solution, while the latter states when a change should benefit a particular player. In Section 2.2, a class of solutions is examined to which the Nash solution belongs, but to which the RKS solution does not belong. For this class of solutions a condition similar to Condition 5.4 is used.

3.2   Bargaining solutions based on invariance with respect to a reference point

In the game (H, d), the threat point, d, plays the role of reference point for the Nash solution. Although Condition 5.4 has traditionally been called independence of irrelevant alternatives, it might be more aptly named dependence on the threat point. In Section 3.2.1, a condition of *dependence on the reference point* is formulated and a large class of reference points is considered. Section 3.2.2 establishes the existence and uniqueness of solutions based on the class of reference points from Section 3.2.1. Then an example is presented for which several solutions are computed and compared, each for a different reference point, in Section 3.2.3, and finally, comparisons of these solutions with noncooperative equilibria are made in Section 3.2.4.

3.2.1   Conditions defining a class of reference points

The concept of reference point can be formulated abstractly, following Thomson (1981). Let $g(H, d)$ be an element of H that is not in the Pareto set of H (i.e., there is some $y \in H$ such that $y \gg g(H, d)$). Two examples of reference points are the point of minimal expectations, $m(H, d)$, and a convex combination of d and $m(H, d)$, $g(H, d) = kd + (1 - k)m(H, d)$ for $k \in [0, 1]$. The reference point $g(H, d)$ is required to obey two conditions that are obviously satisfied by d. They are

CONDITION 5.7   *Let $(H, d), (H', d') \in W$, $a_1, a_2 \in R_{++}$, $b_1, b_2 \in R$, $d'_i = a_i d_i + b_i$, $i = 1, 2$, and $H' = \{x \in R^2 \mid x_i = a_i y_i + b_i, i = 1, 2, y \in H\}$. Then $g_i(H', d') = a_i g_i(H, d) + b_i, i = 1, 2$.*

This condition states that when two games are related by an affine transformation, their reference points are related by the same affine transformation.

CONDITION 5.8   *Let (i) $\delta \in R$ be defined by the conditions that $(\delta, \delta) \in H$ and $(\delta + \varepsilon, \delta + \varepsilon) \notin H$ for all $\varepsilon > 0$, (ii) $(H, d) \in W$, (iii) $g_1(H, d) = g_2(H, d)$, and (iv) $x \notin H$ if $x_1 + x_2 > 2\delta$. Then there exists $(H', d') \in W$ satisfying (a) $H \subset H'$, (b) if $(x_1, x_2) \in H'$ then $(x_2, x_1) \in H'$, (c) if $x \in H'$ then $x_1 + x_2 \leqslant 2\delta$, and (d) $g(H, d) = g(H', d')$.*

For a game (H, d), suppose a line of slope -1 is drawn that is tangent to the upper right boundary of H. If this tangency point, x, is symmetric (i.e., $x_1 = x_2$), and the reference point is symmetric (i.e., $g_1(H, d) = g_2(H, d)$), then the game is *almost symmetric*. Condition 5.8 states that the game (H, d) can be enlarged into the symmetric game (H', d') with the two games having the same reference point $(g(H, d) = g(H', d'))$ and with $[u_1 - g_1(H, d)][u_2 - g_2(H, d)]$ maximized on H at the same point u^* where $[u_1 - g_1(H', d')][u_2 - g_2(H', d')]$ is maximized on H', if the original game (H, d) is almost symmetric.

Condition 5.9 is parallel to Condition 5.4; it is a condition of independence of irrelevant alternatives in which the reference point d is replaced with the reference point $g(H, d)$. Let

$$W_g = \{(H, d) \in W \mid g(H, d) \in H \text{ and } y \gg g(H, d) \text{ for some } y \in H\} \quad (5.20)$$

W_g is the subset of W in which the reference point of a game $(H, d) \in W_g$ is not Pareto optimal.

CONDITION 5.9   *If* $(H, d), (H', d') \in W_g$, $g(H, d) = g(H', d'), H \subset H'$, *and* $f(H', d') \in H$, *then* $f(H, d) = f(H', d')$.

Results parallel to Lemma 5.1 and 5.2 and Theorem 5.1 hold, but with W_g replacing W and $g(H, d)$ replacing d. The counterparts to Lemma 5.1 and Theorem 5.1 are stated below as Lemma 5.3 and Theorem 5.5; however the proofs are omitted because they trivially repeat the earlier proofs. In parallel to Condition 5.1:

CONDITION 5.10 $f(H, d) \geqslant g(H, d)$.

3.2.2   *Existence and uniqueness of solutions to games based on reference points*

With the conditions defining a class of reference points stated, attention can now be turned to existence and uniqueness of solutions based on them. This is done in Theorem 5.3, but first an intermediate result is needed.

LEMMA 5.5   *Let* $(H, d) \in W_g$, *let* $u^* = f(H, d)$ *satisfy Conditions 5.2, 5.3, 5.9 and 5.10, and let* $g(H, d)$ *satisfy Conditions 5.7 and 5.8. Then if* $u \in H$ *and* $u \neq u^*$ *either* $u_1^* > u_1$ *or* $u_2^* > u_2$.

THEOREM 5.3   *Let* $(H, d) \in W_g$ *be a game with reference function* $g(H, d)$ *that satisfies Conditions 5.7 and 5.8. Then* (H, d) *has a unique solution* $u^* = f(H, d)$ *satisfying Conditions 5.2, 5.3, 5.9, and 5.10. The solution satisfies*

$$(u_1^* - g_1(H, d))(u_2^* - g_2(H, d)) > (u_1 - g_1(H, d))(u_2 - g_2(H, d)) \quad (5.21)$$

for all $u \in H, u \geqslant g(H, d)$, *and* $u \neq u^*$.

Thomson (1981) names several reference functions that satisfy Conditions 5.7 and 5.8, including (a) the point of minimal expectations, $m(H, d)$,

(b) the *point of minimal compromise*, given by

$$\left(\frac{M_1(H, d) + m_1(H, d)}{2}, \frac{M_2(H, d) + m_2(H, d)}{2}\right) \qquad (5.22)$$

(c) the center of the smallest rectangle containing H, and (d) the center of gravity of H. These reference functions share a common characteristic: Each depends on the shape of H, but has no dependence on the threat point d. It is proved in Thomson (1981: 438) that a reference function that is a convex combination of reference functions satisfying Conditions 5.7 and 5.8 will also satisfy these conditions. Thus many reference functions can be constructed by combining d and one or more of the four foregoing reference functions.

3.2.3   An example to compare different solutions

Suppose two players can attain any utility pair that lies on or below the curve $u_2 = 7.5 + u_1 - .1u_1^2$ and is also on or above the u_1 axis. The threat point is fixed at the origin. Figure 5.6 depicts this set. In the figure, five solutions are shown and each is denoted by a letter. The letter appears in uppercase on the payoff frontier at the solution point itself and in lowercase at the reference point for the solution. The solutions and their accompanying letters are (1) the Nash solution (N), (2) the Raiffa–Kalai–Smorodinsky solution (R), (3) the minimal expectations reference point solution (E), (4) the minimal compromise reference point solution (C), and (5) the middle of the smallest rectangle containing H reference point solution (M). Note that two reference points are specified for the

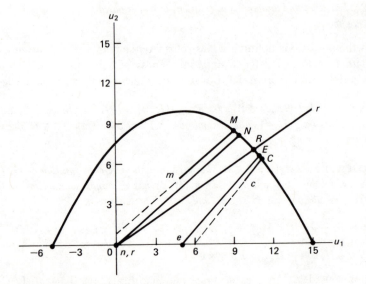

FIGURE 5.6   A comparison of several solutions.

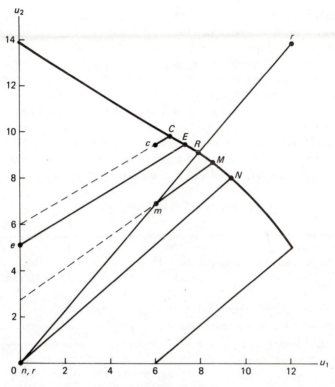

FIGURE 5.7   A further comparison of several solutions.

Raiffa–Kalai–Smorodinsky solution. This is because both the threat point and the point (15, 10), giving the ideal point for the two players, are both reference points. The solution is on the frontier where the straight line from the threat point to (15, 10) intersects it.

Contrast the game just described with the game shown in Figure 5.7. For this game, the set *H* is bounded below and on the left by the two axes. The

TABLE 5.1   Location of reference and solution points for models in Figures 5.6 and 5.7

	Figure 5.6				Figure 5.7			
	Reference Point		Solution Point		Reference Point		Solution Point	
	Player		Player		Player		Player	
Solution name	1	2	1	2	1	2	1	2
Nash	0	0	9.34	8.11	0	0	9.34	8.11
Raiffa–Kalai–Smorodinsky	0	0	10.49	6.99	0	0	7.91	9.16
	15	10			12	13.9		
Minimal expectation	5	0	10.77	6.67	0	5.1	7.33	9.5
Minimal compromise	10	5	11.08	6.31	6	9.5	6.67	9.9
Middle of rectangle	5	5	9.08	8.33	6	6.95	8.54	8.75

upper right boundary of H is given by $u_2 = 7.5 + u_1 - u_1^2$, as before, from $u_1 = 8$ to $u_1 = 12$. Going leftward from $u_1 = 8$ and $u_2 = 9.1$, the boundary is a straight line with slope $-.6$ until it reaches the u_2 axis at $u_2 = 13.9$. From $u_1 = 12$ and $u_2 = 5.1$, the boundary goes downward and to the left at a slope of $+1$ until the u_1 axis is reached at $u_1 = 6.9$. The solutions and reference points for both games are shown in Table 5.1. Note the change in the relative positions of the solutions between the two games. Except for the middle of the smallest rectangle solution favoring player 2 relative to the Nash solution in both games, the solutions appear in reversed order. The best three for player 1 in Figure 5.6 are C, E, and R, in that order, but in the game in Figure 5.7, C, E, and R are the best for player 2 *in that order*.

3.2.4 *Comparison of cooperative solutions with noncooperative games*

It is instructive now to compare the bargaining models described above with noncooperative games. Within a bargaining game to which a specific solution is applied, there is no action for a player to take. The structure of the game (specification of H and d) along with the definition of the solution concept decide the outcome. Why, then, should these solution concepts be of any interest? There are three answers explored below: fairness, efficiency, and descriptive accuracy.

Fairness was discussed in Section 1.1. Clearly, if the members of a group regard a particular solution as fair, they have an incentive to adopt it as an arbitration scheme in order to achieve efficiency (Pareto optimal outcomes) in a generally acceptable way. As noted earlier, this makes sense as an aspect of a group's operating rules when it is believed that a sequence of games will be encountered in the future and there is no idea in advance of which games they will be.

On descriptive accuracy, it is possible that the empirical investigation of cooperative game situations will reveal that certain solutions are persistent outcomes. Such a finding would be very important and would be a compelling reason to give a special place of importance to these solutions; however, as far as I know, results of this type have not yet surfaced.

This discussion is not likely to leave anyone feeling compelled to accept a particular solution. Game theory presently offers many cooperative game solution concepts; in addition to the bargaining solutions covered above, additional solutions are discussed in the remainder of this chapter and in the next chapter. Those covered in this book do not exhaust the literature. None is widely accepted as preeminent, and perhaps the brief discussion of fairness, acceptability as an arbitration scheme, and descriptive accuracy makes clear why no single solution has conquered the field.

4 Bargaining over time

To this point, the only model of the bargaining process that has been reviewed is Zeuthen's. In the present section a model of the bargaining process due to Rubinstein (1982) is discussed; however, his results are not presented in complete detail. The problem Rubinstein takes up is very simple: Two players can split between them a unit of a good that both of them value. If player 1 gets $s_1 \in [0, 1]$, then player 2 gets $s_2 = 1 - s_1$, but neither player receives anything unless the two players come to an agreement. The game is modeled as a noncooperative game, played over time, in strategic form. In the first period, player 1 proposes a division of the good to which player 2 responds by accepting or rejecting. If player 2 accepts, the game ends with player 1 getting s_1 and player 2 getting $1 - s_1$. If player 2 rejects the proposal, then the game continues with player 2 making the next proposal, which player 1 can accept or reject. Each period consists of a proposal being made by one player followed by the acceptance or rejection of it by the other player. The game ceases as soon as one player accepts the offer of the other. Prior to termination, player 1 makes an offer in each even numbered period $t = 0, 2, 4, \ldots$, and accepts or rejects offers of player 2 in each odd numbered period $t = 1, 3, \ldots$. Player 2 makes offers in each odd-numbered period and passes on offers of player 1 in each even-numbered period. The value of an outcome to a player depends on what he receives and on the time period in which agreement is reached. Naturally, the value rises with the amount received and falls with time. There are no rules concerning how one offer is related to another; in particular, the offer of player i in period t need not concede as much as the offer he made in period $t - 2$. The game is cooperative in the sense that if one player states an offer and the other accepts, the offer is a binding agreement for both of them.

4.1 The strategy spaces and payoff functions

In presenting the assumptions of Rubinstein's model, one alteration is made. He does not give an explicit payoff function for each player; rather, he defines an ordering on outcomes for each player. In the presentation that follows, each player has a payoff function.

ASSUMPTION 5.1 $u_i(s_i, t)$ *is the payoff function of player i. It is continuous and strictly increasing in s_i, strictly decreasing in t, defined for $s_i \in [0, 1]$ and $t \in \{0, 1, 2, \ldots\}$, and satisfies*
(a) $u_i(0, \infty) < u_i(s_i, t)$ *if $s_i > 0$ and $t < \infty$*
(b) $u_i(s_i, t) = u_i(s_i', t + 1)$ *if and only if $u_i(s_i, t') = u_i(s_i', t' + 1)$*
(c) *if $u_i(s_i + \varepsilon, 1) = u_i(s_i, 0)$, $u_i(s_i' + \varepsilon', 1) = u_i(s_i', 0)$, and $s_i < s_i'$, then $\varepsilon < \varepsilon'$*

Assumption 5.1 asserts that the good to be divided is strictly valuable, the passage of time is strictly costly, and the payoff of a player is continuous in the amount of the good received. In addition, (a) to (c) stipulate that (a) any positive amount of the good received at any finite time is preferred to obtaining nothing, (b) the payoff functions are stationary with respect to time, and (c) the amount of compensation required for a one-period delay in receiving the good increases with the amount of the good.

The game is played noncooperatively in the sense that each player has a strategy set from which she chooses a strategy. Rubinstein is interested in subgame perfect noncooperative equilibria for the game. For player 1, a strategy has the form $\sigma_1 = (f_{10}, f_{11}, f_{12}, f_{13}, \ldots)$ where

$f_{10} = s_{10}$, the offer of player 1 at time 0

f_{11} is a function whose argument is $(s_{10}, s_{21}) \in [0, 1]^2$ and whose value is *accept* or *reject*

f_{1t} is a function whose argument is $(s_{10}, s_{21}, s_{12}, s_{23}, \ldots, s_{2,t-1}) \in [0, 1]^t$ and whose value is $s_{1t} \in [0, 1]$ when t is even, and when t is odd, the argument is $(s_{10}, s_{21}, \ldots, s_{2t}) \in [0, 1]^{t+1}$ and the value is *accept* or *reject*

Strategies for player 2, $\sigma_2 = (f_{20}, f_{21}, \ldots)$, are analogous to strategies for player 1. For even values of t, f_{2t} has $(s_{10}, s_{21}, \ldots, s_{1t}) \in [0, 1]^{t+1}$ as its argument and takes the value *accept* or *reject*. For odd values of t, f_{2t} has $(s_{10}, s_{21}, \ldots, s_{1,t-1}) \in [0, 1]^t$ as its argument and takes a value $s_{2t} \in [0, 1]$.

4.2 Equilibrium and perfect equilibrium outcomes

In this game, any division of the good can be associated with a noncooperative equilibrium. This is discouraging in the sense that one usually hopes for equilibrium conditions to greatly narrow the field of possible outcomes. Ideally, that field is narrowed to one. If any outcome can be associated with equilibrium, then the model totally lacks predictive power. In the present case, σ^* is an equilibrium point where: $\sigma_i^* = (f_{i0}^*, f_{i1}^*, \ldots)$

For even t

$$f_{1t}^* = s_1^*$$
$$f_{2t}^* = accept \text{ if } s_{1t} \geq s_1^*$$
$$f_{2t}^* = reject \text{ if } s_{1t} < s_1^*$$

For odd t

$$f_{1t}^* = accept \text{ if } s_{2t} \geq s_2^* = 1 - s_1^*$$
$$f_{1t}^* = reject \text{ if } s_{2t} < s_2^* = 1 - s_1^*$$
$$f_{2t}^* = s_2^* = 1 - s_1^*$$

It is obvious that these equilibria are not perfect equilibria and are supported by a knife-edge quality built into the terms of accpetance. Player 1 proposes s_1^* and, if this is rejected, will accept in the future only agreements giving himself s_1^* or more. Player 2 will, likewise, accept $1 - s_1^*$ or more and will propose this amount in any odd-numbered period. Clearly, neither player can unilaterally increase her payoff by the use of an alternate strategy.

To be a subgame perfect equilibrium, the following conditions should be met at any time t, following a sequence of offers and rejections. (a) The player whose turn it is to make an offer has no superior alternative to offering what his strategy prescribes. (b) The other player, if she planned to accept the offer at time t, cannot do better by rejecting it. (c) If she planned to reject, she could do no better than reject. As an example of an equilibrium that is not subgame perfect, consider the equilibrium discussed by Rubinstein (1982: 103). Let $u_i(s_i, t) = s_i - c_i t$ with $c_1 = .1$ and $c_2 = .2$, and let $s_1^* = .5$. If player 1 offered $s_1^* = .6$ player 2 would reject it, expecting settlement in the next period at $s_1^* = .5$. But the payoff that player 2 rejects is $(1 - .6) - .2t = .4 - .2t$ and what she would receive instead is $(1 - .5) - .2(t + 1) = .3 - .2t$. Player 2 would lose .1 by this behavior, which violates (c) above.

Rubinstein proves that the final outcome of a perfect equilibrium strategy combination must be a pair $(s_1^*, 1 - s_1^*)$ where s_1^* is the first member of a pair (s_1^*, s_2^*) that simultaneously satisfies two equations, $s_2 = d_1(s_1)$ and $s_1 = d_2(s_2)$ that are defined as follows:

$$d_1(s_1) = 1 \text{ if, for all } s_2 \in [0, 1], u_1(1 - s_2, 0) > u_1(s_1, 1)$$
$$= s_2 \text{ if } u_1(1 - s_2, 0) = u_1(s_1, 1) \tag{5.23}$$
$$d_2(s_2) = 1 \text{ if, for all } s_1 \in [0, 1], u_2(1 - s_1, 0) > u_2(s_2, 1)$$
$$= s_1 \text{ if } u_2(1 - s_1, 0) = u_2(s_2, 1) \tag{5.24}$$

Any such $(s_1^*, 1 - s_1^*)$ can be a perfect equilibrium realization, and any game satisfying Assumption 5.1 has at least one such realization. An example of a perfect equilibrium is

$$
\left.
\begin{aligned}
f_{1t}(s_{10}, \ldots, s_{2,t-1}) &= s_1^* \\
f_{2t}(s_{10}, \ldots, s_{1t}) &= accept \text{ if } s_{1t} \leq s_1^* \\
&= reject \text{ if } s_{1t} > s_1^*
\end{aligned}
\right\} \quad t = 0, 2, 4, \ldots
$$

$$
\left.
\begin{aligned}
f_{1t}(s_{10}, \ldots, s_{2t}) &= accept \text{ if } s_{2t} \leq s_2^* \\
&= reject \text{ if } s_{2t} > s_2^* \\
f_{2t}(s_{10}, \ldots, s_{1,t-1}) &= s_2^*
\end{aligned}
\right\} \quad t = 1, 3, 5, \ldots
$$

where $s_1^* = d_2(s_2^*)$ and $s_2^* = d_1(s_1^*)$. Note that the equilibrium allocation is $(s_1^*, 1 - s_1^*)$; however, this is because player 1 is the first to propose an offer. If player 2 were to be the first to make an offer, then the equilibrium allocation would be $(s_2^*, 1 - s_2^*)$, which, in general, would be better for player 2 than $1 - s_1^*$ would be.

4.3 *Examples of the model of bargaining over time*

It appears that bargaining will usually end in the first round ($t = 0$), that a player will do better if she is first to make an offer, and that a player's equilibrium amount of the good is higher, the smaller is the drop in payoff she suffers by postponing receipt of the good by one period. These

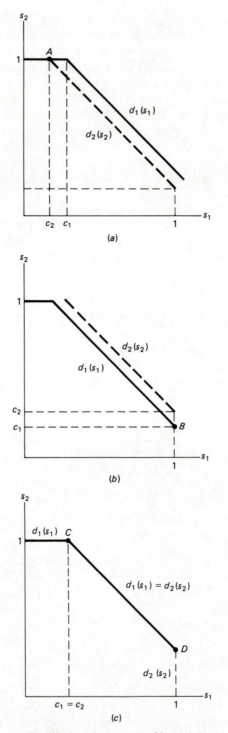

FIGURE 5.8   Equilibrium in a game of bargaining over time.

conclusions are not proved for all games satisfying Assumption 5.1, but they are borne out by two examples Rubinstein discusses and that are examined below. In the first example, the payoff functions are $s_1 - c_1 t$ for player 1 and $s_2 - c_2 t$ for player 2. The functions d_1 and d_2, defined in equations (5.23) and (5.24), are shown in Figure 5.8. In Figure 5.8a, $c_1 > c_2$ and the only point satisfying equations (5.23) and (5.24) simultaneously is A where $s_1^* = c_2$ and $s_2^* = 1$. Thus, with player 1 making the first offer, the outcome would be $(c_2, 1 - c_2)$; however, if player 2 were able to make the first offer, the outcome would be $(0, 1)$. In Figure 5.8b, $c_1 < c_2$ and the only point satisfying the equilibrium requirements is B. With player 1 going first, the outcome is $(1, 0)$ and with player 2 going first, it is $(1 - c_1, c_1)$. Finally, if $c_1 = c_2$, as in Figure 5.8c, any point on the line from C to D can be associated with an equilibrium point.

For the second example, let $\delta_1, \delta_2 \in (0, 1)$ and let the two payoff functions be $s_1 \delta_1^t$ for player 1 and $s_2 \delta_2^t$ for player 2. Equations (5.23) and (5.24) are plotted in Figure 5.9 where the only point giving rise to an equilibrium is at A. The equilibrium payoffs are $(s_1^*, 1 - s_1^*)$ if player 1 offers first and $(1 - s_2^*, s_2^*)$ if player 2 offers first. Note that with $\delta_1 < \delta_2$, player 1 places less weight on the future relative to the present than player 2. This favors player 2 in the sense that $s_1^* < s_2^*$. That is, if player 1 were to offer first, his equilibrium payoff would be less than if player 2 were to offer first.

In thinking about the process of bargaining, it is difficult to imagine it as anything but a noncooperative procedure, with the essential distinction

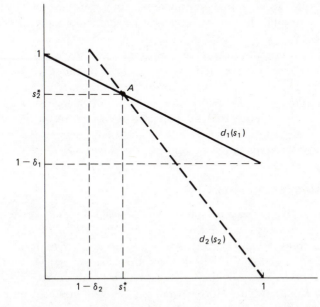

FIGURE 5.9 A second illustration of equilibrium in a game of bargaining over time.

from most noncooperative games being that the players are allowed to make binding agreements. As in the Rubinstein model, each player forms a strategy that dictates his move at each stage of the process, and the strategy is chosen to maximize his payoff at the final cooperative outcome to which the bargaining process leads. Were it found that actual bargaining processes tended toward a particular cooperative solution, it would become very important to discover noncooperative game formulations of bargaining that would lead to the same solution.

By way of comment on Rubinstein's model, it does give an explicit value to time that may differ between the two players and may differ for one player according to the size of the player's payoff. A value for time may enter for either of two reasons. First, the actual quantity of good to be divided may shrink over time. This can occur because the good is subject to deterioration or, as in labor-management negotiations taking place during a strike, each day that passes without an agreement is a day in which the productive power of both sides is wasted. The second reason for time having a value is the economists' usual one: A given reward received today is valued higher than the same reward would be valued today if it were to be received tomorrow.

An important phenomenon that the Rubinstein model does not touch on is the failure to make agreements or the making of agreements at later than the optimal time. In labor-management negotiations, strikes are observed, and in most instances it would undoubtedly be better for both parties if the contract that was finally agreed on would have been accepted in time to avert a strike. If the bargainers have incomplete or inaccurate information concerning one another's payoff functions, coming to an agreement might be made more difficult and strikes might be understandable. Indeed, even the failure to agree at any time might be understandable. The labor-management example has a feature that goes beyond the scope of cooperative games studied in this book: The bargaining over a contract may be seen by both players as a single episode in an ongoing sequence of contract negotiations. Therefore, the outcome of one particular contract would naturally be evaluated for its effect in the future on the remaining contracts. Seen in this light, one side or both may be quite willing to have an occasional strike to avoid the appearance of weakness.

5   Variable threat games

It is easy to imagine two-person games in which binding agreements are possible, but in which each player has considerable scope for action in the absence of an agreement, and in which the decision of each player affects both of them. Nash (1953) dealt with this class of games from several angles, all of which provided justification for a revised version of his bargaining solution. The approach taken here combines arbitration with a noncooperative game. Suppose each of the two players has a strategy set, S_i for player i, that is compact and convex, and assume that $P_i(s_1, s_2)$ is the payoff function for player i in the absence of an agreement. Thus the game

$(\{1, 2\}, S, P)$ is a default noncooperative game that the two players must play if they cannot agree. There is no threat point as such. Suppose further that there is a compact, convex set $H \subset R^2$ consisting of all the payoff points that the two players can reach by means of binding agreements. H would naturally contain as a subset all those points attainable in the default game.

DEFINITION 5.6 $\Gamma = (N, S, P, H)$ *is a* **variable threat two-person cooperative game** *where* (N, S, P) *is a two-person noncooperative game that is played if no agreement is reached and the compact, convex set H is the cooperative attainable payoff set. H contains $\{P(s) \in R^2 \mid s \in S\}$.*

The Nash arbitration game proceeds by having the two players simultaneously choose strategies for the default game, $s_i^T \in S_i$, which are used to determine a threat point, $P(s^T)$. The arbitrated outcome to the game is the Nash bargaining solution to $(H, P(s^T))$. Thus the players are not interested in the payoffs $P_i(s)$ for their own sakes; they care about the effect on the final outcome that is due to their choices of s_i^T. Potentially, any point on the Pareto optimal frontier of H could be an arbitrated outcome. Figure 5.10 shows a useful and interesting relationship between points on

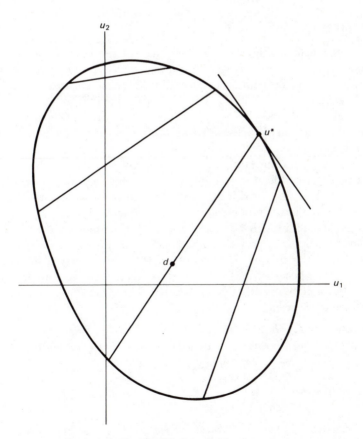

FIGURE 5.10 The Nash variable threat game.

the Pareto optimal frontier of H and the points in H which could serve as threat points. This relationship is that the slope of a line from the threat point to the Nash solution is equal in absolute value and opposite in sign to the slope of the payoff possibility frontier at the Nash solution point. This property is stated formally and proved in the following lemma.

LEMMA 5.6   *Let (H, d) be a two-person bargaining game whose Nash bargaining solution is u^*. Then for all $u \in H$ such that $u \geq d$ and $u \neq u^*$, $(u_1 - d_1)(u_2 - d_2) < (u_1^* - d_1)(u_2^* - d_2)$ implies that no points of H lie above a line of slope $-(u_2^* - d_2)/(u_1^* - d_1)$ through u^*. The slope of the line from d to u^* is $(u_2^* - d_2)/(u_1^* - d_1)$.*

Proof   Consider the rectangular hyperbola $(x_1 - d_1)(x_2 - d_2) = (u_1^* - d_1)(u_2^* - d_2)$. The slope of this curve at u^* is $-(u_2^* - d_2)/(u_1^* - d_1)$; therefore any point on the curve other than u^* lies above the straight line with this slope that passes through u^* (i.e., the tangent to the rectangular hyperbola at u^*). If some point y of H other than u^* lay above this tangent line, then, by the convexity of H, there would be a point on the line connecting u^* and y that lay on or above the rectangular hyperbola. This contradicts the condition that u^* is the unique Nash product maximizer. That the slope of the line from d to u^* is $(u_2^* - d_2)/(u_1^* - d_1)$ follows from the definition of the line.   QED

With the help of Figure 5.10, it is easy to see the nature of a Nash variable threat cooperative equilibrium and to see the nature of the threat strategies that would be associated with it. Suppose the strategy combination s' results in d in Figure 5.10 as the threat point. That is, suppose the players choose s' and, by the arbitration procedure, u^* is the resulting cooperative outcome. Whether s_1' is an optimal choice of threat strategy for player 1 depends on whether there is some $s_1'' \in S_1$ such that $P(s_1'', s_2')$ would lie below the line connecting d and u^*; for any point below this line, as a threat point, would lead to a cooperative outcome that was more favorable to player 1. Therefore, if s' is an optimal threat point, all points $P(s_1', s_2'')$ lie on or below the line through d and u^* for all s_2'' and all points $P(s_1'', s_2')$ lie on or above the line through d and u^* for all s_1''. Furthermore, if the game has a solution, which is the same as there being an optimal threat, then the solution payoff is unique. Uniqueness of the solution payoff follows from Theorem 2.2, because the noncooperative game whose outcome is the cooperative solution is strictly competitive. These facts are summarized in the following theorem.

THEOREM 5.4   *Let (N, S, P, H) be a two-person variable threat game. If u^* is the Nash solution to the game and s^T is the optimal threat strategy combination, then*

(a) $\dfrac{u_2^* - P_2(s_1^T, s_2)}{u_1^* - P_1(s_1^T, s_2)} \geq \dfrac{u_2^* - P_2(s^T)}{u_1^* - P_1(s^T)} \geq \dfrac{u_2^* - P_2(s_1, s_2^T)}{u_1^* - P_1(s_1, s_2^T)}$ (5.25)

for all $s_1 \in S_1$ and $s_2 \in S_2$, and
(b) *all cooperative Nash variable threat solutions yield the same payoff pair.*

Proof The first part, (a), follows from the fact that the arbitration scheme requires the final outcome to be the Nash bargaining solution to $(H, P(s^T))$. To see part (b), note first that, given the arbitration scheme, the cooperative payoff can be regarded as functions of s^T, thus the payoff functions $P_i^*(s)$ may be understood to be the Nash cooperative payoffs associated with the threat strategy combination s. Clearly, $P^*(s)$ is continuous in s, although this is not needed to prove uniqueness of the equilibrium payoffs. Uniqueness follows using precisely the same argument that establishes uniqueness of the equilibrium payoffs in two-person, strictly competitive games. The crucial point in both instances is that the payoff structure is perfectly competitive. In the present case, $P_1^*(s) < P_1^*(s')$ if and only if $P_2^*(s) > P_2^*(s')$. QED

Note that there is no assurance of existence of a Nash cooperative solution; Theorem 5.4 applies to games having such equilibria. Existence is assured if the strictly competitive game whose payoff function is $P^*(s)$ satisfies the usual concavity conditions: that $P_i^*(s)$ is concave in s_i.

6 Applications of two-person cooperative games

Contract negotiations between a union and a firm have been mentioned several times as an example of a two-person cooperative game. This is most strictly correct if the union is the only source of labor for the firm and the firm is the only place where the union members can be employed. In Section 6.1, this situation is examined using a simple model. Then, in Section 6.2 a two-country arms race is modeled.

6.1 Labor-management, an example of bilateral monopoly

Imagine a firm that is a monopolist in the market for its output and that is a monopsonist in the labor market. At the same time, a labor union is a monopolist in the labor market. Thus, the situation in the labor market is one of bilateral monopoly. Letting L denote the level of employment and w, the wage rate, suppose the union has a utility function $u(L, w) = (Lw)^{.5}$. In other words, the union values both numbers employed and the rate of pay per unit of work. The firm values profits, and utility for it is measured by profit. The inverse demand function facing the firm is $p = 100 - q$, where p and q are price and output, respectively. The firm's production function is $q = L$; that is, output is proportional to employment. Thus the firm's profit function is $\pi = L(100 - L) - wL$.

In this situation, the most natural threat on the part of the firm is to cease production, which means the union members will all be without jobs. Similarly, the union can refuse to supply any labor to the firm, and, again, there will be neither production nor jobs. Looking for a Nash solution, then

$(0, 0)$ is the threat point, and the game is a Nash bargaining game. The Pareto optimal curve can be found by maximizing

$$F(L, w) = \rho\pi + (1 - \rho)u = \rho(100 - L - w)L + (1 - \rho)(Lw)^{.5} \quad (5.26)$$

with respect to L and w for values of ρ between zero and one. Carrying out the maximization, the first-order conditions are

$$\frac{\partial F}{\partial L} = \rho(100 - 2L - w) + .5(1 - \rho)w(Lw)^{.5} = 0 \quad\quad (5.27)$$

$$\frac{\partial F}{\partial w} = -\rho + .5(1 - \rho)L(Lw)^{-.5} = 0 \quad\quad (5.28)$$

Both of the first-order conditions can be solved for ρ, then the two expressions for ρ can be equated and the resulting equation depends only on u and π. This can be solved to obtain

$$\pi = 2500 - u^2 \quad\quad (5.29)$$

which is the equation of the Pareto optimal curve. Now the Nash solution is easily found by maximizing

$$u\pi = 2500u - u^3 \quad\quad (5.30)$$

with respect to u. The outcome is $u = 16.67(3)^{.5}$ and $\pi = 1666.67$. These payoffs are associated with employment of $L = 50$ and a wage rate of $w = 16.67$.

6.2   An illustration of an arms race

A usual presumption in an arms race is that each party values the extent to which it is stronger than its rival. This sounds like a zero-sum situation, and it would be if only arms were without cost. Let x denote the arms level of player 1 and y the arms level of player 2. For each player, utility consists of two terms. The first is the contribution to utility that comes from the relative arms strength of the players, and the second is a negative term that results from the cost of the arms that the player purchases. The two players' utility levels are

$$u_1 = 20(x - y) - x^{1.5} \quad\quad (5.1)$$

$$u_2 = 10(y - x) - y^{1.5} \quad\quad (5.32)$$

The Pareto optimal curve is found in the same way as in the bilateral monopoly example: Maximize $\rho u_1 + (1 - \rho)u_2$ with respect to x and y. The first-order conditions are

$$(30 - 1.5x^{.5})\rho - 10 = 0 \quad\quad (5.33)$$

$$-30\rho - 1.5(1 - \rho)y^{.5} + 10 = 0 \quad\quad (5.34)$$

Solving for u_2 as a function of u_1 is not easy in this case, so instead, equations (5.33) and (5.34) can be used to obtain x and y as functions of ρ.

These give

$$x = \left(\frac{60\rho - 20}{3\rho}\right)^2 \tag{5.35}$$

$$y = \left(\frac{20 - 60\rho}{3(1 - \rho)}\right)^2 \tag{5.36}$$

Both x and y must be nonnegative, so equation (5.35) is correct for $\rho \geqslant 1/3$ and $x = 0$ otherwise. Likewise, equation (5.36) holds for $\rho \leqslant 1/3$ and $y = 0$ otherwise. This makes sense, because it can never be Pareto optimal for *both* players to have positive arms expenditure. It will always be possible to reduce both players' arms expenditure by the amount of the smaller expenditure of the two. This keeps the value of $x - y$ constant and reduces costs for both of them.

Figure 5.11 shows the Pareto optimal frontier for this game. Unlike the bilateral monopoly example, these players can spend on arms whether or not they make an agreement; therefore, the threat situation may be more complicated. There are two ways to look at their threat behavior. On one hand, in the absence of agreement, they may simply play noncooperatively. If so, they may take the Nash noncooperative equilibrium as the threat point for a Nash bargaining game. The noncooperative equilibrium payoffs are $u_1 = 296.3$ and $u_2 = -1629.6$, and the Nash bargaining solution, based on the noncooperative equilibrium as a threat point, is $u_1 = 870.7$ and $u_2 = -779.5$.

Whether there is a Nash variable threat outcome depends on the ability of the players to choose threat outcomes at will. Choosing arbitrary threat

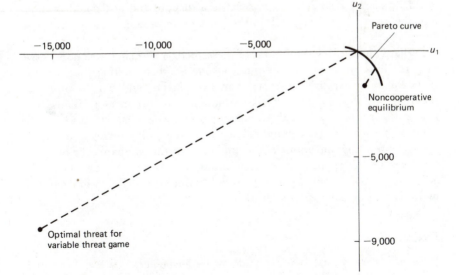

FIGURE 5.11 Optimal threats in a variable threat arms race.

outcomes is possible if the players are able to make commitments, or if they have agreed to a binding arbitration under which they must take the Nash cooperative solution that is based on whatever threat point results from threat strategies. The latter is not plausible in the context of an arms race, because some higher authority must be present to enforce the binding arbitration. The former can be imagined. Each country might set in motion internal policies that cannot be changed and that force selection of arbitrary threat strategies should there fail to be an agreement. Supposing this case, it is easily checked that the optimal threats are $x^T = 711.1$ and $y^T = 177.8$, with the threat payoffs being $u_1^T = -15{,}592.6$ and $u_2^T = -8{,}296.3$. The associated Nash solution is $x = 0$ and $y = 0$, where the payoffs are $u_1 = 0$ and $u_2 = 0$.

7 Concluding comments

The foregoing models are often called bargaining models as if the outcomes they prescribe are the likely outcomes of a bargaining process; however, the reader can easily see that most of these models describe a solution, or equilibrium, without showing any kind of actual sequential bargaining process. The two exceptions are Harsanyi's interpretation of Zeuthen and the model of Rubinstein. The Zeuthen process is not convincing as a process that bargainers, acting in their own interests, are likely to follow. Rubinstein's model is more convincing on this score. Of course, the absence of a convincing process to lead to a particular outcome does not mean that outcome cannot be the end point of such a process; it only means nothing has yet been found.

The various solutions also have interest apart from bargaining. Any one could be used by an arbitrator to settle a dispute and any could be built into the laws of a society or into the rules of an organization to deal with situations fitting the model.

Perhaps the greatest limitation of these models is their restriction to two players. This objection can be met, on one hand, by noting that some of them can be generalized to more than two players, and, on the other, by pointing out that many gamelike situations are two person. Thus two-person theory has considerable scope for practical application. Indeed, the word *bargaining* brings to mind, above all, a pair of people (or organizations) confronting one another: the union versus the company, the owner of a house versus a person who is interested in purchasing it, a city government and a county government allocating responsibility for road and highway maintenance, and so forth.

Exercises

1. Suppose Barbara and Don can trade apples for oranges, but they must trade integer quantities. Barbara has two apples and no oranges, while Don has no apples and two oranges. The utility each attaches to apple-orange commodity bundles is listed as follows.

		Utility for	
Apples	Oranges	Barbara	Don
0	0	0	5
1	0	4	10
0	1	6	8
2	0	10	11
0	2	12	15
1	1	14	25
1	2	20	36
2	1	16	35
2	2	21	37

   a. Describe as a Nash bargaining game the situation that Barbara and Don face.

   b. What is the Nash solution of the game?

2. a. For the game in problem 1, find the point of minimal expectations and the ideal point.

   b. What is the Raiffa–Kalai–Smorodinsky solution of the game?

3. a. For the game in problem 1, find the solution and reference point associated with the center of the smallest rectangle.

   b. Find the solution and reference point associated with the point of minimal compromise.

4. Suppose the set H consists of the points lying on and within a circle of radius 2, having a center at $(2, 2)$. If the threat point, d, is at $(2, 2)$, what are the Nash, Raiffa–Kalai–Smorodinsky, minimal expectations, minimum compromise, and smallest rectangle solutions? What are the reference points?

5. Suppose H is as in problem 4, except that $d = (0, 2)$. What are the Nash, Raiffa–Kalai–Smorodinsky, minimal expectations, minimum compromise, and smallest rectangle solutions? What are the reference points?

Notes

1. It is possible to distinguish between the status quo, denoting a pair of utility levels that were achieved prior to the start of bargaining, and the threat point, where the players will be if they bargain and fail to agree. Given that they will bargain, it is not clear that the status quo concept should be relevant to the outcome. Brito et al. (1977) analyze a model in which the status quo and threat point are different.

2. It is, in fact, possible that reasonable persons will be able to make binding agreements and fail to achieve a Pareto optimal outcome. This could occur when a bargaining process allows players to make mutually incompatible demands and, when such demands are made, leaves the players at the threat point. Where solutions are explored in the absence of a bargaining process, the Pareto optimality requirement is easy to accept.

3. If $d = 0$ were not assumed, equation (5.1) would use

$$x_i = \frac{u_i^* - d_i}{y_i^* - d_i}(y_i - d_i)$$

to define H', and suitable changes would be required in the remainder of the proof. Details are left to the reader.

6

n-Person cooperative games with transferable utility

In this chapter and Chapter 7, *n*-person cooperative games are examined and several solution concepts are reviewed. The distinction between the two chapters is that the present chapter assumes *transferable utility*, while Chapter 7 does not maintain this restriction. As compared with the material in Chapter 5, this chapter is more general in dealing with *n*-, rather than two-, person games, but it is less general in that the models of Chapter 5 did not require transferable utility.

To assume transferable utility is to require that the payoffs attainable by any particular coalition (subset of N) consist of all individual payoffs that sum to no more than a particular number. For example, suppose a five-player game and a coalition consisting of players 1 and 4. Each player has his own utility scale; however, if the transferability condition is met, then there will be a number, $v(\{1, 4\})$, that describes the payoff possibilities of the coalition $\{1, 4\}$. They can achieve any payoff (x_1, x_4) that satisfies the condition $x_1 + x_4 \leq v(\{1, 4\})$. This condition is dropped in Chapter 7, but, in the meantime, it greatly simplifies the analysis in this chapter. If the players in the game are firms in a market, it may seem reasonable to assume transferable utility on the ground that income in money measures utility for each firm, and does so in the same way for all firms. Additionally, many models from this chapter are useful in developing results for the nontransferable utility games covered in Chapter 7.

1 An overview of the chapter

The *core*, due to Gillies (1953), is the first solution concept studied below. It is an appealing solution; however, it suffers from two faults: Some games have no outcomes in the core and others have annoyingly many outcomes in the core. The groups of players that may form and act in concert are called *coalitions*. In general, a coalition is a subset of players that has the right to make binding agreements with one another, and it is usually assumed that any subset of players can do this. Another aspect of the core is that it does not appear to take into consideration which particular coalitions will actually form. In this respect, a closely related solution concept, the *stable set* (also called the von Neumann–Morgenstern (1944) solution) takes some cognizance of actual coalition formation. In comparison with the core, the stable set has the advantage that many games with empty cores have (nonempty) stable sets.

Similar advantages are associated with the *bargaining set*, a solution that exists for a large class of games and that takes explicit account of the way that players divide themselves into coalitions. A payoff vector is considered in conjunction with a specific division of the players into coalitions. Such a division of players is called a *coalition structure*. A particular payoff vector-coalition structure pair is in the bargaining set (i.e., is a solution) if no subset of players who are already members of the same coalition can find a way of improving their payoffs. There are specific rules for improving payoffs that involve passing two hurdles. The first is that these players, who are said to form an *objection*, are able to do better for themselves with the aid of a few other players, called their *partners*, who also benefit from the change. The second hurdle is that the other players cannot mount a successful *counterobjection*. A counterobjection is successful if these other players can do as well as they did originally and can assure more to the partners of the objectors. Closely related to the bargaining set are the *kernel* and the *nucleolus*.

A solution concept that yields a unique outcome in a large class of games is the *Shapley* (1953*b*) *value* and the somewhat similar solution proposed by Banzhaf (1965) and axiomatized by Owen (1978). The Shapley value differs markedly from the solutions covered earlier in the chapter by being unique. It is defined by several conditions, called the Shapley axioms, and is characterized by a specific function that gives the payoff to each player as a function of the characteristic function of the game. All of these solutions are discussed in the balance of the chapter.

Summarizing the remainder of this chapter, Section 2 contains basic concepts used in the study of characteristic function games. Section 3 introduces the core and gives conditions for a nonempty core. The stable set is taken up in Section 4, and Section 5 is devoted to the bargaining set and its cousins, the kernel and the nucleolus. The Shapley and Banzhaf values are discussed in Section 6, an example of political power is in Section 7, and summary comments are in Section 8.

2 Basic concepts for cooperative games

In this section some concepts are introduced that are used generally in the study of *n*-person cooperative games. Section 2.1 formally defines coalitions. Section 2.2 takes up the *characteristic function* and also defines the *characteristic function form*, or *coalitional form* of a game. Then, in Section 2.3, a class of feasible payoff vectors, called *imputations*, is introduced. These constitute a subset of payoffs that are of particular interest, because they are Pareto optimal and give each player at least as much as he could assure himself on his own. In the same section the distinction between *essential* and *inessential* games is made, the former being the class of games in which coalition formation has a chance of benefiting the players who join together. Finally, in Section 2.4 *domination*, a key concept in the definition of several solutions, is discussed.

2.1 Coalitions

As in previous chapters, $N = \{1, 2, \ldots, n\}$ is the set of players. Subsets of players, called *coalitions*, are denoted K, L, M, and so forth. The corresponding lowercase letter denote the number of players; thus K has k players, L has l players, and M has m players. The actual members of, say, K are $\{i_1, \ldots, i_k\}$ where each i_j is distinct from all the others and is an integer between 1 and n. For example, suppose $n = 50$ and $K = \{1, 3, 5, 8, 12, 24, 46\}$. Then $k = 7$, $i_1 = 1$, $i_2 = 3$, ..., $i_7 = 46$. The coalition consisting of all players other than those in K, called the *complementary coalition of K*, is denoted by $N \backslash K$ and also by $\bar{K}$. The notation $K \backslash L$ denotes the players who are in K but are not in L. Thus $K \backslash L = K \cap \bar{L}$.

DEFINITION 6.1   A **coalition** *is a subset of the set of players, N, that is able to make a binding agreement.*

ASSUMPTION 6.1   *Any subset of N, including N itself, can form a coalition.*

2.2 Characteristic functions

There is an important sense in which our point of view naturally changes when examining cooperative games: The actual strategies available to the players recede into the background; instead, attention focuses on what payoffs the players and coalitions are able to achieve for themselves. These possibilities are summarized in the *characteristic function*, which is defined as follows.

DEFINITION 6.2   *The* **transferable utility characteristic function** *of a game having the set of players N is a scalar valued function, $v(K)$, that associates $v(K) \in R$ with each $K \subset N$. The characteristic function value for the empty coalition is zero. That is $v(\phi) = 0$.*

In the rest of this chapter, the term *characteristic function* always means *transferable utility characteristic function*. In Chapter 7, the characteristic function for nontransferable utility games is defined. The quantity $v(K)$ is interpreted in the present chapter as the maximum payoff to members of the coalition K that the coalition can guarantee to itself.

Describing the way that characteristic functions can be related to games in strategic form requires that some useful concepts be developed. First, a notion of what a player alone can guarantee herself is needed. This is commonly done in one of two ways. Both ways are described in Section 2.2.1. Then Section 2.2.2 defines the characteristic function form of the game.

2.2.1 The α and β characteristic functions

There are two usual ways of deriving a characteristic function from a game in strategic form. The first, giving rise to the *α-characteristic* function, is based on what a player (or coalition) can guarantee to himself when the remaining players act to minimize his payoff. The second, called the *β-characteristic* function, is based on the payoff to which the remaining players can hold a player (or coalition).

The α-characteristic function is the more frequently encountered concept, and is defined first. Let $\Gamma = (N, S, P)$ be a game in strategic form, and let the joint strategy space of the players in a coalition K be $S^K = \times_{i \in K} S_i$. Elements of S^K are denoted s^K. It will be convenient to use the notation $(s \backslash t^K)$ to denote the strategy combination in which player i is using s_i if $i \notin K$ and t_i if $i \in K$. Also, $(s \backslash t_i)$ is defined to be $(s \backslash t^{\{i\}})$. A player can be utterly certain of no more than her *maximin* value in this game. That is, imagine that player i is in a situation where the remaining players, $N \backslash \{i\}$, form a coalition with the express purpose of minimizing the payoff of player i. Then the largest payoff that player i can assure herself is

$$\underline{u}_{\alpha i} = \max_{t_i \in S_i} \min_{s^K \in S^K} P_i(s \backslash t_i) \qquad \text{for } K = N \backslash \{i\} \tag{6.1}$$

Let u^K denote a payoff vector in R^k giving payoffs for members of the coalition K, and let $\underline{u}^K$ be the vector of maximin payoffs of the members of K.

ASSUMPTION 6.2 *If $u^K \in R^K$ can be achieved by the coalition K, then K can achieve any u'^K satisfying*

$$\sum_{i \in K} u'_i \le \sum_{i \in K} u_i \tag{6.2}$$

Assumption 6.2 embodies two conditions. The first is the transferable utility condition that, if K can achieve u^K, then it can achieve any other outcome (u'^K) in which the players' payoffs sum to the same total $(\sum_{i \in K} u'_i = \sum_{i \in K} u_i)$. The second condition is free disposal. If u^K can be achieved and $u'^K < u^K$, then u'^K can also be achieved. Assumption 6.2 allows a very compact way to represent the payoffs attainable by a coalition. For a given game, each coalition has associated with it the largest total payoff that it is capable of attaining. To define the α-characteristic function, these are maximin payoffs for the coalition. The α-characteristic function is:

$$v_\alpha(K) = \max_{t^K \in S^K} \min_{s^{\tilde{K}} \in S^{\tilde{K}}} \sum_{i \in K} P_i(s \backslash t^K) \tag{6.3}$$

By definition, $v_\alpha(\{i\}) = \underline{u}_{\alpha i}$; however, equation (6.3) is defined for all coalitions K.

Equations parallel to (6.1) and (6.3) that define the β-characteristic function are

$$\underline{u}_{\beta i} = \min_{s^K \in S^K} \max_{t_i \in S_i} P_i(s \backslash t_i) \qquad \text{for } K = N \backslash \{i\} \tag{6.4}$$

$$v_\beta(K) = \min_{s^{\tilde{K}} \in S^{\tilde{K}}} \max_{t^K \in S^K} \sum_{i \in K} P_i(s \backslash t^K) \tag{6.5}$$

In contrasting the α and β forms, it is helpful to do a thought experiment in which K for α (or $N\backslash K$ for β) moves first. In defining v_α, suppose that K must choose s^K and announce it to $N\backslash K$, and then, knowing s^K, $N\backslash K$ can select $s^{N\backslash K}$. With this procedure, K knows that, for any s^K it chooses it can be held to

$$\min_{s^{\bar{K}}\in S^{\bar{K}}} \sum_{i\in K} P_i(s\backslash s^K) \tag{6.6}$$

K can guarantee itself the maximum over s^K of equation (6.6), which is equation (6.3). By contrast, to define v_β, suppose that $N\backslash K$ chooses $s^{N\backslash K}$, announces it to K, and then K selects s^K. Then $N\backslash K$ can hold K down to

$$\max_{s^K\in S^K} \sum_{i\in K} P_i(s\backslash s^K) \tag{6.7}$$

In general, $v_\alpha(K) < v_\beta(K)$ for all K. This is entirely analogous to the security levels of the two players in a two-person, zero-sum game. In defining $v_\alpha(K)$ and $v_\beta(K)$, the technique is to treat K and $N\backslash K$ as the two players in a zero-sum game in which the payoff to player K is $\sum_{i\in K} P_i(s)$ and to player $N\backslash K$ is $-\sum_{i\in K} P_i(s)$.

2.2.2 The characteristic function form

The following results and assumptions are stated for characteristic function games in general, and hold whether the α or β form is used. To simplify notation, $\underline{u}$ is used in place of $\underline{u}_\alpha$ and $\underline{u}_\beta$, and v is used in place of v_α and v_β. It is generally assumed that coalitions can achieve at least as much as the sum of what their members can achieve. This condition is called *superadditivity* and is defined in terms of any partition of a subset. That is, if K and L are subsets of N with $K\cap L=\varnothing$, then $v(K\cup L)\geqslant v(K)+v(L)$.

ASSUMPTION 6.3   *The characteristic function, $v(K)$, for a game (N,S,P) is superadditive. That is, for any disjoint coalitions, K and L contained in N, $v(K\cup L)\geqslant v(K)+v(L)$.*

It is convenient to refer to the characteristic function and set of players, (N,v), as a game, rather than mentioning (N,S,P), because $\Gamma=(N,v)$ contains all the needed information. This description of the game is called the *characteristic function form* or the *coalitional form*.

DEFINITION 6.3   *For transferable utility games, the* **characteristic function form** *of a game, also called the* **coalitional form**, *is given by $\Gamma=(N,v)$. It is characterized by the set of players, N, and the characteristic function, v.*

2.3 Imputations and essential games

Certain payoff vectors are naturally singled out for study as the set containing all reasonable outcomes for a cooperative game; this is called the *set of imputations*. An *imputation* is a payoff vector that gives each player at least as much as he can guarantee himself and gives all players together $v(N)$.

DEFINITION 6.4   *A payoff vector,* $x \in R^n$, *is an* **imputation** *in the game* $\Gamma = (N, v)$ *if* $x_i \geq \underline{u}_i$ *for all* $i \in N$ *(i.e., x is individually rational) and* $\sum_{i \in N} x_i = v(N)$ *(i.e., x is group rational). The set of imputations is denoted* $I(N, v)$.

In this chapter and Chapter 7, a payoff vector is sometimes called an *allocation*. This terminology is natural in the sense that an imputation, in particular, is a payoff vector in which $v(N)$ is allocated among the n players.

Characteristic function games are naturallly divided into two categories, depending on whether there is anything of interest in them to analyze. A game satisfying Assumptions 6.1 to 6.3 in which $\sum_{i \in N} v(\{i\}) = v(N)$ is a game in which no coalition can possibly achieve more than the individual members can do on their own, and such a game is called *inessential*. Games in which $v(N)$ is strictly greater than $\sum_{i \in N} v(\{i\})$ are called *essential*, and it is these games that are the center of attention below.

2.4 Domination

A key concept in the study of n-person cooperative games is *domination*, which refers to the power a coalition can exert through its ability to go it alone. Recalling that $I(N, v)$ denotes the set of imputations, suppose that $x, y \in I(N, v)$. Then x is dominated by y via the coalition K if y gives more to the members of K than does x and y^K is achievable by K.

DEFINITION 6.5   *For* $x, y \in I(N, v)$, y **dominates** x **via** K *if* $y^K > x^K$ *and* $\sum_{i \in K} y_i \leq v(K)$.

The definition of domination is:

DEFINITION 6.6 y **dominates** x *if, for some* $K \subset N$, y *dominates* x *via* K.

If y dominates x via K, it is sometimes said that K can *improve on* x.[1] Domination is used below to define the core.

3   The core and the epsilon core

It will be seen below that many games have empty cores, which, of course, is a drawback of the core as a solution concept. Facing a game with an empty core, one is tempted to ask the question of how "close" the game is to having a nonempty core. This query naturally leads into the study of the ε-core, introduced in Section 3.3. In the meanwhile, Section 3.1 has an interesting historical example that is an early instance of the core, while the core itself is taken up in Section 3.2. Finally, Section 3.4 is concerned with a special class of games called *simple games*.

3.1 Edgeworth and the core

The core is a cooperative game solution concept that predates formal game theory and appears a century ago in the economics literature in Edgeworth

(1881). He discusses equilibrium for a pure trade economy in which traders are not forced to transact with one another through conventional markets utilizing competitive prices over which they have no individual control. Instead, Edgeworth places no restrictions on the institutions of the economy, and any group of traders can engage in any trade that falls within the resources at their command. That is, a particular collection of traders (Mary, Harry, Barry, Larry, and Cary, for example) can agree to redistribute among themselves the resources that they own in any fashion they wish. Prices need not enter such an arrangement, and no trader need be able to transact in a conventional competitive market. With this setup, Edgeworth argued that certain trades could, and others could not, be ruled out as final trades for the economy. This set of possible equilibria consisted of trades that gave to each trader a level of utility no lower than the trader would achieve by consuming his or her own commodity bundle, and, in addition, gave to each subset of consumers utility levels that the group could not better on its own.

This last point can be illuminated by an example. Suppose that trader i (i = Mary, Harry, etc.), has an endowment of m goods, $w^i = (w^i_1, \ldots, w^i_m)$, that the utility of that endowment bundle is $u_i(w^i) = 0$, and that there is a trade available to Mary, Harry, and Larry as a group that gives them, respectively, utilities of 5, 2, and 8. Then Edgeworth argued that no acceptable final outcome could (a) give any trader a utility less than zero and (b) simultaneously give Mary a utility of less than 5, Harry less than 2, and Larry less than 8. The reasoning behind (a) is that no one is forced to trade; hence, cannot be forced to end up worse off than $u_i(w^i)$. The reasoning behind (b) is that such a proposal would never get the agreement of the three of them, nor could they be forced to accept it; for, on their own, they could provide themselves with $(5, 2, 8)$.

Similar reasoning can be applied to any outcomes achievable by any subset of traders, including the subset consisting of all players. The trades that are left as possible outcomes constitute trades associated with payoff vectors in the core. Edgeworth believed that competitive equilibrium points were always in the core and that, as the number of traders became very large, the core converged to the set of competitive equilibria. Subsequent research has proved Edgeworth's conjecture to be correct (see Debreu and Scarf (1972)). Edgeworth's game is one of nontransferable utility, and, in the applications at the end of Chapter 7, a model in the spirit of his is discussed.

3.2 The core

In this section, attention is restricted to essential games satisfying Assumptions 6.1 to 6.3. The *core* of a game is the set of undominated imputations. Section 3.2.1 contains a commonly used example of a game that has no core and a closely related example that does have a core. Then, in Section 3.2.2, the core is formally defined and it is shown how to determine whether the core is empty.

3.2.1 Two examples illustrating empty and nonempty cores

Given a game $\Gamma = (N, v)$, there is a well-defined sense in which the core, $C(N, v)$, is not empty if $v(N)$ is sufficiently large relative to the values of the $v(K)$ for other coalitions K. This is obvious after a little thought. Consider a family of games that are identical in every way except for the value of $v(N)$. That is, any two games (N, v) and (N', v') have the same set of players $(N = N')$, and for all K having fewer than n players, $v(K) = v'(K)$. If $v(N)$ is small relative to the $v(K)$, then there will be no core. As an example, look at the game in which three players are told they can divide \$100 any way they wish. An agreement signed by two or more players that gives a division of the money into three parts is binding on all three of them. Suppose that utility is measured by money in this game. Then $v(\{i\}) = 0$ for all i and $v(K) = 100$ for any coalition having two or three members. No matter what imputation is tentatively proposed, there is a way for two players to form a coalition that dominates it. For instance, if $(50, 50, 0)$ is proposed, players 1 and 3 can dominate it with $(75, 0, 25)$. Consider any imputation, (x, y, z). If, for example, $x, z > 0$, then players 2 and 3 can dominate (x, y, z) with $(0, y + x/2, z + x/2)$; however, this can be dominated by players 1 and 2 proposing $(z/2, x + y + z/2, 0)$, and so it goes.

Now imagine a variant of this game, denoted (N, v'), in which contracts signed by two players remain binding and determine the allocation of payoffs to all three players, but suppose that a contract signed by all three players can distribute \$150. That is, the rules of this new game state that a pair of players can receive \$100, split between the two of them as they agree, but that three players can receive \$150, split among them as they agree. Thus $v'(\{1, 2\}) = v'(\{1, 3\}) = v'(\{2, 3\}) = 100$ and $v\{i\} = 0$ $(i \in N)$ as before, and $v'(\{1, 2, 3\}) = 150$. For this game, the imputation $(50, 50, 50)$ is in the core, because each two-person coalition receives 100, and each individual receives at least zero. Similarly, suppose the coalition of three can achieve \$$y \geq 0$, while, as previously, two-person coalitions can achieve \$100. Then an allocation (a, b, c) is in the core if $a, b, c \geq 0$, $a + b$, $a + c$, $b + c \geq 100$, and $a + b + c = y$.

3.2.2 Existence of the core

The core is formally defined below:

DEFINITION 6.7 *The **core** of the game $\Gamma = (N, v)$, denoted $C(N, v)$, is a subset of the set of imputations consisting of the imputations that are not dominated.*

Another way of stating Definition 6.7 is that an imputation y is in the core if $\sum_{i \in K} y_i \geq v(K)$ for all coalitions K. It is possible to determine if a game $\Gamma = (N, v)$ has a nonempty core by solving a linear programming problem in which the objective function is the minimal value of $v(N)$ that allows a nonempty core. The form of the problem is

$$\text{minimize} \sum_{i \in N} x_i \tag{6.8}$$

$$\text{subject to } \sum_{i \in K} x_i \geq v(K) \text{ for all } K \in N, K \neq N \qquad (6.9)$$

For the family of three-person games discussed above, this linear programming problem is

$$\text{minimize } x_1 + x_2 + x_3 \qquad (6.10)$$

Subject to

$$
\left.
\begin{aligned}
x_1 & & & \geq 0 \\
& x_2 & & \geq 0 \\
& & x_3 & \geq 0 \\
x_1 + x_2 & & & \geq 100 \\
x_1 & & + x_3 & \geq 100 \\
& x_2 + x_3 & & \geq 100
\end{aligned}
\right\} \qquad (6.11)
$$

Clearly, if Assumptions 6.1 to 6.3 hold for a game $\Gamma = (N, v)$, the problem posed in equations (6.8) and (6.9) can be solved. Any solution is bounded below by $\sum_{i \in N} u_i$, and there are obviously large, finite values for the x_i that will satisfy all constraints (see, for example, Hillier and Lieberman (1974)). Let Z denote the solution to the linear programming problem posed in equations (6.8) and (6.9). Then:

LEMMA 6.1 *Let (N, v) be a game satisfying Assumptions 6.1 to 6.3. Then the core, $C(N, v)$, of the game is nonempty if and only if $Z \leq v(N)$.*

Proof Obvious from the structure of the programming problem. QED

3.3 The ε-core

The *epsilon core*, introduced by Shapley and Shubik (1966), consists of imputations that are within ε of being in the core. Thus, any game satisfying Assumptions 6.1 to 6.3 has an ε-core for a large enough ε. To be in the core, an imputation must give at least $v(K)$ to each coalition K, but to be in the ε-core, an imputation need only give $v(K) - \varepsilon$.

DEFINITION 6.8 *The ε-core of a game (N, v), denoted $C_\varepsilon(N, v)$, is a subset of the set of imputations. $y \in I(N, v)$ is an element of $C_\varepsilon(N, v)$ if $\sum_{i \in K} y_i \geq v(K) - \varepsilon$ for all coalitions K.*

As an example, recall the game in which three players divide \$100. If $\varepsilon = 33\frac{1}{3}$, then the ε-core is not empty and consists of the single point $(33\frac{1}{3}, 33\frac{1}{3}, 33\frac{1}{3})$.

There is nothing inherent in the definition of the ε-core that requires ε to be nonnegative, and, if negative values are also admitted, there is a unique value ε^* such that $C_\varepsilon(N, v) \neq \varnothing$ if and only if $\varepsilon \geq \varepsilon^*$.

LEMMA 6.2 *Let (N, v) be a game satisfying Assumptions 6.1 to 6.3. For this game* *there is a unique ε^* such that the ε-core of the game is not empty if and only if $\varepsilon \geq Z - v(N)$.*

Proof By the definition of the ε-core, there is a finite value of ε sufficiently large that the ε-core is not empty. Similarly, there is a finite value, possibly negative, small enough that the ε-core is empty. It also follows that if the ε-core is not empty for ε', then it is not empty for any larger value of ε. Therefore, it is clear that there exists a value ε^* such that, for $\varepsilon > \varepsilon^*$, the ε-core is not empty and for $\varepsilon < \varepsilon^*$, the ε-core is empty. It remains to show that the ε-core is not empty for $\varepsilon = \varepsilon^*$. This follows from the inequalities defining the ε-core being weak inequalities. QED

The ε-core associated with the value ε^* from Lemma 6.2 is called the *least core* because it is the smallest nonempty core associated with the game (N, v).

3.4 Simple games and the zero-one normalized form

There are some games in which a coalition is naturally described as either *winning* or *losing*. Such games are called *simple games* and are the focus of most of this section. Prior to taking them up, a normalized form of the characteristic function, called the *zero-one normalized form*, is defined in Section 3.4.1. If two games have the same normalized form, then they are equivalent from the point of view of many solution concepts. For the study of simple games, the normalized form is particularly natural and convenient. Section 3.4.2 defines simple games, Section 3.4.3 gives examples, and Section 3.4.4 has results on the core of such games.

3.4.1 The zero-one normalized form

Two games may have different characteristic functions and be the same in their essentials. Whether this is true for a given pair of games is determined by transforming each game to its *zero-one normalized form*. If the two games reduce to the same zero-one normalized form (or *zero-one normalization*), then they are regarded as belonging to the same equivalence class and as being the same in their essentials. For instance, the cores, the bargaining sets, and the Shapley values of the two games will be related by the transformations that define their common zero-one normalization.

DEFINITION 6.9 *Let (N, v) be a game. Then the* **zero-one normalization of** (N, v), *denoted* (N, v^*), *is given by*

$$v^*(K) = \frac{v(K) - \sum_{i \in K} v(\{i\})}{v(N) - \sum_{i \in N} v(\{i\})}, \qquad K \subset N \tag{6.12}$$

Games having identical zero-one normalizations are called *S-equivalent*. *S*-equivalence is proved in Lemma 6.3 to be an equivalence relation. That is, a relation that is reflexive (Γ is S-equivalent to Γ), symmetric (if Γ is S-equivalent to Γ', then Γ' is S-equivalent to Γ), and transitive (if Γ is S-equivalent to Γ' and Γ' is S-equivalent to Γ'', then Γ is S-equivalent to Γ'').

DEFINITION 6.10 *Two games, $\Gamma = (N, v)$ and $\Gamma' = (N, v')$, that have the same zero-one normalized form are S-**equivalent.***

It is proved in Lemma 6.4 that the core of (N, v) and the core of its zero-one normalization, (N, v^*), are related by the transformation in equation (6.12). That is, $u \in C(N, v)$ if and only if $u^* \in C(N, v^*)$, where

$$u_i^* = \frac{u_i - v(\{i\})}{v(N) - \sum_{i \in N} v(\{i\})} \tag{6.13}$$

LEMMA 6.3 *S-equivalence is an equivalence relation.*

Proof That S-equivalence is reflexive and symmetric is obvious. For transitivity, note that, if Γ and Γ' have the same zero-one normalized form, and Γ' and Γ'' do also, then Γ and Γ'' must share the same zero-one normalized form.   QED

LEMMA 6.4 *Let (N, v) be any game satisfying Assumptions 6.1 to 6.3 whose zero-one normalization is (N, v^*), and let $u^* \in I(N, v^*)$ be related to $u \in I(N, v)$ by*

$$u_i^* = \frac{u_i - v(\{i\})}{v(N) - \sum_{i \in N} v(\{i\})} \tag{6.14}$$

Then $u^* \in C(N, v^*)$ if and only if $u \in C(N, v)$.

Proof u is in the core of (N, v) if and only if $\sum_{i \in K} u_i \geq v(K)$ for all K. Let $\sum_{i \in K} u_i = v(K) + a_K$. Then u is in the core if and only if none of the a_K is negative. From equation (6.14),

$$\sum_{i \in K} u_i^* = \frac{\sum\limits_{i \in N} [u_i - v(\{i\})]}{v(N) - \sum\limits_{j \in N} v(\{i\})} \tag{6.15}$$

Using $\sum_{i \in K} u_i = v(K) + a_K$ in equation (6.15) gives

$$\sum_{i \in K} u_i^* = \frac{v(K) - \sum\limits_{i \in N} v(\{i\})}{v(N) - \sum\limits_{i \in N} v(\{i\})} + \frac{a_K}{v(N) - \sum\limits_{i \in N} v(\{i\})}$$

$$= v^*(K) + \frac{a_K}{v(N) - \sum\limits_{i \in N} v(\{i\})} \tag{6.16}$$

Thus $u^* \in C(N, v^*)$ if and only if all the a_K are nonnegative, which means that $u^* \in C(N, v^*)$ if and only if $u \in C(N, v)$.   QED

3.4.2   Simple games

There is a category of games, called *simple games* in which a coalition is either *winning* or *losing*. These games are characterized by a fixed gain from coalition formation that a winning coalition obtains.

DEFINITION 6.11 $\Gamma = (N, v)$ *is a* **simple game** *if the zero-one normalization of* (N, v), *denoted* (N, v^*), *satisfies (a)* $v^*(K) = 1$ *or* $v^*(K) = 0$ *for all* $K \subset N$. *(b) If* $v^*(K) = 1$, *then* K *is called a* **winning coalition,** *and if* $v^*(K) = 0$, *then* K *is called a* **losing coalition.** *(c)* (N, v) *is superadditive. (d)* $v^*(N) = 1$.

In the definition of a simple game, the notion that a coalition K is winning is captured by $v(K) = 1$ and that it is losing by $v(K) = 0$. If the game were not zero-one normalized, the payoff to a winning coalition would be $v(K) = a + \sum_{i \in K} v(\{i\})$ and to a losing coalition would be $v(K) = \sum_{i \in K} v(\{i\})$. Winning would add a fixed amount, a, to the sum of what the individual members could achieve on their own. The definition implies (from superadditivity) that the complement of a winning coalition is a losing coalition; however, note that the converse need not hold, as an example discussed below will illustrate. The superadditivity condition means that if K is a winning coalition, then adding members to K will result in a coalition that is still winning. Therefore, if K is winning, then $N \backslash K$ must be losing. Otherwise, $v(K) = v(N \backslash K) = 1$ and superadditivity would be violated. The definition implies that the game is essential; that is, that there exists at least one winning coalition, N, and at least one losing coalition. This is because, for $n \geq 2$, both $\{1\}$ and $\{2\}$ cannot be winning. If they were, then $v(\{1\}) = v(\{2\}) = v(N) = 1$, which violates superadditivity.

3.4.3   Examples of simple games

As an example of a simple game, imagine a committee or a legislature in which a simple majority of the members has full power. Then $v(K) = 1$ if $k > n/2$ and $v(K) = 0$ if $k \leq n/2$. For a study of politics under the assumption that some political processes are characterized by simple games, see Riker (1962). Other examples of voting situations as simple games include majority games in which substantially more than half the votes are required to win, and weighted majority voting games in which player i has a weight $w_i > 0$. If a vote total of w_0 $(> \sum_{i \in N} w_i/2)$ is required to win in a weighted majority game, $v(K) = 1$ if $\sum_{i \in K} w_i \geq w_0$ and $v(K) = 0$ otherwise. The winning majority could be anything larger than a half, including 100% of the weighted votes.

As an example of a game in which the complement of a losing coalition is a winning coalition, consider a simple majority voting game where each player has one vote and the number of players is odd. Then $v(K) = 1$ if and only if $v(N \backslash K) < n/2$; for either $k > n/2$ or $(n - k) > n/2$. Now consider a majority voting game in which each player has one vote, but a winning coalition requires 75% of the votes. If a coalition K has 60% of the votes and $N \backslash K$ has 40%, then both K and $N \backslash K$ are losing.

3.4.4   The core of a simple game

A key fact about simple games is that they always have empty cores if they
are at all interesting. Roughly speaking, interesting simple games are those
having some (nonempty) losing coalitions and at least two winning
coalitions. A player i can be thought of as a *dictator* if she is essential to all
winning coalitions. In other words, for i to be a dictator means that if i does
not belong to the coalition K, then K cannot be winning. If N is the only
winning coalition, then all players are dictators. It is proved below that a
simple game that has no dictators has an empty core. The proof is carried
out in two steps. The first, Lemma 6.5, establishes the result for normalized
games. Then, Lemma 6.6 extends Lemma 6.5 to all simple games having
no dictators.

LEMMA 6.5   *Let $\Gamma = (N, v)$ be a zero-one normalized simple game. If $v(N \setminus \{i\}) = 1$ for all $i \in N$, then the core of (N, v) is empty.*

Proof   Let $u \in I(N, v)$. Then at least one player has a positive payoff under
u. Suppose, without loss of generality, that $u_1 > 0$. Then u is dominated by
u' where $u'_i = u_i + u_1/(n-1)$ for $i > 1$ and $u'_1 = 0$.   QED

   In a simple game, (N, v), the reader can easily verify that K is winning if
$v(K) = a + \sum_{i \in K} v(\{i\})$ and losing if $v(K) = \sum_{i \in K} v(\{i\})$, where a is a
positive constant.

LEMMA 6.6   *If (N, v) is a simple game in which $N \setminus \{i\}$ is a winning coalition for
all i, then the core of the game is empty.*

Proof of this lemma is left to the reader.[2]

4   The stable set

The stable set, also known as the von Neumann–Morgenstern solution,
was proposed by von Neumann and Morgenstern (1944), and is closely
related to the core. Recall that the core is the set of undominated
imputations. Thus, an allocation in the core is not dominated by another
allocation in the core, nor is it dominated by an allocation outside of the
core. Let I^* be a subset of $I(N, v)$. Then I^* is a *stable set* if no allocation in
I^* is dominated by any other allocation in I^*, and each allocation outside
of I^* is dominated by an allocation in I^*. Two important differences
between the stable set and the core are, first, that the stable set is not a
unique set, and, second, many games have stable sets that also have empty
cores.

DEFINITION 6.12   *A **stable set**, $C^*(N, v)$, is a subset of the set of imputations
that satisfies two conditions: (a) If $u \in C^*(N, v)$ then u is not dominated by any other
member of $C^*(N, v)$. (b) If $u \notin C^*(N, v)$, then there exists $u' \in C^*(N, v)$ such that
u' dominates u.*

   As an example, recall the three-person game in which any two players can determine the division of $100 between all three players. One stable set for this game is

$$\{u \in R_+^3 \mid u_1 + u_2 = 100 \text{ and } u_3 = 0\} \tag{6.17}$$

Other stable sets are:

$$\{u \in R_+^3 \mid u_1 + u_2 = 100 - a \text{ and } u_3 = a\} \text{ for } 0 < a < 50 \tag{6.18}$$

For a while it was wondered if all games had stable sets; however, Lucas (1969) found a game having none. (See also Owen (1982).)

In thinking about cooperative games, it is natural to think about coalition formation and to wonder which coalitions will, in fact, form. One might expect a *coalition structure* to emerge—that is, a partition of the players into coalitions. The underlying notion here is that the players subdivide themselves into groups, with each group carrying out some binding agreement. With respect to the core as a solution concept, the natural coalition structure often seems to be N all by itself. In other words, for a game having a core, and in which the core is the solution, the players would, in many instances, seem to form the coalition of the whole, N, and to choose some core point. Even if none of the smaller coalitions form, their potential plays a role in determining the outcome. The influence of the smaller coalitions is seen in the definition of the core, where an allocation is ruled out of being in the core if it does not provide to each coalition a total payoff at least as large at that coalition could guarantee itself.

The stable set looks as if it might be closer to saying something about actual coalitions, other than the coalition of the whole, that might form. In the game where two or three players can divide $100, the stable set consisting of all allocations giving player 3 nothing and splitting the $100 between players 1 and 2 is a set that looks like the options that are open to the coalition $\{1, 2\}$, with player 3 taking it on the chin because he is left out by the others. Still, coalitions appear in the stable set in an implicit way. The definition of a stable set does not rest on stipulating a particular coalition structure and then determining an outcome, or set of outcomes, based on some "reasonable" criteria. The latter approach is taken in the bargaining set and the kernel, which are discussed below in Section 5.

5 The bargaining set and related solutions

The stable set hints at taking into account coalitions that might actually form; however, such an interpretation is implicit, not explicit, in the solution concept. In contrast, the *bargaining set* is clearly concerned with the actual coalitions that might form, because an equilibrium outcome is defined in relation to a particular partition of the players into coalitions. There are several different bargaining set concepts, only one of which is described below.

Closely related to the bargaining set are the *kernel* and the *nucleolus*. These latter two solutions can be used to show the bargaining set to be nonempty; the kernel can be proved to be contained in the bargaining set, which means a nonempty kernel implies a nonempty bargaining set; and, the nucleolus is always associated with a payoff configuration in the kernel (hence, also in the bargaining set). Thus, if the nucleolus exists, then the bargaining set is not empty. Connections among the bargaining set, the kernel, the nucleolus, and some other constructs are in Maschler, Peleg, and Shapley (1979).

The kernel and the nucleolus may have independent appeal as solution concepts in addition to their role in proving the bargaining set nonempty. For example, the nucleolus is generally unique, and its formulation may make it attractive as a fair division concept. The bargaining set is covered in Section 5.1, the kernel in Section 5.2, and the nucleolus in Section 5.3. Examples are given in Section 5.4.

5.1   The bargaining set

A feature of the bargaining set is that it is not enough for some players to be able to improve on a particular allocation in order to rule it out. To rule out an allocation, a coalition must be able to improve on it, and it must be impossible for members of that coalition to be enticed away by another coalition that can improve on what the first coalition proposed as an alternative to the originally proposed allocation. Furthermore, only certain coalitions are allowed to try to improve on an allocation.

For example, suppose an allocation x is under review, and imagine that a coalition K proposes the allocation y as an alternative to x, where y gives all members of K as much or more than they get under x and y^K is enforceable by K. It is next determined whether there exists an allocation z and coalition L having the properties that some, but not all, members of K can be in L and all members of L get as much under z as they did under x and y. The members of K who are in L must get at least what y afforded them and the remaining members of L must get at least what x afforded them. The proposal y is called an *objection* and the proposal z is called a *counterobjection*. An allocation x is in the bargaining set if any objection to x can be met with a counterobjection. The preceding description gives a rough notion of the bargaining set, but some details are left out. Of course, they will be filled in below. There are actually several different bargaining set concepts that vary according to the exact manner in which the missing details are specified.

In treating this topic, concepts needed to define the bargaining set are introduced in Sections 5.1.1 and 5.1.2, and then the bargaining set is defined in Section 5.1.3.

5.1.1   Coalition structures and payoff configurations

The bargaining set is intimately related to what various coalitions can achieve, given that the set of players is partitioned into several coalitions.

In other words, a payoff vector is examined in relation to a particular partition of the players into subsets. Such a partition is a *coalition structure* and is defined as follows.

DEFINITION 6.13 *A* **coalition structure** $\mathcal{T} = (T_1, \ldots, T_m)$ *is a partition of the set of players into coalitions. Each set T_k is nonempty, $T_j \cap T_k = \varnothing$ for all $j, k \in \{1, \ldots, m\}$ with $j \neq k$, and $\bigcup_{k \in N} T_k = N$.*

To make it easier to think about payoff vectors in the presence of a given coalition structure, the *payoff configuration* is defined below. A payoff configuration is merely a particular payoff vector paired with a particular coalition structure. The payoff vector must also give to each coalition in the associated coalition structure precisely as much as the coalition can assure itself.

DEFINITION 6.14 *A* **payoff configuration** *is a pair $(x, \mathcal{T})$ where $x \in R^n$, $\mathcal{T}$ is a coalition structure, and $\sum_{i \in T_k} x_i = v(T_k)$ for $k = 1, \ldots, m$.*

A payoff configuration is a payoff vector that is group rational in a local sense that is defined by its associated coalition structure. For a payoff configuration $(x, \mathcal{T})$, each coalition in $\mathcal{T}$ receives a total payoff that is equal to what that coalition can achieve. The next definition refines this concept by adding individual rationality.

DEFINITION 6.15 *An* **individually rational payoff configuration** *is a payoff configuration, $(x, \mathcal{T})$ for which $x_1 \geq v(\{i\})$ for all $i \in N$. The set of all individually rational payoff configurations for the game (N, v) relative to a coalition structure $\mathcal{T}$ is denoted $I_{\mathcal{T}}(N, v)$.*

5.1.2 Objections and counterobjections

The bargaining set consists of individually rational payoff configurations that pass a certain test. Roughly speaking, the test is that no *allowable coalition* has an effective complaint against the proposed payoff configuration. An allowable coalition is one that is a subset of a coalition in the coalition structure. An effective complaint is an *objection* to which there is no *counterobjection*. On the way to defining these last two concepts, the notion of *partners* of a coalition with respect to a coalition structure is needed. Partners of K in $\mathcal{T}$ are all those players who are in coalitions that also contain members of K.

DEFINITION 6.16 *For a coalition structure $\mathcal{T}$ and coalition K, the* **partners of K** *in $\mathcal{T}$ are the members of the set $P(K, \mathcal{T}) = \{i \mid i \in T_j, T_j \cap K \neq \varnothing\}$.*

For example, let $\mathcal{T} = (\{1, 2, 5\}, \{3, 6, 9\}, \{4, 7, 8\})$ and let $K = \{1, 2, 6\}$. Then $P(K, \mathcal{T}) = \{1, 2, 3, 5, 6, 9\}$.

An *objection* of K against L is an individually rational payoff configuration $(y, \mathcal{U})$ under which the members of K all get more than they get at $(x, \mathcal{T})$ and all partners of K get at least as much as they get under $(x, \mathcal{T})$. K and L are both subsets of the same member, T_j, of $\mathcal{T}$. An intuitive notion underlying the objection is that the members of K believe they are getting less of the payoff going to their coalition (T_j) than is fair and that the members of L are getting more than K thinks they deserve.

DEFINITION 6.17 *Suppose that* $(x, \mathcal{T}) \in I_{\mathcal{T}}(N, v), K, L \subset T_j \in \mathcal{T}$, *and* $K \cap L = \varnothing$. *Then an* **objection of K against** L *is* $(y, \mathcal{U}) \in I_{\mathcal{U}}(N, v)$ *such that (a)* $P(K, \mathcal{U}) \cap L = \varnothing$, *(b)* $y_i > x_i$ *for all* $i \in K$, *and (c)* $y_i \geqslant x_i$ *for all* $i \in P(K, \mathcal{U})$.

Note that the members of K are not restricted to choosing a $\mathcal{U}$ of which K is a member, nor must K be a subset of member of $\mathcal{U}$, but they must be sure that all other players in coalitions with them under $\mathcal{U}$ are sufficiently well treated.

Roughly speaking, a *counterobjection* is a proposal of L that is similar to an objection and that leaves all interested players at least as well off as they would otherwise have been. This means that the partners of L must get at least as much as they get under $(x, \mathcal{T})$, and those partners of K under $(y, \mathcal{U})$ that are partners of L under $(z, \mathcal{V})$ must get at least as much as they would get under $(y, \mathcal{U})$. In effect, the counterobjection is good enough to dissuade some of the partners of K from joining K in the objection and good enough to keep the allegiance of L's partners.

DEFINITION 6.18 *Suppose that* $(x, \mathcal{T}) \in I_{\mathcal{T}}(N, v)$, $K, L \subset T_k \in \mathcal{T}$, $K \cap L = \varnothing$, *and* $(y, \mathcal{U}) \in I_{\mathcal{U}}(N, v)$ *is an objection of K against L. Then a* **counterobjection of L against** K *is* $(z, \mathcal{V}) \in I_{\mathcal{V}}(N, v)$ *satisfying (a)* $K \not\subseteq P(L, \mathcal{V})$, *(b)* $z_i \geqslant x_i$ *for* $i \in P(L, \mathcal{V})$, *and* $z_i \geqslant y_i$ *for* $i \in P(K, \mathcal{U}) \cap P(L, \mathcal{V})$.

Provision (a) in Definition 6.18 indicates that some members of K can be partners of L under $(z, \mathcal{V})$, but at least one member of K is excluded.

5.1.3   Definition of the bargaining set

The bargaining set consists of all individually rational payoff configurations for which every objection can be met with a counterobjection. Loosely speaking, a plan is in the bargaining set if, when a group of dissidents tries to bribe a few others to go along with a second plan that benefits all of them, it is possible for another group to profitably offer a third plan containing a larger bribe to those whom the dissidents need.

DEFINITION 6.19 *The* **bargaining set** $\mathcal{M}_1^{(i)}$ *is the set of all individually rational payoff configurations* $(x, \mathcal{T}) \in I_{\mathcal{T}}(N, v)$ *such that whenever some coalition K has an objection against a coalition L, at least one member of L has a counterobjection.*

To recapitulate, imagine a particular coalition structure, $\mathcal{T}$, and a payoff vector, x. These form an individually rational payoff configuration $(x, \mathcal{T})$. Thus, x gives to each coalition in $\mathcal{T}$ a payoff just equal to what the coalition can achieve for itself. If some coalition K is a subset of $T_j \in \mathcal{T}$, it may have an objection against a coalition L that is a subset of the same member of $\mathcal{T}$. K and L must be disjoint. That K has an objection against L can be interpreted as saying that the members of K believe they are not getting as much as they think they should and that the members of L are getting too much. The objection itself is a new coalition structure $\mathcal{U}$ and an individually rational payoff configuration $(y, \mathcal{U})$ under which all members of K get more than before ($y_i > x_i$ for i in K), and all partners of K gets at least as much as before ($y_i \geq x_i$ for partners). Any player i is a partner of K if the coalition U_j to which i belongs also contains one or more members of K. In other words, the members of K need not be in the same single coalition in the structure $\mathcal{U}$ even though they had to be in the same coalition under the structure $\mathcal{T}$. The payoff requirements for partners of K reflects the notion that K needs the active cooperation of all players who appear in coalitions with members of K under the new coalition structure $\mathcal{U}$ that K proposes.

Now turning to the counterobjection of L to K, L must propose $(z, \mathcal{V})$ where z gives all members of L and all partners of L at least what they received under x ($z_i \geq x_i$ for members of L and partners of L). In addition, any members of K who are also partners of L must receive at least as much as they were to get from y ($z_i \geq y_i$ for partners of L who are members of K). If L has a counterobjection for a particular objection of K, then the objection is not considered to be viable. The reason is that K cannot get its members and its partners to go along with the objection if L can offer a counterobjection under which the counterobjectors do sufficiently well, and, in so doing, deprive K of some of the supporting players it needs for its objection. If $(x, \mathcal{T})$ is in the bargaining set, then for any objection of any coalition K against any coalition L, the coalition L has a counterobjection.

As an example, look at the game in which three players divide \$100, with two or three players able to dictate the payoff vector. First, $[(0, 0, 0), (\{1\}), \{2\}, \{3\})]$ is in the bargaining set. The reason is that no player is in a coalition with another player against whom she can make an objection. The payoff configuration $[(50, 50, 0), (\{1, 2\}, \{3\})]$ is also in the bargaining set. Obviously, player 2 can make an objection against player 1 and propose $[(0, 50 + a, 50 - a), (\{1\}, \{2, 3\})]$ where $0 < a \leq 50$. To this, proposal player 1 can make the counterobjection $[(50, 0, 50), (\{1, 3\}, \{2\})]$. Thus, any payoff configuration consisting of a coalition structure and an allocation that gives 50 to each of two players who form a coalition and zero to the remaining player, who is in a coalition alone, is in the bargaining set. In the same vein, it can be shown that $[(a, a, b), (\{1, 2\}, \{3\})]$ for $0 \leq b < 100$ and $2a + b = 100$ is in the bargaining set. Interestingly, $[(50 + a, 50 - a, 0), (\{1, 2\}, \{3\})]$ for $a > 0$ is not in the bargaining set. To see this, notice that $[(0, 50 - a/2, 50 + a/2), (\{1\}, \{2, 3\})]$ can be put forth by player 2 as an objection against player 1, but this cannot be countered by player 1. A successful counterobjection by player 1 must give at least $50 + a$ to player 1 and at least $50 + a/2$ to player 3. Clearly, this cannot be done within the constraint that there is 100 to divide. Similarly, any individually rational payoff configuration $[(a, b, c), (\{1, 2, 3\})]$ is in the bargaining set, because any objection can be met with a counterobjection.

The bargaining set is an appealing concept, because of the interpretations given to its definition. The notion that players are, in fact, sorted out into particular coalitions is attractive. Given a coalition structure and a payoff vector, objections can be mounted only by players who are inside the same coalition, and they are objections against one or more other members of the same coalition. This makes sense from the standpoint that these are the players who are contracting with one another at the moment. But, if an objection is to be made, the objectors can go outside the immediate coalition and propose a whole new global structure (i.e., a new coalition structure and payoff vector); however, the new proposal is successful only if it cannot be countered by the group against which the objection was originally made. Thus, it is not good enough to propose a change that benefits those taking part in it; the change must be impervious to a counterproposal. All these provisions have the flavor of bargaining processes, although they are not actual processes.

A simple alternative formulation of the bargaining set is based on requiring that both K, the objecting coalition, and L, the coalition against which K objects, each consist of one player. There remains the fundamental question of whether a given game has a bargaining set, and, more importantly, whether all games within a large class can be shown to possess a bargaining set. This question is handled indirectly by moving on to the kernel and the nucleous. They can be used to settle the issue.

5.2   The kernel

Turning now to the *kernel*, Section 5.2.1 introduces concepts used in defining the kernel, and then the kernel is defined. In Section 5.2.2, it is proved that an individually rational payoff configuration that is in the kernel is also in the bargaining set.

5.2.1   Basic definitions for the kernel

Two useful concepts are defined that are related to the gains from forming various coalitions and to the comparative importance of pairs of players in coalitions. The first of these is the *excess*, in Definition 6.20. It measures the payoff potential of a coalition relative to a particular payoff vector.

DEFINITION 6.20 *In a game* (N, v) *the* **excess of the coalition** K **with respect to the payoff vector** u *is*

$$e(K, u) = v(K) - \sum_{i \in K} u_i \qquad (6.19)$$

The *surplus of i against j* can be thought of as a measure of the bargaining power of player i relative to player j. In comparing i and j in this way, one can also look at the surplus of j against i.

DEFINITION 6.21 *In a game* (N, v) *the* **surplus of** i **against** j *is* $s_{ij}(u) = max\{e(K, u) \mid K \subset N, i \in K, j \notin K\}$.

The excess $e(K, u)$ measures the amount by which the members of a coalition can improve their joint payoff over what they receive under a proposed payoff vector u. The surplus of i against j is the largest excess $e(K, u)$ over all coalitions which include i but exclude j. Relative to the payoff vector u, K is the most profitable coalition that has i as a member and that lacks j as a member. In thinking about players i and j, keeping other things equal, and evaluating the worth of player i by herself, without the help of j, relative to the payoff vector u, $s_{ij}(u)$ measures the largest contribution to a coalition that can be associated with i and has no connection with j. Two players i and j are in a kind of balance, relative to u, if $s_{ij}(u) = s_{ji}(u)$, and this balance is the basis of the *kernel*.

DEFINITION 6.22   *The* **kernel,** $\mathcal{K}$, *consists of all* $(u, \mathcal{T})$ *such that, if* $i, j \in T_k \in$ $\mathcal{T}$, *then* (a) $s_{ij}(u) = s_{ji}(u)$ *or* (b) $s_{ij}(u) < s_{ji}(u)$ *and* $u_i = v(\{i\})$ *or* (c) $s_{ji}(u) <$ $s_{ij}(u)$ *and* $u_j = v(\{j\})$.

The conditions in Definition 6.22 are stated for each pair of players i and j who are in the same coalition T_k. Either the surplus of i against j $(s_{ij}(u))$ equals the surplus of j against i $(s_{ji}(u))$, or, if this is not the case, the player whose surplus is smaller is already receiving the minimum possible payoff (i.e., $u_i = v(\{i\})$ if player i has the smaller surplus). The reasoning behind this specification is that if $s_{ij}(u) < s_{ji}(u)$ and $u_i > v(\{i\})$, then player j is in a position to make an objection to which i has no counterobjection. In doing this, j will increase her payoff at the expense of i. If their surpluses are equal, then a successful objection by either one is impossible. Also, if $s_{ij}(u) < s_{ji}(u)$ with $u_i = v(\{i\})$, it is impossible for j to make a successful objection because i is already at the lowest payoff to which he can be driven.

5.2.2   The relationship between the kernel and the bargaining set

Theorem 6.1 shows that the kernel is contained in the bargaining set.

THEOREM 6.1   *For a game* (N, v) *the kernel is contained in the bargaining set.*

Proof   This theorem is proved in several steps. The first shows that if a coalition K has an objection against another coalition L, then there must be a single member subset of K, $\{i\}$, that has an objection against a single member subset of L, $\{j\}$. After this is established, it is shown that, for a point in the kernel $(x, \mathcal{T})$ and for any objection of $\{i\}$ against $\{j\}$, (where i and j are in the same set T_k) $\{j\}$ has a counterobjection.

Suppose that $(x, \mathcal{T})$ is in the kernel, that K and L are disjoint subsets of the same $T_k \in \mathcal{T}$, and that K has an objection against L. Then, by the definition of objection, precisely the same objection could be made by any $\{i\} \subset K$ against any $\{j\} \subset L$.

Now let $(y, \mathcal{U})$ be an objection of $\{i\}$ against $\{j\}$. Clearly the partners of $\{i\}$ will coincide with the members of the set U_k to which i belongs. Consequently, $\sum_{l \in U_k}(y_l - x_l)$ can be no larger than $s_{ij}(x)$. But $\{j\}$ has a counterobjection if there is $(z, \mathcal{V})$ under which each partner, l, of j receives at least x_l and, among them, any that were partners of i under the objection receive at least y_l. It is possible to mount such a counterobjection if $s_{ji}(x) \geq s_{ij}(x)$, because this latter amount is the amount by which the payoff of a carefully chosen coalition containing j, but not containing i, can receive above what they received under the original proposal $(x, \mathcal{T})$. Furthermore, this is at least as large as the amount by which i can reward those who join her in her objection, and, thus j can win back any of those she needs and also sufficiently reward any other required players to sustain the counterobjection.

It remains to cover the case where $s_{ij}(x) > s_{ji}(x)$. In this case, $x_j = v(\{j\})$ as well; therefore, in the face of an objection by $\{i\}$, $\{j\}$ can counterobject with a $(y, \mathcal{U})$ under which $y_j = v(\{j\})$ and $\{j\} \in \mathcal{U}$.   QED

An appealing feature of the kernel is that it is stated in terms of pairs of players. An individually rational payoff configuration is in the kernel when no pair of players in the same coalition is in a position where one can make a successful objection against the other. Of course, it is important that the kernel is always in the bargaining set. This fact, in conjunction with the nucleolus being in the kernel, is useful in showing the bargaining set is not empty.

5.3   The nucleolus

The kernel, like the bargaining set, can have many elements; however, for a large class of games the nucleolus consists of just one point. The nucleolus is defined in relation to a given set of payoff vectors that can be an arbitrary set. This differs from both the kernel and the bargaining set, which are defined in relation to sets $I_{\mathcal{T}}(N, v)$. The idea behind the nucleolus is very simple: a payoff vector is in the nucleolus if, in a sense to be defined below, the excesses for all coalitions for that payoff vector are made as small as possible. The nucleolus is defined in Section 5.3.1. Section 5.3.2 contains conditions assuring its existence and uniqueness, then, in Section 5.3.3, any payoff vector in the nucleolus is shown to be in a payoff configuration contained in the kernel. The significance of the latter result is that any game having a nucleolus has a nonempty kernel and a nonempty bargaining set.

5.3.1   Definition of the nucleolus

The definition of the nucleolus rests on comparisons among the excesses associated with various payoff vectors; therefore, these comparisons must first be described. To make a comparison between various payoff vectors, a function is constructed, $\theta(u) = (e_1(u), e_2(u), \ldots, e_{2^n}(u)) \in R^{2^n}$ that has one coordinate for each of the 2^n coalitions contained in N (including the coalitions N and ϕ). Order the 2^n coalitions $K_1, K_2, K_4, \ldots, K_{2^n}$ so that

$\theta_j(u) = e(K_j, u)$ and $\theta_j(u) \geqslant \theta_{j+1}(u)$ for $j = 1, \ldots, 2^n - 1$. This can be done for any u in the set, X, of payoff vectors being considered. Note that $\theta_j(u)$ and $\theta_j(u')$ may be associated with different coalitions, in general. In both instances, however, the jth coordinate is the jth largest excess relative to u and u', respectively.

$\theta(u)$ and $\theta(u')$ can be compared using the *lexicographic ordering*. Under this ordering, $\theta(u)$ is smaller than $\theta(u')$ if $\theta_1(u) < \theta_1(u')$ or, for $j > 1$, $\theta_j(u) < \theta_j(u')$ and $\theta_i(u) = \theta_i(u')$ for $i = 1, \ldots, j-1$. This relation is denoted $\theta(u) <_L \theta(u')$. If $\theta_j(u) = \theta_j(u')$ for all j, then $\theta(u) =_L \theta(u')$, and $\theta(u) \leqslant_L \theta(u')$ means $\theta(u) <_L \theta(u')$ or $\theta(u) =_L \theta(u')$. For example, suppose that $n = 3$ and let $\theta(u^0) = (100, 62, 60, 50, 40, 36, 32, 30)$, $\theta(u^1) = (100, 62, 60, 52, 0, 0, 0, 0)$, $\theta(u^2) = (99, 98, 97, 96, 95, 94, 93, 92)$, and $\theta(u^3) = (120, 50, 45, 40, 35, 30, 25, 20)$. The lexicographic ordering of these four elements is $\theta(u^2) <_L \theta(u^0) <_L \theta(u^1) <_L \theta(u^3)$.

DEFINITION 6.23 *For a set of payoff vectors X, the* **nucleolus over X** *is* $nuc(X) = \{u \in X \mid u' \in X \text{ implies } \theta(u) \leqslant_L \theta(u')\}$.

Thus, the nucleolus over X consists of those payoff vectors, $u \in X$, having the lexicographically smallest associated excesses.

5.3.2 Existence and uniqueness of the nucleolus

There are two results in this section. The first is that, if X is compact, then $nuc(X)$ is nonempty. The second is that $nuc(X)$ is a single point if X is convex as well as compact.

THEOREM 6.2 *Let X be a nonempty compact subset of R^n. Then $nuc(X)$ is not empty.*

Proof Let $A_1 = \{\theta(u) \in R^{2^n} \mid u \in X\}$ and let $z_1 = \inf_{y \in A_1} y_1$. Because X is compact, there must be elements of A_1 having z_1 as the first coordinate. Let $X_2 = \{u \in X \mid \theta_1(u) = z_1\}$. It is easily seen that X_2 is compact: For each coalition K, the set $B_1(K) = \{u \in X \mid e(K, u) \leqslant z_1\}$ is compact. Some, but not all, of the $B_1(K)$ may be empty. Clearly, $X_2 = \bigcup_K B_1(K)$ and X_2 is not empty. Now define $A_2 = \{\theta(u) \in A_1 \mid u \in X_2\}$.

From here, the proof proceeds by induction. Suppose that $X_i \subset X_{i-1}$ is nonempty, compact, and consists of all payoff vectors in X_{i-1} for which $\theta_j(u) = \theta_j(u')$ for all $u, u' \in X_{i-1}$ and all $j < i$, and that, if $u \in X_i$, then $\theta_{i-1}(u) = z_{i-1}$ where z_{i-1} is the minimum value of $\theta_{i-1}(u')$ for all $u' \in X_{i-1}$. Let $A_i = \{\theta(u) \in R^{2^n} \mid u \in X_i\}$. Note that, for $\theta(u), \theta(u') \in A_i$, $\theta_j(u) = \theta_j(u')$, $j = 1, \ldots, i-1$ and that $\theta_j(u), \theta_j(u') \leqslant \theta_{i-1}(u)$ for $j \geqslant i$. Now let $z_i = \inf_{y \in A_i} y_i$. Because X_i is compact, there must be elements of A_i having z_i as the ith coordinate. Let $X_{i+1} = \{u \in X_i \mid \theta_i(u) = z_i\}$. As with X_2, X_{i+1} is compact and nonempty. A_{i+1} is defined recursively as $A_{i+1} = \{\theta(u) \in R^{2^n} \mid u \in X_{i+1}\}$, and, thus for $y \in A_{i+1}, y_j = z_j, j = 1, \ldots, i$.

Letting $X_1 = X$, it is clear $nuc(X) \subset X_i$ for $i = 1, \ldots, 2^n + 1$, that

$\mathrm{nuc}(X) = X_{2^n+1}$, and that $\theta(u) = (z_1, z_2, \ldots, z_{2^n})$ for $u \in \mathrm{nuc}(X) = X_{2^n+1}$. QED

COROLLARY *If X is also convex, then $\mathrm{nuc}(X)$ contains exactly one point.*

Proof Suppose that u and u' are elements of $\mathrm{nuc}(X)$; hence $\theta(u) =_L \theta(u')$. In the vector $\theta(u)$, there are s distinct values of the coordinates, with k_1 occurrences of the largest number, k_2 occurrences of the second largest, and so forth. Of course, $\sum_{i=1}^{s} k_i = 2^n$. With respect to $\theta(u)$, let the order of the coalitions be $K_1, K_2, \ldots, K_{2^n}$ (i.e., $\theta_j(u) = e(K_j, u)$ for all j), and, similarly, let the order of the coalitions with respect to $\theta(u')$ be $K_1', K_2', \ldots, K_{2^n}'$. Letting $\lambda \in (0, 1)$ and $u^\lambda = \lambda u + (1 - \lambda)u'$, note that $\theta(u^\lambda)$ can have, at most, k_1 occurrences of $\theta_1(u)$, and $\theta(u^\lambda)$ has exactly k_i occurrences of $\theta_{k_1+\cdots+k_{i-1}+1}(u)$, $i = 1, \ldots, j-1$, then it can have, at most, k_j occurrences of $\theta_{k_1+\cdots+k_{j-1}+1}(u)$.

The reasons for this are as follows: Take the occurrences of $\theta_1(u)$. There are k_1 of these in $\theta(u^\lambda)$ if and only if the two sets of coalitions $\{K_1, \ldots, K_{k_1}\}$ and $\{K_1', \ldots, K_{k_1}'\}$ have precisely the same members. If the two collections of coalitions are not identical in their membership, there is some coalition, K_i ($i \leqslant k_1$), from the first list such that $e(K_i, u) > e(K_i, u')$. If this inequality holds, then there are fewer than k_1 coordinates of $\theta(u^\lambda)$ having the value $\theta_1(u)$. There can be no coordinates of $\theta(u^\lambda)$ with a value higher than $\theta_1(u)$; therefore, $\theta(u^\lambda) <_L \theta(u)$.

If the collections of coalitions $K_1, \ldots, K_{k_1}$ and $K_1', \ldots, K_{k_1}'$ are the same, then the argument can be repeated for the coordinates achieving $\theta_{k_1+1}(u)$. Either the collections of coalitions, $K_{k_1+1}, \ldots, K_{k_1+k_2}$ and $K_{k_1+1}', \ldots, K_{k_1+k_2}'$ are the same or $\theta(u^\lambda) <_L \theta(u)$. This argument can be repeated inductively with the conclusion that $\theta(u^\lambda) =_L \theta(u)$ if and only if $u = u'$, and otherwise $\theta(u^\lambda) <_L \theta(u)$. The latter inequality implies the contradiction that neither u nor u' are elements of $\mathrm{nuc}(X)$; hence, $\mathrm{nuc}(X)$ consists of just one point. QED

5.3.3   The nucleolus is contained in the kernel

To see better what is going on, consider the individually rational payoff configurations, relative to the coalition structure $\mathcal{T}$, for the game $(N, v): I_{\mathcal{T}}(N, v)$. The payoff vectors associated with $I_{\mathcal{T}}(N, v)$ are the elements of $A_{\mathcal{T}}(N, v) = \{u \in R^n \mid (u, \mathcal{T}) \in I_{\mathcal{T}}(N, v)\}$, which is compact, so $\mathrm{nuc}[A_{\mathcal{T}}(N, v)]$ is not empty and is in both the bargaining set and the kernel. In fact, this result not only establishes that the bargaining set is nonempty, but that there is at least one element in the bargaining set relative to each coalition structure.

THEOREM 6.3   *Let $\mathcal{K}(N, v)$ be the kernel of the game (N, v), let $\mathcal{T}$ be a coalition structure, and let $u \in \mathrm{nuc}[A_{\mathcal{T}}(N, v)]$. Then $(u, \mathcal{T}) \in \mathcal{K}(N, v)$.*

Proof Suppose that $(u, \mathcal{T}) \in I_{\mathcal{T}}(N, v)$ and $(u, \mathcal{T}) \notin \mathcal{K}(N, v)$. Then there is a pair of players, $i, j \in N$ such that $s_{ij}(u) > s_{ji}(u)$ and $u_j > v(\{j\})$. Let δ equal the smaller of $(s_{ij}(u) - s_{ji}(u))/2$ and $u_j - v(\{j\})$, and define u' as follows;

$$u'_i = u_i + \delta \tag{6.20}$$

$$u'_j = u_j - \delta \tag{6.21}$$

$$u'_k = u_k \text{ for } k \neq i, j \tag{6.22}$$

Let K^* be a coalition with $i \in K^*, j \notin K^*$, and having the largest excess among all coalitions that contain i and exclude j. Finally, in ordering the coordinates of the function $\theta(u)$ suppose that K^* is placed after any coalitions L for which $e(K^*, u) = e(L, u)$. The coordinate of $\theta(u)$ corresponding to K^* is k^*.[3]

Now compare $\theta(u)$ and $\theta(u')$: $\theta_k(u) \leq \theta_k(u')$ for $k < k^*$. The coalitions coming before K^* can fall into any of three categories: (a) they contain both i and j, (b) they contain neither i nor j, and (c) they contain i but not j. No such coalition can contain j and omit i because of the condition $s_{ij}(u) > s_{ji}(u)$. For any coalition falling into (a) or (b), $\theta_k(u) = \theta_k(u')$, and for any coalition in category (c), $\theta_k(u) < \theta_k(u')$. Meanwhile, for $k > k^*$, $\theta_k(u') < \theta_k^*(u)$; therefore, $\theta(u') <_L \theta(u)$ and so u is not in the nucleolus. This establishes that u is not in the nucleolus if $(u, \mathcal{T})$ is not in the kernel, which implies that $(u, \mathcal{T})$ is in the kernel if u is in the nucleolus.   QED

COROLLARY   *Let (N, v) be a game in characteristic function form. (N, v) has a nonempty bargaining set, and, for each coalition structure $\mathcal{T}$, there is a payoff configuration in the bargaining set.*

Proof   This corollary follows from Theorems 6.1 to 6.3. By Theorem 6.2 $\text{nuc}[A_{\mathcal{T}}(N, v)]$ is not empty, because it is compact. Compactness follows from two things: First, the payoff space is bounded because the $v(K)$ are finite. Second, $I_{\mathcal{T}}(N, v)$ is, by definition, closed; hence $A_{\mathcal{T}}(N, v)$ is also closed. By Theorem 6.3, $u \in \text{nuc}[A_{\mathcal{T}}(N, v)]$ implies that $(u, \mathcal{T})$ is in the kernel, and by Theorem 6.1 the kernel is in the bargaining set. Thus $(u, \mathcal{T})$ is in the bargaining set. That there is a point in the nucleolus for any coalition structure follows from $\text{nuc}[A_{\mathcal{T}}(N, v)]$ being nonempty.   QED

5.3.4   *The nucleolus of S-equivalent games*

The nucleolus is defined with reference to both a game and a set of outcomes. Thus $\text{nuc}(X)$ is the nucleolus over the set of outcomes X that are a subset of the outcomes that can be achieved in some particular game (N, v). In speaking of "the nucleolus of a game (N, v)" it would be natural to mean $\text{nuc}(X)$ for that game with X being the set of achievable outcomes. In fact, it is sufficient to examine $\text{nuc}[I(N, v)]$, the nucleolus over the set of imputations of the game, $I(N, v)$. Now let (N, v^*) be a zero-one normalized game and consider the *S-equivalence class of (N, v^*)*. This class is the set of games that have (N, v^*) as their zero-one normalized form. The nucleolus of each of the members of this set of games are related by equation (6.13).

LEMMA 6.7   *Let (N, v) be S-equivalent to the zero-one normalized game (N, v^*).*

Then $u \in nuc[I(N, v)]$ *if and only if* $u^* \in nuc[I(N, v^*)]$ *where* u *and* u^* *are related by*

$$u_i^* = \frac{u_1 - v(\{i\})}{v(N) - \sum\limits_{i \in N} v(\{i\})} \tag{6.23}$$

Proof For any $u \in I(N, v)$, there is exactly one $u^* \in I(N, v^*)$ that is related to u by equation (6.23). Conversely, for each $u^* \in I(N, v^*)$, there is one corresponding $u \in I(N, v)$. These facts are clear from the definition of S-equivalence. For such a pair, $e(K, u^*)$ is given by

$$e(K, u^*) = \frac{v(K) - \sum\limits_{i \in K} v(\{i\}) - \sum\limits_{i \in K} [u_i - v(\{i\})]}{v(N) - \sum\limits_{i \in N} v(\{i\})}$$

$$= \frac{v(K) - \sum\limits_{i \in K} u_i}{v(N) - \sum\limits_{i \in N} v(\{i\})} \tag{6.24}$$

Now let $u, w \in I(N, v)$ and let u^* and w^* be the corresponding elements of $I(N, v^*)$, related by equation (6.23). Then, from equation (6.24), it follows that $\theta(u) \leq_L \theta(w)$ if and only if $\theta(u^*) \leq_L \theta(w^*)$, which proves the lemma. QED

5.4 Examples

Two three-person game examples are described below for which the nucleolus over the set of imputations is given, and corresponding payoff configurations in the kernel and bargaining set are given. In the first game, $v(K)$ is defined by $v(\{i\}) = 0$ for all $i \in N$, $v(\{1, 2\}) = 4$, $v(\{1, 3\}) = 2$, $v(\{2, 3\}) = 3$, and $v(N) = 6$. The payoff vector $(2, 3, 1)$ is the only element of the nucleolus over $I(N, v)$, the set of imputations. The excesses of $u = (2, 3, 1)$ are $e(\{1\}, u) = -2$, $e(\{2\}, u) = -3$, $e(\{3\}, u) = -1$, $e(K, u) = -.5$ for each two-person coalition, and the excess is zero for both N and $\varnothing$. This gives $\theta(2, 3, 1) = (0, 0, -.5, -.5, -.5, -1, -2, -3)$. For any other imputation, u', the excesses of the three two-person coalitions would still sum to -1.5, but at least one of the coalitions would have an excess greater than $-.5$. This would make the third coordinate of $\theta(u')$ larger than $-.5$ without changing the first two coordinates; therefore, $\theta(2, 3, 1) <_L \theta(u')$ for such a u'. Note, too, that if we consider the set of all individually rational payoffs, any such u' that is not an imputation would also have a vector of excesses that is lexicographically larger than $\theta(2, 3, 1)$, because $e(N, u')$ would be strictly positive. The payoff configuration $((2, 3, 1), \{1, 2, 3\})$ is in the kernel and the bargaining set.

For the second example, let $v(N) = 4$ and let the characteristic function be otherwise unchanged from the preceding example. The payoff vector $(2, 2, 0)$ is in $nuc[I(N, v)]$. The argument to support this claim is similar to that used in the first example: The excesses are -2 for the coalitions $\{1\}$,

$\{2\}$, $\{1,3\}$, and $\{2,3\}$ and zero for all remaining coalitions. Thus $\theta(2,2,0) = (0,\ 0,\ 0,\ 0,\ -2,\ -2,\ -2,\ -2)$. If $u \in I(N,v)$ is chosen with $u_1 + u_2$ less than 4, then $e(\{1,2\}, u)$ is strictly positive; therefore, $\theta(u) >_L \theta(2,2,0)$ and only $(2,2,0)$ is in the nucleolus. The payoff configuration $((2,2,0), \{1,2\}, \{3\})$ is in the kernel and the bargaining set.

6 The Shapley value and the Banzhaf index

The Shapley (1953b) value can be calculated for any superadditive game (N, v) in characteristic function form having a finite number of players, and it has the further advantage of giving a unique outcome that satisfies both individual rationality and group rationality. The payoff to each player is a weighted average of the contributions that the player makes to each of the coalitions to which she belongs with the weights depending on the number of players, n, and the number of members in each coalition. Another appealing aspect of the Shapley value is that it can be characterized by three easily understood conditions.

The Shapley value is defined in Section 6.1, and in Section 6.2 its existence and uniqueness are shown. Section 6.3 looks at the Banzhaf power index, which is defined for simple games and is somewhat similar to the Shapley value.

6.1 Description of the Shapley value

The value itself is denoted $\phi(v)$ where $\phi(v) \in R^n$ and $\phi_i(v)$ is the Shapley value payoff to the ith player. The formula is:

$$\phi_i(v) = \sum_{K \subset N} [v(K) - v(K \backslash \{i\})] \frac{(k-1)! \, (n-k)!}{n!} \tag{6.25}$$

The Shapley value is defined by four conditions, given in Definition 6.25, and following the definition, it is proved that the conditions imply that the Shapley value is characterized by the formula in equation (6.25). The four conditions are (a) group rationality, $\sum_{i \in N} \phi_i(v) = v(N)$, (b) if a player, i, adds nothing more than $v(\{i\})$ to any coalition, then the player receives only $v(\{i\})$, (c) if two games are identical except for the order in which the players are listed, then the Shapley values for the players are the same, and (d) if a game is formed by adding two games together, then the Shapley value of the new game is the sum of the values of the two original games. To formally state condition (c) above, it is necessary to say what is meant by two games that differ only with respect to the order of the players. This is done in Definition 6.24.

DEFINITION 6.24 *Let i^* and j^* be a specific pair of players and suppose the games (N, v) and (N', v') are related in the following way: (a) $n = n'$, (b) $v(K) = v'(K)$ if $i^*, j^* \in K$ or if $i^*, j^* \notin K$, and (c) $v(K \cup \{i^*\}) = v'(K \cup \{j^*\})$ if $i^*, j^* \notin K$. Then (N, v) is a **simple permutation** of (N', v'). Players i^* and j^* are the **permuted players**.*

The conditions defining the Shapley value are enumerated below in Definition 6.25. These conditions are sometimes called the *Shapley axioms*.

DEFINITION 6.25   *For a game* $\Gamma = (N, v)$ *the* **Shapley value** $\phi(v)$ *is defined by*:

(a) $\sum_{i \in N} \phi_i(v) = v(N)$.

(b) *If, for some* $i \in N$, $v(K) = v(K \backslash \{i\}) + v(\{i\})$ *for all* $K \subset N, i \in K$ *then* $\phi_i(v) = v(\{i\})$.

(c) *If* (N, v) *is a simple permutation of* (N', v') *with* i^* *and* j^* *being the permuted players, then* $\phi_{i*}(v) = \phi_{j*}(v')$, $\phi_{i*}(v') = \phi_{j*}(v)$, *and, for all* $i \in N \backslash \{i^*, j^*\}$, $\phi_i(v) = \phi_i(v')$.

(d) *If* (N, v) *and* (N, w) *are two games having the same player set* N, *and* (N, z) *is defined by* $z(K) = v(K) + w(K)$ *for all* $K \subset N$, *then* $\phi(z) = \phi(v) + \phi(w)$.

It is surprising that the four conditions enumerated in Definition 6.25 are enough to determine a unique payoff vector. The first asserts group rationality. The second requires that a player i who contributes only $v(\{i\})$ to each coalition must get a payoff of $v(\{i\})$. The third condition is a symmetry condition in the sense that it forces the solution point payoffs to depend on the structure of $v(K)$, but not on how the individual players are numbered. If, for example, a game (N, v) is rearranged in the sense that Al, who is player 1, is to become player i_1, and Betty, who is player 2, is to become player i_2, and so forth, the solution point payoffs to the players in the new game are the same as in the old game. That is, the new game (N', v') is to have the feature that $v(\{\text{Al, Betty, George}\}) = v'(\{\text{Al, Betty, George}\})$, and so on for all coalitions; and $\phi_{\text{Al}}(v) = \phi_{\text{Al}}(v')$, and so forth for all coalitions. The final condition requires a natural consistency among triplets of games that are related in the manner that the games (N, v), (N, w), and (N, z) are related. If the characteristic function z equals the sum of the characteristic functions v and w, then $\phi(z) = \phi(v) + \phi(w)$.

6.2   Existence of the Shapley value

Proof of existence and uniqueness of the Shapley value is done in several steps. In Section 6.2.1, existence is proved for simple games. This is useful, because in Section 6.2.2 it is shown that any game can be treated like a sum of simple games, and the Shapley value for a game that is the sum of several games is the sum of their respective Shapley values.

6.2.1   The Shapley value for simple games

To prove the existence of a Shapley value and to derive its expression, a handy concept to use is the *marginal value of a coalition*, which is defined recursively, as follows:

$$c_{\{i\}}(v) = v(\{i\}) \qquad \text{for all } i \in N \qquad (6.26)$$

$$c_K(v) = v(K) - \sum_{\substack{L \subset K \\ L \neq K}} c_L(v) \qquad \text{for all } K \subset N \text{ with } k \geqslant 2 \qquad (6.27)$$

Thus the marginal value of a coalition K is $v(K)$ minus the marginal values of all conditions that are both smaller than K and are subsets of K. Equation (6.27) can be rewritten as

$$c_K(v) = \sum_{L \subset K} (-1)^{k-l} v(L) \qquad \text{for } K \subset N \qquad (6.28)$$

Deriving existence of the unique Shapley value is accomplished by showing that a game (N, v) can be regarded as a weighted sum of a number of simple games (N, v_K) defined as follows:

$$v_K(L) = 1 \qquad \text{if } K \subset L \text{ and} \qquad v_K(L) = 0 \text{ otherwise} \qquad (6.29)$$

The game (N, cv), for a scalar c, has a characteristic function $cv(K)$.

LEMMA 6.8 *For the game* (N, cv_K), *the Shapley value is* $\phi_i(cv_K) = c/k$ *if* $i \in K$ *and* $\phi_i(cv_K) = 0$ *if* $i \notin K$.

Proof If $i \notin K$, then by (b) of Definition 6.25, $\phi_i(cv_K) = 0$, and if $i \in K$, $\phi_i(cv_K) = c/k$ by condition (c). QED

6.2.2 *The Shapley value for superadditive games*

Extending Lemma 6.8 to general superadditive games is accomplished by showing that any characteristic function can be represented as a weighted sum of characteristic functions for simple games. This is done in Lemma 6.9. Next, in Lemma 6.10, it is seen that if a characteristic function equals one characteristic function minus another, then the Shapley value for this game is also the one characteristic function minus the other.

LEMMA 6.9 *The characteristic function,* v, *of a game* (N, v) *satisfies*

$$v = \sum_{\substack{K \subset N \\ L \neq \varnothing}} c_K(v) v_K \qquad (6.30)$$

where the function $c_K(v)$ *is defined by equation* (6.28) *and the* v_K *are defined by equation* (6.29).

Proof Proving the lemma requires showing that

$$v(K) = \sum_{\substack{L \subset K \\ L \neq \varnothing}} c_L(v) v_L(K) \qquad \text{for all } K \subset N \qquad (6.31)$$

Using equation (6.28) in equation (6.31) gives

$$v(K) = \sum_{L \subset K} \sum_{M \subset L} (-1)^{l-m} v(M)$$

$$= \sum_{M \subset K} \left[\sum_{l=m}^{k} (-1)^{l-m} \frac{(k-m)!}{(l-m)!\,(k-l)!} \right] v(M) \qquad (6.32)$$

The term in brackets in equation (6.32) is always zero when $m < k$; therefore, equation (6.32) reduces to $v(K) = v(K)$ which establishes the lemma. QED

LEMMA 6.10   *Let (N, v), (N, w), and (N, z) be games where $z = v - w$. Then $\phi(z) = \phi(v) - \phi(w)$.*

Proof   This follows from Definition (6.25d).   QED

THEOREM 6.4   *A superadditive game has a unique Shapley value given by*

$$\phi_i(v) = \sum_{K \subset N} [v(K) - v(K \setminus \{i\})] \frac{(k-1)! \, (n-k)!}{n!}, \qquad i \in N \qquad (6.33)$$

Proof   Using Lemmas 6.8 and 6.10 in equation (6.31) gves

$$\phi_i(v) = \sum_{\substack{K \subset N \\ i \in K}} \frac{c_K(v)}{k}, \qquad i \in N \qquad (6.34)$$

And using equation (6.28) in equation (6.34), the latter becomes

$$\phi_i(v) = \sum_{\substack{K \subset N \\ i \in K}} \frac{1}{k} \left[\sum_{K \supset L} (-1)^{k-l} v(L) \right]$$

$$= \sum_{K \supset L} \sum_{K \subset N} \frac{(-1)^{k-l}}{k} [v(L) - v(L \setminus \{i\})]$$

$$= \sum_{l=0}^{n-k} \frac{(-1)^l (n-k)!}{(k+l)(n-k-l)! \, l!} [v(K) - v(K \setminus \{i\})] \qquad (6.35)$$

To evaluate the coefficient of $[v(K) - v(K \setminus \{i\})]$, denote $(n-k)!/[(n-k-l)! \, l!]$ by C_l^{n-k} and note

$$\sum_{l=0}^{n-k} \frac{(-1)^l}{k+l} C_l^{n-k} = \sum_{l=0}^{n-k} (-1)^l C_l^{n-k} \int_0^1 x^{k+l-1} \, dx$$

$$= \int_0^1 \sum_{l=0}^{n} (-1)^l C_l^{n-1} x^{k+l-1} \, dx$$

$$= \int_0^1 x^{k-1} \sum_{l=0}^{n} (-1)^l C_l^{n-k} x^l \, dx$$

$$= \int_0^1 x^{k-1} (1-x)^{n-k} \, dx = \frac{(k-1)! \, (n-k)!}{n!} \qquad (6.36)$$

Using equation (6.36) in equation (6.35) completes the proof.   QED

As an exercise, the reader might wish to prove that if (N, v) has the zero-one normalized form (N, v^*), and u is the Shapley value of (N, v), then the Shapley value of (N, v^*) is given by equation (6.13). Table 6.1 contains a game in characteristic function form, along with information useful in computing the Shapley value for the game.

TABLE 6.1 A four-person game and its Shapley value

Coalition	$v(K)$	kC_k^n	$v(K) - v(K\backslash\{i\}$ for Player 1	2	3	4
$\{1\}$	0	4	0	0	0	0
$\{2\}$	0	4	0	0	0	0
$\{3\}$	0	4	0	0	0	0
$\{4\}$	0	4	0	0	0	0
$\{1, 2\}$	2	12	2	2	0	0
$\{1, 3\}$	5	12	5	0	5	0
$\{1, 4\}$	3	12	3	0	0	3
$\{2, 3\}$	6	12	0	6	6	0
$\{2, 4\}$	8	12	0	8	0	8
$\{3, 4\}$	5	12	0	0	5	5
$\{1, 2, 3\}$	7	12	1	2	5	0
$\{1, 2, 4\}$	11	12	3	8	0	9
$\{1, 3, 4\}$	9	12	4	0	6	4
$\{2, 3, 4\}$	10	12	0	5	2	4
$\{1, 2, 3, 4\}$	15	4	5	6	4	8

Shapley value: $\phi_1 = \dfrac{33}{12}$, $\phi_2 = \dfrac{49}{12}$, $\phi_3 = \dfrac{41}{12}$, $\phi_4 = \dfrac{57}{12}$

6.3 The Banzhaf power index

The Banzhaf (1965) index is defined for simple games and is based on counting, for each player, the number of coalitions for which the player is crucial to winning. Let (N, v) be a zero-one normalized simple game and recall from Definition 6.11 that a winning coalition is one for which $v(K) = 1$ and a losing coalition is one for which $v(K) = 0$. Each coalition K that wins when $K\backslash\{i\}$ loses is called a *swing* for player i, because the membership of player i in the coalition is crucial to the coalition winning. For a game (N, v) let $\sigma_i(N, v)$ be the number of swings for i, and let $\sigma_0(N, v) = \sum_{i \in N} \sigma_i(N, v)$ be the total number of swings of all players in the game. Then the normalized Banzhaf index is $b_i(N, v) = \sigma_i(N, v)/\sigma_0(N, v)$.

The Banzhaf index can be generalized to nonsimple games. On this, see Owen (1978) who also provides axioms for the index that are along the lines of the conditions defining the Shapley value. The generalization is by the formula $b_i(N, v) = \sum_{K \subset N} [v(K) - v(K\backslash\{i\})]/(2^{n-1})$. This formula has in common with the Shapley value that a player's value is computed as a weighted sum of his marginal contributions to all the coalitions of which he is a member; however, the Banzhaf weights are different from the Shapley weights. For Banzhaf, all coalitions are weighted equally, no matter what their size, while the Shapley value weights vary with the size of the coalition.

7   An application to power in government

Table 6.2 shows the Shapley and Banzhaf values for several related games that have interesting interpretations relating to the U.S. govenment. To pass a law at the federal level, it is necessary to have a bare majority in the House of Representatives, a bare majority in the Senate, and the agreement of the president. A second way to pass a law requires a larger two-thirds majority in both the House and Senate, but does not require the agreement of the president. Suppose that a coalition K having the power to pass a law has a characteristic function value of $v(K) = 1$ and that any other coalition L has a value $v(L) = 0$.

The table contains the Shapley and Banzhaf values for three sets of rules. The rules differ only with respect to the votes needed to override a presidential veto. With the president's agreement, only a bare majority of both houses is needed in each case. The Shapley and Banzhaf values for the

TABLE 6.2   The Shapley and Banzhaf power indexes for an election game

Shapley 1	Total	With president	Without president	Single value	Total value
House	40	21	22	.0118	.4704
Senate	15	8	9	.0324	.4857
President				.0439	
Shapley 2					
House	40	21	27	.0119	.4741
Senate	15	8	10	.0261	.3914
President				.1345	
Shapley 3					
House	40	21	40	.0076	.3022
Senate	15	8	15	.0187	.2797
President				.4181	

Banzhaf 1	Total	With president	Without president	Single value	Total value
House	40	21	22	.0152	.6092
Senate	15	8	9	.0235	.3525
President				.0383	
Banzhaf 2					
House	40	21	27	.0146	.5852
Senate	15	8	10	.0212	.3176
President				.0972	
Banzhaf 3					
House	40	21	40	.0145	.5806
Senate	15	8	15	.0212	.3182
President				.1012	

situation approximating the U.S. government rules are in the table as Shapley 2 and Banzhaf 2. These calculations are done on the basis of a 40-member House and 15-member Senate, which, of course, are not the actual sizes of these two bodies. Thus $v(K) = 1$ if K includes 21 or more House members plus 8 or more Senate members plus the president, and $v(K) = 1$ if K includes 27 or more House members plus 10 or more senators. Otherwise, $v(K) = 0$.

Note that the Banzhaf value accords much less weight to the president: .1345 for Shapley versus .0972 for Banzhaf, because the Banzhaf value weights each coalition equally, whereas, the Shapley value weights a coalition inversely to the number of coalitions that exist of the given size. Because the president is crucial, on the whole, in smaller winning coalitions (because with the president, many fewer House and Senate members are needed), the Shapley value will favor him relative to the Banzhaf value.

Shapley 1 and Banzhaf 1 are based on different rules for overriding a veto. The president's power is greatly reduced by allowing only 22 House members with 9 senators to override a presidential veto. Correspondingly, the Shapley value for the president is .0439, roughly a third of the Shapley 2 value, and the Banzhaf value is .0383, also greatly reduced and, of course, less than the corresponding Shapley value. Curiously, in both cases, most of the power lost by the president is gained by the Senate. The power of the House is changed very little.

This may be contrasted with Shapley 3 and Banzhaf 3 where, without the president, all members of both House and Senate are required to pass a law. The president's power, of course, rises, but the two indices behave very differently. The Shapley value of the president rises from .1345 to .4181, nearly threefold, but the Banzhaf value goes up only slightly.

In circumstances such as those of the example, the two indices are often called power indices, the idea being that the sum of the values across players is 1, and the value of a particular player or coalition gives the slice of total power wielded by that player or coalition. Individuals must decide for themselves whether they find such an interpretation congenial.

8 Conclusions

In this chapter, various cooperative game solutions have been examined for transferable utility games in characteristic function form. The solutions fall into several interesting categories. First, the core is based on criteria with which it is difficult to quarrel. A point is in the core if it gives to each player and coalition at least as much as that player or coalition could guarantee for itself. These minimal criteria are both too much and too little; too much because the core in many games can be very large, and too little because there are many games that have no core. Also, the core leaves one with little sense of how bargaining processes might proceed and affect the outcome.

The stable set goes a little way toward remedying the undesirable aspects of the core. It seems a bit more connected with the bargaining process, and, for many more games than for the core, the stable set is not empty. But, as with the core, the stable set can include very many points, and, additionally, a game can have more than one stable set.

The bargaining set gets closer to the bargaining process than the stable set. As with all solution concepts in Chapters 6 and 7, the bargaining process is not formally modeled, but the definition of a solution can be suggestive as to the kind of bargaining that might be expected in the background. With the bargaining set, players are conceived as being divided into coalitions, and whether a particular payoff vector is a solution payoff depends on the coalition structure, $\mathcal{T}$, that accompanies it. Thus one considers pairs, $(u, \mathcal{T})$, and, to some extent players are locked into the coalition structure $\mathcal{T}$. The bargaining set gets closer to the bargaining process and it exists for a large class of games, but, like the core and the stable set, there can be many possible outcomes in the solution.

The kernel and the nucleolus are related to the bargaining set, and the kernel, in particular, shares much with it. The nucleolus is unique when the coalition structure is given and the set of payoff vectors being considered is convex. In essence, the nucleolus gives a method for picking one element from the bargaining set among the elements in the bargaining set that are associated with a given coalition structure $\mathcal{T}$. One must decide whether the criterion used for choosing this element is appealing.

The Shapley value goes in a quite different direction. It has little to say about bargaining processes, but is, instead, based on conditions that are, and are meant to be, reasonable. The value exists and is unique for a large class of games, but, again, one must decide whether the conditions that define it are ultimately acceptable. Like the core, the Shapley value outcome seems based on an action by the coalition of the whole, with lesser coalitions never forming, but, nonetheless, affecting the outcome. Nothing has the status quo nature that the coalition structure has for the bargaining set.

In sum, then, these cooperative game solutions are quite diverse and no one commands the field; yet each has appealing features.

Exercises

1. Suppose a three-person game with the characteristic function $v(\{1\}) = 5$, $v(\{2\}) = 8$, $v(\{3\}) = 4$, $v(\{1, 2\}) = 15$, $v(\{1, 3\}) = 20$, $v(\{2, 3\}) = 15$, $v(\{1, 2, 3\}) = 30$.
   a. Find a point in the core of this game.
   b. What is the zero-one normalization of this game?
   c. Assuming that superadditivity must hold and that the $v(K)$ are fixed for all $K \neq N$, what is the lowest value to which $v(N)$ can be changed? If $v(N)$ is changed to this value, is the core empty or nonempty?
2. Calculate the Shapley value for the game in part (a) of problem 1. Is the Shapley value in the core?

3. Is superadditivity either necessary or sufficient for a nonempty core?
4. Prove that the following is a necessary condition for a nonempty core: Let $(T_1, \ldots, T_m)$ be any partition of N. Then $v(N) \geqslant \sum_{i=1}^{m} v(K)$.

Notes

1. In some of the earlier literature, coalition K is called a *blocking coalition* and is said to *block x*.
2. Let K and L be coalitions, each of which contains at least one player who is not in the other coalition. Lemmas 6.5 and 6.6 can be easily extended to any simple game in which K and L are both winning.
3. These specifications on placing K^* are not restrictions on the model; they make the remainder of the proof easier to state without affecting the substance.

7

n-Person cooperative games without transferable utility

This chapter generalizes Chapters 5 and 6 in the sense that the models studied here are *n* person, going beyond the two-person setting of the former, and assume nontransferable utility, which expands on the latter. Just as some of the models of Chapter 5 do not have counterparts in Chapter 6, not all models from either of the preceding chapters have counterparts in the current chapter. In particular, the major topics presented below are on the core and on a generalized Shapley value for nontransferable utility games.

1 Introduction to nontransferable utility games

In Section 1.1, some remarks are made to help clarify the difference between transferable and nontransferable utility. The difference is further highlighted in Section 2 where the characteristic function is redefined to capture the concept of nontransferable utility. Section 1.2 gives an overview of the remaining sections of the chapter.

1.1 A brief comparison of transferable and nontransferable utility

Transferable utility is an unwelcome assumption to make in many economic situations. For example, where two or more consumers are involved, transferable utility requires that there must be a commodity with respect to which the utility of each consumer is linear and that enters into each consumer's utility function separately from other commodities. Where x_i, y_i and z_i are amounts of three goods, X, Y, and Z, the utility function of each consumer, i, needs to be of the form $u_i(x_i, y_i, z_i) = x_i + w_i(y_i, z_i)$. Transferable utility is built into this formulation because all players' utility functions are separably linear in the same good X; thus one person can increase the utility of any other person by one unit at a cost of just one unit to himself. Sometimes the commodity X that plays this special role is called *money* and it is said that a unit of money is equivalent to a unit of utility for each person. While this might be acceptable in some circumstances, one would be reluctant to have all results in economics based on such a condition. Fortunately, some of the cooperative game solutions examined in Chapter 6 can be restated for models lacking the transferable utility restriction, and others can be generalized.

1.2 Overview of the chapter

This chapter explores some of these nontransferable utility models. As a first step, Section 2 deals with the reformulation of the characteristic function; for, when transferable utility is given up, it is no longer possible to describe the payoffs available to a particular coalition as a sum of utility that the group can guarantee. Instead, each coalition K has a set of k-dimensional payoff vectors in R^k that it can achieve. It is easily seen in Section 2 that the characteristic function for a transferable utility game is a special case of the characteristic function for a nontransferable utility game. The remaining sections look at the solutions that were examined in Chapter 6; however, not all of them will be seen to carry over. In Section 3, the core is redefined in terms of the generalized characteristic function and a theorem is stated and proved on existence of a nonempty core. Redefining the core is easy and natural, but the existence proof becomes a much more formidable task than was the case for transferable utility. Section 4 looks at the stable set, which is easily recast. In Section 5, the bargaining set, kernel, and nucleolus are briefly discussed. Section 6 deals with a generalization of the Shapley value to the nontransferable utility case. Section 7 contains applications of the core, and Section 8 contains concluding comments.

2 The characteristic function and other basic tools

The characteristic function for nontransferable utility games is defined in Section 2.1. Following that, imputations and domination are defined with reference to the newly recast characteristic function. Then, in Section 2.2 a class of games called *balanced games* is defined. This class of games plays an important role in Section 3 where it is proved that balanced games have nonempty cores.

2.1 Imputations, domination, and the characteristic function

The characteristic function for a nontransferable utility game must specify all obtainable payoff vectors for each coalition, and this must be done by actually specifying a set of payoff vectors. Note, for example, that the ability of the coalition $\{1, 2, 3\}$ to attain the payoff $(4, 8, 12)$ does not, in the absence of transferable utility, impart any information on that coalition's ability to achieve, say $(5, 9, 10)$, a payoff vector whose component payoffs also sum to 24. On the one hand, this second payoff vector could be beyond the set of payoffs that $\{1, 2, 3\}$ can reach, or, on the other, it may be interior to the coalition's attainable set of payoffs even if $(4, 8, 12)$ is on the frontier of that set. Letting $V(K)$ denote the characteristic function, $V(K)$ is the *set* of all k-dimensional vectors of payoffs that the coalition K can guarantee to itself. As with the games of Chapter 6, there is a payoff that each player, i, can guarantee himself. As before, it is denoted u_i, and $V(\{i\}) = \{u_i\}$ for all $i \in N$.

Suppose, for example, that the three-player game where any two or three players can dictate the division of \$100 is being examined, and assume that the utility for money of each of the three players is $U_1(x_1) = \ln(x_1 + 1)$ for player 1, $U_2(x_2) = \sqrt{x_2}$ for player 2, and $U_3(x_3) = -1/(x_3 + 2)$ for player 3. Then $V(\{1\}) = \{0\}$, $V(\{2\}) = \{0\}$, and $V(\{3\}) = \{-.5\}$. For the coalition $K = \{1, 2\}$, $V(K)$ consists of all utility pairs that can be obtained by distributing between 0 and \$100 the two players. That is,

$$V(\{1, 2\}) = \{(u_1, u_2) \mid u_1 = \ln(x_1 + 1), u_2 = \sqrt{x_2}, 0 \leqslant x_1, x_2, \text{ and}$$
$$x_1 + x_2 \leqslant 100\} \quad (7.1)$$

This set is depicted in Figure 7.1 and its upper right boundary is given by the equation $u_2 = (101 - e^{u_1})^{.5}$.

If x is a payoff vector in R^n, then x^K denotes the k-dimensional payoff vector for coalition K implied by x. Thus $x^K = (x_{i_1}, x_{i_2}, \ldots, x_{i_k})$ where $K = \{i_1, i_2, \ldots, i_k\}$. A transferable utility game can have its characteristic

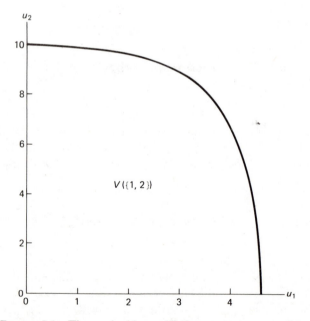

FIGURE 7.1   The attainable payoffs for a two-person coalition.

function represented by a set function $V(K)$; however, such a set function is related to $v(K)$ by the rule

$$V(K) = \{x^K \in R^k \mid x_i \geq v(\{i\}), i \in K, \sum_{i \in K} x_i \leq v(K)\} \qquad (7.2)$$

Thus, for example, $V(\{1, 2\})$ in a transferable utility game is always a right triangle with vertices at $(\underline{u}_1, \underline{u}_2)$, $(\underline{u}_1 + v(\{1, 2\}), \underline{u}_2)$, and $(\underline{u}_1, \underline{u}_2 + v(\{1, 2\}))$. Parallel to the practice in Chapter 6, a game in characteristic function form will be denoted $\Gamma = (N, V)$.

DEFINITION 7.1 *The* **characteristic function** $V(K)$ *for a nontransferable utility game* (N, V) *is a set valued function where, for each coalition K, $V(K)$ is the set of all payoff vectors u^K that the coalition K can achieve and which satisfies the condition $u_i^K \geq \underline{u}_i$ for all $i \in K$.*

Imputations are defined essentially as in Chapter 6. They consist of all payoff vectors in $V(N)$ that are not strongly dominated. That is, $u \in I(N, V)$ if $u \in V(N)$ and there is no $u' \in V(N)$ for which $u \ll u'$.

DEFINITION 7.2 *A payoff vector $u \in V(N)$ is an* **imputation** *in the game $\Gamma = (N, V)$ if there is no $u' \in V(N)$ such that $u_i < u_i'$ for all $i \in N$. The set of imputations is denoted $I(N, V)$.*

Domination can also be defined in the present setting. The idea remains the same: That one payoff vector dominates another via the coalition K if the first vector gives more to each player in K than does the second, and if the first vector is attainable by K.

DEFINITION 7.3 *For $x, y \in I(N, V)$, y* **dominates** *x* **via** *K if $y^K \gg x^K$ and $y^K \in V(K)$.*

DEFINITION 7.4 *y* **dominates** *x if, for some coalition K, y dominates x via K.*

2.2 Balanced games

Balanced games are important because it can be proved that such games have nonempty cores. This is done in Section 3. Balanced games are defined in relation to *balanced collections of coalitions*. In a game (N, V) there are 2^{n-1} possible coalitions, not counting the null coalition, $\emptyset$. A collection of coalitions is a subset of this family of coalitions. For example, in a game with four players, the set of (nonempty) coalitions is $W = \{\{1\}, \{2\}, \{3\}, \{4\}, \{1, 2\}, \{1, 3\}, \{1, 4\}, \{2, 3\}, \{2, 4\}, \{3, 4\}, \{1, 2, 3\}, \{1, 2, 4\}, \{1, 3, 4\}, \{2, 3, 4\}, \{1, 2, 3, 4\}\}$, and a collection of coalitions is a subset of W such as $W_1 = \{\{1\}, \{4\}, \{1, 3\}, \{2, 3, 4\}, \{2, 3\}\}$ or $W_2 = \{\{2\}, \{3\}, \{1, 4\}, \{2, 4\}, \{3, 4\}, \{1, 2, 3\}\}$. A collection of coalitions is balanced if it is possible to assign a positive number to each coalition in the collection so that the assigned numbers add to unity when summed over the coalitions to which any one player belongs.

DEFINITION 7.5 *Let W be the set of coalitions in the game $\Gamma = (N, V)$ and let W_1*

be a subset of W. W_1 is a **balanced collection of coalitions** *if there are* numbers $\delta_K > 0$, $K \in W_1$ *such that* $\sum_{\{K \in W_1 | i \in K\}} \delta_K = 1$ *for each* $i \in N$.

For example, $W_1 = \{\{1\}, \{4\}, \{1, 3\}, \{2, 3, 4\}, \{2, 3\}\}$ is not a balanced collection, but W_2 is. To see that $W_2 = \{\{2\}, \{3\}, \{1, 4\}, \{2, 4\}, \{3, 4\}, \{1, 2, 3\}\}$ is balanced, let

$$\delta_{\{2\}} = \frac{1}{6} \qquad \delta_{\{3\}} = \frac{1}{12} \qquad \delta_{\{1,4\}} = \frac{5}{12}$$

$$\delta_{\{2,4\}} = \frac{1}{4} \qquad \delta_{\{3,4\}} = \frac{1}{3} \qquad \delta_{\{1,2,3\}} = \frac{7}{12}$$

Summing the weights for the coalitions containing player 1 yields $\frac{5}{12} + \frac{7}{12} = 1$, doing the same for player 2 yields $\frac{1}{6} + \frac{1}{4} + \frac{7}{12} = 1$, for player 3 yields $\frac{1}{12} + \frac{1}{3} + \frac{7}{12} = 1$, and, finally, for player 4 yields $\frac{5}{12} + \frac{1}{4} + \frac{1}{3} = 1$. To see that W_1 is not balanced, note that positive numbers must be found so that $\delta_{\{2,3\}} + \delta_{\{2,3,4\}} = 1$ (this sum is over the coalitions containing player 2) and $\delta_{\{1,3\}} + \delta_{\{2,3\}} + \delta_{\{2,3,4\}} = 1$ (this sum is over the coalitions containing player 3). It is impossible to find three such positive numbers, which shows that W_1 is not a balanced collection.

A *balanced game* is a game in which a special relationship exists between $V(N)$ and the $V(K)$; however, this special relationship needs to hold only with respect to balanced collections of coalitions. To see the gist of this relationship, suppose $u \in R^n$ is a payoff vector and W_1 represents any balanced collection of coalitions. Then if $u^K \in V(K)$ for all K in any balanced collection W_1, it is required that $u \in V(N)$.

DEFINITION 7.6 *A game* $\Gamma = (N, V)$ *is* **balanced** *if* $u \in V(N)$ *whenever, for any balanced collection* W_1 *and any* $K \in W_1$, $u^K \in V(K)$.

With these basics in hand, attention can turn to the core.

3   The core

This section is further divided into several subsections. The assumptions that are of primary interest are listed and discussed in Section 3.1 where the core is also defined. In order to prove the core of a game in this class is not empty, a more restricted class of games is examined in Section 3.2. It is proved that this smaller class has a core, and then, in Section 3.3, the result is extended to the games described in Section 3.1.

3.1   The assumptions and the definition of the core

The class of games to be considered here is described by Assumptions 7.1 to 7.4, which specify that (a) there be a finite number of players, (b) the sets $V(K)$ be nonempty and compact, (c) that any payoff vector in $V(K)$ can be altered by reducing a player's payoff, and the resulting payoff vector is still in $V(K)$ if the player's payoff is not reduced below $\underline{u}_i$, and (d) the game is balanced.

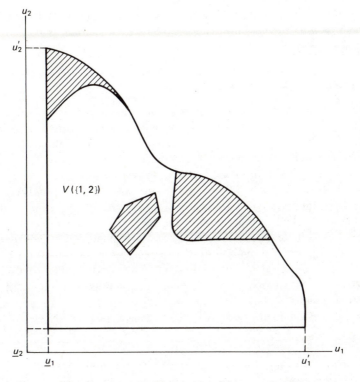

FIGURE 7.2   An illustration of Assumption 7.3.

ASSUMPTION 7.1   *In the game (N, V) the number of players is finite.*

ASSUMPTION 7.2   *In the game (N, V), for each $K \subset N$, $V(K)$ is nonempty and compact. For each $i \in N$, $V(\{i\}) = \{\underline{u}_i\}$, and, for any $u^K \in V(K)$, $u^K \geq \underline{u}^K$.*

ASSUMPTION 7.3   *In the game (N, V) if $u^K \in V(K)$ and $\underline{u}^K \leq u'^K \leq u^K$, then $u'^K \in V(K)$.*

ASSUMPTION 7.4   *The game (N, V) is balanced.*

Figure 7.2 illustrates Assumption 7.3 for a two-player coalition. The assumption would be violated if any of the three shaded regions were not part of $V(\{1, 2\})$. For this two-player coalition, Assumption 7.3 implies that $V(\{1, 2\})$ is bounded below by a horizontal line through $\underline{u}_2$, on the left by a vertical line through $\underline{u}_1$, and above and to the right by a curve from $(\underline{u}_1, u_2^*)$ to $(u_1^*, \underline{u}_2)$ that never slopes upward. Assumption 7.3 is sometimes called a *free disposal* assumption, because it is analogous to economic axioms of that name. The core is defined essentially as in Chapter 6:

DEFINITION 7.7   *The **core** of the game (N, V), denoted $C(N, V)$, is the subset of the set of imputations consisting of imputations that are not dominated.*

As in Chapter 6, u is in the core of the game (N, V) if it is both group and individually rational (i.e., $u \in I(N, V)$), and if it gives to each coalition at least as much as the coalition can assure itself (i.e., there is no $x^K \in V(K)$ such that $x^K \gg u^K$).

3.2 The core for a finite-cornered game

The nonemptiness of the core is proved following Scarf (1967, 1973) using an algorithm that relies on there being only a finite number of points to check. This algorithm is an extension of the algorithm developed by Lemke and Howson (1964) for bimatrix games. It cannot work directly on all games satisfying Assumptions 7.1 to 7.4; however, the larger class of games is dealt with in Section 3.3 via a limiting argument. A set $V(K)$ that satisfies Assumptions 7.1 to 7.4 can be approximated using a finite number of points in R^k. This is illustrated in Figure 7.3. For an arbitrary coalition K, a set $V(K)$, analogous to Figure 7.3 can be defined by means of $\underline{u}$ and m_K payoff vectors, $u^{K,1}, \ldots, u^{K,m_K}$. In Figure 7.3, $m^K = 3$, and $u^K \in V^K$ if (a) $\underline{u}^K \leq u^K \leq u^{K,1}$ or (b) $\underline{u}^K \leq u^K \leq u^{K,2}$ or (c) $\underline{u}^K \leq u^K \leq u^{K,3}$. The part of $V(K)$ satisfying (a) is shaded with diagonal lines, that satisfying (b) with horizontal lines, and that satisfying (c) with vertical lines. A characteristic function based on such points is called a *finite-cornered characteristic function*,

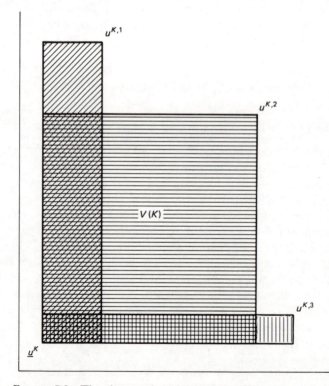

FIGURE 7.3   The characteristic function in a finite-cornered game.

and a *finite-cornered game* is a game whose characteristic function is finite cornered.

DEFINITION 7.8 *V is a* **finite-cornered characteristic function** *for the game* (N, V) *if, for each* $K \subset N, k \geq 2$, *there exist* $u^{K,j} \in R^k$, $j = 1, \ldots, m_K$, *such that* $\underline{u}^K \leq u^{K,j}$ *for all j and*

$$V(K) = \bigcup_{j=1}^{m^K} \{x^K \in R^k \mid u^K \leq x^K \leq u^{K,j}\} \tag{7.3}$$

DEFINITION 7.9 (N, V) *is a* **finite-cornered game** *if V is a finite-cornered characteristic function for the game.*

3.2.1 A two-matrix representation of finite-cornered games

There is a way to represent a finite-cornered game using two matrices, each having n rows and $n^* = \sum_{K \subset N} m_K$ columns, where $m_{\{i\}} = 1$ for all i and $m_\varnothing = 0$. This representation will be used to introduce Scarf's algorithm and to prove existence of a nonempty core for a finite-cornered game satisfying Assumptions 7.1 and 7.4. Note, by the way, that a finite-cornered game automatically satisfies Assumptions 7.2 and 7.3.

One matrix, called the *incidence matrix*, I, identifies all the coalitions. The first n columns each correspond to one of the single-player coalitions, with column i having a *one* in the ith row and *zero* everywhere else. The next $m_{\{1,2\}}$ columns correspond to the coalition $\{1, 2\}$, the next $m_{\{1,3\}}$ to $\{1, 3\}$ and so forth through all coalitions of two or more players. A column corresponding to a particular coalition has a *one* in any row corresponding to a member of the coalition and a *zero* in each other row. Thus in a column for $\{1, 2, 4\}$, the first, second, and fourth row entries are *one*, and all the other entries are *zero*.

The second matrix, called the *payoff characterization matrix* B, has a column for each of the vectors, $u^{K,j}$, that are upper right corners of $V(K)$. Each one-player coalition has one column in the B matrix. For $\{i\}$ the assigned column is column i and it has $\underline{u}_i$ in the ith row and M_{ji} in the jth row. The remaining columns are ordered as they are in the incidence matrix. After the first n columns of B, the next $m_{\{1,2\}}$ columns correspond to the coalition $\{1, 2\}$, and so forth, as with the incidence matrix I. Thus each of the m_K columns corresponding to a particular coalition K is devoted to a different vector among the $u^{K,j}$. For a particular $u^{K,j}$, corresponding to column r of the matrix B, the lth row entry (b_{lr}) is the payoff to player l in $u^{K,j}$ if $l \in K$ and equal to M_{lr} if $l \notin K$. The entries M_{ij} are dummy entries whose values are all larger than any of the other entries, and, in addition, chosen so that no two of the M_{ij} are equal. One further restriction is placed on the entries M_{ij}: In each row of B, the M_{ij} $(j \leq n)$ occurring in the first n columns, corresponding to the coalitions $\{i\}, i \in N$, are larger than are the M_{il} $(l > 0)$ for entries in other columns.

An illustration is presented in Table 7.1. The first part of the table shows the payoff vectors that define the characteristic function. The vector

TABLE 7.1   The basic data for a finite-cornered game

Payoff vectors defining the $V(K)$

				Coalition											
Player	1	2	3	1, 2				1, 3		2, 3			1, 2, 3		
1	5	*	*	15	13	9	7	10	8	*	*	*	20	16	11
2	*	2	*	3	5	6	9	*	*	10	7	4	8	11	12
3	*	*	4	*	*	*	*	10	12	5	6	13	16	14	8

Incidence matrix

				Coalition											
Player	1	2	3	1, 2				1, 3		2, 3			1, 2, 3		
1	1	0	0	1	1	1	1	1	1	0	0	0	1	1	1
2	0	1	0	1	1	1	1	0	0	1	1	1	1	1	1
3	0	0	1	0	0	0	0	1	1	1	1	1	1	1	1

Payoff characterization matrix

				Coalition											
Player	1	2	3	1, 2				1, 3		2, 3			1, 2, 3		
1	5	97	95	15	13	9	7	10	8	87	86	85	20	16	11
2	99	2	94	3	5	6	9	89	88	10	7	4	8	11	12
3	98	96	4	93	92	91	90	10	12	5	6	13	16	14	8

$y = (5, 2, 4)$, and, for player 1, $V(\{1\}) = \{5\}$. This set is defined by the vector (5) in R^1. The first column, headed by $\{1\}$, has * in rows 2 and 3 to denote that there are no entries corresponding to players 2 and 3. The upper right boundary of $V(\{1, 2\})$ is defined by the corners $(15, 3)$, $(13, 5)$, $(9, 6)$, and $(7, 9)$, which are vectors in R^2, the two-dimensional space with coordinates corresponding to payoffs to players 1 and 2. The information in this part of the table provides the material to form the incidence matrix I and the payoff characterization matrix B. For I, there is a column corresponding to each column at the top of the table. For each column, the entry in a row is "1" if the corresponding player is in the coalition to which the column belongs, and is "0" otherwise. Thus "*" in the top matrix of the table corresponds to "0" in the incidence matrix. The matrix B repeats all the *numbers* from the top matrix of the table, but where "*" appears at the top matrix of the table, the corresponding entry in B is a large number. Each of these large numbers must be bigger than any number appearing in the payoffs in the top matrix of the table in the payoff vectors defining the $V(K)$, and the large entries in the first three columns must be larger than all the rest of these special entries.

3.2.2 Defining a basis for each matrix

The way that the matrices I and B are used is that each matrix has associated with it a *basis*, which is a set of n columns from a matrix; a basis for I is a set of n columns of I and similarly for B. If the same set of columns is a basis for both, then it defines a core point. Specifically, let $\delta \geqslant 0$ be a vector with exactly as many components as there are columns of I (i.e., $\delta \in R_+^{n^*}$), and let $e \in R^n$ be a vector whose components are all equal to 1. Then the n columns of I numbered $j_1, \ldots, j_n$ comprise a *feasible basis* for I if there exists δ such that $I\delta = e$, $\delta_j > 0$ for $j = j_i$, $i \in N$, and $\delta_i = 0$ otherwise. Recall that in I a column really denotes a coalition, so a collection of columns $\{j_1, \ldots, j_n\}$ corresponds to a collection of coalitions. Thus a feasible basis is a balanced collection of coalitions. Note that $\sum_{j=1}^{n^*} b_{ij} \delta_j$ is the sum of the weights assigned to the coalitions in the collection $\{j_1, \ldots, j_n\}$ that correspond to those coalitions to which player i belongs.

Now turning to B, a collection of columns of B, $W = \{j_1, \ldots, j_n\}$, is an *ordinal basis* of B if a vector β defined using the columns in W satisfy a special condition. Let

$$\beta_i = \min\{b_{ij_1}, \ldots, b_{ij_n}\}, \qquad i \in N \qquad (7.4)$$

and define $\beta = (\beta_1, \ldots, \beta_n)$. Denote the lth column of B by b_l. If $\beta \ll b_l$ does not hold for any l, then the columns $j_1, \ldots, j_n$ are an ordinal basis. In other words, for β associated with an ordinal basis, there is no column of B that is strictly larger, component by component. If β were attainable (i.e., if $\beta \in V(N)$), then β would be in the core.

Thus, if W is a feasible basis, it is a balanced collection of coalitions and if W is an ordinal basis, the associated β would, if attainable, be in the core. However, if W is *both a feasible and an ordinal basis* then $\beta \in V(N)$ (i.e., $\beta \in C(N, V)$). This follows from the game being balanced.

DEFINITION 7.10 *Let* $W = \{j_1, \ldots, j_n\}$ *be a collection of columns of the incidence matrix* I. W *is a* **feasible basis** *for* I *if there exists* $\delta \in R_+^{n^*}$ *such that* $I\delta = e$.

DEFINITION 7.11 *Let* $W = \{j_1, \ldots, j_n\}$ *be a collection of columns of the characterization matrix,* B, *and let* β *be defined by* $\beta_i = \min_{l \in N} b_{ij_l}$, $i \in N$. *Then* W *is an* **ordinal basis** *for* B *if, for each column* j *of* B, *there is at least one index* i *such that* $\beta_i \geqslant b_{ij}$.

3.2.3 Scarf's algorithm

The purpose of the algorithm, then, is to find a collection of columns, W, that is simultaneously a feasible and an ordinal basis. The method of the algorithm is to start with two collections of columns, W_f^0 and W_o^0. The former being a feasible basis and the latter an ordinal, with the two sets having $n - 1$ of their members in common. As will be seen, it is easy to start in this way. In a sense, one is close to finding a core point at this beginning place. The algorithm proceeds by removing that member of W_o^0 that is not found in W_f^0. This is called a *pivot* on the ordinal basis. The rules of proceeding are such that there is exactly one possible column to add to the ordinal basis when the mismatched column is removed. This results in a new ordinal basis, W_o^1. One of two things must be true about W_o^1: (a) the newly added column corresponds to the (formerly) mismatched column in W_f^0, or (b) the newly added column is not one of the columns found in W_f^0. If (a) holds, then the search is over, and the corresponding β^1, defined by equation (7.4) using W_o^1, is an element of the core. If (b) holds, then the next step is to *pivot* on the feasible basis. This is done by adding to W_f^0 the mismatched column of W_0^1. As with the pivot on the ordinal basis, there is only one possible column to remove, resulting in either a complete matching between W_o^1 and W_f^1 or a mismatch in one column. Again, in the former case β^1 is a core point, and in the latter, another pivot step must be taken. This time the pivot step is on the ordinal basis. This process continues, with ordinal and feasible pivots alternating. The process must end in a finite number of pivot steps with a core point being found, because there are only a finite number of ordinal and feasible bases and the pivoting process can never cycle back and repeat some pair of bases for a second time.

3.2.4 Preliminary results

The next several lemmas and Theorem 7.1 go through in detail the things that are sketched above. To simplify the process of proof, the games that are examined first are finite-cornered games in which elements of B in any given row are distinct and in which the δ_j associated with the n columns of a feasible basis are all strictly positive and different from one another. These extra conditions are later removed, but they simplify proofs and make it easier to see why the results hold. To summarize the results proved in this section, Lemma 7.1 establishes that when a new column is added to a feasible basis, there is only one column that can possibly be removed. Then, in Lemma 7.2, it is shown that when a column is removed from an ordinal basis, there is only one possible column that can replace it to form a new ordinal basis.

LEMMA 7.1 *Let (N, V) be a finite cornered game that satisfies Assumptions 7.1 and 7.4, and let I and B be the incidence and payoff characterization matrices. Assume that no two elements of the ith row of B have the same value $(i \in N)$ and that, for any feasible basis $W = \{j_1, \ldots, j_n\}$, the weights $\delta(W)$ associated with W corresponding to the columns in W are positive and unique. For any column $j^* \notin W$, there is a unique feasible basis consisting of j^* and $n - 1$ of the columns in W if the convex set $\Delta = \{\delta \in R^{n^*} \mid \delta \geqslant 0, I\delta = e\}$ is bounded.*

Proof The introduction into the basis of j^* and the adjustment of the positive δ_j to keep $I\delta = e$ satisfied is precisely a linear programming pivot step. The condition that the positive elements of $\delta(W)$ are also distinct from one another guarantees that, as the weight on j^* is increased and the other weights are appropriately altered, two weights cannot reach zero simultaneously. The condition that Δ is bounded implies that, as the weight on j^* increases, the weight on at least one column in the original basis, W, must decline. This, in turn, means that the weight on j^* must rise to a point at which one of the previous columns drops out of the basis. QED

LEMMA 7.2 *Under the conditions of Lemma 7.1, let* $W = \{j_1, \ldots, j_n\}$ *be an ordinal basis of B. For an arbitrary column of the basis, say* j_1, *suppose that the remaining columns are not all contained in* $\{1, \ldots, n\}$. *Then there is a unique column* $j^* \neq j_1$ *such that* $W^* = \{j^*, j_2, \ldots, j_n\}$ *is an ordinal basis.*

Proof Three things are done in this proof. The first is to define an ordinal pivot step. After that, it is shown that such a step is unique and must lead to a new ordinal basis. Finally, it is shown that nothing but an ordinal pivot step can lead to a new ordinal basis.

From the definition of an ordinal basis, there must be exactly one column among $j_2, \ldots, j_n$ that contains two entries that are the smallest entries in their respective rows. Although one of these row minimizers, occurring in row i^*, is a row minimizer in W, the other, occurring in row i', is not. Denote by j_l the column in which these two row minimizers are found, and let β be the vector of row minimizers for W. Thus the new row minimizer in row i', after removal of j_1, is $b_{i'j_l}$. Next, look among all the columns *not* in W and, among them, find all the columns for which $b_{ij} > \beta_i$ $(i \neq i^*)$ and $b_{ij} > b_{ij_l}$. From these columns, select the one in which b_{i^*j} is maximized and denote the column j^*. This completes the specification of the ordinal pivot step.

Now it is shown that the ordinal pivot step described above leads to a unique new basis. Letting β' denote the vector of row minimizers for $W' = \{j^*, j_2, \ldots, j_n\}$, note that for $i \neq i^*$, i', we have $\beta'_i = \beta_i$, and that $\beta'_{i'} = b_{i'j_l}$ and $\beta'_{i^*} = b_{i^*j^*}$. The columns not included in W can be divided into two groups. There are those selected for examination in the search for j^* and those not selected. For those not selected, each one has $b_{ij} < \beta'_i$ for at least one $i \neq i^*$; therefore, introducing one of these would force out some member of W other than j_1. Among those selected, if any column apart from j^* had been introduced, $b_{ij^*} > \beta'_i, i \in N$, which would violate the definition of ordinal basis. Thus the pivot step is unique and leads to a new ordinal basis.

It remains to see that a new column other than j^* could not have been chosen with its row minimizer in row i'. Supposing there is such a row, then the resulting β' would be identical to the old β in all entries except i'. Therefore, $b_{ij^*} \geq b_{ij_1}$, which means that column j_1 could not improve on β'. On the other hand if j^* is introduced, $b_{i'j^*} \leq \beta_{i'}$ which implies that $b_{i'j^*} = b_{i'j_1}$; thus j^* could only be j_1. Therefore, a new column $j^* \neq j_1$ cannot be chosen with its row minimizers in i^*. QED

3.2.5 Existence of a nonempty core

Putting Lemmas 7.1 and 7.2 together, suppose there is a W_o^0 (ordinal basis) and W_f^0 (feasible basis) that form a starting point for the present discussion, and assume that the two bases have $n - 1$ columns in common. Two methods are allowed by the algorithm for pivoting to a new basis: (1) add to the feasible basis the mismatched column from the ordinal basis or (2) remove the mismatched column from the ordinal basis. Thus, either the mismatched column from W_o becomes matched by putting it into W_f or it ceases to be mismatched by removing it from W_o. Both of these steps are unique. When the algorithm is applied, there is only one step to take at each point, because one of the two possible pivots moves the algorithm *backwards* to the previous pair of bases. Thus, the only way to attain a new pair of bases is to take the one step that does not reverse the previous pivot.

Going through this in more detail, assume that the two special conditions of the lemmas are met (that the set Δ is bounded and, if a column is removed from W_o^0, then at least one remaining column is not among columns $1, \ldots, n$). Denote by j_o^0 the column in W_o^0 that is not also found in W_f^0 (the mismatched column in W_o^0) and by j_f^0 the mismatched column from W_f^0. From the lemmas, there are only two possible pivot steps to take: (a) One step is to drop j_o^0 from W_o^0 and the other is to add j_o^0 to W_f^0. Supposing that the next pivot step does not result in a core point, dropping j_o^0 causes (a unique) j_o^1 to be added and it is a new mismatch in the new ordinal basis W_o^1. (b) Adding j_o^0 to W_f^0 causes some other (unique) member to drop out. If that member is not j_f^0, then $j_f^0 (= j_f^1)$ remains the mismatch in the new W_f^1, and some new j_o^1 (corresponding to the column that was removed from W_f^0) is the mismatch in W_o^0.

Consider the possibilities if pivot (a) were taken. After the pivot step, j_o^1 is the mismatch in W_o^1 and the two possible pivots are (i) drop j_o^1 from W_o^1 or (ii) add j_o^1 to W_f^0. Taking step (i) merely puts the bases back to their previous position; therefore, the only *new* alternative is (ii). Similarly, if pivot (b) were taken, W_o^0 acquires a new mismatched column, j_o^1. After this pivot, two steps can be taken: (i) drop j_o^1 from W_o^0 and (ii) add j_o^1 to W_f^1. Step (ii) simply reverses what was just done, so step (i) is the only new alternative.

It is now possible to prove that a game satisfying the extra restrictions assumed in Lemmas 7.1 and 7.2 has a nonempty core. The technique of proof is to show that one can always find a special pair of bases W_f^0 and W_o^0, having $n - 1$ columns in common, from which only one pivot step is possible. This starting point ensures that the pivoting process must always move forward to bases that have not already been encountered, and the finite corneredness of the game guarantees that pivoting cannot go on forever. The process must reach a termination, but it can only terminate at a core point.

LEMMA 7.3   *Let (N, V) be finite cornered game satisfying Assumptions 7.1 and 7.4, in which no two elements of any row of B have the same value and in which the weights $\delta(W)$ associated with any column in a feasible basis W are positive and distinct. Then $C(N, V)$ is not empty.*

Proof   Let $W_f^0 = \{1, \ldots, n\}$ and $W_o^0 = \{2, \ldots, n, j_o^0\}$ where j_o^0 is chosen to be that (unique) column among columns $n + 1, \ldots, n^*$ having the largest first row entry. Thus $\beta = (b_{1j_o^0}, \underline{u}_2, \ldots, \underline{u}_n)$, and this is clearly the only ordinal basis that can have columns $2, \ldots, n$ as members. From this starting point, only one pivot is possible; removing j_o^0 from W_o^0 is ruled out, because only j_o^0 can be put with columns $2, \ldots, n$ to form an ordinal basis. Any other column used in place of j_o^0 will result in an associated β vector that is strongly dominated by column j_o^0. This violates the definition of an ordinal basis.

Note, too, that Δ must be bounded, which means that Lemma 7.1 can be applied. Next note that in taking the other pivot step, adding j_o^0 to W_f^0, one of the columns $2, \ldots, n$ becomes the mismatch in W_o^0; therefore, the special condition in Lemma 7.2 is met for the next pivot step. With Lemmas 7.1 and 7.2 applying, there is, after the first pivot step (which is unique) only one possible pivot step that does not backtrack. Because there can only be a finite number of possible bases of either type, and, aside from the special starting point for the algorithm and a core point, there must always be two possible pivots, there must be a collection of n columns that is simultaneously a feasible and an ordinal basis.   QED

Moving from Lemma 7.3 to a theorem establishing that $C(N, V)$ is not empty for any game satisfying Assumptions 7.1 to 7.4 is easy and rests on using Lemma 7.3 with sequences of games. This is carried out in two steps. For the first step, taken in Lemma 7.4, finite-cornered games are retained with the special conditions mentioned in Lemma 7.1 being dropped. Then Theorem 7.1 makes the final extension.

LEMMA 7.4 *Any finite-cornered game (N, V) satisfying Assumptions 7.1 and 7.4 has a nonempty core.*

Proof Let I^l and B^l, $l = 1, 2, \ldots$, be a sequence of incidence and payoff characterization matrices that converge to I and B, respectively. The members of the sequence are chosen to satisfy all the conditions of Lemma 7.1 and I and B represent a finite-cornered game and satisfy Assumptions 7.1 and 7.4. For the game (N^l, V^l), represented by I^l and B^l, let β^l be the core point found by the algorithm and let δ^l be the corresponding set of weights. A cluster point of the sequence $\{\delta^l\}$ is a solution for $I\delta = e$. Let the sequence $\{\beta^l\}$ be the companion sequence to the convergent subsequence of $\{\delta^l\}$. This subsequence of core points has a convergent subsequence whose limit may be denoted β. The payoff vector β is a core point of the game represented by I and B.   QED

3.3   The core of a balanced game

Lemma 7.4 provides a foundation from which the final result can easily be built. Essentially, the class of games covered by Lemma 7.4 can be used to approximate any game satisfying Assumptions 7.1 to 7.4. For an arbitrary game (N, V) satisfying these assumptions, it is possible to find a convergent sequence of games satisfying the conditions of the lemma that has the game (N, V) as its limit. Then it is proved that the limiting game has a nonempty core if the members of the convergent sequence have nonempty cores.

THEOREM 7.1   *A game (N, V) satisfying Assumptions 7.1 to 7.4 has a nonempty core.*

Proof   Let $\{(N^l, V^l)\}$ be a sequence of finite-cornered games satisfying Assumptions 7.1 and 7.4, the members of which are represented by I^l and B^l (respectively), and suppose that the members of this sequence are chosen to converge to a game (N, V) that satisfies Assumptions 7.1 to 7.4. This sequence can be selected to be dense in the limit. Letting β^l be a core point of (N^l, V^l), a cluster point of the sequence $\{\beta^l\}$ is a core point of (N, V).   QED

The algorithm can be illustrated using the game in Table 7.1. The initial feasible basis is $W_f^0 = \{1, 2, 3\}$ and the initial ordinal basis is $W_o^0 = \{2, 3, 10\}$. In choosing this ordinal basis, any two of the first three columns can be used, but once the two columns are selected, there is only one possible choice from the remaining 12 columns. Were any column other than 10 used with 2 and 3, the resulting β vector would be strictly dominated by column 10. From this starting point, the only possible pivot step is to put column 10 into the feasible basis, which results in the removal of column 2 and $W_f^1 = \{1, 3, 10\}$.[1] Now the mismatched column in the ordinal basis is column 2, which is removed. Column 14 is added, resulting in $W_o^1 = \{3, 10, 14\}$. Next, column 14 is added to the feasible basis and column 1 is dropped, resulting in $W_f^2 = \{3, 10, 14\}$. At this point, the two bases are the same, so the β vector associated with the ordinal basis $(16, 10, 4)$, is a core point. Note that a point is in the core if it is not strongly dominated, and this core point is, in fact, weakly dominated by column 14.

4   The stable set

It was seen above that the definition of the core is essentially the same for nontransferable utility games as for transferable utility games. In both situations, the core is based on domination. The same holds for the stable set. Just as in Chapter 6, a stable set for a game (N, V) consists of a subset B of the set of imputations that satisfies two conditions: First, if an imputation x is in B, then there is no imputation in B that dominates x. Second, if an imputation y is not in B, then there is some imputation x in B that dominates y.

5   The bargaining set, the kernel, and the nucleolus

The situation is largely the same with the bargaining set as with the stable set. One can nearly carry over all definitions for the bargaining set with no alteration; however, it is necessary to restate the definition of individually rational payoff configurations to put it in terms of the characteristic function V.

DEFINITION 7.12 *An* **individually rational payoff configuration** *is a pair* $(x, \mathcal{T})$ *where* $x \in R^n$, $\mathcal{T}$ *is a coalition structure, and* $x^K \geqslant y^K$ *for all* $y^K \in V(K)$ *and all* $K \in \mathcal{T}$. *The set of all individually rational payoff configurations for the game* (N, V) *relative to the coalition structure* $\mathcal{T}$ *is denoted* $I_{\mathcal{T}}(N, V)$.

From here, the definitions of *objection*, *counterobjection*, and of the *bargaining set* from Section 5 of Chapter 6 can be used with $I_{\mathcal{T}}(N, V)$ substituted for $I_{\mathcal{T}}(N, v)$.

For the kernel and the nucleolus, it is much less obvious how to generalize. Both are based on the concept of *excess*, which is intimately bound to the transferable utility characteristic function.

6   Extending the Shapley value to games without transferable utility

The extension of the Shapley value presented below is due to Shapley (1969) and uses a concept from Harsanyi (1959). Harsanyi found a generalizaton of the Shapley value to nontransferable utility games that also generalizes the Nash bargaining solution to *n*-person games. This was later refined in Harsanyi (1963), and his formulation has considerable appeal for the way that it balances off all the two-person games that can be found embedded in the original game by (a) taking each coalition K with $1 \leqslant k < n$ and considering a two-person game in which the players are K and $N \backslash K$, and (b) for each pair of players, i and j, holding fixed the circumstances of all but these two players and looking at a two-person game between i and j. The details of Harsanyi's model are formidable, which accounts for some of the appeal of Shapley's much simpler formulation. In addition to Harsanyi's original articles, expositions can be found in Friedman (1977: Chapter 11) and Harsanyi (1977: Chapter 12). The latter treatment is exceptionally fine. Another extension of the Shapley value is due to Owen (1972).

The concept borrowed from Harsanyi is called the *λ-transfer value*, and the two approaches differ with respect to the rules defining how the value is characterized. The assumptions of the model and Shapley's definition are found in Section 6.1; then, in Section 6.2 existence of a λ-transfer value is proved. The model is illustrated in Section 6.3 by a simple example.

6.1   The assumptions of the model and the λ-transfer value

Shapley's own version is extremely simple and is, perhaps, as easily justified as any of the others. His basic device is to define a family of transferable utility games that can be associated with the original game.

Each such game is based on giving weights to the players. Each game has a Shapley value; however, for most of these games, the Shapley value cannot be achieved in the (suitably weighted version of the) original game. A λ-transfer value for the original game is, essentially, the Shapley value of a member of this family that can be attained in the original game. Assumptions 7.1 and 7.2 are retained and supplemented by Assumptions 7.5 and 7.6. Both concern $V(N)$, the former being Assumption 7.3 applied only to $V(N)$ and the latter being convexity.

ASSUMPTION 7.5   *If $u' \in V(N)$ and $\underline{u} \leqslant u \leqslant u'$, then $u \in V(N)$.*

ASSUMPTION 7.6 $V(N)$ *is convex.*

To define the family of transferable utility games that are associated with (N, V), let Λ denote the unit simplex in R^n. That is, $\Lambda = \{\lambda \in R^n \mid \lambda \geqslant 0, \sum_{i \in N} \lambda_i = 1\}$. For $\lambda \in \Lambda$, (N, v_λ) is a transferable utility game with a characteristic function defined by

$$v_\lambda(K) = \max_{u^K \in V(K)} \sum_{l \in K} \lambda_l u_l^K, \qquad K \subset N \qquad (7.5)$$

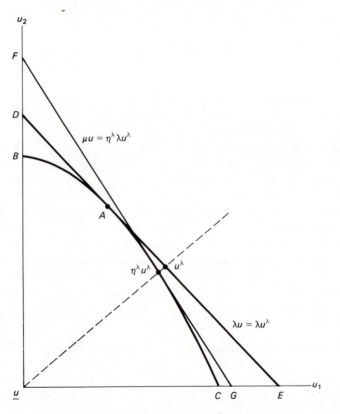

FIGURE 7.4   An illustration of the λ-transfer value.

The weights λ assign a relative importance to each of the players and equality would mean $\lambda_i = 1/n$ for each player. Denote the Shapley value of the game (N, v_λ) by $\phi(N, v_\lambda)$, and define for $\lambda' \in \Lambda$ the payoff vector

$$u' = (\phi(N, v_{\lambda'})/\lambda_1', \ldots, \phi_n(N, v_{\lambda'})/\lambda_n') \in V(N) \qquad (7.6)$$

Then if $u' \in V(N)$ it is the λ-*transfer value* of the game (N, V) and is Shapley's proposed value solution for nontransferable utility games.

DEFINITION 7.13 *For a nontransferable utility game (N, V) and for $\lambda \in \Lambda$, (N, v_λ) is a companion transferable utility game where v_λ is defined by equation (7.5). If the Shapley value of (N, v_λ) satisfies equation (7.6), then*

$$u' = (\phi_1(N, v_\lambda)/\lambda_1, \ldots, \phi_n(N, v_\lambda)/\lambda_n) \in V(N) \qquad (7.7)$$

*is the λ-**transfer value** of the game (N, V) if $u' \in V(N)$.*

Figure 7.4 illustrates the relationship between the game (N, V) and the game (N, v_λ). For the coalition $\{1, 2\}$ the region bounded above by the curve BAC is $V(\{1, 2\})$. The point A is where $\lambda_1 u_1 + \lambda_2 u_2 = v_\lambda(\{1, 2\})$ is maximized on $V(\{1, 2\})$, and the straight line DAE satisfies $\lambda_1 u_1 + \lambda_2 u_2 = v_\lambda(\{1, 2\})$. Thus the set with upper right boundary DAE is the set of attainable payoff vectors for $\{1, 2\}$ in the game (N, v_λ). What is done here for the coalition $\{1, 2\}$ must be repeated for all coalitions K, including the coalition of the whole, N, in order to form v_λ. For the sake of illustration, it is supposed that the Shapley value for the game (N, v_λ) awards u^λ to $\{1, 2\}$ in the diagram.

6.2 Existence of the λ-transfer value

The means of proving that a game satisfying Assumptions 7.1, 7.2, 7.5, and 7.6 has a λ-transfer value is to define a correspondence that takes elements of Λ into subsets of Λ, and to show that this correspondence has a fixed point that must be the weights associated with the λ-transfer value. This is carried out in two steps, the first of which is Lemma 7.5 where it is proved that $\phi(N, v_\lambda)$ is continuous in λ. When the Shapley value of (N, v_λ) is outside $V(N)$, it is possible to give a scalar measure of how far outside it is. A measure is defined in Lemma 7.6 and shown to be continuous in λ. Then, in Theorem 7.2 an appropriate correspondence is defined, using the measure from Lemma 7.6, and shown to be upper semicontinuous. From this the existence of the λ-transfer value is established.

LEMMA 7.5 *Under Assumptions 7.1, 7.2, 7.5, and 7.6, $\phi(N, v_\lambda)$ is a continuous function of λ for all $\lambda \in \Lambda$.*

Proof The characteristic function, v_λ is continuous in λ, because $\max_{u^K \in V(K)} \sum_{l \in K} \lambda_l u_l^K$, which defines the characteristic function, is continuous in λ. From equation (6.25), giving the Shapley value, it is clear that $\phi(N, v_\lambda)$ is continuous in each $v(K)$; therefore, $\phi(N, v_\lambda)$ is continuous in λ, which establishes the lemma. QED

LEMMA 7.6   *Let $u^\lambda = (\phi_1(N, v_\lambda)/\lambda_1, \ldots, \phi_n(N, v_\lambda)/\lambda_n)$. For $\lambda \in \Lambda$ define $\eta^\lambda \in R_+$ by the condition that $\eta^\lambda(u^\lambda - \underline{u}) + \underline{u}$ is on the upper right boundary of $V(N)$. That is, $\eta(u^\lambda - \underline{u}) + \underline{u} \in V(N)$ for η equal to η^λ and $\eta \notin V(N)$ for $\eta > \eta^\lambda$. Then, η^λ is continuous in λ.*

Proof   The lemma follows from the continuity of $\phi(N, v_\lambda)$ with respect to λ.   QED

THEOREM 7.2   *A game (N, V) satisfying Assumptions 7.1, 7.2, 7.5, and 7.6 has a λ-transfer value.*

Proof   Note first that $u^\lambda = (\phi_1(N, v_\lambda)/\lambda_1, \ldots, \phi_n(N, v_\lambda)/\lambda_n)$ is a continuous function of λ and that either u^λ lies on the upper right boundary of $V(N)$ or it is above and to the right of $V(N)$. With that in mind, let

$$T(\lambda) = \left\{ \mu \in \Lambda \; \middle| \; \sum_{i \in N} \mu_i u_i^\lambda = \sum_{i \in N} \lambda_i u_i^\lambda \quad \text{and} \right.$$
$$\left. \sum_{i \in N} \mu_i u_i \leqslant \eta^\lambda \sum_{i \in N} \mu_i u_i^\lambda, u \in V(N) \right\} \quad (7.8)$$

If $\lambda \notin T(\lambda)$, then $u^\lambda \notin V(N)$ and u^λ cannot be the λ-transfer value of the game; however, if $\lambda \in T(\lambda)$, then $u^\lambda \in V(N)$ and u^λ is the λ-transfer value. The only remaining question is whether $T(\lambda)$ has a fixed point. Clearly, it is a mapping from Λ to subsets of Λ, because $\eta^\lambda u^\lambda$ is a Pareto optimal element of $V(N)$. The continuity of $\eta^\lambda u^\lambda$ in λ assures that $T(\lambda)$ is upper semicontinuous, and, finally, the convexity of $V(N)$ implies that the sets $T(\lambda)$ are convex. Therefore, the Kakutani fixed point theorem can be applied to assure that $T(\lambda)$ has a fixed point, which completes the proof.   QED

The proof of Theorem 7.2 is illustrated in Figure 7.4. For λ, recall that the point A in the figure is where the weighted sum of the players' payoffs, using the weights λ, is maximized. The payoff vector u^λ, which is a weighted transformation of $\phi(N, v_\lambda)$ (again, using the weights λ) lies on the line DAE that is tangent to $V(N)$ (i.e., the supporting hyperplane through A), and it is used to obtain the weights μ into which λ maps by drawing a straight line from $\underline{u}$ to u^λ. The point on this line that intersects the upper right boundary of $V(N)$, $\eta^\lambda u^\lambda$, is used to obtain the new weights μ. A tangent to $V(N)$ at $\eta^\lambda u^\lambda$ (the line FG) gives the new weights. Figure 7.5 illustrates a situation in which these weights would not be unique; however, they are assured to be nonnegative by Assumption 7.5.

Note that a coalition K, smaller than N, can receive a payoff vector lying outside of $V(K)$. It is only for $K = N$ that the coalition's payoff must lie on the upper right boundary of $V(K)$. It is tempting to interpret the weights λ as the relative importance of the players. Certainly within the confines of the model, such a procedure may be useful; however, establishing the "worth" of a player within a game context and transferring that "worth" to other situations may be unwarranted.

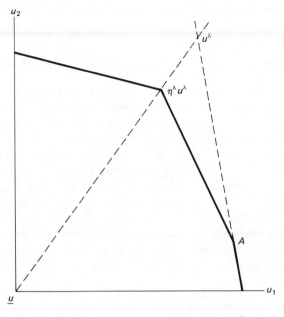

FIGURE 7.5   Nonunique weights for $T(\lambda)$.

6.3   An example

An example is easily constructed for three players. Suppose a characteristic function where $\underline{u} = (0, 0, 0)$ and the upper right boundary of the sets $V(K)$ for the two- and three-player coalitions are $u_2 = 16 - u_1^2/6$ for $V(\{1, 2\})$, $u_3 = 14 - .02u_1^2$ for $V(\{1, 3\})$, $u_3 = 10 - .045u_2^2$ for $V(\{2, 3\})$, and $u_3 = 14 - u_1^2/87.5 - .036u_2^2$ for $V(\{1, 2, 3\})$. For weights $\lambda = (.2, .3, .5)$, the λ-transfer value of the game is $(35/2, 25/3, 8)$. This can be seen by first finding the characteristic function for the game (N, v_λ), then obtaining the Shapley value, $\phi(N, v_\lambda)$, for this game, and, finally, noting that $(35/2, 25/3, 8) = (\phi_1(N, v_\lambda)/\lambda_1, \phi_2(N, v_\lambda)/\lambda_2, \phi_3(N, v_\lambda)/\lambda_3)$.

When $.2u_1 + .3u_2$ is maximized on $V(\{1, 2\})$, the resulting maximum is $v_\lambda(\{1, 2\}) = 5$. Doing the same for the remaining coalitions of two and three players yields $v_\lambda(\{1, 3\}) = 8$, $v_\lambda(\{2, 3\}) = 6$, and $v_\lambda(\{1, 2, 3\}) = 10$. The Shapley value for this game is $\phi(N, v_\lambda) = (3.5, 2.5, 4)$ and the λ-transfer value is $(3.5/.2, 2.5/.3, 4/.5) = (17\frac{1}{2}, 8\frac{1}{3}, 8)$.

7   Applications of the core

Two examples are discussed in this section. The first is an old and well-known core application: Edgeworth's model of general equilibrium without production. This is the classic case, mentioned earlier in this volume, of an economy in which there are consumers who can trade with one another, but there are no producers. The second example is from the literature of political science and relates to decision making by majority vote in a committee or a society.

7.1 A model of general economic equilibrium with trade

The first example is based on Edgeworth's (1881) general equilibrium model of pure trade. Within this framework he invented the core. His approach was to postulate a two-person economy, depicted in the Edgeworth box in Figure 7.6, and to ask which trades ought one expect the traders to make. In the figure, E is the endowment point of the traders, indicating that Ann has 50 apples and 100 bananas, while Ben has 80 apples and 60 bananas. For Ann, the origin is the lower left corner of the box, and quantities rise for her as one moves up and to the right. The reverse holds for Ben, for whom the upper right corner of the box is the origin and quantities rise as one moves down and to the left. A point in the box represents an allocation of the total resources of the community (130 apples and 160 bananas) among the two traders.

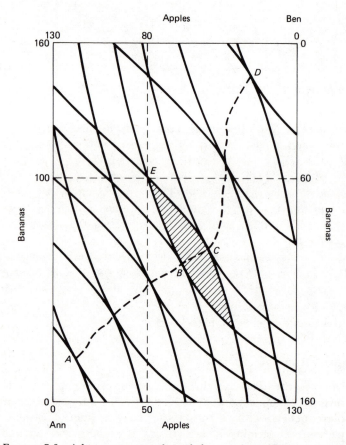

FIGURE 7.6   Advantageous trade and the core in an Edgeworth box.

Edgeworth postulated two criteria for the acceptability of an allocation. First, a final allocation should yield to each trader at least as much utility as he obtains from his endowment. Second, it should be impossible to find a trade that Pareto dominates a final allocation. The shaded region in Figure 7.6 satisfies the first criterion and the curve $ABCD$ satisfies the second. Thus the curve BC satisfies both. For the two-person game, the segment BC is the set of commodity allocations corresponding to payoff vectors in the core.

Note that the discussion has been carried out without reference to markets or prices. This is natural in the sense that markets in which prices are used as a mechanism of trade ought to be competitive, or at least competitive on one side (i.e., on the buyers' side or on the sellers' side). In the two-person setting, it is not particularly natural for one trader to tell another he will trade at a predetermined ratio any quantities the other person wishes. This could happen, but traders need not be constrained to such behavior.

The next step Edgeworth took was to consider an economy with $2k$ traders. Half of them have both the same endowment and the same preferences as Ann, the other half share these characteristics with Ben. Edgeworth conjectured, and others later proved (see Debreu and Scarf (1963, 1972)), that, as k goes to infinity the core commodity allocations converge to the set of commodity allocations associated with competitive equilibria. In other words, this remarkable result says that when the number of traders is extremely large, the set of "acceptable" trades consists of those trades that are achievable as equilibrium outcomes in competitive economic markets with prices.

The Edgeworth model with two types of traders and k of each type can be adequately represented in the Edgeworth box in Figures 7.6 and 7.7, because all core allocations must give identical commodity bundles to all the traders of a single type. The importance of this fact is that the commodity allocations in the core can be fully represented in a space of unchanging dimension as k increases. Similarly, the payoff vectors in the core give identical payoffs to all traders of a single type; therefore, at a core allocation one need only know the utility received by a representative member of each type. More generally, if there are n types of traders, m commodities, and k traders of each type, then the core can be represented in a space of dimension $n \cdot m$, no matter what the value of k. Thus, it is meaningful to talk of the core becoming smaller as k increases.

To see why all traders of a given type must receive identical commodity bundles at a Pareto optimal allocation, suppose an allocation z that does not have this feature. Let z^{ih} denote the commodity bundle assigned to player h of type i, where the index h can go from 1 to k. From each i form the commodity bundle $\bar{z}^i = \sum_{h=1}^{k} z^{ih}/k$. Thus, $\bar{z}^i$ is the mean bundle received by the players of type i. Now form a coalition L having n members, one of each type, with the member of each type i being that one receiving the least desirable commodity bundle among all of his type. Note that the allocation

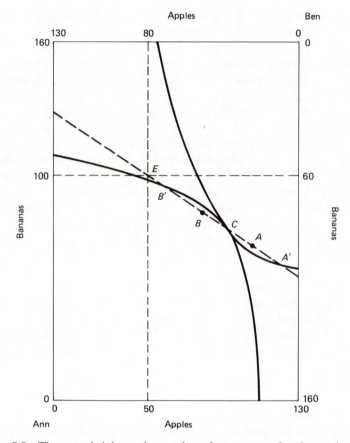

FIGURE 7.7   The core shrinks as the number of consumers of each type increases.

$(\bar{z}^1, \ldots, \bar{z}^n)$ is achievable by L and each member i finds $\bar{z}^i$ at least as desirable as his original assignment. Furthermore, if member i's original assignment was different from $\bar{z}^i$, then $\bar{z}^i$ is superior, due to convexity of preferences.

To see how the core shrinks as k increases and why any outcome that is not a competitive equilibrium will eventually be dropped from the core as k rises, consider the commodity allocation C in Figure 7.7. This point is not a competitive equilibrium, as can be seen from the price line through C and E. (Recall that E is the endowment point.) On that price line, the point A is preferred to C by the players of type Ann and the point B is preferred to C by the players of type Ben. Now measure the distances EA and EB, and suppose a coalition L made up of k_A type-Ann players and k_B type-Ben players. If $k_A \cdot EB = k_B \cdot EA$, then a trade among the members of L is feasible that places the type-Ann players at A and the type-Ben players at B. If this coalition can be formed, then the point C cannot be a core commodity allocation, but EA and EB need not stand in a ratio that allows this coalition. This problem is remedied by noting that A could be placed anywhere in the (open) interval from C to A', and B could be placed anywhere in the interval from C to B'. Therefore, k must be large enough that two integers k_A and k_B can be chosen to satisfy $1 < k_A/k_B < EA'/EB'$. Clearly, as k increases, a threshold value $k(C)$ is reached such that, for all $k > k(C)$, the point C cannot be in a core commodity allocation, but for smaller values of k, C is a core commodity allocation. A commodity allocation corresponding to a competitive equilibrium cannot be eliminated from the core in this way, no matter how many consumers there are of each type.

7.2 Group decision and the core

The second example is from political science and deals with characteristics of group decision practices. A democratic political organization ought to make decisions that are best for the group that the organization represents; however, there are at least two obstacles to this end. One is that the persons who actually make decisions for the organization may have objectives that are at variance with the best interests of the group. Another is that it may be very difficult to determine what is, in fact, in the best interests of the group. Where the group is democratic, finding the "best" policy must come down to aggregating the preferences of the group members in some fashion. To make a simple example, suppose there are three persons, Ann, Ben, and Carrie, and three alternatives among which they must choose, I, II, and III. Suppose that these three alternatives are mutually exclusive and are joint in nature, as would be the case if the three people were the citizens of a medieval town and the issue were the sort of wall to be built around their village for their defence. I might be *no wall*, II could be a *wooden wall*, and III could be a *stone wall*. If, for instance, all three ranked the alternatives in the order, from best to worst, III, II, I, then decision would be trivial. It is when everyone is not in agreement that an interesting group decision issue arises.

Voting is a common method for group decision in democratic organizations. If the three-person village uses majority voting as a means of ranking each pair of alternatives, it is well known that no clear-cut social ordering need emerge. If Ann's preferences are I, II, III, Ben's are II, III, I, and Carrie's are III, I, II, then, in pairwise votes, I beats II, II beats III, and III beats I. This, of course, is the *Condorcet paradox* (see Black (1958)), and is intimately related to Arrow's (1951) General Possibility Theorem. The Condorcet paradox can be stated in game theoretic terms by noting that I dominates II, II dominates III, and III dominates I; thus, the core of the game is empty. If, on the other hand, the decision criterion were unanimity instead of majority vote, then the paradox would dissolve. No alternative would beat any other, which would leave all three tied for "best." Put in terms of the core, no alternative would dominate another; hence, all would be in the core.

The model elaborated below is a voting game with n voters. It is possible for each voter to have different weight from any other voter; however, the decision structure is similar to that of a *simple game*. Any coalition is either *winning* or *not winning*. A winning coalition has the power to select any policy from the set of policies, X. The set $X \subset R^m$ is called the *policy space* and should be pictured in these terms: Imagine that the group has m issues that it must decide. Each issue is quantifiable. For example, one might be the height of the town wall, another could be the budget of the fire department, another could be the surface area of the town swimming pool, and so forth, Each voter i has preferences over the policy space that are represented by a utility function $u_i(x)$. Following Schofield (1978), conditions are given below that guarantee the core is empty.

CONDITION 7.1   *The policy space $X \subset R^m$ is convex.*

CONDITION 7.2   *Each player i has preferences over X that are represented by a continuously differentiable utility function $u_i(x)$. Each function u_i achieves a maximum and a minimum on X. The minimum is $\underline{u}_i$. The first partial derivatives of u_i are zero only at extreme points.*

CONDITION 7.3   *For a coalition K, $V(K) = \{u^K(x) \in R^k \mid x \in X\}$ if K is winning and $V(K) = \{\underline{u}^K\}$ otherwise. N is winning. For at least one player i, $\{i\}$ is not winning. If K is winning and $K \subset L$, then L is winning. If K is winning, then $N \backslash K$ is not winning.*

In Condition 7.2 it is specified that each $u_i(x)$ achieves a maximum on X. This states that some policy in X is preferred by player i to all others. Figure 7.8 illustrates the preferences of a player in a two-dimensional issue space with the player's most preferred policy vector at B. The structure set up in Condition 7.3 affords a very natural way to say whether a policy x^1 wins over policy x^2. One policy wins over another if there is a winning coalition that prefers one policy to the other. Let

$$K(x^1/x^2) = \{i \in N \mid u_i(x^1) > u_i(x^2)\} \qquad (7.9)$$

Then x^1 wins over x^2 if and only if $K(x^1/x^2)$ is a winning coalition. Note that $K(x^1/x^2)$ and $K(x^2/x^1)$ cannot both be winning, and that neither need be winning. In the political context, policy x^1 wins over x^2 when x^1 would win an election against x^2. In terms of cooperative game theory, winning is the same as domination. That x^1 wins over x^2 is the same as x^1 dominates x^2 (via $K(x^1/x^2)$).

Now suppose that there is a finite sequence of policies $x^0, x^1, \ldots, x^r$ with $x^r = x^0$. If x^{j-1} wins over x^j for $j = 1, \ldots, r$, then *cyclic group preferences* occur. This is like the situation in the Condorcet paradox, and none of the policies in the list is a group winner, because each is beaten by some other policy. Any policy that can be made part of a preference cycle, as in this example, cannot be in the core, and cannot be a "best" choice for the group. An important concern in political theory is over characterization of conditions where "best" outcomes must be (or cannot be) available. Schofield (1978)

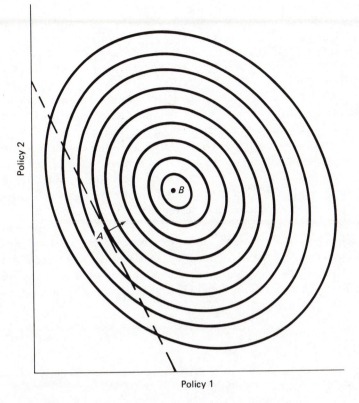

FIGURE 7.8   The preference contours of one player.

gives conditions under which local and global cyclic group preferences will occur. These results are based on examination of the directions of movement from a given policy that increase the utility of a player.

The continuity and differentiability conditions assumed on the u_i make it easy to tell the directions of movement from a given policy that will increase a player's utility. Consider the policy at point A in Figure 7.8. The dashed line through A is tangent to the indifference curve on which A lies, and the arrow, perpendicular to the tangent at A, shows the direction in which u^i increases most rapidly. Any direction that lies above and to the right of the dashed line is a direction in which u_i increases, as long as the size of the move is not too large. To see this, first define

$$u'_i(x) = \left(\frac{\partial u_i(x)}{\partial x_1}, \ldots, \frac{\partial u_i(x)}{\partial x_m} \right) \tag{7.10}$$

and let $\delta \in R^m$. The vector δ defines a direction of movement from x. This direction is one in which u_i increases, for sufficiently small change, if the inner product $\delta \cdot u'(x) > 0$. In general, the improving directions from x define an open half space, the declining directions form another open half space, and the directions in which utility does not change form a hyperplane that is the boundary between the two open half spaces. The set of improving directions for player i from x is

$$C_i(x) = \{\delta \in R^m \mid \delta \cdot u_i'(x) > 0\} \qquad (7.11)$$

for any x for which $u_i'(x) \neq 0$. If x is a local minimum, then $C_i(x) = X$ and if it is a local maximum, then $C_i(x) = \varnothing$. In the former case, all directions are improving, and in the latter, none are.

The set of improving directions from x for a coalition K is the intersection of the improving directions for the members of K: $C_K(x) = \bigcap_{i \in K} C_i(x)$. Such sets are illustrated in Figure 7.9 for the two-player coalitions in a three-player game. The indifference contours are not drawn, because they would add unnecessary confusion to the diagram; however, the tangent to each indifference curve at x is drawn, as is the gradient. For player 1, the dashed line $11'$ is the tangent and the arrow labeled u_1' is the gradient. Parallel notation applies to the other two players. The shaded region labeled $C_{\{1,2\}}$ is the region of improving directions from x for the coalition $\{1, 2\}$. Improving directions for $\{1, 3\}$ and $\{2, 3\}$ are similarly shown.

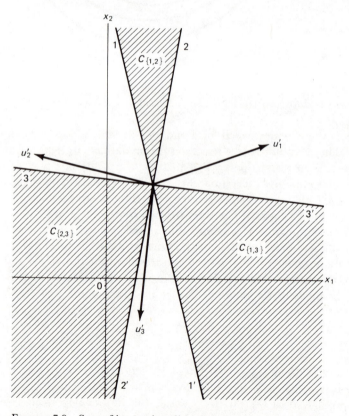

FIGURE 7.9   Sets of improving directions for various coalitions.

The set of directions that is of particular interest is the union of all the $C_K(x)$, taken over winning coalitions. In other words, the set of directions that is improving for at least one winning coalition. Denote this set $C_W(x)$, and denote the convex hull of $C_W(x)$ by $\bar{C}_W(x)$. A principal result in Schofield (1978) is if $\bar{C}_W(x) = X$ then x is part of a preference cycle. The result is proved by showing that it is possible to find a (continuous) path that begins and ends at x, along which at least one coalition is improving continually. As a rule, the path is divided into several segments, the union of which is the whole path. Each segment is identified with a particular coalition, and that coalition has its members' utility increasing as one moves along that segment of the path. What makes it possible to show that such a path exists is that there must be a (nonempty) neighborhood of x such that $\bar{C}_W(y) = X$ for all y in the neighborhood. In Figure 7.9, $\bar{C}_W(y) = X$.

As the result stands, it is not clear whether preference cycles must be small and close to x, or whether they may range quite far. Suppose, for example, that $X = R^m$ and that $\bar{C}_W(x) = R^m$ for all $x \in R^m$. Is there a way to know if a cycle can be found that arbitrarily includes any pair of policies x and y? The answer is that a cycle can be found among any such pair. In general, where C^* is the set of all elements of X for which $\bar{C}_W(x) = X$, if two points of C^* can be connected by a continuous curve that lies entirely in C^*, then those two points can be part of a preference cycle. Finally, Schofield gives conditions under which $C^* = X$.

8 Concluding comments

The cooperative game solutions reviewed in this chapter for nontransferable utility games are, I believe, interesting and useful for applications to economics and politics. The examples presented in this and other chapters are far from exhaustive, but they do represent a few interesting illustrations. And they firmly make the case that game theory has contributed greatly to the clarification and development of important problems in both disciplines.

Looking back over the cooperative game solutions in Chapters 5 to 7, the variety of them still stands out. On the positive side, several important solutions have been successfully adapted from transferable to nontransferable utility models. On the negative side, no single solution concept comes close to attaining acceptance as *the* solution. Of course, the wall of uniform acceptance of the noncooperative equilibrium of Nash for noncooperative games has some cracks in it. These pertain mainly to issues surrounding perfection and to the extreme and superb rationality that must be assumed of the players.

Still, looking back over the 40 years since the first publication of *The Theory of Games and Economic Behavior* I think it is fair to say the promise von Neumann and Morgenstern held out is well on the way to being fulfilled.

Exercises

1. Let there be a three-person nontransferable utility game in which the characteristic function is defined as follows:

   $V(\{i\}) = \{0\}$ for $i \in N$

   $V(\{1, 2\}) = \{(u_1, u_2) \in R_+^2 \mid u_2 \leqslant 48 + u_1 - \frac{1}{8}u_1^2\}$

   $V(\{1, 3\}) = \{(u_1, u_3) \in R_+^2 \mid u_3 \leqslant 10 + \frac{2}{3}u_1 - \frac{2}{27}u_1^2\}$

   $V(\{2, 3\}) = \{(u_2, u_3) \in R_+^2 \mid u_3 \leqslant 10 + u_2 - \frac{1}{45}u_2^2\}$

   $V(N) = \{(u_1, u_2, u_3) \in R_+^3 \mid u_3 \leqslant 33 + \frac{1}{3}u_1 + \frac{2}{3}u_2 - \frac{1}{28}u_1^2 - \frac{1}{49}u_2^2\}$

   Find a λ-transfer value for this game. Is the solution you have found in the core of the game?

2. For the game in problem 1, what is the tranferable utility game (N, v_λ) associated with the solution you found? What is the Shapley value for (N, v_λ)?

Note

1. Some of the special restrictions in Lemma 7.1 are intended to rule out various forms of degeneracy. These are that all row entries are distinct and that the weights associated with a feasible basis are strictly positive. The latter condition is actually violated at the first pivot step, and inevitably so. The pivot adds a two-player coalition, $\{2, 3\}$, and must remove one of the one-player coalitions. It turns out that the weights on $\{2\}$ and $\{3\}$ reach zero simultaneously; therefore, it cannot happen that one falls out while the other remains with a positive weight. To deal with this, it is all right to use an arbitrary rule to decide which to drop, and then to leave the other in the basis with a weight of zero.

Mathematical notation and brief review

In this appendix are gathered some mathematical notation, definitions, and a few theorems that are used throughout the text. All notation, definitions, and theorems are stated for points, sets, functions, and so forth, defined for finite dimensional Euclidean spaces, unless the contrary is explicitly noted.

Notation

R	The set of finite real numbers.
R^n	The set of vectors that have n real-valued components. $R^n = \{x = (x_1, \ldots, x_n) \mid x_i \in R, i = 1, \ldots, n\}$. The n-dimensional Euclidean space.
R^n_+	The set of vectors in R^n that have nonnegative components. $R^n_+ = \{x \in R^n \mid x \geq 0\}$.
R^n_{++}	The set of vectors in R^n that have strictly positive components. $R^n_{++} = \{x \in R^n \mid x \gg 0\}$.
$\{\ \}$	Notation designating a set of points. $\{a, b, c\}$ is "the set of points consisting of a and b and c." $\{a \in R \mid a < 4\}$ is "the set of real numbers that are less than 4."
$\in$	Denotes membership in a set. $a \in A$ means that "a is an element of the set A."
$\subset$	Denotes set inclusion. $A \subset B$ means "the set A is contained in the set B."
$\cup$	Denotes the union of two sets. $A \cup B$ is the set of all points that are in A, or in B, or in both.
$\cap$	Denotes the intersection of two sets. $A \cap B$ is the set of all points contained in both A and B.
$x \backslash u_i$	Where x is a vector, $x \backslash u_i$ denotes the vector $(x_1, x_2, \ldots, x_{i-1}, u_i, x_{i+1}, \ldots, x_n)$.
$K \backslash L$	Where K and L are sets, $K \backslash L$ denotes the set of points that are members of K but are not members of L. $K \backslash L$ is the intersection of K and the complement of L.
$\varnothing$	Denotes the empty set.
$\tilde{K}$	Denotes the complement of K. The set of points that are not in K.
$\times$	Cartesian product. $A \times B$ denotes the set of points (a, b) where $a \in A$ and $b \in B$.

$\leqslant$ applied to vectors, $x \leqslant y$ means $x_i \leqslant y_i$, $i = 1, \ldots, n$.

$<$ Applied to vectors, $x < y$ means $x \leqslant y$ and $x \neq y$.

$\ll$ Applied to vectors, $x \ll y$ means $x_i < y_i$, $i = 1, \ldots, n$.

$|$ This symbol is used with other symbols to reverse the meaning of the other symbol. For example $\neq$ means "is not equal to," $\notin$ means "is not an element of," $\not<$ means "is not smaller than," etc.

$[a, b]$ Denotes the closed interval. $[a, b] = \{x \in R \mid a \leqslant x \leqslant b\}$.

$[a, b)$ Denotes the half-open interval. $[a, b] = \{x \in R \mid a \leqslant x < b\}$.

$(a, b]$ Denotes the half-open interval. $(a, b] = \{x \in R \mid a < x \leqslant b\}$.

(a, b) Denotes the open interval. $(a, b) = \{x \in R \mid a < x < b\}$.

$f^i(x)$ Denotes the partial derivative of $f(x)$ with respect to the jth argument of the function.

f^{ij} Denotes the second partial derivative of $f(x)$ with respect to the ith and jth arguments of the function.

$\max_{x \in A} f(x)$ Denotes the largest value achieved by the function f on the set A. In other words, $\max_{x \in A} f(x) = f(x^*)$ if and only if $x^* \in A$ and $f(x^*) \geqslant f(x)$ for all $x \in A$.

Definitions

affine function   Let $x \in R^n, y, a \in R^m$, and let A be a $m \times n$ matrix. Then $y = a + Ax$ is an affine function.

bounded set   The set A is bounded if, for all $a, b \in A$, $d(a, b) \leqslant M < \infty$. That is, a set is bounded if there is a finite upper bound on the distance between any two points in the set.

Cartesian product   The Cartesian product of two sets, A and B, consists of all ordered pairs (a, b) such that $a \in A$ and $b \in B$. If $A \subset R^m$ and $B \subset R^n$, then $A \times B \subset R^{m+n}$.

closed set   A set is closed if, for any convergent sequence of points in the set, the limit is in the set.

cluster point   A cluster point of a sequence is the limit point of a subsequence. Suppose that $\{x^i\}$ is a sequence of points. If a subsequence of $\{x^i\}$ converges to a limit then that limit is a cluster point of the original sequence.

compact set   A set in R^n is compact if and only if it is closed and bounded.

concave function   Let f be a function with domain $A \subset R^n$ and range contained in R. The function is concave if, for any $x, y \in A$ and any $\lambda \in [0, 1]$, $f[\lambda x + (1 - \lambda)y] \geqslant \lambda f(x) + (1 - \lambda)f(y)$. The function is strictly concave if, for any $x, y \in A$ and any $\lambda \in (0, 1)$, $f[\lambda x + (1 - \lambda)y] > \lambda f(x) + (1 - \lambda)f(y)$.

contraction   Let f be a function with domain $A \subset R^n$ and range contained in R^m. The function is a contraction if, for any $x, y \in A$, $d(f(x), f(y)) < d(x, y)$. A contraction is a function that obeys a Lipschitz condition with ratio $k < 1$.

convex function   Let f be a function with domain $A \subset R^n$ and range contained in R. The function is convex if, for any $x, y \in A$ and any $\lambda \in [0, 1]$, $f[\lambda x + (1 - \lambda)y] \leqslant \lambda f(x) + (1 - \lambda)f(y)$. The function is strictly convex if, for any $x, y \in A$ and any $\lambda \in (0, 1)$, $f[\lambda x + (1 - \lambda)y] < \lambda f(x) + (1 - \lambda)f(y)$.

convex combination   A convex combination of the points $x^1, \ldots, x^n$ is $\lambda_1 x^1 + \cdots + \lambda_n x^n$ where $\lambda_i \geqslant 0$, $i = 1, \ldots, n$, and $\sum_i \lambda_i = 1$.

convex hull   The convex hull of a set A is the smallest convex set that contains A. The convex hull of A consists of all points that are convex combinations of members of A.

convex set   A set is convex if any convex combination of points in the set is also in the set. A convex set is the convex hull of itself.

correspondence   A correspondence is a mapping that associates a subset of R^m with each point in its domain.

disjoint sets   Two sets are disjoint if their intersection is empty.

distance   The distance between two points in a set, $d(x,y)$, is defined by a norm: $d(x,y) = \|x - y\|$. Distance must satisfy three properties: $d(x,y) \geq 0$, $d(x,x) = 0$, and $d(x,z) \leq d(x,y) + d(y,z)$.

domain   The domain of a function or a correspondence, $f(x)$, is the set of values of x for which the function or correspondence is defined.

equivalence relation   An equivalence relation is a binary relation that is reflexive, symmetric, and transitive. For example, "=" is an equivalence relation. Reflexivity means that $a = a$. Symmetry means that, if $a = b$, then $b = a$. Transitivity means that if $a = b$ and $b = c$, then $a = c$.

function   A function is a mapping that associates a point in R^n with a point in R^m.

infimum   The infimum of a set of points is the greatest lower bound of the set.

interior   The interior of a set A is the largest open set contained in A. A point a is in the interior of A, denoted $\mathring{A}$, if, for some small positive ε, all points b such that $d(a, b) < \varepsilon$ are in A.

limit   The point x^0 is the limit of the sequence of points $\{x^i\}$ if, for any positive ε, there is a finite k such that $d(x^0, x^i) < \varepsilon$ for all $i > k$.

linear function   A linear function is an affine function for which $a = 0$.

Lipschitz condition   Let f be a function with domain $A \subset R^n$ and range contained in R^m. The function obeys a Lipschitz condition with ratio k if, for any $x, y \in A$, $d(f(x), f(y)) \leq kd(x,y)$.

norm   A norm, denoted $\|x\|$, is a function defined on the elements of a set A that satisfies: $\|x\| \geq 0$ for all $x \in A$, $\|0\| = 0$, and $\|x + y\| \leq \|x\| + \|y\|$.

quasiconcave function   Let f be a function with domain $A \subset R^n$ and range contained in R^m. The function is quasiconcave if, for any $x, y \in A$ and any $\lambda \in [0, 1]$, $f[\lambda x + (1 - \lambda)y] \geq \min\{f(x), f(y)\}$. The function is strictly quasiconcave if, for any $x, y \in A$ and any $\lambda \in (0, 1)$, $f[\lambda x + (1 - \lambda)y] > \min\{f(x), f(y)\}$.

partition   A partition of a set A is a division of A into pairwise disjoint subsets, $B_1, \ldots, B_n$, whose union equals A. That is, $\bigcup_i B_i = A$, and for all i, j with $i \neq j$, $B_i \cap B_j = \varnothing$.

range   Let f be a function with domain $A \subset R^n$ and range contained in R^m. The range of $f(x)$ is $\{y \in R^m \mid y = f(x), x \in A\}$.

supremum   The supremum of a set of points is the least upper bound of the set.

unit simplex   The unit simplex in R^n is $\{x \in R^n \mid x \geq 0, \sum_i x_i = 1\}$.

Theorems

Theorem 1. Let f be a function with compact domain $A \subset R^n$ and range contained in R^m. Then there is $x^* \in A$ such that $f(x^*) \geq f(x)$ for all $x \in A$.

Theorem 2. Let $\{x^i\}$ be an infinite sequence of points contained in a compact subset of R^n. Then $\{x^i\}$ has a cluster point.

Theorem 3. Let f and g be concave functions with domain $A \subset R^n$ and range contained in R^m. Then, for $a, b \in R_+$, $h = af + bg$ is concave on A.

Answers to exercises

Chapter 2

1. a. $v = \frac{20}{7}$, $s_1^* = \left(\frac{2}{7}, \frac{5}{7}\right)$, $s_2^* = \left(\frac{4}{7}, \frac{3}{7}\right)$

   b. $v = \frac{20}{7}$, $s_1^* = \left(\frac{2}{7}, \frac{5}{7}\right)$, $s_2^* = \left(\frac{4}{7}, \frac{3}{7}, 0\right)$

   c. $v = \frac{11}{4}$, $s_1^* = \left(\frac{1}{4}, \frac{3}{4}\right)$, $s_2^* = \left(\frac{1}{4}, 0, \frac{3}{4}\right)$

3. $s_1^* = \left(\frac{1}{9}, \frac{8}{9}\right)$, $s_2^* = \left(\frac{4}{7}, \frac{5}{7}\right)$, $P(s^*) = \left(\frac{20}{7}, \frac{16}{3}\right)$

4. $r_1(s) = 3.125 + 1.875 s_2$, $r_2(s) = 50 - .5 s_1$, $s^* = (50, 25)$

5. $r_1(s) = 3.125 + 1.875 s_2$, $r_2(s) = 50 - .5 s_1$, $s^* = (30, 35)$

6. $r_1(s) = 10 + 1.25 s_2$, $r_2(s) = 25 - 1.5 s_1$, $s^* = \left(\frac{330}{23}, \frac{80}{23}\right)$

7. The Rosen theorem can be applied to the game in problem 6, because the Jacobian of the best reply mapping is negative quasi-definite.

Chapter 3

1. a. $(1, 1)$, $(3, 2)$, $(4, 3)$

   b. Yes, with $s^0 = (4, 3)$, $s^1 = (1, 1)$, $s^2 = (3, 2)$

   c. 6 periods

   d. .95, .805

2. If $s^* = (2, 4)$ and $s^c = (4, 3)$, then $\alpha_1 > \frac{5}{14}$ and $\alpha_2 > \frac{3}{16}$. If $s^* = (2, 4)$, but $(1, 1)$ is chosen if player 1 abandons the trigger strategy and $(3, 2)$ is chosen if player 2 does, then $\alpha_1 > \frac{1}{3}$ and $\alpha_2 > \frac{3}{17}$.

3. a. $s^* = (10, 10)$ is a unique equilibrium point. The best reply mapping is a contraction. $P(s^*) = (1000, 1500)$

   b. For $\alpha_1 > \frac{3}{4}$ and $\alpha_2 > \frac{49}{85}$ a subgame perfect trigger strategy equilibrium can be maintained. $s^* = (35, 30)$ and $P(s^*) = (1750, 3000)$

Chapter 4

1.
$$s_{1t} = \frac{5 - 5 s_{1,t-1} + s_{2,t-1} - 4 s_{1,t+1}}{28}$$

$$s_{2t} = \frac{10 - 6 s_{1,t-1} - 2 s_{1t}}{16}$$

$$s^* = (.15, .55)$$

Chapter 5

1. a. The threat point is $d = (10, 15)$. The attainable set H is the convex hull of the utility pairs associated with the points in the set of possible trades. These are

$u^1 = (0, 37)$, $u^2 = (4, 36)$, $u^3 = (6, 35)$, $u^4 = (10, 15)$, $u^5 = (12, 11)$, $u^6 = (14, 25)$, $u^7 = (20, 10)$, $u^8 = (16, 8)$, and $u^9 = (21, 5)$; therefore, $H = \{u \in R^2 \mid u = \sum_{i=1}^{9} \lambda_i u^i,$ $\sum_{i=1}^{9} \lambda_i = 1$, $\lambda \geqslant 0$, $i = 1, \ldots, 9\}$. The subset of H containing payoffs weakly dominating the threat point, $H^* = \{u \in H \mid u \geqslant d\}$, is the convex hull of $(10, 15)$, $(10, 30)$, $(14, 25)$, and $(18, 15)$.
  b. $(14, 25)$
2. a. $m = (10, 15)$, $M = (18, 30)$
  b. $(\frac{102}{7}, \frac{165}{7})$
3. a. Reference point: $(10.5, 21)$; solution: $(13.85, 25.1875)$.
  b. Reference point: $(14, 22.5)$; solution: $(14.5, 23.75)$.

4.

Solution	Reference point	Solution Payoffs
Nash	$(2, 2)$	$(3.4142, 3.4142)$
R–K–S	$(2, 2)$, $(4, 4)$	$(3.4142, 3.4142)$
min expectations	$(2, 2)$	$(3.4142, 3.4142)$
min compromise	$(3, 3)$	$(3.4142, 3.4142)$
smallest rectangle	$(2, 2)$	$(3.4142, 3.4142)$

5.

Solution	Reference Point	Solution Payoffs
Nash	$(0, 2)$	$(3.49, 3.334)$
R–K–S	$(0, 2)$, $(4, 4)$	$(3.6, 3.2)$
min expectations	$(2, 2)$	$(3.4142, 3.4142)$
min compromise	$(3, 3)$	$(3.4142, 3.4142)$
smallest rectangle	$(2, 2)$	$(3.4142, 3.4142)$

Chapter 6

1. a. $(10, 10, 10)$
  b. $v(\{i\}) = 0$ for $i = 1, 2, 3$, $v(\{1, 2\}) = \frac{2}{13}$, $v(\{1, 3\}) = \frac{11}{13}$, $v(\{2, 3\}) = \frac{3}{13}$, $v(N) = 1$
  c. $v(N) = 28$ is the minimum. $(8, 8, 10)$ is in the core.
2. $\phi(v) = (10.5, 9.5, 10)$. The Shapley value of this game is in the core.
3. Superadditivity is neither necessary nor sufficient. The following three-person game violates superadditivity and has $(2, 2, 2)$ in the core: $v(\{i\}) = 2$ for all i, $v(K) = 3$ for all two-player coalitions, and $v(N) = 6$. On the other hand, simple games are superadditive and generally have empty cores. For example, the three-person game in which $v(\{i\}) = 0$ for all i and $v(K) = 1$ for all two- and three-player coalitions has no core.
4. If this inequality is violated for a partition, then no imputation can be found that gives at least $v(T_i)$ to each coalition in the partition.

Chapter 7

1. The weights are: $(\frac{1}{3}, \frac{1}{6}, \frac{1}{2})$ and the associated payoffs are $u = (14, 49, \frac{43}{3})$. This payoff vector cannot be improved on by any coalition; hence, it is in the core.
2. For $\lambda = (\frac{1}{3}, \frac{1}{6}, \frac{1}{2})$ $v_\lambda(\{i\}) = 0$ for $i \in N$, $v_\lambda(\{1, 2\}) = 10$, $v_\lambda(\{1, 3\}) = 8$, $v_\lambda(\{2, 3\}) = 15$, and $v_\lambda(N) = 20$. The Shapley value is $\phi(v_\lambda) = (\frac{28}{6}, \frac{49}{6}, \frac{43}{6})$.

References

Abreu, Dilip, 1983, *Repeated Games with Discounting*, Ph.D. dissertation, Department of Economics, Princeton University.

Arrow, Kenneth J., 1951, *Social Choice and Individual Values*, New York: Wiley.

———, 1971, *Essays in the Theory of Risk Bearing*, Chicago: Markham.

Arrow, Kenneth J. and Gerard Debreu, 1954, "Existence of an Equilibrium for a Competitive Economy," *Econometrica* 22: 265–290.

Aumann, Robert J., 1959, "Acceptable Points in General Cooperative n-person Games," in A. W. Tucker and R. D. Luce, eds., 1959, *Contributions to the Theory of Games* IV, Princeton: Princeton University Press.

———, 1961, "The Core of a Cooperative Game without Side Payments," *Transactions of the American Mathematics Society* 98: 539–552.

———, 1976, "Agreeing to Disagree," *Annals of Statistics* 4: 1236–1239.

———, 1981, "Survey of Repeated Games," in Aumann et al., *Essays in Game Theory*, Mannheim: Bibliographisches Institut.

Banzhaf, J. F. III, 1965, "Weighted Voting Doesn't Work: A Mathematical Analysis," *Rutgers Law Review* 19: 317–343.

Bartle, Robert G., 1964, *The Elements of Real Analysis*, New York: Wiley.

Benoit, Jean-Pierre and Vijay Krishna, 1985, "Finitely Repeated Games," *Econometrica* 53: 905–922.

Berge, Claude, 1957, *Théorie Générale des Jeux à n Personnes*, Paris: Gauthier-Villars.

Black, Duncan, 1958, *The Theory of Committees and Elections*, Cambridge: Cambridge University Press.

Blackwell, David, 1965, "Discounted Dynamic Programming," *Annals of Mathematical Statistics* 36: 226–235.

Brito, D. L., A. M. Buoncristiani, and M. D. Intriligator, 1977, "A New Approach to Nash's Bargaining Problem," *Econometrica* 45: 1163–1172.

Champsaur, Paul, 1975, "Cooperation versus Competition," *Journal of Economic Theory* 11: 394–417.

Cournot, Augustin, 1838, *Recherches sur les Principes Mathématiques de la Théorie des Richesses*, Paris: Hachette.

———, 1960, *Researches into the Mathematical Principles of the Theory of Wealth*, English edition of Cournot (1838), translated by Nathaniel T. Bacon, New York: Kelley.

Crawford, Vincent P., 1979, "A Procedure for Generating Pareto-Efficient Egalitarian-Equivalent Allocations," *Econometrica* 47: 49–60.

————, 1980, "A Self-administered Solution of the Bargaining Problem," *Review of Economic Studies* 47: 385–392.

Debreu, Gerard, 1952, "A Social Equilibrium Existence Theorem," *Proceedings of the National Academy of Science* 38: 886–893.

————, 1959, *Theory of Value*, New York: Wiley.

Debreu, Gerard and Herbert E. Scarf, 1963, "A Limit Theorem on the Core of an Economy," *International Economic Review* 4: 235–246.

————, 1972, "The Limit of the Core of an Economy," in C. B. McGuire and Roy Radner, eds., *Decision and Organization*, Amsterdam: North-Holland.

Denardo, Eric V., 1967, "Contraction Mappings in the Theory Underlying Dynamic Programming," *SIAM Review* 9: 165–177.

Dieudonné, J., 1960, *Foundations of Modern Analysis*, New York: Academic Press.

Edgeworth, Francis Y., 1881, *Mathematical Psychics*, London: Kegan Paul.

Fan, Ky, 1952, "Fixed-point and Minimax Theorems in Locally Convex Topological Linear Spaces," *Proceedings of the National Academy of Sciences* 38: 121–126.

Fellner, William J., 1949, *Competition Among the Few*, New York: Knopf.

Flaherty, M. Thérèse, 1980, "Industry Structure and Cost Reducing Investment," *Econometrica* 48: 1187–1209.

Friedman, James W., 1971, "A Non-cooperative Equilibrium for Supergames," *Review of Economic Studies* 38: 1–12.

————, 1974, "Non-cooperative Equilibria in Time-dependent Supergames," *Econometrica* 42: 221–237.

————, 1977, *Oligopoly and the Theory of Games*, Amsterdam: North-Holland.

————, 1981, "A Note on the Turnpike Properties of Time Dependent Supergames," *Econometrica* 49: 1087–1088.

————, 1983, *Oligopoly Theory*, New York: Cambridge University Press.

————, 1984, "On Characterizing Equilibrium Points in Two Person Strictly Competitive Games," *International Journal of Game Theory* 12: 245–247.

————, 1985, "Cooperative Equilibria in Finite Horizon Noncooperative Supergames," *Journal of Economic Theory* 35: 390–398.

Fudenberg, Drew and Eric Maskin, 1983. "The Folk Theorem in Repeated Games with Discounting and with Incomplete Information," MIT and Berkeley.

Gale, David, and Hukukane Nikaido, 1965, "The Jacobian Matrix and the Global Univalence of Mappings," *Mathematische Annalen* 159: 81–93.

Gillies, D. B., 1953, *Some Theorems on n-Person Games*, Ph.D. dissertation, Department of Mathematics, Princeton University.

Green, Edward J., 1980, "Noncooperative Price Taking in Large Dynamic Markets," *Journal of Economic Theory* 22: 155–182.

Green, H. A. John, 1976, *Consumer Theory*, rev. ed., London: Macmillan.

Green, Jerry, and Jean-Jacques Laffont, 1979, *Incentives in Public Decision-Making*, Amsterdam: North-Holland.

Groves, Theodore and John Ledyard, 1977, "Optimal Allocation of Public Goods: A Solution to the 'Free Rider' Problem," *Econometrica* 45: 783–809.

Harsanyi, John C., 1956, "Approaches to the Bargaining Problem Before and After the Theory of Games," *Econometrica* 24: 144–156.

————, 1959, "A Bargaining Model for the Cooperative *n*-Person Game," in A. W. Tucker and R. D. Luce, eds., *Contributions to the Theory of Games IV*, Princeton: Princeton University Press.

————, 1963, "A Simplified Bargaining Model for the n-person Cooperative Game," *International Economic Review* 4: 194–220.

————, 1967, 1968a, 1968b, "Games with Incomplete Information Played by 'Bayesian' Players, Part I: The Basic Model," *Management Science* 14: 159–182; Part II, *Management Science* 14: 320–334; Part III, *Management Science* 14: 486–502.

————, 1977, *Rational Behavior and Bargaining Equilibrium in Games and Social Situations*, Cambridge: Cambridge University Press.

Hildenbrand, Werner and Alan Kirman, 1976, *Introduction to General Equilibrium Analysis*, Amsterdam: North-Holland.

Hillier, Frederick S. and Gerald J. Lieberman, 1974, *Operations Research*, San Francisco: Holden-Day.

Hume, David, (1739–40), 1888, *A Treatise of Human Nature*, edited by L. A. Selby-Bigge, Oxford: Clarendon Press.

Johnson, Samuel, 1755, *A Dictionary of the English Language*, London: W. Strahan.

Kakutani, Shizuo, 1941, "A Generalization of Brouwer's Fixed Point Theorem," *Duke Mathematical Journal* 8: 457–459.

Kalai, Ehud and Dov Samet, 1982, "Persistent Equilibria in Strategic Games," unpublished paper, Northwestern University.

Kalai, Ehud and Meir Smorodinsky, 1975, "Other Solutions to Nash's Bargaining Problem," *Econometrica* 43: 513–518.

Kelley, John L., 1955, *General Topology*, New York: van Nostrand.

Kirman, Alan P. and Matthew J. Sobel, 1974, "Dynamic Oligopoly with Inventories," *Econometrica* 42: 279–287.

Kreps, David M. and Robert Wilson, 1982a, "Reputation and Imperfect Information," *Journal of Economic Theory* 27: 253–279.

————, 1982b, "Sequential Equilibrium," *Econometrica* 50: 863–894.

Kuhn, Harold W., 1953, "Extensive Games and the Problem of Information," in H. W. Kuhn and A. W. Tucker, eds., *Contributions to the Theory of Games II*, Princeton: Princeton University Press.

Kurz, Mordecai, 1976, "Altruistic Equilibrium," in Bela Balassa and Richard Nelson, eds., *Economic Progress, Private Values and Public Policy*, Amsterdam: North-Holland.

Lambson, Val E., 1984, "Self-Enforcing Collusion in Large Dynamic Markets," *Journal of Economic Theory* 34: 282–291.

Lemke, C. E. and J. T. Howson, 1964, "Equilibrium Points of Bimatrix Games, *SIAM Journal of Applied Mathematics* 12: 413–423.

Lucas, William F., 1969, "The Proof that a Game may not have a Solution," *Transactions of the American Mathematical Society* 136: 219–229.

Luce, R. Duncan and Howard Raiffa, 1957, *Games and Decisions*, New York: Wiley.

McKenzie, Lionel, 1960, "Matrices with Dominant Diagonals and Economic Theory," in Kenneth J. Arrow, Samuel Karlin, and Patrick Suppes, eds., *Mathematical Methods in the Social Sciences*, 1959, Stanford: Stanford University Press, 47–62.

Maschler, Michael, Bezalel Peleg, and Lloyd Shapley, 1979, "Geometric Properties of the Kernel, Nucleolus, and Related Concepts." *Mathematics of Operations Research* 4: 303–338.

Milgrom, Paul, 1981, "An Axiomatic Characterization of Common Knowledge," *Econometrica* 49: 219–222.

Miller, Charles L., 1982, "A Reaction Function Equilibrium for a Simple Dynamic Duopoly Model with Random Demand," unpublished paper, Department of Economics, Johns Hopkins University.

Myerson, Roger B., 1978, "Refinements of the Nash Equilibrium Concept," *International Journal of Game Theory* 7: 73–80.

Nash, John F., Jr., 1950, "The Bargaining Problem," *Econometrica* 18: 155–162.

———, 1951, "Non-Cooperative Games," *Annals of Mathematics* 54: 286–295.

———, 1953, "Two-Person Cooperative Games," *Econometrica* 21: 128–140.

Nikaido, Hukukane and Kazuo Isoda, 1955, "Note on Noncooperative Convex Games," *Pacific Journal of Mathematics* 5: 807–815.

Nishimura, Kazuo and James Friedman, 1981, "Existence of Nash Equilibrium in n Person Games without Quasiconcavity," *International Economic Review* 22: 637–648.

Owen, Guillermo, 1967, "An Elementary Proof of the Minimax Theorem," *Management Science* 13: 765.

———, 1972, "Values of Games without Side Payments," *International Journal of Game Theory* 1: 95–109.

———, 1978, "Characterization of the Banzhaf–Coleman Index," *SIAM Journal of Applied Mathematics* 35: 315–327.

———, 1982, *Game Theory*, 2nd ed., New York: Academic Press.

Peleg, Bezalel and Menaham Yaari, 1973, "On the Existence of A Consistent Course of Action when Tastes are Changing," *Review of Economic Studies* 40: 391–401.

Porter, Robert H., 1983, "Optimal Cartel Trigger Price Strategies," *Journal of Economic Theory* 29: 313–338.

Prescott, Edward C., 1973, "Market Structure and Monopoly Profits: A Dynamic Theory," *Journal of Economic Theory* 6: 546–557.

Radner, Roy, 1980, "Collusive Behavior in Noncooperative Epsilon-Equilibria of Oligopolies with Long but Finite Lives," *Journal of Economic Theory* 22: 136–154.

Riker, William H., 1962, *The Theory of Political Coalitions*, New Haven: Yale University Press.

Rives, Norfleet W., Jr., 1975, "On the History of the Mathematical Theory of Games," *History of Political Economy* 7: 549–565.

Roberts, A. Wayne and Dale E. Varberg, 1973, *Convex Functions*, New York: Academic Press.

Rogers, Philip D., 1969, "Nonzero-Sum Stochastic Games," ORC 69-8, Operations Research Center, University of California, Berkeley.

Rosen, J. B., 1965, "Existence and Uniqueness of Equilibrium Points for Concave n-person Games," *Econometrica* 33: 520–534.

Rosenthal, R. W., 1979, "Sequences of Games with Varying Opponents," *Econometrica* 47: 1353–1366.

———, 1981, "Games of Perfect Information, Predatory Pricing and the Chain-Store Paradox," *Journal of Economic Theory* 25: 92–100.

Roth, Alvin E., 1977, "Individual Rationality and Nash's Solution to the Bargaining Problem," *Mathematics of Operations Research* 2: 64–66.

———, 1979, *Axiomatic Models of Bargaining*, Berlin: Springer.

Rubinstein, Ariel, 1979, "Equilibrium in Supergames with the Overtaking Criterion," *Journal of Economic Theory* 21: 1–9.

———, 1982, "Perfect Equilibrium in a Bargaining Model," *Econometrica* 50: 97–109.

Scarf, Herbert E., 1967, "The Core of an n-Person Game," *Econometrica* 35: 50–69.

————, 1973, *The Computation of Economic Equilibria*, New Haven: Yale University Press.

Schmeidler, David, 1973, "Equilibrium Points of Nonatomic Games," *Journal of Statistical Physics* 7: 295–300.

Schofield, Norman, 1978, "Instability of Simple Dynamic Games," *Review of Economic Studies* 45: 575–594.

Selten, R., 1975, "Reexamination of the Perfectness Concept for Equilibrium Points in Extensive Games," *International Journal of Game Theory* 4: 25–55.

————, 1978, "The Chain Store Paradox," *Theory and Decision* 9: 127–159.

Shapley, Lloyd, 1953a, "Stochastic Games," *Proceedings of the National Academy of Science* 39: 1095–1100.

————, 1953b, "A Value for n-Person Games," in H. W. Kuhn and A. W. Tucker, eds., *Contributions to the Theory of Games II*, Princeton: Princeton University Press.

————, 1969, "Utility Comparison and the Theory of Games," in G. Th. Guilbaud, ed., *La Décision, Aggregation et Dynamique*, Colloques Internationaux du Centre de la Recherche Scientifique No. 171, Editions C.N.R.S.

Shapley, Lloyd and Martin Shubik, 1966, "Quasi-cores in a Monetary Economy with Nonconvex Preferences," *Econometrica* 34: 805–827.

Shubik, Martin, 1982, *Game Theory in the Social Sciences*, Cambridge: MIT Press.

————, 1984, *A Game-Theoretic Approach to Polictical Economy*, Cambridge: MIT Press.

Simon, Herbert A., 1957, *Models of Man*, New York: Wiley.

Sobel, Matthew J., 1971, "Noncooperative Stochastic Games," *Annals of Mathematical Statistics* 42: 1930–1935.

Thomson, William, 1981, "A Class of Solutions to Bargaining Problems," *Journal of Economic Theory* 25: 431–441.

Tideman, T. Nicolaus and Gordon Tullock, 1976, "A New and Superior Process for Making Social Choices," *Journal of Political Economy* 84: 1145–1159.

van Damme, Eric, 1983, *Refinements of the Nash Equilibrium Concept*, Berlin: Springer.

Varian, Hal R., 1978, *Microeconomic Analysis*, New York: Norton.

von Neumann, John, 1928, "Zur Theorie der Gesellschaftsspiele," *Math. Annalen* 100: 295–320.

————, 1959, "On the Theory of Games of Strategy," English version of von Neumann (1928), translated by Sonya Bargmann, in A. W. Tucker and R. D. Luce, eds., *Contributions to the Theory of Games IV*, Princeton: Princeton University Press.

von Neumann, John and Oskar Morgenstern, 1944, *Theory of Games and Economic Behavior*, Princeton: Princeton University Press.

Zeuthen, Frederik, 1930, *Problems of Monopoly and Economic Warfare*, London: Routledge & Kegan Paul.

Subject index

Author index